D1571044

~ Traditional Buildings ~

~

TRADITIONAL BUILDINGS

~

A Global Survey of Structural Forms and Cultural Functions

ALLEN G. NOBLE

I.B. TAURIS

LONDON · NEW YORK

Published in 2007 by I.B.Tauris & Co Ltd
6 Salem Road, London W2 4BU
175 Fifth Avenue, New York NY 10010
www.ibtauris.com

In the United States of America and Canada
distributed by Palgrave Macmillan, a division of St Martin's Press
175 Fifth Avenue, New York NY 10010

International Library of Human Geography 11

ISBN 978 1 84511 305 6

A full CIP record for this book is available from the British Library
A full CIP record is available from the Library of Congress

Library of Congress Catalog Card Number: available

Typeset in Palatino by JCS Publishing Services
Printed and bound in Great Britain by TJ International Ltd, Cornwall

Contents

List of Figures

Acknowledgments

The creation of a book is never the product of one person's efforts. I have benefited from the help of several talented individuals who have solved many problems for me, and taught me how to avoid other difficulties, which I might not otherwise have recognized. Linda Bussey is foremost among these persons. With her artistic sense, computer skills and cheerful outlook, she performed a wide variety of tasks, which significantly enhanced this book. Subsequently, Marlene Harmon took over many of these duties, becoming invaluable with her competence and good nature. Kevin Butler, a perceptive and talented friend, greatly aided in the production of illustrations. I am indebted to the late M. Margaret Geib for many exceptionally clear sketches, to Keith Pitts, Amy Rock, Iraida Galdon Soler, Angela Gotch, Drew Flater, and Matthew Goyder for other outstanding cartographic and artistic contributions. Several persons worked diligently and faithfully to convert the manuscript to an acceptable text form. They include Nicole Schoeppner, Amos Scarfo, Desmond Wayome, Chapman Owusu-Sekyere, Jeffrey Idom, Agyemang Frimpong, and Josh Van Duser. Jonathan McCray, Mahmut Gokmen, and Risa Patarasuk searched for source materials and provided evaluations. Atit Shah provided excellent technical assistance to an author whose computer competence is decidedly limited. I am indebted to Robert Kent, chairperson of the Department of Geography and Planning, University of Akron, for providing the facilities and student personnel that enabled me to undertake this work.

Finally, I must acknowledge the advice and guidance of David Stonestreet of I.B.Tauris Publishers, who early on recognized that such a volume might have value. An indispensable asset was the copy-editing of Jessica Cuthbert-Smith, which rectified many of my slips. I found her expertise to be world-wide in scope and always accurate. I am obligated to all those individuals.

My greatest thanks and appreciation must go to my wife, Jane, who has searched through the manuscript to lead me clear of potential pitfalls and to a clearer style of expression. To her this volume is dedicated.

Preface

To discuss the traditional dwellings of the entire world is a daunting task. Examining in detail buildings at a local, country, or even macro-regional scale, would produce a work of encyclopedic scope. Time also presents a problem. Many traditional buildings are occupied today, providing accommodations to millions of individuals. Some of these structures follow original modes of construction, or at least those processes and guideposts that have persevered for centuries, and certainly deserve attention. Even more, inhabited structures, which may still be called traditional, possess modifications that have altered their original form.

Another group of traditional buildings has only recently – during the past century or so – been abandoned and may still be seen in the landscape by the dedicated observer. But some traditional structures are so old that they have been unoccupied for hundreds or even thousands of years. They still fall clearly within the scope of traditional dwellings. Only with the guidance of the archeologist can we understand and appreciate these structures, which may possess valuable clues to features of more recent buildings.

I have been most fortunate during my careers as a US Foreign Service officer and as a university professor to have lived and traveled in many parts of the world. This has enabled me to examine traditional buildings at close range and to make comparisons over a wide spectrum of examples. I have entered loess cave homes in central China, stilt houses in the shore waters of Dahomey, wattle-and-daub huts in lowland Ecuador, Tanzania and Sri Lanka, housebarns in Europe and North America, mud and stone circular-plan houses in highland Ethiopia, and many other buildings that stand out in my memory. Additionally, visits to fine open-air or Skansen museums throughout Europe, North America, and at least two in Africa, offered me the opportunity to study structures otherwise no longer in existence. The steady disappearance of traditional buildings across the entire world makes the expansion of these museums, and the establishment of new ones in other parts of the world, a critical necessity for governments and NGOs. By so doing, a heritage as well as cultural links can be preserved for future generations.

In order to present a study of maximum utility, rather than a mere catalog, however useful the latter might be, a few organizing concepts must be employed in a project of such diverse scope. First of all, the reader must realize that the work offers no new ideologies or theories. That is not to say that existing theories are not accepted or rejected herein. I hope I have been clear when I differ with earlier authors. To focus the discussion, I have arranged the text material around certain themes, concepts or characteristics. Most chapters of this volume examine two closely related general items or topics, or they explore a single topic in somewhat greater depth. Using such an approach enables the reader to understand various processes, developments, and the rationale for traditional building. Examples are drawn from widely separated geographical locations and often from entirely unrelated peoples. In some instances, the examples are complementary, demonstrating the universal application of a principle. Alternatively, they may suggest the presence of axioms at variance with one another.

No reader should consider this volume as definitive. It explores what I think are interesting aspects and points the way to fuller treatments of certain features. I have tried to retain much of the original wording from the sources that I cite and use. In this way the approach of original researchers should be clear even though my own interpretation may differ. The text is supplemented with photos, maps, sketches, and diagrams to help clarify and expand materials. The study of traditional buildings is always greatly assisted by having illustrations to confirm, or make clear in another fashion, the written word.

One of the most serious problems facing the student of traditional buildings is that source materials are scattered over thousands of books and journals. Indices for these, by and large, do not exist and most bibliographies are narrow, fragmentary, or highly specific as to topic. I hope the current volume will bring some of the vast material on traditional buildings together in a useful and coherent fashion. To this end I have included references to a very large number of sources. I hope readers will consult these resources, which usually go into much more detail than is possible here. Citations in the text allow the reader, with a little effort, to consult the sources of my research and to determine whether or not I have accurately interpreted the material, and also to understand for themselves the argument of the original writer. The list of these references cited is an integral part of the present work and increases enormously whatever value it may have. I have also included a large number of illustrations, some original but many taken from cited works. I wish I could have doubled, or even tripled, the number of illustrations, but such action might be burdensome to the reader and would certainly be cost prohibitive. When you wish a more elaborate explanation than I have given, or you feel additional illustration would make the discussion clearer, please refer to the references cited, which will often contain other illustrations and usually a fuller discussion.

I hope this volume provides information, answers unasked questions and stimulates the reader to pursue further the fascinating topic of traditional building.

Allen G. Noble

~ 1 ~
Introduction: Terminology and Disciplines

Considerable confusion exists in the discussion of *traditional buildings* and it seems wise at the outset to establish the limits of terms and definitions in order to avoid further confusion. The word *traditional* refers both to procedures and material objects that have become accepted as a norm in a society, and whose elements are passed on from generation to generation, usually orally, or more rarely by documents that have codified orally transmitted knowledge, instructions, and procedures. This is not to imply that traditional processes and objects do not change over time (Figure 1-1). They often do, but usually slowly enough that their provenance is clearly seen or easily established. Though change is a constant in any society, it is the rate at which a society is forced to absorb the new that determines whether it can retain its integrity (Carver 1981, 27).

In traditional societies,

> people have to make do with whatever is at hand. The form and arrangement of dwellings, for example, are constrained by the availability of local materials, the nature of the local climate and the socioeconomic facts of life. To a modern observer, the material world thus created can have enormous appeal because everything in it has a purpose, and because its aesthetic qualities emerge unobtrusively out of the serious business of living. (Tuan 1989, 28).

The concept of "traditional dwelling," normally employed to describe a simple structure, often can be quite a complex conception. In warm environments where so much of daily life is lived in the open, the concept of a house as a structure is not as important as that of the entire compound, "the idea of a bit of land which is screened for privacy and which contains some enclosed internal space, and some outside space. This whole thing taken together is thought of as the home environment. Each part within is used as seems most appropriate in the

1-1. *The low, black tent favored by nomadic peoples in central Turkey is traditional, but evidences of modern influences are abundant. For example, just over the roof of this tent and adjacent to another tent is an automobile used to get food and supplies from nearby towns and to market handicrafts, weaving, and sheep products. The propane tank and the sheets of plastic hanging over the tent ropes are other indications of modernity (photo by the author, 1999).*

1-2. *The interior of the tent shown in Figure 1-1. Except for a bit of ceiling plastic, the furnishings are entirely traditional (photo by the author, 1999).*

circumstances" (Rodger 1974, 105). Such a view is common through-out many traditional societies in areas of warmer temperature, and is especially strong where individuals live in extended family groups, or even clans (Thompson 1983, 204). The concept is further clarified by Alison Shaw's (1988, 54) observation that "in Pakistan ownership of land is more important than ownership of a house."

The cooler climate equivalent of this extended concept of the dwelling is the notion of the farmstead, with all its buildings and facilities, as the unit of residence, rather than the emphasis being placed on just the dwelling. These expanded concepts of the traditional dwelling will reappear throughout subsequent chapters.

"Tangible evidence of the past found in extant architecture enhances the present by providing a time perspective and by creating through contrast and harmony a feeling of location or situation. Furthermore, a sense of continuity and permanence conveyed by sur-viving material culture provides psychological security" (Robinson 1981, xviii). Also, some secondary elements may change, but at the same time others do not, thus verifying the traditional nature of the object or procedure (Figure 1-2). "By its relative immutability the dwelling offers a sustaining sense of security against the uncertainties of a milieu in which change is inevitable, but directions are imper-fectly perceived and mechanisms are poorly understood" (Steward 1965, 28).

One of many such examples that could be cited is what happened with the log cabins built early on by the Scots-Irish in eastern North America (Evans 1965, 34). In Ireland, the Scots-Irish had built partly excavated sod huts, or much less often, stone huts, but in North America they rapidly shifted to the widespread construction of log houses. However, in the process they retained the floor-plan dimen-sions of the old-country huts (Figure 1-3), which made it easier and more acceptable culturally for them to use the new material (Noble 1984, 1:44). Certainly, other factors also played their part: the abun-dance of timber, the easier construction with logs versus stone, and the successful example of the neighboring Germans, Finns, and Swedes, who came to North America with long traditions of log building.

Fred Kniffen (1960, 22) reported a similar traditional tenacity from Louisiana, asserting "that the form of a structure persists even when the materials change." The hand of tradition is a strong one. Still another aspect of cultural tenacity has been reported by Ake Camp-bell (1935, 68), who noted the continuing custom in Ireland of "having farm-animals housed under the family-roof." He further observed, "this custom cannot be ascribed to poverty as it is still commonly met with among people who, if they so desired, could easily afford

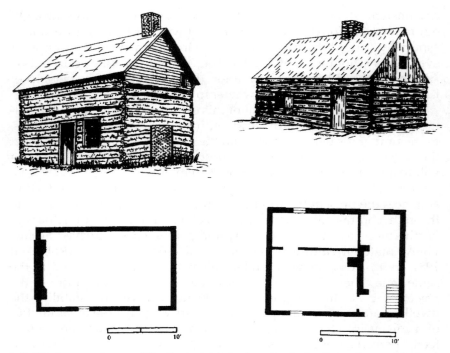

1-3. *The log pen house of the Scots-Irish in America had a floor-plan ratio of about 1:2. The hearth and chimney were at one gable. The interior was sometimes divided into two rooms of unequal size. The German log house's plan ratio was approximately 2:3, the hearth and chimney were interior, and the plan consisted of three rectangular rooms of unequal size and dimensions (drawings by M. Margaret Geib).*

separate accommodation for the domestic animals. They prefer, however, to cling tenaciously to the old custom."

One term that, thankfully, is less and less often encountered is *primitive architecture* or *primitive building*. These words are frequently used in a way that implies negatively the "intention or mental equipment of the builder." Properly, the term describes only the cultural and technical development of a society (Brodrick 1954, 100). Even when used correctly, the terms are vague (Raglan 1964, 3–4), and reflect negatively upon structures, that are often precisely designed, symbolically executed, and more carefully fitted to the local environment than so-called "professionally" planned structures. "Too often we view the products of a past pioneer technology as primitive and crude when they are in fact quite complex and exacting" (Welsch 1967, 335). Too often "the notion of the 'primitive hut' is commonly introduced as a hazy stereotype in many standard works of architectural history, as the supposed link with 'the cave' in the lineal ascent towards today's cityscape" (Duly 1979, 5).

In discussing traditional buildings one encounters other terms that appear from a hasty glance to have a somewhat similar meaning. *Folk building* or *folk architecture* is usually employed to describe practices or structures which are the products of persons not professionally trained in building arts, but who produce structures or follow techniques which basically have been accepted by a society as the correct or "best" way.

Speaking of the folk builder, Alan Gowans (1966, 10) says that he

> builds not so much functionally as adaptably – that is, not so much consciously thinking out solutions to particular problems of light, air or circulation (like a modern architect), as embodying in his work inherited generations of experience and with adjustments to local climate, materials, and social customs. . . . If the folk builder expresses his building materials frankly, it is not from any conscious convictions about architectural honesty or the virtues of handicraft (he will not hesitate for example, to cover stone walls with plaster or whitewash if that will protect them from frost).

One author, perhaps with unconsciously clever wit, has characterized folk architecture as "the architecture of habit" (Gamble 1990, 23). Even an outsider, after limited exposure, can recognize some buildings as belonging to a particular ethnic group. Just how strong this connection is, and how significant is folk architecture, has been emphasized by Peter Just (1984, 30), who – speaking of Indonesia – noted that "traditionally, each of the scores of Indonesian ethnic groups had a distinctive architectural standard for every house built by a member of the group, which constituted an active expression of that group's ethnic identity. The design of a house often had deep symbolic resonance for its inhabitants." Speaking of a different people in a different place, geographer Peirce Lewis (1975, 2) labels "common houses as cultural spoor," thereby emphasizing the house to be a cultural identifier.

Although folk houses are rarely identical to one another, they follow conventions accepted by their society and passed down orally. An unconscious recognition of this fact has been recorded by Sylvia Grider (1975, 51), who quoted a shotgun house carpenter as saying that such houses, for which no blueprints or drawings were ever used, "were always built by ear." Individualized expression is of limited value in folk building, but the overall similarity is symbolic of identification with the group that resides within them (Oliver 1977, 12).

Again, the example of the Scots-Irish in North America differentiates them from both the Germans and the Finns. The Scots-Irish log house is immediately identifiable as different from that of the Germans or the Finns or any other ethnic group (Noble 1984, 1:41–5, 121–2). The Scots-Irish utilized a rectangular, one- or two-room plan, typically with one door and one window, gable hearth and chimney, and horizontal logs or boards above the plate-log level in the gable. The Germans employed a three-room, less rectangular floor plan, a massive, centered, interior-positioned hearth and chimney, and vertical boards enclosing the gable (Brumbaugh 1933; Bucher 1962) (Figure 1-3). The Finns built log houses with extremely tightly fitted logs, which to a large extent eliminated the need for the considerable chinking required by the other groups. Corner notching used by the Finns also was usually more complex (Figure 1-4).

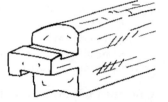

1-4. Sketch of a tooth notch. This and other complex notches are found throughout the Baltic Sea basin. In North America, they are most often seen in Fenno-Scandinavian areas (drawing by M. Margaret Geib).

Among the earliest scholars to recognize the cultural significance of traditional buildings, as expressed in folk architecture, are those folklorists who were exponents of the *folk-life* approach. Together with cultural anthropologists, they studied, in the words of Gwyn Meirion-Jones (1982, 3) referring to British folklore scholars, "not only the fabric of the building, its materials, construction and plan, as well as the archaeological and architectural evidence of change, but also the folkways of those who inhabited it, their customs, superstitions, habits of work and play, their music, literature and oral traditions."

Vernacular architecture is a term widely used in the United Kingdom, and less so in North America (Ennals and Holdsworth 1998, 241f). Paul Oliver (1969, 10–11) reminds us that the term was employed as long ago as 1858. The expression was widely used and popularized by archeologists "to describe buildings that are built according to local custom to meet the personal requirements of the individuals for whom they are intended" (Carson 1974, 185). Its differentiation from the designation *"formal architecture"* is emphasized by Michael Karni and Robert Levin (1972, 92): "the study of vernacular architecture is not the study of intellectualized styles and modes as they are manifested in grand buildings. Rather, it is the study of how skilled craftsmen have met the building needs of their group by using the materials available to them."

In a more expanded discussion, the eminent Irish cultural geographer F.H.A. Aalen (1973, 27) expands the definition and its application by noting,

> Within regions there is marked and voluntary adherence by the majority of society to a single model or ideal pattern of house form. Even though professional builders may be operating, the basic model is not seriously questioned by builder or peasant. The model has no designer but is part of the anonymous folk tradition and tends to be persistent in time. Conformity, anonymity, and continuity may be seen as the hallmarks of regional vernacular architecture, reflecting the cultural coherence, simplicity, and conservatism of present communities and the deep rooted traditions within the building craft.

Geographer Martha Henderson (1992, 15) offers the observation that "vernacular architecture is an historical and geographical record of a culture group's relationship to physical and social environment." Gwyn Meirion-Jones (1982, 166) further suggests that vernacular architecture is an outgrowth and refinement of very early building, which is labeled "primitive." The author further wrote, "there can be no clear divide between the 'primitive' and the 'vernacular' in architecture. The one merges into the other as skill improves and the tradesman, be he carpenter or mason, is increasingly brought into the construction process."

In its most precise usage the term refers to types of structures that occur in a limited area. The usage was borrowed from linguists who used the term "vernacular" to refer to language limited to a particular region (Haase 1992, 11). Thus, words, phrases or grammatical constructions in English found only in Cornwall, for example, comprise the Cornwall vernacular language (i.e. its version of the more widely spoken standard English language).

> When it is said that someone is speaking their "vernacular tongue," it is widely understood that the person is speaking a language indigenous to his or her area of upbringing. It is not normally a term which many people might associate with a style of architecture. At the same time, however, a vernacular building and a vernacular language share many characteristics. Both belong to a recognizable tradition that has evolved over many generations and both have features that are particular to the locality in which they are found. (Dublin Heritage Group 1993, 4)

Building skills also "resemble language to the extent that they are taught by demonstration and learned by imitation so that the idiosyncrasies of teachers are passed on to pupils, thereby consolidated in a generation or two and perpetuated in the long term" (Mason 1973, 15). Jay Edwards (1993, 18) has observed,

> traditions of American vernacular architecture, and low-level polite traditions which function like them, are formulated principally from the perspective of shared geometric regularities rather from that of stylistic attributes. Such traditions are implicitly recognized and understood by their designers, and are identified by their users primarily in terms of consistent geometric forms and spaces and the conventional relationships which obtain between them. Other aspects of a vernacular tradition remain variable and even expendable.

One of the distinctive characteristics of vernacular architecture study is its interdisciplinary or multidisciplinary focus. "Vernacular architecture has been examined from the perspectives of art and architectural history, social history, folklore, anthropology, historical and cultural geography, archaeology, architectural theory, and sociology to name only those disciplines that come immediately to mind" (Upton 1983, 263).

The initial scholarly studies of American vernacular architecture appeared in the 1890s, following the approach that has come to be recognized as object-oriented research. Such a method continues to be important "for there is much data to be gathered, much remaining to be understood about the physical history of buildings. This understanding forms the basis of all other vernacular architecture research" (Upton 1983, 277), although socially, culturally, and symbolically oriented studies are steadily gaining the attention of students of vernacular architecture.

In Great Britain, architectural historian Anthony Quiney (1990, 6–7) draws a line between folk building, which he disparages as "mere building," and vernacular architecture, which he assigns to structures created by the formally untrained, but skilled, craftsmen/builders. At the same time, he recognizes that "the line which separates mere building from architecture [is] impossibly vague." In North America the term vernacular architecture is usually applied more loosely to mean "of the people" – hence folk architecture, although Kingston Heath (1988) objects. Often the exact differentiation between vernacular architecture and folk building is not at all clear, although some researchers have attempted to label folk building as the product of persons who reside in the structure themselves, and vernacular architecture as the term to be used to describe buildings that are built according to local custom by local builders (Weeks 1996, 16). Obviously the terms overlap and often refer to the same process. Paul Oliver (1987, 68) has summarized nicely the process that applies to both:

Tradition establishes a broad matrix, the individual builder designs and constructs to suit his requirements within it. Such dwellings are neither slavish copies of their predecessors, nor willful deviants from them. Construction is not a matter of intuition as if the builders were like birds making their nests, but the result of deliberate decisions related to perceived needs.

Speaking of research methodologies employed in North America for studying traditional buildings, James Shortridge (1980) identified two dominant ones: "the wide-ranging, informal survey designed to get a feel for variation over a large area; and the meticulous measured drawing system often used by students of historical preservation." An intermediate-level approach has been largely lacking. One suspects that the reason for this has much to do with the enormous size of the North American study area.

The term vernacular architecture (in its regional sense) works well in England and some other countries where settlement has been more or less homogeneous with only wide regional differences. "Although there is evidence of widespread overall contact between craftsmen and an obvious exchange of ideas, there was also a good deal of regional insularity [up to the 19th century] leading to pronounced localized mannerisms" (Mason 1973, 15). Particular combinations of elements were "likely to recur throughout a district, thus producing a regional style of building, while the apprenticeship system of training craftsmen and the conservative tastes of most middle-and-lower-class country dwellers ensured that a style . . . tended to be repeated for many years with only minor variations. Regional building styles can, therefore, be identified" (Sheppard 1966, 33).

However, in North America concentrated settlements derived originally from numerous immigrant peoples are decidedly more limited geographically and are scattered across the landscape in a checkerboard fashion. Each group introduced structures which were uniquely or primarily its own. Thus in Wisconsin, for example, there is no regional or vernacular architecture (in the British sense), but a series of ethnically related structures. In the outstanding open-air museum of Old World Wisconsin, where structures of early ethnic groups in Wisconsin are displayed, one experiences the distinctly different structures of the Finns, Norwegians, Germans, and Danes, because each is in its own cluster or setting and physically apart or shielded by vegetation from the others, although located closely enough for comparison. *Ethnic architecture* is a term that works well here, as well as for many studies elsewhere, where strong ethnic characteristics apply. It is especially useful in those places where more than one early ethnic group settled.

Cultural anthropologists have contributed some of the most useful studies of ethnic architecture because of the intimate connection between group culture and buildings. Schooled to investigate all aspects of culture, they recognize its influence on building. Selection of site, orientation of structure, choice of building materials, methods of construction, use of decorative elements, and many other characteristics are all intimately related to culture and vary from group to group within the same area.

The use of a seemingly straightforward term, such as *building*, also may engender some confusion. Scholars who study traditional buildings tend to view them, as Henry Glassie (1972, 31) has suggested, as "internally usable space rather than externally viewed art." Usage of the term *architecture* in phrases such as folk architecture and vernacular architecture is looked on askance by some scholars, especially architects. A quotation from John Harvey (1975, 2) illustrates the point quite well:

> two separate words do exist side by side: *architect* and *builder*, and their products architecture and building. This is fitting, since Architecture is acknowledged as the Mistress Art. Building, with all its component skills such as masonry, carpentry, glazing, is a collective technique taught by the members of one generation to those of the next. It may be greatly modified in course of time by the discovery of new materials or the invention of improved methods, but these changes come from outside. Architecture, however, is not simply the control and supervision of buildings; its primary function is the creation of solutions to fresh problems posed by patrons who wish to have not standardized but specially designed works put up in answer to their requirements.

Architecture is thus viewed as an art form, while building is not. Such an obviously class-derived differentiation is especially attractive to professional architects in the UK and elsewhere, who usually make little effort to discuss traditional buildings, or, when they do, often fail to understand or appreciate them. I must quickly, and in the interest of fairness, add that not all architects evidence such a narrow view.

Pamela Simpson (1990, 78), an art historian, speaking of the difficulties that she and a co-author had, says the following:

> Standard American architectural books proved of little value. Although the seventeenth century was treated in these books in its vernacular manifestations (when nothing else existed to treat), once the high-style bandwagon got underway in the eighteenth century, vernacular forms were ignored. To study vernacular forms, we found it necessary to turn

to non-art historical fields – to anthropology, folklore, and cultural geography.

Perhaps it is because traditional buildings were not designed by professional architects that they seem to be neglected by many of them. Of course, as noted above, exceptions to this narrow perspective exist. Susan Denyer (1978, 4) comments, "Today more and more architects are turning to vernacular architecture for inspiration . . . because it is recognized that these structures obviously satisfied their communities' psychological needs far better than most modern suburban settlements do." Others have noticed the same awakening of interest among some architects, but as architectural scholar Ronald Haase (1992, 10) observes, "in a rush to add depth and meaning to a new post-modern architecture, much that is inappropriate and ineffectual is being borrowed from history and applied without concern for context," demonstrating a lack of appreciation of the vernacular.

An example from Sudan of such misapplication is provided by Allan Cain et al. (1975, 208–9), which they term "formalistic mimicry" or "pseudo vernacular." They recount the construction of low-cost housing in the time-honored circular plan with adobe-like walls. However, the huts are arranged in a formalistic and absolutely straight line with walled backyards rather than in the traditional open cluster arrangement. Additionally, the conical roof is of reinforced concrete rather than thatch. The new roof conducts heat while the old one did not. Finally, the new roof has no overhanging eave to shade much of the wall, so that now the entire wall is exposed to the heat of the sun. The walling material looks like adobe but is of cement, which more readily conducts heat to the interior.

Structural engineers also often find it difficult to appreciate the process of traditional building, which they label *low technology*. R.J.S. Spence and D.J. Cook (1983) accurately point out the differences of the low technology approach, but unfortunately they use as their example the manufacture of fire brick, not a very useful illustration because such brick is far less used in traditional building than other materials.

Architectural historians also seem largely to have neglected traditional building (Roberts 1972, 282). "What was legitimate in architectural history fell within the architect's realm; what was not encompassed by professional architecture was illegitimate" (Upton 1991, 195). Over 30 years ago John Maas (1969, 4) noted "architectural historians do not yet pay attention to the anonymous architecture of early and rural societies." In the years since, a painfully slow movement of architectural historians toward recognition of traditional building is evident, but the tilt towards the formal still persists.

> Most histories of architecture have ignored the traditional common house; yet it is among man's most complex and ubiquitous creations – a product of physical and emotional relationship with human existence that has been constant, intimate and profound.
>
> As shelter, folkhouses were essential to survival by moderating the extremes of climate, by keeping the terrors of the outside world at bay, and by providing the spaces that made life and work possible in an uncertain world. (Carver 1984, 7)

As it was almost 40 years ago (Maas 1969, 7), architectural history today remains a branch of art history. The problem of the basic orientation of many architects and architectural historians has been incisively identified by Gowans (1966, xvii):

> Too often writers on architecture begin by paying lip service to the principle that architecture is the most social of all the arts, that unlike painting or sculpture it cannot be the expression of purely private taste or personal ideas, but must by its nature grow out of and uniquely witness to the common life and thought of its period, etc., etc. – then, having said this, they proceed to chose and write about precisely those works that were not typical of their periods, but that were great and original, and led on to the future.

The problem for architectural historians and architects in investigating vernacular architecture (Upton 1979, 173–5) may be that the widely held "elitist idea that architectural styles gradually filter down to the folk, who employ them as an imitation of high style, is erroneous" (Bronner and Poyser 1979, 118). Thus, these structures do not fit conveniently into architectural style classification systems.

One of the enduring strengths of traditional structures is their intimate relationship with their environment. As James Ayres (1981, 17) notes, "Before houses were 'designed' they evolved, with a sensitivity towards their environment that may be seen as truly organic. It is such values that we have lost today and thus it is, that we so cherish them." Barry Dawson and John Gillow (1994, 19) make the influence of the environment even more critical by stating that "traditional architecture is a product of its environment; each regional variant develops in response to the conditions and materials determined by the local climate and vegetation."

Anthropologists, folklorists and other similarly oriented scholars, however, hold out for culture-determined building strategies. The true relationship probably lies somewhere among these viewpoints. Ronald Knapp (1986, 1) offers a context that provides a solid rationale for the examination of traditional buildings. He says the following in reference to Chinese structures: "Rising out of frugality rather than riches, vernacular forms, despite their nondescript appearance, none-theless document a tradition in which experience and practical wisdom predominate."

Cultural and social historians seem to be much more sensitive to traditional structures and their significance to historical development. Carl Lounsbury (1983, 186) has identified the difference that exists between traditional building and formal architecture, as in the way research materials must be approached:

> The study of vernacular architecture must proceed with a systematic and careful investigation of a large sample of buildings in a given area in order to distinguish common house types, materials, and structural systems. Unlike the study of academic architecture where emphasis is placed on the analysis of individual buildings of exceptional character, the study of vernacular forms depends on the recognition of the repeti-tive and commonplace. Too few buildings in a survey may distort the overall picture.

Architectural historian Dell Upton (1991, 197) carries this idea even further observing "each of the senses may perceive a different land-scape in which the individual building is irrelevant." Therefore, the architectural historian needs to accept as the "unit of analysis the entire *cultural landscape*." Thus, he comes quite close to the approach followed by cultural geographers, as noted below.

Amos Rapoport (1980, 283–4) earlier carried the argument for extensive surveys even further. "Generalizations based upon limited samples are suspect. The broader our sample in space and time, the more likely we are to see regularities in apparent chaos and to under-stand better those differences which are really significant." He further emphasized that high style architectural elements "can be fully and properly understood only in the context of the vernacular matrix which surrounds them, and to which they were related, at the time they were created."

Both "architecture" and "building" operate in a broad area, which is often termed *material culture*. Several definitions of this term have been offered, but the simplest and, at the same time, most comprehen-sive and widely applicable, is that put forward by James Deetz (1977, 10). He simply defines it as "that segment of man's physical environ-ment which is purposely shaped by him according to culturally dictated plans."

Although the term material culture is coming to be widely accepted in North America, other terms with somewhat different meanings also may be found. As Henry Glassie (1968–69, 39), a non-geographer, recognizes, "the establishment of cultural regions provides one of the major reasons for studying material folk culture." Consequently, cultural geographers sometimes use the expression *settlement land-scape* instead of material culture because their orientation is frequently toward analyses of the component parts that make up the cultural landscape. Geographers, to the distress of other scholars, often neglect the details of a building and its particular human connection in their quest for the keys to the cultural landscape (Attebery 1998, 5).

Geographer Daniel Arreola (1988, 299) has proposed the interesting term *"housescape"* to include a house and its immediate landscape. The placing of the building in its surrounding context has strong appeal for geographers. They frequently are more interested in how the structure reflects regional patterns of culture, economy, and environment (Buchanan 1963) than they are in the human dimensions and history of the building. This also creates unease among anthropologists, folklorists, and historians.

Another expression sometimes encountered is *built environment*. It serves to identify that part of material culture which treats entire buildings and their man-made context, as differentiated from the natural environment. The term, although apparently coined originally by sociologists, is favored by planners, engineers, and some landscape architects.

Finally, notice should be taken of the continuum that exists in the phrase *architecture/building*. Traditional building is the product of talented but largely untrained individuals, who build as they do because such knowledge has been more or less informally passed on from generation to generation. The society enforces rules, often unwritten, by group acceptance. Even so, some individuals do not conform, but their structures never characterize the ethnic group's most definitive buildings.

At the opposite pole stands the trained architect who follows stylistic rules, or in rare cases breaks new ground to expand the rules or make new ones. If the society accepts the creations a new style is born or an older one modified. When a particularly responsive chord is struck, the style persists and may come to dominate. Gothic Revival, Classic Revival, Italianate and Second Empire are all examples of long-lived styles recognized in the US. The attitude of society is important only after the structure is completed, and not before, as in the case of folk architecture. In a real sense, the architect is building for the approval of clients and other architects. Structures built by architects are often referred to as *academic* or *formal* architecture.

Folklorist Howard Marshall (1981, 25) helps us to understand the different perspectives by noting that "folk things tend to vary little over time but much over space – and the opposite is true for fashion-

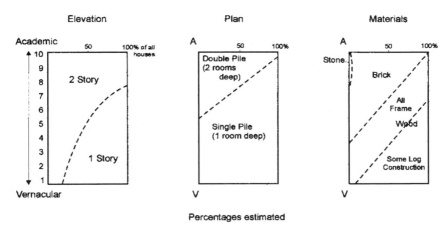

1-5. *The relationship between characteristics of vernacular and academic or formal architecture, emphasizing form and materials (based upon Trimble 1988, 100).*

able things and academic architecture." Writing with regard to middle Tennessee – where both vernacular and academic architecture buildings exist – Stanley Trimble (1988, 98–100), in a valuable idiosyncratic analysis, contrasted academic and vernacular characteristics relating to elevation, plan, materials, and other aspects (Figure 1-5).

Between the poles of folk and academic architecture lies a vast area into which most buildings fall in any classification scheme. Designated as *popular* or *eclectic* architecture, these structures combine components of various architectural styles, sometimes together with elements from traditional building. John Warren and Ihsan Fethi (1982, 21) have summed up this relationship quite nicely:

> There is an indefinite threshold between vernacular building and conscious architecture. The vernacular is the work of the people, the users, without the aid of designers. Conscious architecture is the work of those who design as a deliberate art, often for their livings and usually for others: and between the two lies the work of local builders guided by experience and tradition and working directly to the wishes of their clients. At its one extreme this work rises into the realms of conscious architecture and at the other it reflects the untutored eye of the common man often with the most engaging and practical of results.

While architects may have been remiss in ignoring traditional building, or, when what little attention has been paid, in patronizing (Mason 1973, 12), a wide variety of other scholars have examined these structures. Such investigators include cultural geographers, cultural historians, anthropologists, archeologists, sociologists, historic preservationists, folklorists, and landscape architects. Fortunately, such diverse backgrounds and training permit traditional building to be approached from several perspectives, offering a variety of insights.

With the shift of world population to cities, the emphasis on traditional building began to decline (Aalen 1973, 48). However, the overwhelming number of scholarly studies of such structures treat those of the countryside or in small villages. As geographer Ronald Knapp (1986, 2) puts it, "rural houses by and large have been *built* rather than designed, with tradition acting as the regulator. Experience, practicality, and economy have guided housing form just as local conditions have governed building materials." In these areas patterns usually can be seen more clearly than in the often confusing and mixed urban context. Also, the hold of tradition is strongest in the rural areas, where change and innovation generally occur most slowly. This is not to say that traditional buildings cannot be found in urban areas, but most scholarly attention has been focused elsewhere. Nevertheless, historic preservationists and historic preservation planners have been in the forefront of those working with traditional structures in urban areas.

Above all, it must be remembered that traditional buildings rarely exist in isolation. They make up an *ensemble* of structures as part of a farmstead, a compound, a hamlet, or a small village, and they need to be considered in their context whenever possible. A fundamental error, which many local historical preservation entities make, is to preserve a single building, often moved and reassembled on a new site. Of course, many factors operate against extensive preservation, such as lack of funding, lack of adequate space, radically changed land use, and lack of community interest. Granted, single structure preservation is better than none at all, but how much more useful would be preservation which included context.

The need for archeologists to investigate and understand context has been explained by Robert Barakat (1972, 6). His comments apply equally to scholars of all other disciplines. He says, "The task of the historical archaeologist is to reconstruct the whole life of a town, village, farm or house, and not just selected parts, a goal that is indeed awesome in scope but not so impossible. If his work is to mean anything at all to the world at large, it must accomplish this; he cannot escape his responsibilities to the scientific pursuit of knowledge and to himself."

Over 20 years ago, I ended a two-volume study of the North American settlement landscape (Noble 1984) with a plea for the development of a common research *terminology*. I was certainly not alone in recognizing the problem, which had been identified by frustrated researchers at earlier times (Richardson 1973, 77; Walker 1977, 5–7, for example). It was probably naive of me to expect that such commonality could be achieved in a short space of time. With so many scholars from such widely disparate disciplines and perspectives, a converging research approach remains unlikely, but the need continues. Even the preparation of an extensive and comprehensive multilanguage glossary would be beneficial in enhancing knowledge and research.

Interest, and even awareness, of vernacular architecture is growing, both among professionally trained investigators and among those others who simply have a curiosity about such structures. Not until about the 1960s was such interest sufficient to support much ongoing activity to learn about and then to preserve traditional buildings. Prior to that, efforts were generally oriented toward structures that had an intimate connection with an historical event, or more likely a locally prominent person. The buildings of the folk were largely ignored as unimportant.

The reader will note a heavy emphasis in this volume on earlier studies and the extensive employment of examples to illustrate concepts, processes, and phenomena. These demonstrate the worldwide scope of traditional building practices and the often surprisingly similar approaches in widely separated parts of the world, as well as the informing contrasts. Thus, these examples are so numerous and integral as to form a critical component of this volume. I have included references to these earlier works to enable interested readers to locate them easily and to evaluate the source materials for themselves.

Admittedly it is difficult to attempt to find universal commonalities in traditional building across the entire world. They exist only up to a point, but at the same time their identification may be illuminating, so that a framework is created for investigations of problems of much more local and restricted scope. It is with this hope that the following chapters are presented.

~ 2 ~
Function and Form

Concepts of function and form are central to the study of traditional buildings. The widely repeated dictum that "form follows function" has fine alliteration and a kernel of truth, but on close examination the idea falls short with reference to traditional building. Recognizing this, French scholars of architecture at the Museum of Folk Arts and Traditions in Paris coined the term *functional décalage* to identify the many discrepancies between form and function (Rivière 1954, 9). Furthermore, John Lloyd (1969, 34) notes that in medieval Norway "buildings were differentiated by function rather than by form." Each farmstead consisted of multiple, identically standardized units, each unit being differentiated only by its function. In contrast, Ronald Lewcock and Gerard Brans (1977, 107–16) and others have demonstrated convincingly that house form derived from other sources can persist and be easily adapted to function if the form is sufficiently strong within the cultural background of the society.

Even though *function* remains inflexible, the form is quite variable. Houses may be excavated or erected, or partly both. They may rise to a single story or several. Their floor plans are square, rectangular, round, oval, or combinations of such figures. Roof forms are equally diverse and depend more upon climate and available local materials than on function (Figure 2-1). Wall treatments show almost infinite variations. As an illustration of the significant effect of climate, consider Labelle Prussin's (1974, 185–6) observation that in West Africa there is little temperature change between day and night, or even between wet and dry seasons. This calls for a shelter with a raised floor, open-weave bamboo screen walls, and a floor plan providing for cross-ventilation. In contrast, the interior savannah climate has both rainy and dry seasons, with daily temperature changes in the latter as large as 30 to 35° Fahrenheit. Here, "the earthen roundhouse with its insulating walls can accumulate and store the heat of the day for evening comfort."

One must not, therefore, rely on form and function too singlemindedly. "All houses are dwellings; but all dwellings are not houses" (Oliver 1987, 7). The case of Dutch windmills offers an apt illustration.

2-1. The arched roof traditional dwelling of the Toda people in the Nilgiri Hills, India. The small size of the door is a security feature carried over from earlier, more precarious times (photo by the author, 1976).

The function of a windmill is to provide a reliable source of power. At the same time, many of the older windmills provided living space for the miller's family on the lower levels of the structure. The mills, designed in the 15th century, were of the hollow-post type, and had two entrance doors. Two are "required in order to provide free access and exit with any position of the plane in which the sails are turning. The door past which the sails sweep is then firmly shut, for it would be highly dangerous if someone were to pass through inadvertently" (Stokhuyzen 1963, 30).

Because these early mills were small, the single living/kitchen/sleeping room was very cramped. "A small cottage, the summer house, is often found close to the mill. It is there that the miller and his family live more comfortably in summer. The summer house is low, so as not to interfere with the catching of the wind" (Stokhuyzen 1963, 33). Later on, the mills became considerably larger and two floors could be devoted to living quarters, but space was always at a premium. Even later, larger drainage mills provided more suitable, expanded living accommodation, with the living room/kitchen on the ground floor and bedrooms on the next level. Smoke found its way out of the mill through small apertures high up in the thatched wall/roof.

In some instances, the function of old traditional buildings may have changed while the form continues unaltered. Perhaps the best example occurs among the Ashanti, where dwellings have been converted into fetish houses, now used only for religious purposes (Swithenbank 1969). The form of the structures making up the dwelling is unusual (Rutter 1971). Four small, thatched-roof, rectangular huts of light timber and bamboo frame supporting mud walls are linked by splayed screen walls to enclose a central courtyard, with only one entrance. Only one hut, the sleeping room, is enclosed on the courtyard side.

Form may also change even though function does not. Dorothy Bracken and Maurine Redway (1956, 4 & 158) document the often-encountered change from single-cell log cabin to more complex dog-trot house with the passage of time. The home of the early Texas leader Sam Houston offers a more expanded, specific example. Beginning as a single-cell log cabin, the structure ended up as a six-room, story-and-a-half house. To the original one-room cabin, a second room was later added, with a dogrun between. Porches and other rooms were added still later, as were the attic and the drop siding.

Form is influenced by a number of factors of which function is just one. Environment is also important. It establishes absolute limits: there are no snow houses in the tropics nor palm-leaf huts in the polar regions (Anderson 1961, 46). The influence of the environment cannot be ignored. In northern Korea, for example, the individual rooms of traditional houses are arranged in double rows to conserve internal heat and protect against extreme external cold. In southern Korea, though, the influence of the much hotter summer climate, combined with milder winter, meant that houses were smaller, built in a single row to facilitate cross-ventilation, and typically with raised wooden floors with freely circulating air beneath (Choi et al. 1999, 13). More often, the environment simply exerts a partial influence upon form, although its effect upon building materials is more profound, as will be seen in following chapters.

The influence of environment is more subtle in some areas. In Appalachia, initial settlement by European-derived pioneers was usually in log houses, which continued to predominate into the 20th century in the uplands. In the more fertile valley bottoms, where soils were of better quality, settlers replaced original log cabins with larger frame I-houses. These structures eventually became the standard dwellings identifying the better agricultural areas of Appalachia. I-houses had become so established that when settlement moved westwards into the Midwest, the house type moved with the people.

Today examples can be found throughout the central United States (Noble 1984, 1:52), even as far west as Oklahoma (Crumbie 1987).

The *I-house* is a traditional form, which has not received the careful attention it deserves. It is a structure "gables to the side, at least two rooms in length, one room deep, and two full stories in height" (Kniffen 1965, 555). For Fred Kniffen, who gave this house type its name, the designation of "I" house was appropriate since its tall, narrow gable-end form resembles a block letter "I". More accurately, however, the name was contrived by Kniffen because in semi-annual automobile trips between Louisiana and Michigan using varying routes through Iowa, Illinois and Indiana, he noticed the dominance of these houses which did not occur much to the north or south of the three states whose names began with "I". For convenience sake he called them I-houses. Thus are vernacular features often named!

The I-house is probably the traditional house type with the greatest geographical distribution in North America. It has numerous subtypes (Figure 11-6), which may or may not come from a single origin. A British connection seems to be logical, but other European links, especially German, may also exist. In Appalachia the I-house was especially popular among the more affluent farmers in the 19th century, as a decided step upward from the common log house of that area. Hundreds, perhaps thousands, were built, but this popularity also meant that the structure sometimes was a rebuild of an earlier log house, and not an original frame I-house.

A fine example of such a modification exists in the Sadler house near Bessemer, Alabama. The original house was of log construction. Later a frame room was added across a breezeway, creating a classic dogtrot form (Figure 2-2). A second story, added even later, gave the building its characteristic I-house configuration of two-story elevation, two-room width (if the enclosed breezeway is considered a hall passage), and one-room depth. The final modification was the adding of a rear, one-story shed and a front porch with a small framed-in room. These small front porch rooms were often locally called "prophet's rooms" because they were sometimes used as a bedroom to shelter itinerant preachers (Gamble 1990, 30).

In rural areas the functions of traditional buildings include human shelter, animal shelter, storage of agricultural tools and implements, and food storage. In addition, a few non-agricultural structures are encountered, including churches and chapels, workshops and the odd small mill, usually powered by wind or water. Large-scale structures, on the other hand, are products of the Industrial Revolution and do not fit in with traditional buildings. The scope of the present discussion largely omits the non-agricultural buildings of whatever size.

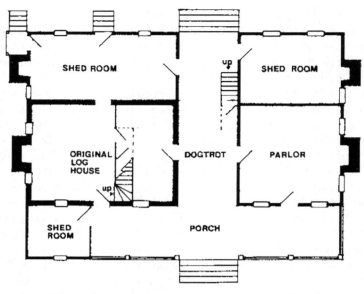

2-2. *Floor plan of the Sadler house in northern Alabama. Four or five stages of remodeling are evident, beginning from the single-room log house and finishing with an expanded I-house (from Gamble 1990, 32. Reprinted with permission of the University of Alabama Press).*

When more than one function is anticipated, the question of form may be even more problematic. Take the example of housebarns, which shelter not only humans but animals as well, and also provide storage for equipment and tools, and often farm products and food. French archeologists use a further term, "mixed house," to refer to a structure in which humans and animals are housed *in the same room* (Chapelot and Fossier 1985, 224). In the current work, the word *house-*

2-3. *Drawing of a koshel, a typical log housebarn of northern Russia. The living quarters are to the left and the farm buildings are to the right. The roofed-over center section is really a large yard. The ramp leads to a hayloft (drawing by M. Margaret Geib).*

barn refers to all structures that house both humans and animals, regardless of room arrangement.

An almost infinite variety of housebarn forms serve these functions. One of the most unusual, the *koshel*, appears in northern Russia. All the parts are arranged in two rows separated by a large central yard. The buildings and enclosed yard form a square space under a common, massive, gabled roof whose two slopes are unequal in length and asymmetrical in profile. The shorter slope over the living quarters is steeper, while the other, longer slope covers both interior yard and the farm structures (Figure 2-3). These log buildings allowed the farmer to follow work routines entirely under cover during the fierce, northern Russian winters (Opolovnikov and Opolovnikov 1989, 45).

In North America the only commonly built housebarns are those of the German-Russian Mennonites in Manitoba and, less frequently, in Saskatchewan. Early on, when Europeans first arrived along the east coast of North America, a few housebarns were constructed by other groups (Leiby 1964, 87), but the housebarn did not persist long. Several reasons may account for its early demise: the abundance of wood from nearby forests encouraged separation of house and barn, so that fire danger was thus reduced and hygiene enhanced; most settlers were poor and did not possess resources sufficient to build large housebarns. Even more fundamental, most early settlers did not own much livestock and availability of land was not a concern, so farmsteads could spread out much more than in Europe. A few housebarns can still be found elsewhere in North America (Koop and Ludwig 1984; Tishler and Witmer 1984; Marshall 1986; Price 1989; Ainsley 2003).

The very earliest German-Russian housebarns in Canada were framed as a single unit, but the separate framing of house and barn, although still joined together, became popular as sawn lumber replaced hewn timber. The typical form is a structure oriented with the gable of the house to the road, but the door on the side, and a higher roof ridge for the attached barn, which was divided into stable and storage areas for grain and equipment (Figure 2-4). The house and the barn have in-line rectangular plans (Figure 2-5) resulting in an elongated overall form (Noble 1992b).

Contrast the form of these housebarns with the four-story, stone-built housebarns of the Italians and Swiss in Piedmont and Engadin (Scheuermeier 1943, 2:2–3). Here, because of mountainous terrain, the housebarn assumes a vertical form. Still a third European form variation is the widely distributed barn called the Hallenhaus (Figure 2-6). Of brick and half-timber construction with a thatched roof, it ranges all across the North German plain from Lower Saxony to the Vistula

2-4. *Drawing of a housebarn typical of German-Russian Mennonite settlements in southeastern Manitoba, Canada. The house part on the left is connected to the barn by an interior door (drawing by M. Margaret Geib).*

2-5. *Floor plan of a typical German-Russian Mennonite housebarn from Manitoba. The ovesid extension is used for extra storage of gear. Note the centrally located black kitchen (drawing by M. Margaret Geib).*

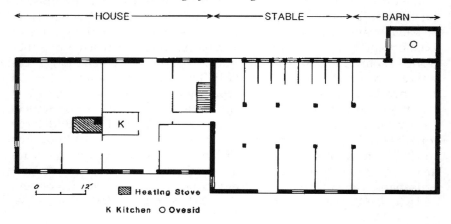

delta. With the entrance door on the gable end, this transverse building has a wide central aisle with stables and stalls lining both sides of one end and the living quarters clustered at the other, also opening off the center aisle of the building (Folkers 1961; Bedal 1980).

An even more impressive housebarn is the *Gulfhaus*, which ranges from northwestern Netherlands, across Germany to southwestern Denmark. The house and barn adjoin but are separately framed (Figure 2-7). The huge, squarish expanse of the barn, designated to hold great quantities of grain and hay for dairy cattle, consists of a heavy timber frame supporting a roof on four massive wooden pillars approximately 15 meters (44 feet) high (Lasius 1885; Folkers 1954, 18; Lerche 1973, 16). In North Holland the Gulfhaus is referred to as a *stolp* farmhouse. In the closely related *stelp* farmhouse version found in Friesland the house and barn are framed together and the barn is rectangular rather than square in plan (Smaal 1979, 98). A fourth dis-

2-6. This brick and half-timber Hallenhaus is preserved in the Cloppenburg Open-Air Museum, Germany. Note the extra layer of thatch along the ridge and the bellcast of the eaves, both features to provide maximum rain protection (photo by the author, 1982).

tinctive and common European form variation is the Bernese Middleland housebarn of Switzerland (Figure 2-8). Two and a half stories high, the building has prominent gable balconies and an immense tent-like, hipped roof hood, reaching almost to the ground (Atkinson 1969, 50–2).

Two, much older, housebarn forms from other parts of Europe also can be mentioned as additional variations. In western Ireland the early housebarns had a roughly oval floor plan and were constructed of turf and stone. These quite basic structures, with no division between the parts housing animals and those housing humans (Aalen 1966, 49), represent a stage in the evolution of larger and more sophisticated housebarns. The other early European housebarn occurs in the Finnmark province of Norway. Encased in turf or sod over a timber frame, the single-story structures called *gamme* have a unique "T" shaped floor plan (Vreim 1937, 189–90).

Housebarns are also characteristic in other parts of the world. In the mountainous areas of central Morocco, a 2:3 ratio rectangular-plan adobe and stone building is most common (Laoust 1935). The animal accommodations are a foot or so lower, and usually downhill from the rest of the house. In winter, women and children sleep in the loft over the stable (Bourdieu 1973, 98). This Berber housebarn from the Atlas Mountains of Morocco is surprisingly similar in general

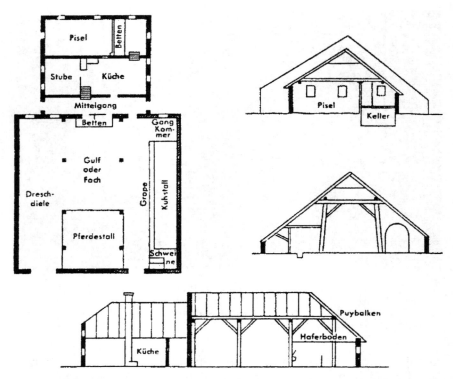

2-7. Cross-sections and floor plan of a Gulfhaus typical of the Netherlands. This
structure is also referred to as a Stolp farmhouse. Although attached, the small
house part is separately framed and quite distinct from the large, attached,
square-plan barn (from Lasius 1885, 5).

features to a totally unrelated housebarn from northwestern Ireland
(Figure 2-9). Such similarity strengthens the idea of the influence of
function upon form. In the Irish barn the byre is separated by a stone
partition from the dwelling part of the structure, but a bedroom occupies a higher level over the byre. In both the Irish and Berber
housebarns the sleeping areas benefit in winter from the upward
moving heat of the animals. Here, in this more limited comparison of
housebarn forms, we do have function determining form: both
humans and animals housed, animals in a lower level so that wastes
are drained away from the human dwelling areas, and sleeping areas
benefiting from the heat of the animals. The more important idea,
though, is to warn researchers not to ascribe a cultural connection
between widely, or even closely, situated examples when the features
may be related more to climate or some other natural factor.

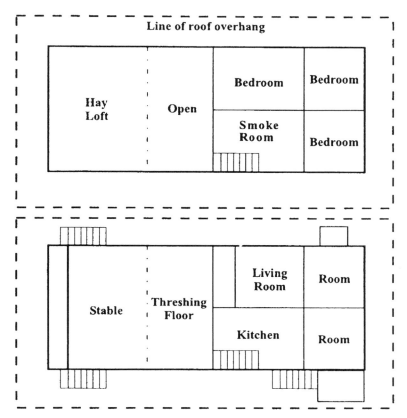

2-8. *Floor plans of a Bernese Middleland housebarn. These structures have immense roofs that are suspended from the main center poles. This type of roof is sometimes called a tent roof. The dashed line represents the extent of the roof overhang (drawn by Amy Rock, based upon Atkinson 1969, 54).*

Even in the Indian sub-continent, where separate sheds or enclosures shelter most cattle, the housebarn form shows interesting variations. These are most evident in the Himalaya Mountains of Nepal. Variations both in form and construction materials appear as altitude changes and agriculture responds. The Tharu people farm and tend animals in the Piedmont plains up to 600 meters (±1800 feet). Their houses occupy both sides of north–south trending, single-street villages. Lined up closely on both sides of the road, and every one oriented to the south (Milliet-Mondon 1982, 153), the rectangular housebarns remind one of a train of box cars, or perhaps more fancifully a parade of circus elephants! The cow-house part of the structure is separated from the habitation by a center "hall" with open fire. This space serves as the public social area of the dwelling.

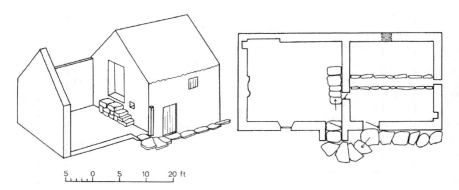

2-9. *Floor plan and diagram of a housebarn from Donegal, Ireland. Note the rough inside stone steps leading to the sleeping area above the byre. In winter the sleeping area gained heat from the animals in the byre (from McCourt 1970, 5. Courtesy of the Ulster Folk and Transport Museum).*

2-10. *Sketch, cross-section and plans of a Sherpa housebarn of the high Himalaya. Note how the structure hugs the mountain slope, taking advantage of the limited level land (from Milliet-Mondon 1982, 162. Reprinted with permission of the Nordic Institute of Asian Studies).*

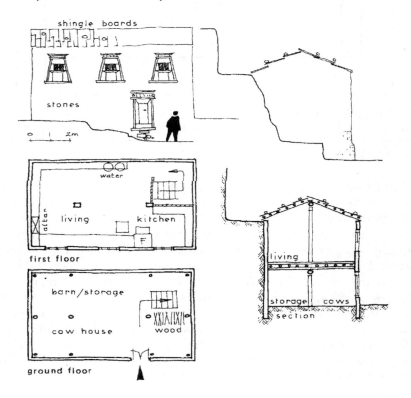

The smaller, more compact, two-story-with-loft dwellings of the Tamang people lie at about 1400 meters (± 4300 feet). Colder temperatures encourage the use of rammed earth, stone, and mortar for walling, and the gable-on-hip roof is thatched to shed the large amount of summer rain. Three sides of the structure are free of windows or doors to help moderate the chill of winter (Milliet-Mondon 1982, 159). Sherpas occupy housebarns up to 4,400m. (± 13,200ft.) in the high Himalaya. Usually built against an over-steepened mountain wall, the two-story housebarn has a door and windows opening out to the downslope valley (Figure 2-10). Only occupied for up to six months a year, these dwellings serve as winter shelter (Milliet-Mondon 1982, 163).

Somewhat similar structures can be found in the Indian areas of the Himalayas. These include the one-and-a-half-story stone houses of the poorer peasants on the hill slopes of Dehra Dun (Dikshit 1965, 46), and the more commodious and elaborate two- and three-story timber and stone structures higher up in Jaunsar, Himachal Pradesh (Tewari 1966, 41–6).

Perhaps the most distinctive and unusual housebarn, although not called that, is a round masonry tower house found in interior Yemen. The ground floor accommodates animals, the next one or two levels are for food storage and processing, and the airy upper stories contain the living quarters (Lewcock 1976, 7, 10). Similar, but rectangular, tower housebarns occur in the Atlas Mountains of Morocco (Hicks 1966). See Chapter 14 for how tower houses are being replaced by houses of quite different design.

Housing animals with humans at night in order to provide maximum security for a critically valuable farm resource has been almost a universal practice throughout the world of subsistence agriculture (Brooke 1959, 70–1, for an example). Where the dwelling sits in an enclosed compound, the courtyard provides the protection for cattle and other livestock (Pawar 1984, 45–6, for an example).

Even in the relatively small area of the United Kingdom considerable variation exists in the form of housebarns. In northwestern England, Wales, and lowland Scotland the predominant example is the narrow, rectangular *longhouse*, with centered hearth and smoke hole or chimney essentially dividing the human domain from that of the animals (Peate 1963; Aalen 1973, 38–9; Whyte 1975, 63). The most critical diagnostic feature of the longhouse is the cross-passage, which served both as entrance to the living area for humans and walkway to the byre area for milk cows (Smith, J.T. 1963, 389).

Along the Scottish–English border a radically different form appears in the *bastle house*. These small, defensible structures, located within 20 miles of the border, were a response to the long unsettled conditions of that area. The building rises a full two stories with animals housed below, an arrangement not found elsewhere in Britain (Quiney 1990, 124–6). An outside stairway gives access to the upper floor, but originally entry was probably by a removable ladder (Ramm, McDowall and Mercer 1970). The third variation in UK housebarns, the *laithe house* form, occurs across the upland area of the Pennines. The laithe house is a two-story dwelling with a one-story animal shelter and barn fully integrated into the structure. The laithe house incorporates a barn as well as a byre, which the other housebarns do not (Smith, P. 1963, 430). Often no internal connection exists between byre/barn and living quarters (Stell 1965, 10, 20–1).

It might be useful at this point to explain differences in terminology in use in the British Isles and in North America. In the latter area the word *barn* is applied to structures that house animals, including cows and horses, as well as equipment and fodder, and often grain. The barn is normally the largest structure on the farmstead, often supplemented by small special-use buildings such as chicken coops, smokehouses, springhouses, and others. The barn often carries a modifier to more specifically designate its particular use, such as dairy barn, sheep barn, potato barn and so on. In the British Isles the word barn is reserved for grain storage structures, and the terms *byre* or *shippon* are applied to cow shelters. Horses are sheltered in a separate *stable* building.

In addition to the housebarns highlighted above, a very wide range of similar structures could be cited across the world. The further in time a person goes back to examine human habitation, the more likely one is to encounter structures providing shelter to both humans and domestic animals, even though the structures appear to be smaller and smaller. As agricultural income gradually improved, societies became more stable, and as the need for security lessened, animals increasingly were sheltered in a separate building. However, according to Jean Chapelot and Robert Fossier (1985, 211), in parts of Europe true housebarns (as opposed to "mixed houses") were not the earliest prominent dwellings. Their growing popularity was the result of the need for more powerful horses to draw the newly invented (12th–13th century) mould board plows, the more general use of horses for all kinds of activities, the growing trade in milk and milk products, and an increased demand for meat.

The farther one moves from Europe, the more non-descript and unremarkable the barn or byre becomes, except for North America where fertile soils, abundant land, bountiful harvests, and growing agricultural markets in developing urban areas combined to encourage the construction of these as separate structures in the late 18th and throughout the 19th centuries. Initially, in North America barns were transplanted forms brought by early immigrant settlers. Each group introduced structures they knew from their origins in Europe, so that a number of distinctly ethnic barns are easily identified today in North America. They range from the English three-bay threshing barn to the German *grundschier* and bank barn with forebay, to the Dutch squarish-plan, gable-entry structure, to the French long barn, and a number of less common types (Noble 1984, 2:15–35).

The study of traditional buildings is difficult enough when examples are still extant, even though altered from original form. However, the research is much more difficult and problematic when only traces of the structure remain. Archeologists, although they may seem at times to be overly preoccupied with pottery fragments and copper coins, perform a critically useful service to all other students of traditional buildings by pushing the frontier of knowledge backwards to illuminate early features, thus helping others to understand much later buildings. Nevertheless, much of the work of archeologists, at least in the beginning of research, must necessarily remain conjectural.

P.V. Addyman (1972, 302–7) provides a nice example of conjectural investigation. He offers three drawings to illustrate the possible evolution of early Anglo-Saxon houses of which virtually nothing remains today. The earliest buildings appear to have had paired posts in individual post-holes. Later, more closely spaced poles were erected in a continuous trench. In late Saxon times a timber frame with a sill replaced the poles and the plan was sometimes "boat-shaped." Throughout, the function of the building remained the same even though the form changed.

The observer of traditional buildings quickly recognizes that the functions of a structure may change over time. For most structures the changes will be downward. A dwelling that outlives its usefulness as the family grows may be converted to storage if its structure is still sound. This may also happen if the economic position of the family improves (Richmond 1932, 96). A recently discovered New World Dutch timber-frame house in Schohaire, New York illustrates such conversion and the difficulty of its identification without close interior inspection. The structure today represents a 19th-century carriage barn, but the exterior conceals a circa 1740 Dutch house.

> In the 19th century the house frame was stripped. Its mud-and-straw infill and riven lath removed. The walls were raised 5½ feet, the pitch of the roof lowered and the structure converted into a carriage barn. Its present appearance is a complete disguise, but its interior displays a

> remarkably preserved and easily accessible New World Dutch house frame. (Sinclair 2004, 1–3)

On the American frontier, log houses might be replaced by more elaborate and fashionable dwellings as family fortunes increased, or as time permitted (Bonar 1983, 213), or as alternative materials became available (Dickinson 1990, 5). A similar process ocurred in rural Ontario (Coffey 1985) in the middle of the 19th century, when rural prosperity as a result of high wheat prices enabled settlers to replace early log houses with larger and more fashionable frame, brick or stone ones (Blake and Greenhill 1969, 3). The progression from temporary shelter in a dugout or hut, to semi-permanent log house, and finally to permanent timber or lumber frame, or brick or stone house is such a common theme in North America that it is commented upon by numerous scholars (Carter 1975, 339; Bakerdsay 1979, 131–2; Carson et al. 1981, 140, as examples). Another possibility, as noted above, was simply to use the log cabin as a nucleus and to construct a new house around it (Jones 1979, 48).

If the structure remained sound, the logs frequently were covered by clapboards, sawn planks, stucco or even a facing of bricks, providing a tighter building able to withstand deterioration better. The most compelling reason for such modification, however, was not heat retention but to gain status. "Although straightforward log and adobe structures are admired today, in their time they were not much appreciated for their rustic beauty" (Robinson 1981, 51). "Jacksonian democracy made it socially acceptable for a presidential candidate to have been born in a log cabin, but it was most assuredly not fitting for the candidate to continue living in one" (Jordan 1978, 5). W. Calvin Dickinson (1990, 5) puts it more bluntly, "Log houses were considered a symbol of poverty."

In any case, if deterioration of the building occurs, especially with minimal maintenance, it may be relegated further to basic animal shelter or livestock confinement (Macrae and Adamson 1963, 4; Everest 1966, 59), or in drier environments simply to store grain and other feed for livestock (Attebery et al. 1985, 48). Thus it was in North America that early log cabins often ended up as pig sties or chicken coops. On the other hand, the reverse is possible, although not as frequent. Witness the modern conversion and renovation of barns to become upscale dwellings (Schmertz 1974).

A commonly encountered change of structural form is one that accompanies either growth in family size or increase in household income. Both situations encourage expansion of the dwelling by adding floor levels, or by horizontal expansion of the original plan. Several advantages of vertical expansion may encourage its use.

Because heat rises, an upper floor benefits in winter without the necessity to provide an additional heat source. Also, extra roofing is not required. Upper stories have greater security than horizontal wings. Finally, there is no loss of agricultural land or no necessity to clear additional forest.

One Appalachian solution to the problem of adding needed living space to an existing small cabin was the *dogtrot*, sometimes called the dogrun, possum trot, two pens-and-a-passage, double house, or erroneously the double pen (Latham 1977, 8). A second log or frame pen

2-11. Sketch and generalized floor plan of a dogtrot house. The dashed line indicates the extent of the overhanging roof. The dogtrot itself is the roofed, but otherwise open, area between the two pens (drawing by M. Margaret Geib).

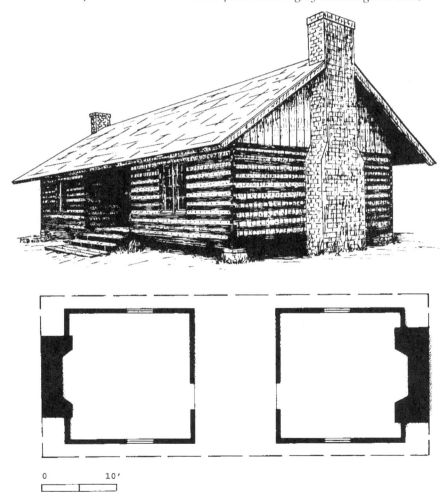

0   10'

was built in line with the first but several feet away (Figure 2-11). The roof of the first structure was then extended over the open space (the dogtrot) and the additional building (Hulan 1975). When a floor was provided to the central passage, two new, roofed, living/working areas were created. The dogtrot was protected from the rain and, because its front and back were open, the Bernoli principle provided a cooling effect, desirable in the long Appalachian summers. However, the dogtrot was not limited to Appalachia (Weslager 1969, 72, 240–1, 345–8; Hulan 1977, 25–32), with numerous early examples in Pennsylvania and the eastern Midwest. From Appalachia the dogtrot spread across the upland areas of the southeastern United States, into the Ozark uplands of Arkansas and Missouri (Marshall 1981, 55) and as far west as Texas (Bracken and Redway 1956), Oklahoma (Henderson et al. 1978) and Kansas (Koch 1982, 26).

All of the factors mentioned above as promoting the building of dogtrot houses may also have played a part in the popularity of single-room-plan, two-story dwellings, termed *stack houses* (Figure 2-12). These structures have been discussed by R.W. Brunskill (1954, 174–5) as they occur in the Eden Valley in northern England, where they consist of kitchen and pantry separated by a light internal partition on the ground floor and a single bedroom on the upper floor. Houses of a similar floor plan are reported from colonial Virginia (Lounsbury 1977, 24), colonial Maine and New Hampshire (Candee 1976, 44–51), and later in German-settled areas of Missouri (Roark and McCutchen 1993). Perhaps the most unusual example of vertical expansion occurs very rarely in Appalachia, where a few dogtrot houses have had a story added, creating a two-story-high breezeway (O'Malley and Rehder 1978, 113; Tate 2002, 51). Adding stories to other house types is common and unremarkable, a sensible way to add space.

Horizontal expansion is also a commonly employed technique everywhere (Figure 2-13). Polish-occupied houses in Buffalo, New York built in the early 20th century are characterized by an add-on form to accommodate growing extended families as well as newly arrived immigrant Polish males (Noble 1992a, 23–4). Horizontal expansion also produced the extended *chattel house* in Barbados (Fraser 1990, 6–14). The original wooden frame dwellings are typically very small, twice as wide as deep, gable-roofed, with a central door flanked by windows. They developed as a response to the freeing of African slaves by the British in the 19th century. Because most of the cultivatable land was owned by sugar plantations, the only locations for the slaves to build their own houses were small plots of marginal land in the vicinity of the plantations where they now worked as tenants (Ainsley 1996, 33).

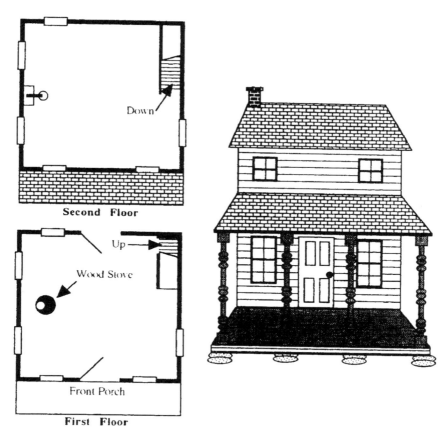

Second Floor

First Floor

2-12. *Sketch and floor plans of the German stack house-type found in Missouri. Each floor normally has just a single room (from Roark and McCutchen 1993, 63. Courtesy of the Pioneer America Society).*

Because the tenants could not own the land on which they built their houses the structures had to be small, easily dismantled, and readily moveable to a new location if necessary, hence the local name of chattel house. The word "chattel," meaning moveable property, is derived from the word "cattle." The idea goes back to Roman times when the only significant item of personal property was the animal. "The cattle could be accumulated and bought and sold and given to any son or daughter the man chose. Cattle were negotiable and could be translated into cash, and one reason they were negotiable was that they were mobile" (Jackson 1984, 92). In Barbados, original chattel houses could be disassembled, lifted in parts onto a cart, and easily moved. Over time, rear room units were added to accommodate additional family members. They were identical to the original unit,

2-13. *Add-on houses are typical of Polish neighborhoods in Buffalo, NY. Additions were added as the family expanded, and also to provide additional sleeping rooms for single male boarders (from Noble 1992a, 24).*

except often a bit wider to encourage cross-ventilation. This final room addition typically had a more easily built shed roof rather than the gable roofs that covered each of the other earlier units (Figure 2-14).

Construction is a dynamic activity that responds to human demands. Thus, building types are not static; or jokingly "they are not set in stone." While construction of a building follows "approved standards of traditional craftsmanship" (Agorsah 1985, 105), constant alteration and improvement is normal, the result of on-going occupa-

2-14. *Sketch of a chattel house, Barbados. Although not shown in this drawing, the rear sections are sometimes a bit wider than the original front section in order to provide better ventilation. Each section can be disassembled quickly for moving to a new site. Most chattel houses do not have basements. (drawing by Amy Rock).*

tion and adjustment. The influence of people in determining building form is so great that many scholars assign it first rank, surpassing even climate and availability of construction materials (Arreola 1988, 313). Edward Chappell (1980, 55) categorically states "form in folk architecture is primarily determined by the traditions and the symbolic needs of the people who construct and live in buildings." Many other scholars will agree.

The building of a traditional house, although the original responsibility of the owner, may involve the entire local community:

> The owner of a house is his own architect, designer, and builder. He not only determines the house's original form, but, as he lives in it, constantly alters and improves upon it. He has at his disposal a local supply of labor and materials. . . . The women and girls supply water from the river, and the men provide timber, rope, puddled earth, and thatch and other roofing materials, depending on what each can afford at the time. A few villagers have developed skills in building and are often invited to help in exchange for a few days' free labor on their farms or some kind of extra reward beyond the party usually held for all who help after each day's work. (Agorsah 1985, 105)

Human needs, wants, and affluence constantly change as do fashions, and this is reflected in changes in construction methods, the popularization of new plans, the acceptance of different building styles, the use of new construction materials, and adoption of innovations derived from outside sources. "Domestic architecture, like all manifestations of human resource and activity, never remains static; development proceeds as habits and conditions of life change; adaptation to changing standards is constantly evident" (Sinclair 1953, 14). Jae-pil Choi (1987, 19–20) has cataloged the extensive changes which took place in Korean traditional houses after the Korean War of the early 1950s. These included sliding doors replaced by swinging doors, the introduction of brick and concrete block as building materials, incorporation of an attached bathroom, water piped into the dwelling, entry to the kitchen inside the house, and the replacement of the courtyard by a front yard.

Even such seemingly esoteric factors as changes in taxation may affect structural form. The part that taxation has played is often overlooked in studies of the design of traditional buildings. Most readers will readily recognize that property taxes vary with the number of rooms and size of a building. In some rural areas of the United States and Canada, disused or relict structures are removed in order to lower property taxes (Mann and Skinulis 1979, 27), which may be, in part, based upon the number of buildings on a property. This act may also lower insurance rates. It may also have the unintentional consequence of removing potentially significant buildings, making them unavailable for future investigators to study.

In northern India on the Bhutan border, taxes in an earlier period were assessed on the basis of the number of shrines or household worship rooms in a dwelling (Sen and Dhar 1997, 250). Needless to say, the number was kept to an absolute minimum, except in the most affluent houses. Taxation has even determined the roof type at certain times and in certain locations. In both Europe and America use of the gambrel roof was often a strategy to avoid taxation based upon number of living floors. The gambrel roof gave much more headroom in an upper floor than the gable roof, but a room under the roof was considered an attic and thus not taxed (Eberlein 1915, 26; Kauffman 1975, 31).

Similarly, tax laws made the one-and-a-half-story log house the most common dwelling in Ontario in the first half of the 19th century.

> Buildings, after 1811, were assessed on the number of storeys, and the type of material used (wood, stone or brick), and this one-and-a-half storey cabin made from round logs (squared on two sides) became the lowest taxable category on the Assessor's Roll from 1811 until 1854. Buildings of entirely round logs (peeled but not dressed), which required about a foot of chinking, and were never very airtight, were removed from the tax roll in 1811. The side effect was to produce a rash of round log stables and outbuildings where draught – and appearance – were not the primary concerns.
>
> In order to get the most out of their cabins and still stay within the law, settlers increased the head room in the attic sleeping loft by increasing the height of the outside walls. This gave them the same superficial space and number of rooms as a two-storey house at a fraction of the cost. For a man with a large family (this could mean as many as 21 children) it was the most economical minimum shelter available. (Ondaatje and Mackenzie 1977, W6)

Brian Coffey (1985, 312), however, is of the opinion that tax had little to do with the form and materials of the building, but availability and cheapness of construction materials were far more important.

Much better known is the effect of window and chimney or hearth taxes in medieval Europe. However, Pamela Simpson (1992) notes that sometimes window taxes have been used incorrectly to explain the presence of bricked-in windows. She calls attention to the 1845 Campbell house in Lexington, Virginia, which has four false windows on its gable end. The window tax of 1697 to 1851 in Britain is offered by Campbell house guides as the explanation for this Virginia feature, but in fact no window tax was ever levied in Virginia.

Window taxes were, however, levied in Britain in the 17th (Cook 1971, 46), 18th and early 19th centuries (Camesasca 1971, 6), in Ireland beginning in 1810 (Gailey 1984, 34; Patterson 1960, 11), and were employed in some parts of the New World (Eberlein 1921, 140). In the UK a window tax was instituted in 1697 to make up for a deficiency in revenue caused by defaced coins as silver was recoined in the reign of William III. Levied on the number of windows, "any house having more than six windows and worth more than £5 per annum was liable" (Cook 1971, 46). Although this tax was abolished in 1850–51, bricked-up windows of early structures may still be seen. The window tax levied in France was based upon the size of the opening. This tax is given by Gerard Morisset (1958, 181) as the rationale for the extremely small gable windows appearing on early French settlers' houses in Quebec.

Even more widespread in Europe and elsewhere were hearth or fireplace taxes. About 1700 in Denmark the government decreed that every hearth had to have a chimney. In part this was an attempt to reduce fire risks from open-hearth fires that burned in several rooms of each farmhouse or housebarn. Equally important, however, was the desire on the part of officials to simplify the collecting of the tax. Tax collectors, henceforth, only had to count the number of chimneys from outside the single-story structure. The strategy adopted by many farmers in new houses was to gather hearths together in the black kitchen and use a single chimney for all. "The concentrated fireplace was the easiest and cheapest answer to the government requirement that each hearth must have a chimney" (Lerche 1973, 13–14). In the early years of the 19th century, fireplace taxes were introduced as assessments on residential dwellings in the province of Ontario, Canada.

> There is no doubt that this method of assessment had some effect on the types of houses favoured in Upper Canada. . . . By establishing what amounted to a hearth tax, it tended to limit the overall size of houses and to ensure that, in some cases, they were inadequately heated. It also served to increase the popularity of the storey-and-a-half house, and to make it the usual type of farm dwelling in this province. . , ,   the fact that a house of less than two stories paid appreciably less tax than a house of two storeys with the same superficial area and the same number of rooms, and that this disparity increased with each additional fireplace, certainly influenced some settlers to decide to forgo the added comfort and superior status derived from possession of a house of two full storeys. (Blake and Greenhill 1969, 25)

Another tax that had an unusual effect on building was the brick tax in force in the UK from 1784 to 1850 (Forrester 1959, x). Because

the tax was enforced on the *number* of bricks used, builders adopted
the strategy of using oversized bricks "with conspicuous detriment to
the appearances of the buildings erected during that period" (Oliver
1929, 62). It had the further and wider effect for traditional buildings
of virtually eliminating bricks as a major construction material in
rural areas. The abolition of the brick tax in 1850 resulted in a much
greater employment of smaller and thus cheaper brick as a building
material in England in the latter half of the 19th century and throughout the 20th (Seaborne 1964, 217).

Other aspects of legislation or official policy also affect the form of
buildings. In Grenada in the Caribbean traditional buildings have tile
roofs rather than the wooden shingles typical on other Caribbean
islands. Their use dates to serious fires in 1771 and 1778 and a subsequent law requiring houses to be built only with brick and stone and
to have tile roofs (Acworth 1949, 22).

Governmental restrictions or feudal policies have also served to
keep building activity confined in certain directions. In Thailand, for
example, before the reign of King Chulalonghorn "only the upper
classes were permitted to build timber houses. The ordinary people
had to make do with other materials or woven panels of left-over timber [wattle?]" (Charernsupkul and Temiyabandha 1979, 48). Similarly,
in early Korea the monarch set the rules for housing, including permitted size, form, and building materials. House decoration was
prohibited for most households (Choi et al. 1999, 36, 60). In Spain "A
significant number of older, grander houses [in seventeenth century
Castile] possessed only one storey for living accommodation. Second
or third storeys were added only after the repeal of the law requiring
the owners of houses more than one storey high to place half their
home and its furniture at the disposal of the [royal] court" (Laws
1995, 102).

Restrictions took a different direction in Yemen, where religion was
the paramount consideration. "The height of Jewish houses was regulated by precise laws based upon the principles expressed in the
Koran (Sura 9/29) that the house of the unbelievers should be lower
and smaller than those of Moslems" (Costa and Vicario 1977, 17).
Therefore, Jewish houses typically have a low cellar or basement,
allowing the upper floors to be a half story lower than Muslim
dwellings.

Another religiously inspired, but quite differently controlled, feature in Jewish houses in Yemen is the placement of a large enclosed
courtyard on the uppermost floor of the structure. "During the so-
called 'tabernacle' festivities celebrated for a week in September or
October, Jews were supposed to take their meals and spend their

nights in a room covered only by leafy branches or matting" (Costa and Vicario 1977, 19). The courtyard provided the necessary space and offered an airy, spacious yet intimate place the rest of the year.

"Typologies of buildings are necessary ingredients of any successful project in the study of vernacular architecture" (Barakat 1972, 8). It is thus that the form and functions of structures can be best understood in their widest context. The problem is that the worldwide study of traditional buildings is such a vast undertaking that it has been done only partially and piecemeal hitherto. Hence, many different classification systems have been proposed and adopted. Perhaps the most critical problem now facing students of traditional building is to relate disparate terms and reconcile classification systems. Such an objective cannot be achieved immediately; it requires the agreement of many, many investigators. Furthermore, while scholars may eventually come to agreement, locally used terms will persist. Perhaps the best answer is the compilation of extensive glossaries, but this effort is time consuming and offers little immediate reward to scholars in terms of academic recognition.

~ 3 ~

Plan and Elevation

The form of a structure may be viewed from two perspectives – horizontally and vertically. Considered together, or even individually, examination of these dimensions provides clues to the possible evolution and relationship of structures (Ragette 1974, 88). Even sketches from widely scattered sources may suggest evolutionary relationships. For example, looking at "black houses" in Ireland and the Hebridean Islands and utilizing both floor plans and elevations, one is tempted to see the side-by-side, but integrated, construction of the barn and house–byre, as reported by Alexander Fenton (1978), as a stage in the complete separation of barn and byre from dwelling, and both as steps in the larger question of the separation of human and animal shelter (Hance 1951, 85), even though only limited evidence exists.

Michael Williams (1991, 65) provides different examples of evolutionary floor-plan development from southwestern North Carolina. Here, many early center-passage dwellings have had the hallway removed to enlarge an existing room and to eliminate perceived "wasted space." Another plan modification was the addition of a kitchen room, either attached or detached, to the small two-room houses common in the region. For many families the addition of a kitchen was directly linked to the acquisition of a cook stove, so that food preparation was no longer done over an open hearth.

The *plan* reveals the shape and horizontal extent of a structure, as well as the internal arrangement of its space. It also may explain, or at least suggest, the function of rooms. The idea of a floor plan revealing or explaining the functions of rooms, however, is basically a Western idea. As Osker Reuther (1910) noted when speaking of houses in Baghdad, the idea of a permanent, unchangeable function for most rooms cannot be applied to most non-Western houses. The function often depends upon the time of day, and it may change with the change of seasons.

Two areas, the kitchen and the toilet, normally require particular attention in a dwelling. The kitchen may be a problem area because the preparation of food involves wastes that attract vermin. Some food also must be cooked, creating a fire hazard and also generating heat that must be dissipated. Preparation of food is normally female activity and in many societies females are secluded. Thus, the kitchen must be secluded as well. In coastal Mid-Atlantic areas, as well as the rest of the US coastal lowland to the south, the kitchen possessed a further feature that favored its removal to the farthest part of the house: most food preparation was performed by slaves.

Originally, in Europe, cooking was done over a small fire in a centrally positioned hearth, which, because it also provided warmth, became the center of the universe of the dwelling. Thus, the hearth achieved the symbolic importance of sanctity. Even today it retains this mystical significance in many societies. As time has passed, however, the location of the kitchen has changed and its quasi-religious connection has diminished in both European and many other societies.

Early on, some people everywhere recognized that prevailing winds could influence location. Kitchens and toilets, with their odors, functioned best on the lee sides of the dwellings (Bourgeois 1980, 75). Even better was to remove the kitchen to a close-by but separate structure (Metraux 1949–51, 12; Forrester 1959, 3; Westmaas 1970, 134; Wilhelm 1971, 18; Edwards 1976–80, 16; Lounsbury 1977, 27). This had additional advantages of reducing both fire risk and, in hot weather, the discomfort of cooking heat in the main structure. This building practice continued in the Chesapeake Bay area well into the 19th century, and "the practice of cooking, and often eating, in a separate building endured into the early twentieth century" (Lanier and Herman 1997, 52).

A fine example illustrating the movement of the kitchen away from the main structure may be found in the Ngadju longhouses in Borneo, where a row of kitchens occupies only the part of a building separated from the living quarters by an elongated, open verandah (Miles 1964, 47). As in many other tropical regions, detached kitchens or cooking places were universal in traditional building areas in Haiti (Metraux 1949–51, 12). A further discussion of kitchens and heating may be found in Chapter 11.

The location of the toilet also required some thought (Figure 3-1). In primitive societies the two tasks of cleansing, washing or bathing, and that of elimination of human wastes, were treated as quite separate functions, although both required some privacy and separation of sexes. Washing was an act of cleansing, while defecation and urinating were polluting acts. Therefore, bathing was first to move within the dwelling itself. The basic problem, of course, was always obtaining sufficient water close by or in the structure itself.

3-1. The well and the privy are conveniently located adjacent to one another. Unfortunately, their proximity is an invitation to contamination of the water supply. A cobocolo farmstead in the Amazonian rain forest near Belem, Brazil (photo by the author, 1963).

Elimination of human waste originally took place in the bush or in the fields. A latrine or toilet structure separated from the dwelling was the first improvement. Only recently have toilets been included within the house. In many parts of the world separated latrines still function (Ragette 1974, 32), or as in south Asia, it may still be the fields that are used, and customarily after dark. Tibetan houses offer an arrangement that seems to be a halfway measure between the bush and incorporation inside the house. Typical two-story Tibetan houses have stairs located on the west sides, and often outside. The toilet space is usually located in an enclosure at the top of the exterior stairs. It "is a simple hole in the floor; every night the excrement is sprinkled with ashes, and it later becomes fertilizer" (Crouch and Johnson 2001, 95).

Even in the United States, considered by many to be a bastion of modernity, "two out of three US rural households relied upon privies" as recently as World War II (Tisdale and Atkins, quoted in Collins 1989, 3). On the Great Plains, privies occupied hidden sites on the farmsteads. "Such socially prescribed privy sites sacrificed convenience and efficiency ... for the more urgent motive of propriety. In every aspect, the privy fulfilled the dictum 'out of sight, out of mind'" (Collins 1989, 4).

Variations in room plan in three simple log dwellings built primarily by the Scots-Irish and common in their early settlement of eastern North America suggest the utility of understanding the plan. Each of the structures contains just two rooms. The double pen house has two fireplaces, one at each gable. There is little formal differentiation of functions in the house. The saddlebag house differs only, but significantly, in having the fireplaces and chimney on the wall separating the two rooms, rather than on the gable. If the central chimneystack has only one fireplace, the room into which it opens serves as the kitchen, while the other room is the work/sleeping room. The third structure, the dogtrot house, has its two rooms separated by an open passageway, although a common roof covers all. The passageway, or dogtrot, is a daytime work and socializing space (Ferris 1973, 106).

In Lebanon, a dwelling called the *liwan* house is quite similar in form to the North American dogtrot. The liwan itself is centrally positioned between two enclosed rooms and is roofed, but open on one side, often to make use of an attractive view (Ragette 1974, 86). The liwan serves as a general living space and an area to receive visitors (El-Khoury 1975). It frequently has benches around the walls and in later and more elaborate versions will have a small, central fountain, reminiscent of the courtyards found elsewhere in the Arab Middle East.

The floor plan may sometimes tell us a great deal about the general background of dwelling builders. For example, three quite distinct floor plans appear in the early log homes of North America erected by three different ethnic groups. The simplest, occurring primarily in the upland areas of the southeastern US, is a single-room, square-plan cabin with strong English connections (Glassie 1963; Glassie 1968). It also exists in many western areas of the US. The English had no tradition of log construction, but single-room, square-plan houses built in other materials were fairly common in some parts of England (Brunskill 1954, 175). These structures appeared in the southeastern US as frame houses as often as they did in log. The eastern US distribution of square cabins has been delineated by Henry Glassie (1968, 353) to include the eastern slopes of the Blue Ridge in Virginia and a less dense pattern throughout the Upland South region. A western US distribution identified by Jennifer Attebery (1982, 27) stretches from Missouri to Texas, Utah, and Idaho. In Idaho square log cabins date from pioneer settlement as recent as the late 19th century (Attebery 1976).

The Scots-Irish log house contains two rooms, usually of unequal size and a distinctly rectangular plan (Wilson 1970). Although similar plans were common to earlier houses throughout much of northern and central Europe, including the British Isles, its distribution across North America as a dwelling made from logs is a legacy of the Scots-Irish (Wright 1958, 111). Widely found throughout eastern North America, its greatest concentration occurs in the uplands of Appalachia. Augmented by Fenno-Scandinavian settlement, a significant landscape of these log buildings also developed in north-central United States (Klammer 1963). The adoption of log construction by the Scots-Irish, who had no tradition of log building in the Old World, came as a result of contacts with Finns, Swedes and especially Germans in the New World (Kniffen and Glassie 1966, 59).

The Germans utilized a quite different floor plan, however. Its dimensions were approximately in a ratio of 2:3, and the interior was divided into three rooms of unequal size, termed by later researchers as the "continental plan." A narrow kitchen (*Kuche*), containing the open fireplace on the interior wall, ran from front to back. The interior position of the fireplace and chimney was one of the features that distinguished this house from the other log dwellings, where these were on the gable. The larger of the two remaining rooms (*Stube*) was an all-purpose living, dining, work, and sleeping room. The smallest and most inaccessible room (*Kammer*) was for sleeping and storage of valuables (Bucher 1962). The plan was so firmly fixed in the Germanic tradition that later houses continued to employ the plan, even though they rearranged the hearth and used quite different building materials (Barakat 1972; Pillsbury 1977).

As settlement proceeded westward in North America groups tended to intermingle, in large part because of the American land policy, which discouraged block grants. Only when a nationality group migrated together at the same time and in large numbers could ethnicity be maintained easily. Log structures did penetrate into the Great Plains (Jordan 1978; Welsch 1980), but halfway across the plains the climate became so dry that suitable trees could no longer be obtained and log construction gave way to sod, adobe, and stone.

Although not an infallible guide, floor plans offer many clues about dwellings. Traditional dwellings are normally small, sometimes very much so. In a 1973 survey in Bangladesh, 63% of all houses in one typical village were smaller than 400 square feet, and three-quarters of all housing units consisted of a single room (44.97%) or just two rooms (30.16%) (Islam et al. 1981, 6 & 14). Earlier dwellings elsewhere had similarly diminutive dimensions. For example, in Ireland in 1841 more than one-third of all houses consisted of just one room and a further 40% had just two to four rooms (Gailey 1984, 8).

Early single-room structures in Britain-influenced areas were usually limited to dimensions of about 15–16 feet because such a span was a traditional measurement (Brown 1979, 20). One hears often that a bay of 16 feet was the space required to house a team of oxen, and presumably such a dimension became standardized. Whether or not this is true, a 15–16-foot bay appears with repeated regularity. In Worcestershire and neighboring counties in the UK Midlands, two- or three-room houses of the later Middle Ages overwhelmingly measured 15 x 30 feet and 15 x 45 feet respectively (Dyer 1986, 23–4). In southwestern Nigeria, a survey of houses by John Vlach (1975) revealed that about 14 feet was the *maximum* width, although length varied between about 14 feet and over 45 feet. Here the governing factor seems to be the length of available building timber components.

This was also probably a major reason for the popularity of houses containing only a single row of rooms throughout Great Britain. However, agricultural prosperity in England allowed the widespread use of bricks for chimneys and glass for window openings to become common after 1600 (Quiney 1990, 116). This change, coupled with greater diversity in room functions, the desire for greater privacy, and the trend to make more rooms useable through increased heating (Brunskill 1988, 43), led to the employment of double-pile floor plans to replace the single-row plans.

In most traditional societies the plan of a structure was rigidly fixed and adhered to closely. One extreme example occurs with the Mongolian *yurt*, which, although consisting of a single room, was by consensus divided into four main spaces.

> The area from the door, which faced south, to the fireplace in the centre, was the junior or low-stratus half, called by the Mongols the 'lower' half. The area at the back of the tent behind the fire was the honorific 'upper' part, named the *xoimor*. This division was intersected by that of the male, or ritually-pure, half which was to the left of the door as you entered, and the female, impure, or dirty section to the right of the door, up to the xoimor. Within these four areas, the tent was further divided along its inner perimeter into named sections. (Humphrey 1974, 273)

Dwellings such as tents, tipis, and yurts, all have well-ordered interior arrangements. Those of the Asian yurt or *kibitka*, much like those of the North American Great Plains Indians, are rationalized by thermal comfort and psychological effect. The door faces south or east in order to give protection from cold winds that blow from the north or west in both northern Asia and the Great Plains. Men and women have their traditionally occupied areas; places closest to the door are work spaces; the south side of the structure is where visitors are received and entertained. "The rear of the tent is divided into special areas. On the left is the house Master and his couch, while the right side in front of the family's precious objects is reserved for honored guests" (Drew 1979, 36).

Within the yurt every item had a proper place and the order was religiously enforced:

> It was considered a sin to move any utensil from its right place into another part of the tent. A woman's object was considered to pollute the men's area and a special [purification] ceremony might have to be performed to erase this. Men were not allowed to touch cooking and other "female" things, while women were forbidden even to step over a whole range of men's goods. There was no single place in the tent where a jumbled heap of things could be put indifferently. There was even a difference in the vertical heights at which objects could be placed: some things had to be wedged behind the roof-poles, some hung from pegs in the wall-lattices, and yet others were placed on the ground (Humphrey 1974, 273).

The plan also helps the investigator understand the roles of family members, and sometimes the social context in which the dwelling's inhabitants operated. For example, the dwelling of the Tharu people of lowland Nepal is constructed to accommodate the welfare, comfort and needs of village and household deities (Zurick and Shrestha 2003, 23). The rectangular-plan houses are situated so that longer walls run north–south. Such position reduces heat buildup, "making the interior a more pleasant place for the [household] deity." The doorway faces east, the direction of the village deity and "the number of rooms in the house must be divisible by an odd number to prevent disturbance to the household god."

Throughout Slavic areas of eastern Europe, early houses of log were single-room cabins, usually identified by the Russian word *izba*. The structure evolved into a two-room building known as a *khata* or *manzanka* (Jorre 1967, 81–2). One room usually contained the oven or stove, which doubled as a bed. Because use of the facility generated smoke and soot, this room became identified as the "black izba." The other room with no fire and no smoke or soot was the "white izba." In Romania, where this two-room dwelling was also built, the room with no fire – called the "clean room" – was devoted to guest and festive use and decorated with ceramics, woven hangings, rugs, icons and the best furniture (Brunvand 1989, 199).

S.K. Chandhoke (1990, 58), drawing upon an earlier study of a tribal people in Manipur state, India, offers the following interpretation of dwelling plans:

> The Purum house is divided length-wise into two parts. The right half is considered to be superior than the left half. The master of the house

with his unmarried sons and daughters sleeps in the right half, while his future sons-in-law, and other casual guests as well as his married daughters whenever visiting their parents' home sleep in the left half. This *Right vs. Left* classification is also observed in every element of the house and is even in its construction method. The very names for the right and left parts of the house, respectively, mean *Private* and *Public*, *Superior* and *Inferior*, *Family* and *Outsiders*.

The Japanese approach interior space quite differently. They view room functions as transitional. The Japanese view has been captured by Frances Earle (1943, 279), who asks on their behalf,

> "Why posses three rooms, two of them continually idle while one is only in use? Why not play the drama of daily living on a single stage, shifting the scenery from human act to human act as needed?" Thus with light internal partitions and minimal furniture, room functions of relaxing, dining, and sleeping can be accommodated in a single room, or several small rooms can be turned quickly into larger ones.

Circular and square or rectangular configurations account for the overwhelming majority of house floor plans across the world. Generally, the circular form is more ancient and persists in areas with the lowest technological levels or the least requirement for adequate shelter, e.g. the tropical rainforest (Andersen 1978). A circular floor plan also predominated in steppe grass areas where structures were portable and frequently moved (Campbell 1915; Drew 1979).

Many scholars have proposed that square or rectangular floor plans are a later development than those of circular form (Mishra 1969, 9–11; Piggott 1945). While it is possible to define large areas where either rectangular or circular floor plans predominate (Bernard et al. 1931, 25; Prussin, 1970, 19), the two forms often occur intermixed. Even so, the square- or rectangular-plan structures can frequently be documented as more recent than the circular ones (Boudier and Minh-ha 1982). Nevertheless, Hiroshi Daifuku (1952, 3) calls attention to early pit houses in Kamchatka of both square and rectangular plan, as well as circular ones of roughly the same age.

The evolution of floor plans in ancient pit houses in Japan does not follow the accepted sequence of most other areas. In Japan the earliest semi-subterranean houses have square floor plans. Later, rectangular plans predominated and the latest, but still early, prehistoric settlements were composed of structures with circular plans (Maringer 1980). Rarely do rectangular and circular rooms occur in the same structure, although Charles DeKay (1908, 107) has provided at least one example from Estonia.

Rather than being governed by time, the floor plans of most traditional houses appear to be associated with several other factors. Level
of technological skills present in a group is, of course, a most strongly
controlling element. Circular huts are, for several technical reasons,
easier to construct than rectangular ones. Also, the available building
materials may restrict or favor certain shapes. Logs or timber, for
example, do not produce circular plans, although by using very short
lengths an approximation of circular can be achieved (Noble 1984,
1:77). Finally, accessibility and contact with other groups from whom
cultural borrowing may take place both have an effect. As an example, Gonzalo Aguirre Beltran (1958, 93) suggests that west-coast
dwelling Mexican Indian peoples borrowed the idea of "round-house
form" from African slaves brought to the east Mexican coast in the
16th century, although this conclusion is based solely on similarity of
form.

L.W.G. Malcolm (1923) offered a sketch map of Cameroon (Figure
3-2), which illustrated these various features. In the more accessible
coastal and southern areas, which are covered by tropical forest, rec-

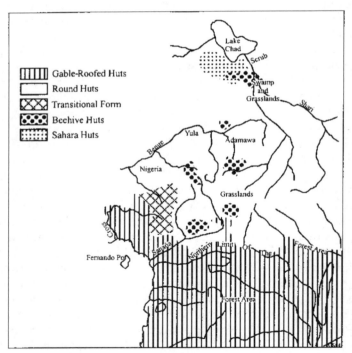

3-2. *Distribution of circular and rectangular dwellings in Cameroon. Both
  accessibility and availability of building materials have influenced the pattern
  (drawing by Iraida Galdon Soler, based upon Malcolm 1923, 26).*

tangular-plan, gable-roof huts predominated. This is also the region that has been exposed to the greatest European colonial influence. Further north and toward the interior, round huts of two types were found. The largest number were light, thatched structures with a conical roof. Smaller areas of mud beehive huts also occurred. Far to the north, simple brush shelters marked the transition from grasslands to desert scrub. The transition between the grasslands and the forest also produced a unique structure built by the Bamileke, consisting of a square, mud-walled hut topped by a conical, thatched roof.

In other areas of the world, oval-plan houses appear to be transitional between circular and rectangular types. James Walton (1952) has proposed a three-fold division of oval plan structures. *Ovate-oblong* structures found in Kenya, southern Africa, Amazonia, the Deccan plateau of India, Italy, and South Yorkshire and the Lake District of England, have semi-circular ends and straight sides. They originate from two vertical-walled, circular huts placed a short distance apart and connected by two straight side-walls (see Chapter 8 for a further discussion).

A second group, the *enlongated circle* houses, is derived from adjacent circular, stone, beehive huts. Numerous examples occur in the Orange Free State, but are uncommon elsewhere, although a few exist in Ireland, the Hebrides, and Italy. The third group, the *rounded-rectangular* houses, occur in Ireland, Scotland, Wales, and Scandinavia. The roof is usually hipped and the floor plan is that of a rectangle with the corners rounded off.

Accessibility is a function of distance, but within a dwelling accessibility is also strongly controlled by social convention. Thus, the dwelling is divided into areas, rooms or spaces that have limitations of various sorts. Almost all societies recognize that free access to non-family members does not extend without special permission beyond the first encountered room. Strangers may not get that far!

> The carefully drawn balance between privacy and interaction with the community [in Rajasthani villages] can also be seen in the treatment of guest rooms in the house. These are locally known as *kothdi,* and are mostly used to accommodate the in-laws of the daughters of the house. Visitors from another village, staying one or two nights in the house are offered a room or set of rooms attached to the house but independently accessed with features of the main house like platforms and an enclosed open space. Significantly there are no doors in the *kothdi,* except sometimes in one room reserved for women, thus emphasizing the independent status of the guests. It provides a place where celebrations can take place involving the larger community without affecting the privacy of the main household. (Ganju 1983, 77)

Even the inhabitants of a house may have conventional restrictions. These may be based on gender, age or seniority, health, lineage, or religion. In northern India, where social norms, even in the Hindu households, are derived from Muslim custom, "the rural dwelling is seen as being divided into 'mardana' (male) and 'zenana' (female) territories, with control by the respective sex group, occupying the front (close to the street) and back of the house respectively" (Sinha 1989, 16).

Similar gender restrictions occur in many traditional societies outside India. The Amazonian Indians reside in communal dwellings with individual family compartments, but entry to the overall structure is via two doors, one for the men (east) and the other for the women (west). Furthermore, the rear and smaller area of the structure is the woman's domain, while the much larger eastern front of the building is male country (Hugh-Jones 1985). Nevertheless, men and women move freely in both territories. Gender separation is carried to an extreme in the dwellings of the Mae Enga peoples in the western highlands of New Guinea, where completely separate structures are built for men and women (Meggitt 1957).

In contrast, Ronald Knapp (1990, 51) observes that little consideration of privacy and separation exists in Chinese dwellings. Women do not have separate structures, rooms or areas of a house, nor do men. What is found in the Chinese dwelling is an order based upon seniority and age, although movement of family members is largely unrestricted. The hierarchical nature of the Chinese house is seen quite clearly in courtyard houses of more prosperous and expanding families in Taiwan (Dillingham and Dillingham 1971). The courtyard and ancestral hall are bisected by an imaginary north–south axis. As the family grows, new rooms are added, often necessitating new courtyards. Accessibility is controlled by social conventions that may be quite rigid (Figure 3-3).

Among the Hausa of northern Nigeria, and elsewhere in much of West Africa, the extended family consists of a male head of household, several wives and numerous unmarried children. Married sons, their wives and children also may be included. "Each wife has her separate hut, the husband having a larger one." The entire collection of huts with granaries, and a reception lodge at the entrance, is surrounded by a compound wall or fence (Tremearne 1910, 179; Denyer 1978). A similar, but not identical, arrangement was identified by Jean-Paul Bourdier and Trinh Minh-ha (1982) among the Lela in Upper Volta (Burkina Faso). The extended family also may consist of brothers, uncles and sons and their wives and children. In the African pattern of circular- (and sometimes also rectangular-) plan houses, the individual hut should be thought of not as the entire dwelling, but

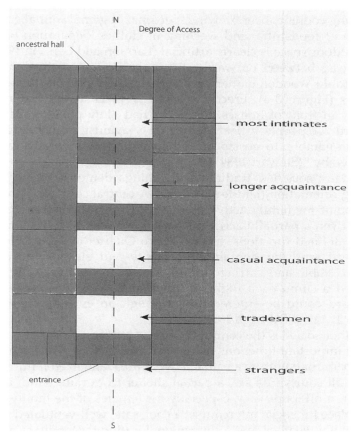

3-3. Generalized plan of a Taiwanese multiple courtyard house. The ancestral hall occupies the innermost place, accessible only after passing through transitional rooms that act as successive social barriers (drawing by Amy Rock).

simply as a sort of room within the dwelling, where the entire compound functions as the dwelling (King 1984, 203). Separate huts for women and men within the compound are reasonably common in tropical African societies. Excellent maps of tribal villages in Mali (Brasseur 1968) clearly show the hierarchical order of settlement components, consisting of numerous well-defined compounds, in their turn made up of multiple huts containing two or even more walled-off spaces, which most Western-trained observers would probably call rooms.

Among the Tswana of modern-day Botswana the compound may or may not be fenced or enclosed by a barrier of vegetation, and often contains only two houses plus a cattle *kraal* and an open cooking place. This "yard" is used for a variety of domestic purposes including cooking, beer brewing, personal hygiene, animal enclosure, storage of foodstuffs, and washing of clothes. Separation of indoor and outdoor space is clearly artificial (Larsson and Larsson 1984, 12).

Midway between outward- and inward-oriented dwellings were the outdoor wooden gathering places of the Pacific Northwest Coast peoples (Figure 3-4). Erected on sturdy piers at the water's edge, directly in front of houses, the decks had "low plank walls sloping outward for people to lean comfortably against, and they gathered there to gamble, to gossip or tell yarns and to generally watch the world go by" (Stewart 1984, 73).

In many societies, traditional dwellings demonstrate an inward-looking orientation (Diddee 2004, 53). A central courtyard provides a focal point for family activities removed from the commerce of the street. Even a partially accessible courtyard may have its limited but clearly defined functions. In the French Quarter of New Orleans the courtyard was the domain of servants and slaves who serviced kitchen, stable and carriage house. Access to the family living area required a climb up a flight of stairs, and from the street even the courtyard could be entered only through an enclosed passageway (Curtis 1933; Al-Sabbagh 1992).

In other societies the central courtyard performs a variety of different but important functions (Subhashini 1987). It provides a protected play space for children; a valuable work area; and even if unroofed, as almost all courtyards are, a partial shelter from rain, wind, and sun. Further, it offers privacy, especially for females of the family; a gathering place for social intercourse; a cool, safe, well-ventilated sleeping place in hot weather, and a convenient location for family celebrations and observances such as weddings and funerals. If small enough and

3-4. Drawing of the wooden outdoor decks located in front of First Nation tribal houses along the Pacific northwest coast, Canada. Raised above the level of high tide, the decks performed an important social function of group interaction in a comfortable environment. The low wooden sides were sloped for ease of sitting (from Stewart 1984, 74. Courtesy of Hilary Stewart from "Cedar," Douglas and McIntyre, BC, Canada and University of Washington Press).

rooms surrounding, it can function as a chimney to
the entire dwelling. As nicely summarized by Sang-
68), "the courtyard was a room without a roof, a
le for the gainful activity of the entire household that
ed to complicated environmental, practical, and sociocultural situations."

Floor plans have long been recognized as among the most important diagnostic characteristics aiding the researcher in a study of
traditional buildings. Even structures that appear to be the same from
the exterior may be placed in different categories by examining the
floor plan, and vice versa (Noble 1984, 1:20–6). Using floor plans,
Caoimhin O'Danachair (1956) suggests that Irish traditional houses
can be grouped into just three types. The first type occurs mainly in
the eastern and southeastern sections of Ireland, and is distinguished
by a short "jamb wall" that protects the fire from wind gusts when the
single door is opened. A small opening in the wall allows inhabitants
to see who is at the door. The second house type, which occurs
throughout the west, is characterized by the addition of a rear door
into the kitchen, offering the possibility of controlling windblasts into
the building. The hearth has shifted to a gable position. The final
house, most evident in the northeastern part of the island, adds
another hearth on the remaining gable. However, F.H.A. Aalen (1997,
149–52) prefers a simpler and later two-fold classification, dividing
traditional Irish houses into a western type, derived from the longhouse and consisting of three rooms, one of which is the byre, with
hearths and chimneys at or near the gable, and an eastern type with a
central hearth and chimney, lobby entrance, hipped roof, a floor plan
of between three and six rooms, and no accommodation for cattle.

Some of the most interesting floor plans belong to the family known
as *shotgun houses*. They include shotguns, double shotguns and camelback houses, and are to be found throughout the Old South of the US
(Sledge 1990) and along the major tributaries of the Mississippi River.
The camelback house gets its name from its form, a one-story, shotgun front area, a two-story middle section, which represents the
camel's "hump", and a low shed roof addition at the back.

Houses quite similar to shotguns and camelbacks are also found in
southern Haiti, from where they were introduced into Louisiana
(Vlach 1976b, 57). Originally a house type associated with Yoruba
areas of Nigeria (Vlach 1976c), these houses in the southern US, Haiti,
and Nigeria consist of a single file of rooms for better ventilation, a
necessity in the tropics. Early versions in both Haiti and Louisiana
possessed a narrow facade, which had no windows, but two doors
(Vlach 1976b, 57). Later ones substituted a window for one of the

doors. Because shotgun houses are just one small room wide but several rooms deep, and with the front door on the narrow end, these structures are often called "straightbacks" in the American South (Moe 1978, 228).

Much more interesting than this name is the etymology of the term shotgun. Because many such houses had doors aligned to each succeeding room, the idea arose that one could stand in the front, fire a shotgun, and the pellets would exit the rear door without hitting any intervening obstruction. Unfortunately, as any hunter knows, there is a lot wrong with this idea. Shotgun charges fan out, which is why hunters love them; even the poorest shot can hit something! If this idea of the blast were true, the building really ought to be called the "rifle house." The answer as to why the structure is called a shotgun has been provided by John Michael Vlach (1977, 56) who notes "in southern Dahomey, the Fan area, the term used to describe houses is *to-gun*." Shotgun then is merely an English language corruption of togun, with a manufactured etymology to match.

In Haiti the togun brought by Yoruba slaves, and with doors mostly on the side of the structure, came into contact with the *bohio*, a similar house type of the Arawak Indians (Figure 3-5). This house had its entry in the end of the building. Gradually the two forms coalesced and it was this compound structure that was brought from Haiti to New Orleans, where the Norman system of roof framing, borrowed from the French, was added (Vlach 1976b, 69). Tracing the migration of the shotgun house from Nigeria to Haiti to Louisiana shows clearly how persistent traditional building types can be. At the same time, the modifications demonstrate the logic of the changes resulting from contact with various ethnic groups and different building approaches.

Elevation is the term used to describe the vertical extent of a structure. Normally the term refers to that part of the building completely above ground. For example, traditional four-room houses in Romania are usually described as single-story structures, although their lower floor is a semi-excavated basement (Camesasca 1971, 243–4). Across the entire world, single-story and story-and-a-half structures predominate. Such dominance is a circumstance of the long history of low income in traditional societies. A survey of 1798 in Harford County, Maryland found 82% of all taxable houses to be of one or one-and-a-half stories (Weeks 1996, 24).

Each floor defines a story, although half-stories may or may not count in different classifications. In at least one system, "façade windows must be present for a floor level to be counted as a story" (Trimble 1988, 99). Above ground, partial stories carry a variety of

3-5. *Sketch of a bohio, a house type of the Arawak Indians of the Caribbean. The bohio joined the togun as ancestors of the shotgun house of the southern US, as reported by Vlach (1976b, 64) (drawing from an early 19th-century Spanish manuscript).*

designations: loft, attic, garret, grenier, alto, sobra techo, pad, upstairs, and so on.

External appearances can be deceiving (Trimble 1988, 99). Levels or positions of windows, for example, may not accurately reflect the number of stories. This is especially true with upper gable windows, which, when no loft floor is present, illuminate the ground story rather than just a loft. Examining Mennonite houses in northern Mexico, Jeffrey Lynn Eighmy (1977, 88) found some with attics or storage areas, which often had an outside window. Although giving "the house the appearance of a second story, the area is seldom high enough to live in and usually no stairway exists for easy access." Similarly, George Gardner (1935, 2) found many early one-room Rhode Island houses to have such a restricted loft headroom that they could be used only for limited storage.

In Fenno-Scandinavia the loft had the important function of acting as a repository for the family valuables (DeKay 1908, 110), even including clothing worn only on festive occasions. The loft, accessible only by ladder or stairs, was the most secure area of the dwelling.

These lofts gained such prestige that they began to be built as an entirely separate structure and given a conspicuous place of honor and decoration in the farmstead. Many still exist on present-day farms throughout Norway. Using the inaccessible, thus secure, space of the attic or loft area to hold valuables is a practice widely followed in many parts of the world (Kana 1980, 227). It is especially common in the humid tropics, enabling treasures to be stored away from the damp earth floor and its population of destructive insects.

The usefulness of the loft often depended in large part on the amount of headroom available (Figure 3-6). In pioneer America, log cabins produced from the Scottish and Irish traditions had a floor constructed at the top of the sidewalls; those following a Continental tradition placed the floor joists from three to five feet below the top of the wall (Glassie 1968, 341; Cohen 1992, 48). This meant the Continental cabin loft was much more useable. Roof type is also an important consideration in loft utilization. During the 17th century in southeastern England, gable roofs began to replace the earlier hipped roofs. The gable loft provided more headroom, and hence utility, than the hipped (Barley 1987, 191). Later on, the expanded gambrel roof continued the drive for greater headroom.

Structures with particularly steep roofs may have a small, narrow upper loft above the main loft. The Albany brick cottage, a structure developed by early Dutch settlers in New York State, is one type of dwelling that normally has such a feature (Noble 1984, 1:31). Early French structures in Quebec are another (Cameron 1982, 2 & 6), as are German stone houses in Pennsylvania (Barakat 1972, 14). Double attics also appear in the Rhenish houses of the Shenandoah Valley of

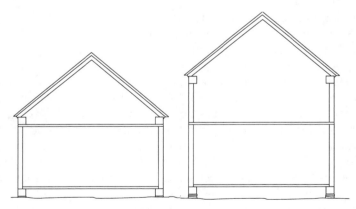

3-6. *Cross-sections showing different amounts of headroom in southern American log cabins. Cabins using Celtic traditions had much less headroom than those based on Continental dwellings. Note the location of the junction of the wall and the upper floor (based on Glassie 1968, 255).*

Virginia where "multi-level storage has survived in the utilization of space above the roof collars, reached by a permanent ladder" (Chappell 1980, 59). Swiss bank houses in Pennsylvania typically have double lofts also (Stevens 1980/81, 80).

The Dutch- and French-derived attics were used principally as storage areas and sometimes for sleeping, especially for children, hired labor or slaves. Using the loft for grain storage was a characteristic found throughout northern and central Europe (Haslova and Vajdio 1974, 40, 55) and in Germanic colonies throughout North America (Huguenot Historical Society 1964; Noble 1992b, 279). The German-derived double-level attics in Pennsylvania held the grain harvest on the lower level, which was called the *Schpeicher* (granary). The upper level, termed the *Rauchkammer* (smoke room), was encased in mud daub or plaster to reduce the fire danger because a small opening in the chimney permitted both smoke and sparks to enter the room. Various meats were hung on built-in racks for curing (Weaver 1986, 254–5). A rather different feature performing essentially the same function was the *beef loft*, found in traditional houses in the Yorkshire Dales (Hartley and Ingilby 1971, 6). Here, a box-like compartment, open to the kitchen below, was constructed adjacent to the fireplace. Joints of beef, hams, and sides of bacon were hung to be dried and lightly smoked by the heat and smoke from the fire.

By the latter part of the 18th century, as settlement matured and the danger of theft of stored grain lessened, a shift from loft stowing to barn storage has been observed for German farms in Pennsylvania (Bucher 1963/64). Facilitating this change was the growing number of sawmills, which supplied tightly fitted sawn boards for barn granaries. Occasionally, American colonial lofts also functioned as workshops (Eberlein 1915, 32), but storage and sleeping remain the universal functions of attics.

In the Dordogne region of France, the *grenier* contains one or more gable-roof dormers, or small triangular-shaped openings in the roof known as *outeaux*. These provide not only light but also valuable ventilation, useful for drying stored hay or grain (Scargill 1974, 173). A variety of uses, including storage of grain and agricultural produce, a place for looms and weaving, and as a dormitory for young males, characterized the grenier in Cajun houses in Louisiana (Rushton 1979, 170). In this latter instance, the loft was referred to as a *garçonière*. Characteristically it had an outside, open stairway leading upward from the front gallery. In the related houses of Acadia, the loft was used as a guest room (Lebreton 1982, 440).

On the Indonesian island of Sumbawa, stilt-elevated, A-frame houses use the attic today for just these purposes (Just 1984, 34). In modern-day America, attics crammed full of cast-off or purposely stored items are frequently cleared, partitioned off, and finished to provide an additional bedroom or two for growing families.

A survey of American farmhouses published in the depths of the 1930s Depression showed a wide regional variation in percentages of one-story and multiple-story dwellings (Melvin 1932). Using a geographical classification then popular, three great regions of the country – the Cotton Belt, the Great Plains and the Great Basin – had 81%, 78%, and 60%, respectively, one-story farmhouses. If number of stories can be taken as a rough measure of rural wealth, the South (Cotton Belt) comes off as the poorest area. Perhaps this is not surprising, given the destruction of that area's economy as a result of the Civil War and the very long period required to recover, the inadequate housing of the now freed former slaves, many in the quarters of pre-war plantations, and the long, hot, humid summers of the South. The upper floor of two-story houses could become unbearably warm in the summer time.

The Great Plains region, never an area of sustained agricultural prosperity, was in the depths of a decade-long period of droughts, crop failures, dust storms, and rural debt and mortgage foreclosure in the 1930s. The Great Basin's environment of mountains and deserts offered only slightly better economic conditions, but to far fewer people. In both of these areas some houses were the original modest structures of the first period of Caucasian settlement.

In the Appalachian–Ozark Highlands, another geographical designation used in the survey, the results were more favorable. Multiple-story and single-story farmhouses were almost balanced, with the former accounting for 55%. The perhaps surprising predominance of multiple-story dwellings may be due to the building of I-houses by prosperous farmers on the limestone-floored valleys in and near Appalachia (Carter 1975, 339; Chappell 1980, 56) and in the Ozark western extension (Crumbie 1987).

The Pacific Northwest and the Tobacco–Bluegrass areas had 15% and 22% single story farmhouses, respectively. The Corn Belt, New England–New York, the Northern Dairy area, and the Central East are all areas that had between 92% and 96% multi-story farmhouses in the 1930s. The reasons for such high percentages probably lie in their long periods of settlement, long enough for rebuilding with better houses, and relative agricultural prosperity.

In addition to economic factors, the environment also plays a role in influencing the elevation of structures. Because of the nature of the terrain, most traditional housing in Ireland, and many other areas, was built on gently to moderately sloping ground. The great advantage of these structures, which served the dual purpose of human and animal shelter, was that liquid and some animal waste drained away downslope from the building. Most of the solid animal waste simply accumulated, and in some cases was cleaned out only once a year. One observer, Lord George Hill in 1887, mentioned accumulations indoors of between 10 to 15 tons of manure (Evans 1939, 216). Slope considerations were important enough to often provide the vernacular names to the two ends of a house – "upper gable" and "lower gable" (Evans 1940, 168).

In Salem County, New Jersey many early houses consisted of a high part and a low part, "to describe them according to local parlance" (Eberlein 1921, 139–40). The low part was entered at ground level and contained the kitchen and a stairway to one or two chambers on an upper floor. The low part was often the original house. The high part, built when the owner's family needed more space and his income had grown, was raised two or three feet with a cellar beneath. The high part contained two rooms on the ground floor and a stairway leading to bedrooms above. The social status attached to affluence plays its part here, even subconsciously!

In northern Sudan, social elements of its culture also influence building elevation. Single-story dwellings are almost universal in rural areas. Several reasons besides the extra labor and cost of building multiple-story mud houses reflect the social and cultural conditions of the area. Pressure of population is so low that expansion of structures is easily accomplished on ground level. Muslim culture places a high value on the need for privacy, especially that of secluding the women of the household from outside observation. "High courtyard walls . . . surround all dwellings. Should a neighbor build a two-story house, this security would be breached." Community social pressure acts to restrict such a development. Also, any man attempting to construct such a large structure would be accused of ostentation (Lee 1974, 244).

Over large parts of the desert Muslim world, however, inhabitants are crowded closely together at oases. Their location and restricted extent are governed by availability of water. Baghdad is a good example. Traditional houses here reflect conditions throughout the desert Muslim world. Dwellings several stories high exist because of land scarcity, and are built around courtyards to assist cooling ventilation. Many of these structures have subterranean basements, which, when not below the local water table, offer cool retreats in the hottest weather. At night, rooftops provide cool sleeping areas.

Plan and elevation together provide a key to help one discover the significance of different components of a structure. In Taiwan and parts of mainland southern China, dwellings are constructed around a courtyard. The entrance is through the compound wall, which faces south and the entire complex is oriented via a dominating central north-south axis, leading ultimately to the most important structure, the ancestral hall. Used for important family functions and for worship, the hall is the equivalent of two stories high, in contrast with other rooms and buildings, which rise only to the height of a single story. The hall is also raised on a plinth to accentuate its symbolic elevation (Dillingham and Dillingham 1971).

One of the most difficult problems in using plan and elevation to understand, or to attempt a typology of, buildings is that many structures are "the result of piecemeal building" so that the original plan and elevation cannot always be determined, and certainly not at first glance (Seaborne 1963, 142). "Architecture is not static. Additions are built; rooms are modified. We must not make the mistake of assuming that because a house has a certain floor plan today, that it always had that floor plan" (Cohen 1992, 40). Nevertheless, it is floor plan and elevation that are the most important features in classifying traditional house types (Sizemore 1994, 49).

~ 4 ~
Location and Orientation

Not all structures of a type find similar locations. *Location* may be governed by several factors, and often by just one of them. Sometimes it is quality and depth of soils that affect placement. In the hill country of northern Appalachia, after the initial pioneer settlement period, the better soils of the broader, limestone-floored valleys permitted construction of substantial I-houses and large timber-frame barns because agricultural incomes were secure. The thin soil cover of the hill slopes reduced income from farming and discouraged most building except for log houses, or simple frame structures and single-crib log barns.

Early houses in Wales were located, not in the best lowland soil areas, but at somewhat higher altitudes where soils were thin and trees largely lacking. The valley locations were tree covered and poorly drained, whereas for early dwellers the slopes "provided sites easily occupied, yet dry and sloping, as was required by their particular agricultural methods" (Gresham 1963, 267). A secondary advantage was the presence in these locations of plentiful supplies of stones and rocks to be used as building materials. Somewhat similarly, farmhouses in Scotland were sited between arable land in valley bottoms and grazing meadows above. A further advantage could be location in the lee of hills as protection against strong prevailing winds (Naismith 1985, 47).

A similar preference for hill slopes by the pioneer settlers in Appalachia is also evident. The rationale for avoiding the best agricultural land there, however, was probably that valleys could be malarial and fever ridden (Dickinson 1990, 10–11). Similarly, on the poorly drained prairies of the American Midwest, pioneer settlers erected their cabins mostly on the western side of rivers and marshes, which were thought healthier than the eastern side, as the prevailing winds are from the west (Oliver 1843, 104).

Avoidance of the best agricultural land for farmsteads can be seen in many parts of America, where the best land – usually valley bottoms – is farmed, while the farmstead occupies the nearby valley slope. Similar situations are reported for the Hebrides (Hance 1951,

80), in Chitral in northern Pakistan (ud-Din 1984, 280) and undoubtedly exist elsewhere. A further advantage of a hill slope site is that both upper and lower levels of barns and houses can be entered directly (Chappell 1980, 60). Throughout the Pennines and other upland areas of the British Isles, houses and housebarns frequently have been located athwart man-made terraces on otherwise sloping land, and prehistoric dwellings have been given the name of *platform houses* (Fox and Fox 1934); the name has been extended to include later buildings elsewhere using terraced locations (Hemp 1939; Walton 1956).

The impact of altitude can be seen more specifically with the location of weavers' cottages in the Huddersfield area of the UK. A survey conducted in the mid-1970s revealed that roughly two-thirds of all such structures were scattered at altitudes of between 750 feet and 1050 feet. The explanation probably lies in the practice of enclosure by estate owners who permitted tenants to secure small freeholdings.

> However, such dispersal had to take place at increasingly higher altitudes onto land which was sub-marginal, even for the predominant pastoral activities. Agriculture alone could not sustain a livelihood for long at higher altitudes and therefore needed to be combined with some other form of economic activity. This, of course, was, or came to be in the majority of cases, the manufacture of cloth. (Barke 1979, 52)

4-1. *A weaver's house, Almondbury, Yorkshire, UK. The large number of windows documents the 18th-century conversion of the dwelling to enable weavers to work with enhanced natural lighting (photo by the author, 1967).*

Weavers' cottages possess rows of tall windows along the front wall (Figure 4-1). In order to permit sunlight to penetrate the structure, the cottages were oriented whenever possible towards the south and southeast.

Not only does altitude influence location of structures, so also does exposure. Jerri Holan (1990, 35) observes that, in Norway, wealthier farmers were located on sunny slopes of mountains and hills and the poorer farmers on shady slopes. Such distributional sorting, however, is probably the result of the better and poorer agricultural growing conditions in the respective areas, so that location determines wealth and not the other way around. Another example occurs in the Alps, where wooden houses predominate on north-facing slopes and stone houses on south-facing slopes (Cereghini 1956, 41). Much of this difference has to do with the amounts of rainfall received on each side of the mountains and the resulting condition of the forest supplying wood for building. Wind also can be a consideration in rough terrain. In Appalachia, "building under a sheltered north slope rather than on the ridge top protected the house from winter winds and facilitated access to water and roads" (Eller 1979, 97).

In India, where most rural settlement is nucleated, villages may be segregated according to caste or the religious community to which individuals belong. In northwestern India, the houses of the highest castes normally are situated in the western part of a village, with doors facing eastwards, the most prestigious direction. Because prevailing winds are from the west, little "pollution" is experienced in such a location. Lower ranking castes occupy the eastern area. The untouchables are segregated to the south, the most negative direction according to Hindu cosmology. Also, because "the least frequent winds are those from the south," chances of their polluting air affecting the rest of the settlement are minimized (Singh and Khan 2002, 100–1).

At times, and especially for prehistoric structures, it is only logical conjecture that offers possible explanations for locational choice. Near Durango in southwestern Colorado, a number of possibilities have been advanced to explain location of pit dwellings at some distance from the critical water source of the Animas valley. These include: avoidance of high water tables in the ground of the valley plain; the need to use level land near the water for farming; escape from cold air drainage in the valley during late fall, winter, and early spring; the better security of higher sites because a greater field of vision allowed dangers to be seen at distance; better soil drainage; numerous small streams and rivulets offered controlled amounts of water, reducing the need to carry water; and finally, safety from periodic flooding (Duke and Matlock 1999, 44).

Most peoples put considerable thought into locational decisions and make prudent and logical choices. Apparently haphazard distributions of houses will be found upon more careful inspection to be well planned and reasoned (Hoskins 1960, 336). The placement of the houses of the Mae Enga in the western highlands of New Guinea on isolated ridge tops or backed against hill slopes serves two important purposes: better defense against attackers and privacy (Meggitt 1957, 168). In the Hebrides "the modern tendency is to align the houses along and near the roads. In the older settlements and where the topography is more rugged, many of the houses are scattered up and down the slope, not necessarily facing the roads which serve them" (Hance 1951, 79). Throughout South Asia, dwellings in low-lying and plains areas are customarily placed on mud plinths in order to raise floors above the flooding that accompanies the sustained rains of the monsoon season. In Bangladesh, Bimal Paul (2003, 101) reports plinth heights to vary between six inches or so in the moribund delta to four feet in the active delta. Similar variations exist across India for the same reason.

Despite the care and thought that most peoples put into their location decisions, inevitably some mistakes are made. One of the most dramatic examples is the Bird House on the Seward Highway near Girdwood, Alaska. "Built on boggy ground, it has sunk so far into the ground that the sill of the window is now below ground" (Hoagland 1993, 108). Elsewhere in Alaska early buildings were frequently constructed above *permafrost*, which subsequently thawed unevenly, producing buckled floors, collapsed walls, fallen roofs, and ultimately often complete destruction of the structures.

Seasonally occupied traditional structures in polar areas suffered less from these problems because they usually avoided permafrost at or near the surface, and were often not heated to a high degree. Nevertheless, to be successful habitation they needed to meet a number of locational constraints. They needed fish and/or game in abundance, an easy waterfront access, good drainage to avoid snow meltwater, some building materials nearby, a source of good drinking water and sufficient space to allow dwellings to have backs to the winds and fronts toward the sun.

Location also has another dimension, that of geographical spatial extent. A map of traditional houses in South Africa illustrates the point nicely (Figure 4-2). The pattern is a result of the simultaneous working of a number of locational factors operating through culture, level of technology, environmental resources, and local economy (Biermann 1971, 96).

4-2. *Several locational factors in South Africa help to explain regional variations in traditional dwellings as seen on this map (modified from Biermann 1971, 96).*

4-3. *On this topographic map of the Mennonite village of Chortitz, Manitoba, the housebarns appear as squares (houses) in front of rectangles (barns). Absence of houses or barns or combined structures is noticeable in the gaps breaking the regular pattern of settlement (section of the Altona, Manitoba topographic quadrangle 62 H/4).*

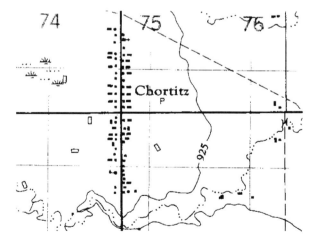

Humans are basically gregarious animals who seek out the company
and potential security of others, especially of the same ethnic group.
In Canada, settlement laws permitted the reservation of blocks of land
to be claimed by homogeneous groups of settlers. Thus, German-
Russian Mennonites established *strassendörfer* (one-street villages) for
their people. All others were effectively excluded in those areas.
About 20 of these villages still persist in southeastern Manitoba (Figure 4-3). On the US Great Plains no such unified settlement was
possible because of different land laws. The pull of heritage and ethnic community was still strong, however. Some German farmers built
their farmsteads at the very corner of their property as did their German neighbors, so that an informal cluster of several homes came
about, "just far enough apart to keep the chickens separated" (Sherman 1974, 193).

People with an intimate connection to the local environment must
change the location of their dwellings when environmental conditions change. Chapter 13 provides examples of groups who move
seasonally to accommodate the grazing animals upon which they
depend for survival. Such movement is often placed under the rubric
of *transhumance*, and most often involves movements upward and
downward in mountain terrain. Other groups move, but only over a
period of several years. The shifting cultivators are normally motivated to change location because of declining fertility of tropical soils.
Their dwellings are of bamboo and thatch, or other similar light materials, which are readily available in new locations and which can be
erected quickly (Ricketson 1927).

Even Plains Indians who sheltered under a simple and moveable
tipi made some elementary decisions. The Blackfoot selected tipi sites
for their good drainage, level land, and absence of rodent and snake
holes (McClintock n.d., 4). Abundance of firewood and ease of its collection has been suggested as the controlling factor for the location of
some Navajo *hogans* (Spencer and Jett 1971, 163). Finnish settlers in
Montana faced their log cabins toward the south or east in order to
avoid the winter winds blowing south out of Canada during the long
winter (Sanford 1991, 46). Early farmers in Iceland placed their dwellings at the base of a hill slope so as to be sheltered from the bitterly
cold winter winds, and also close to a dependable water supply
(Krissdotter 1982, 8).

The importance of water as a locational magnet is hard to overestimate. To cite one example, Cosmos Mindeleff (1898a, 479) noticed
that in the northeast corner of the Navajo territory, 90% of the hogans
were located close to the mostly subterranean water supply of the
Chaco River, where a little digging would find water. At the same
time, hogans were rarely sited next to a spring. In Mindeleff's view

this was a survival from earlier hunting times in order not to frighten away game from these water sources (Mindeleff 1898a, 483). Concealment and location away from water holes became a hallmark of hogan location. In the same general area of southwestern US, the principal requirement among Hopi for locating a permanent pueblo was a dependable water supply (Sanford 1950, 113).

An important consideration influencing farmhouse location in the Central Lowland of the US from western Ohio to Iowa is surface water drainage. In the glaciated areas of these states, moraines, kames and glacial beach ridges provide sites that are just a very few feet above the general surface (Figure 4-4). Such elevation is not only drier but also gives a slight settlement advantage by producing drainage of cold air away from the site in the cool half of the year.

Wayne Kiefer (1972, 491), in a study in northern Indiana, recorded 75% of farmsteads on such slightly elevated sites. A similar adjustment to drainage is reported from Australia, where aborigines located huts on small hillocks and mounds "to insure the more rapid dispersal of the water" (Roth 1909, 49). The corollary, avoidance of low-lying sites, is a worldwide and long-recognized phenomenon controlling site location of dwellings. As early as the first centuries BC, rising water levels forced inhabitants of the low regions in the Frisian part of modern Netherlands to build their houses upon artificial mounds out of reach of the waters (Hekker 1975, 7).

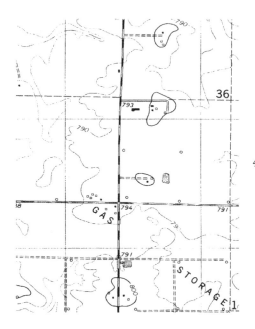

4-4. *A small portion of the Normal East quadrangle, USGS topographic map. Farmhouses along the north–south highway are mostly located on kames, which are identified by the roughly circular 800 foot topographic contour. The 10-foot contour interval is sufficient to provide drier conditions for building on the otherwise poorly drained prairie.*

Characteristics of drainage also have a great deal to do with the design of the dwelling. In the Cajun prairies of southwest Louisiana, a higher water table and consequently poorer drainage in the southern part of the prairies necessitated the storage in above-ground cisterns of cypress wood, of the rainwater collected on the metal roofs of houses. In the northern, better-drained and somewhat higher prairies, the cisterns are tanks placed unobtrusively underground (Post 1962, 24).

In some communities, location of a dwelling is governed by quite specific social regulation. An extreme example is provided by the Sakalava people of western Madagascar. There, a strict order of settlement requires that a village founder or ruling male occupy the northeastern-most location, closest to burial grounds of the group's ancestors. Descendants and subsequent settlers locate houses progressively to the south and west (Feeley-Harnik 1980, 573).

The rules that govern site conditions have been incorporated in many cultures into sacred documents, or into sets of regulations and procedures, which if not actually sacred came to be regarded by the folk as almost divine. Hence, where traditional society still flourishes, one disobeys or ignores them often at great peril. Among Tamils in southern India, these texts admonished that a proper house site must slope downward to the east and the north. They also provided rules for the taste and smell of suitable soils that differed for each group of castes (Chelvadurai-Proctor 1927, 343; Arya 2000, 36–9).

In China, *feng shui* has had an even stronger and more long lasting impact. As late as the 1990s, television stations that I watched in Hong Kong were advertising expensive modern apartments as having "correct feng shui." As far as general location is concerned, feng shui requires that higher elevations be to the north and east of the selected location. "The ideal site nestles into the areas of hills which are shaped like the Azure Dragon in the East and the White Tiger in the West. The dragon is a beneficial force whose formation should be higher than the tiger, a force of danger, which protects only as long as it is balanced by the dragon" (Sullivan 1972, 133).

In Southeast Asia, the proper site location according to geomancy should be on slightly raised ground, with trees in the northeast corner, and a facade facing east without large trees blocking the view. Crossroad sites should be avoided as well as dead-end streets and roads. A rear door must not be aligned with the front entrance (Dumarcay 1987, 14). The practice of feng shui extends beyond principles of harmonious location and orientation to include intricate rules governing design and interior arrangements (Too 1996). An additional brief discussion of feng shui appears in Chapter 12.

Another critical aspect of location among some peoples is that the earth itself is considered to be alive, to possess feeling (Bourdier and Minh-ha 1983, 43). Therefore, it is necessary to propitiate the earth spirit, since construction requires the earth to be broken, dug into, displaced and otherwise roughly handled. In India ceremonies are held on the building site in order to appease the earth spirit *before* any construction takes place (Crooke 1918, 132–3). In Bali a ceremony called *malaspasin* is conducted *after* the structure is erected and includes rituals to bring to life all the materials taken from the earth which were broken, cut or disturbed by the builders (Howe 1983, 154). It would seem that the Indians seek permission, while the Balinese ask forgiveness; shades of Thomas Acquinas!

W. Crooke (1918, 136) offers a scientific explanation for expatiation rites, which are also practiced in various parts of India and perhaps elsewhere, as he explains that "emanations or microbes disturbed in the course of excavation are a source of evil, which primitive men translate into a visitation of demons or evil spirits." A quite different ceremony, but one which also emphasizes the living nature of a house, is reported from northern Thailand (Charernsupkul and Temiyabandha 1979, 57). There a future husband who anticipates building his own dwelling offers "apologies to his wife-to-be's parent's house for loving the daughter of the house" and for taking her away.

The *arrangement of buildings* involves concepts of both location and orientation. Such arrangement is usually culturally controlled, a product of the relationship with the environment, requirements for security, and ethnic group customs and mores. Arnold Alanen and William Tishler (1980) noted a basic difference in arrangements of buildings in farmsteads between western and eastern Finland. "In the western regions of the country, where the influence of Swedish culture was strongest, early farmsteads were organized generally to form a tightly enclosed courtyard. The interior and eastern regions of Finland, however, were characterized by a more scattered or dispersed pattern of farm buildings on the landscape."

Half a world away, the arrangement of farmlands of the Metis and Ukrainians in the Canadian west shows a similar form distinction. The Metis farmstead is characterized by an openness and almost chaotic orientation of buildings, an "informality, lack of rigidly defined structure, and continuity with the landscape," while the "Ukrainian farmsteads are built on a courtyard plan where the house and other farm buildings face inward, and fences are used to separate different functional spaces" (Burley and Horsfall 1989, 27–30).

In Norway, where the courtyard arrangement of farm buildings dominates, "it was rarely formed according to regular plan, as nearly always it had to be adjusted to the terrain and it was practically speaking never symmetrical. But all the farm-buildings always faced the courtyard either broadside or with the narrower [decorative] gable" (Alnaes et al. 1950, 92). In most parts of Norway, farm court-yards were merely open, irregular spaces around which as many as 30 structures on each individual property might cluster (Holan 1990, 46).

Variations in terrain in many parts of the world cause changes, greater or lesser, in the specific location and orientation of buildings. As Alanen and Tishler (1980) noted as they examined Finnish settle-ment in the American Midwest, landscape features such as "the presence of hills, streams and water, marshes, and vegetation types quite often appeared to be the most important factors in determining the spatial configuration of the overall farmstead patterns."

Orientation always means location with reference to something else. This may be a compass direction, a highly visible landmark, such as a volcano or other mountain, an environmentally significant feature, such as the ocean or a prevailing wind, or a particularly auspicious direction, such as that of the rising or setting sun, or an undesirable or repugnant one. To a significant extent, orientation, especially of build-ing clusters, reflects cultural traditions although economic and environmental considerations are important as well.

It should not be surprising that among those communities depend-ing upon fishing for their livelihood houses are oriented toward the sea (Dawson 1880, 146). Wilson Duff and Michael Kew (1958, C45) provide a map of a Haida Indian village on Anthony Island, British Columbia, which offers an excellent example (Figure 4-5). Elsewhere, Harnett Kane (1944, 178) makes the point that Cajun houses in Louisi-ana normally are oriented toward the bayou, a source for fur trapping as well as an easy access route. Orientation to the sea also governs houses in most resort or recreational areas (Bisher 1983) and in ports (Davis 1982, 188).

Just as orientation to the sea is strongly expressed in fishing com-munities, orientation to roadway occurs in those farming communities that increasingly depend for livelihood upon marketing of their products, even if the markets are local. The strength of this orientation, as well as proximity to the road, grows as producers pros-per and become more and more commercially dependent. For example, in Maine, which did not really have a commercial agricul-ture in the 19th century, a general southerly orientation of dwellings at the beginning of the century was replaced as commercial farming grew by the end of that century with an orientation to the road regardless of compass direction (Hubka 1985, 8). In California, where

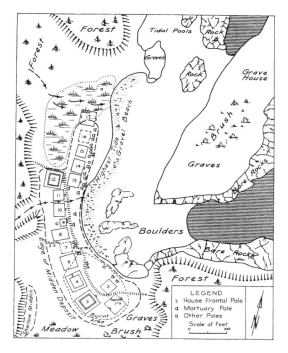

4-5. *The seaward orienta-*
tion of the Haida Indian
village of Ninstints,
Anthony Island, British
Columbia is clearly
shown in this map.
Dwellings line the high-
est tide line and offer
easy access to the sea
(from Duff and Kew
1957, c45).

the ranchers have "grown up with the automobile," fully 69% of the ranchsteads in the mid-20th century fronted directly on the road, also regardless of compass direction (Gregor 1951, 303).

The shift in orientation to the road also may occur in fishing communities. On the island of Scalpay in the Hebrides, "before the roads were built, four out of five houses were oriented to the sea, whereas after the road improvements, five out of six were oriented to the roads" (Beecher 1991, 78). The same attraction elsewhere in the Hebrides is reported by Alexander Fenton (1978, 38), who characterized it as magnetic. Similarly, in Tahiti, "prior to the modern age the preferred house site was the lagoon side; today it is the roadside" (Bell 1973, 109).

In northern Indiana, virtually all rural houses face the road, but "the front door is seldom used, even for guests" (Kiefer 1972, 493). Proximity to the road (location) is more important than orientation. Perhaps this accessibility to the muddy boots of non-family neighbors and others is one reason for the oft-repeated observation of the social significance of the Midwest farm kitchen, or perhaps it is the *result* of that importance.

The precise *orientation* may not, however, be to the roadway, even though the dwelling's *location* may be governed by accessibility. Writing about the UK, M.W. Barley (1967, 740) notes that in the 16th century house orientation – which had been to place the long side toward the road in order to provide a convenient cross-passage-access to the rear farmyard – was changed to present the narrow, gable-end wall to the road. He further suggests that this reordering may have been the result of an attempt to conserve village land front-ages required by the growing population.

It seems reasonable that access should in large part determine orientation. Not only do roadways provide access, other transport facilities do so as well. In the Nubian areas of northern Sudan now flooded by the Aswan Dam, house orientation was strongly toward the river, giving passengers on Nile river boats an excellent view of the elaborately decorated facades (Wenzel 1972, 3).

Perhaps the ultimate example of roadway orientation influence has been offered by Jean Sizemore (1994, 135). Writing of the Ozarks, she says,

> A vivid example of the tenacity of the desire for one's house to face the road is the Will Ford house of 1905. In 1951, when the road in front of their double pen house was rerouted to the rear, the Fords rearranged the house to make what were formerly the two back doors into the front doors. Mrs. Ford said, "Our living room used to be a bedroom; what used to be the living room is now our kitchen".

Orientation toward the roadway, path or street that offers access probably accounts for a majority of traditional houses. In contrast, some structures seek orientation away from the points of access. The Japanese house is, as often as not, oriented to its garden, which has a strong symbolic character (Walker 1940, 338; Taut 1958, 277–87; Ville-minot 1958). In Charleston, South Carolina, so-called *single houses* have the main door opening on to a long, shady verandah, which in its turn fronts a garden removed from the street (Noble 1984, 1:60). Elsewhere, houses that adjoin or surround courtyards usually have an inward orientation (Gebhard 1963, 38) even though entrance doors may face the street or road.

In many societies an orientation away from the road is preferred (Noble 1992b, 274–6). In eastern and south-central Europe, houses rarely face the street or roadway (Williams 1916, 156), although they may be built almost on the thoroughfare. Dwellings among such diverse peoples and locations as rural Poles in the Warsaw area (Noble 1991, 3–5), the Tarascans in the mountains of Michoacan province in Mexico (Beals et al. 1944) and the German-Russian Mennonites of Saskatchewan (Noble 1992b) open onto side yards rather than the road.

In some societies, it is religious tradition more than access that deter-mines orientation. Today, in the leisure-conscious society of the affluent, the setting sun often functions to determine orientation. Houses with picture windows framing the view of a sunset often command higher prices than comparable houses without such an amenity. This operates only in the modern real estate market, although a somewhat similar amenity associated with hill-top sites often determined the direction of traditional buildings. Orientation to the setting sun is rejected in many traditional societies because of its association with death. Interestingly, however, houses in villages in eastern Sumba may face in this direction if on the other side of the street are houses which block the sun's rays (Forth 1981, 55). In a more extreme variation, houses of the Batammaliba in Togo are oriented to face the winter solstice sunset (Blier 1994, 27). I know of no other group oriented in the direction of sunset.

The direction of the rising sun, on the other hand, acted strongly to orient traditional buildings in many societies, including those of the Navajo, so that the entry would receive the first blessing of the rising sun (Wilmsen 1960, 16). David Brugge (1983, 186) has observed that for the Navajo,

> The entry orientation is not to the cardinal direction; rather, it is directed toward sunrise. Thus, it varies somewhat according to the time of year of construction. The direction of sunrise varies from northeast in the summer to southeast in the winter. Similar orientations are used on houses, sweathouses, windbreaks, tents, outhouses and bread ovens, but they are ignored in structures built to shelter livestock, such as cor-rals and chicken coops.

Stephen Jett and Virginia Spencer (1981, 18), too, have observed that for the Navajo northeasterly, and secondarily southeasterly, ori-entations are more common than true easterly compass direction (Figure 4-6). Both hogans and sweat houses utilized a generally east-ward orientation, but summer huts or shelters did not. This confirmed for Cosmos Mindeleff (1898a, 475, 495) that winter hogans were "the real homes of the people." Hogans also have religious func-tions and an orientation toward the east and the rising sun has some religious significance. Nevertheless, Brugge suggested very practical reasons for the hogan entry to face east. Some of his field informants mentioned "the ground does not remain muddy as long in the front of the hogan so orientated, especially if it is on ground sloping slightly to the south or east."

"The additional advantage of a solar orientation avoiding the pre-vailing southwesterly winds of Navajo country is denied by all informants as being a consideration, although it is an effective by-

76 Traditional Buildings

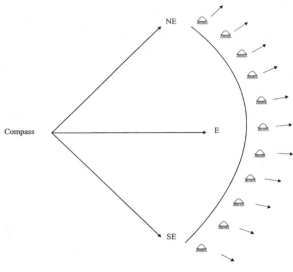

Compass direction of hogan entrance
depending upon date of erection.

4-6. Navajo hogan entrances have somewhat different orientations depending upon the position of the rising sun at the time of the structure's building. Only in rare exceptions is some kind of an eastern directional component lacking (diagram by Iraida Galdon Soler).

product of the tradition" (Brugge 1983, 186). While an eastward orientation applies to the overwhelming number of hogans, a few have a northerly or westerly orientation, which Brugge calls a "reversed orientation." The explanation seems to be "indicative of special religious injunctions associated with dangerous activities such as warfare, some kinds of hunting and certain kinds of curing in which especially powerful and malevolent supernatural forces are to be dealt with." No more specific rationale is needed. The tradition of eastward orientation is so deeply embedded in the Navajo that even modern bungalows and other Western houses built by the Navajo today face to the east (Spencer and Jett 1971, 171).

The Savunese in Indonesia employ more than one orientation for dwellings, but only roughly east or west (Kana 1980, 225). "A house that is positioned incorrectly cuts the land, that is, it crosscuts the lengthwise direction of the island of Savu" and brings bad luck, not only to the house inhabitants but also to the entire community.

An easterly orientation is the one most frequently encountered across the world. It is, or was, predominant among the dwellings of Great Plains Indians (Campbell 1915, 688; Campbell 1927, 94), Moroccan Berbers (Bourdieu 1973), Navajo Indians (Corbett 1940, 107), the

Gond and Bhumia tribal peoples in India (Fuchs 1960, 26), among the Rindi of Sumba, Indonesia (Forth 1981, 55), and many, many, other societies as well. An east-facing orientation has little to do with the compass but a great deal to do with the rising sun, which variously represents rebirth, fertility, light, renewal, energy, even life itself. In India among the Gonds, the east-facing door is constructed to be so low that the peasant exiting in the early morning must bow to the rising sun god (Fuchs 1960, 26).

Obeisance to the sun forms a basic, although often unwritten and even unrecognized, theme of many societies. "The eastern aspect of the house is recognized best to be conducive to prosperity for the family" (Mishra 1969, 13). Throughout India, the east has profound religious significance in addition to being the direction of the sun god. East is the most sacred direction (Chandhoke 1990, 177). The preeminence of eastern and southern directions also can be seen in the Rindi area of Sumba Island, Indonesia. Gregory Forth (1981, 56) took directional readings there and found that "the houses faced between about 105 degrees east and 150 degrees south-east, with the greatest number between 130 and 140 degrees." Forth further found that the variation in orientation was governed by the necessity to prevent the rising sun from directly touching certain structural parts of the dwelling. He notes that "the rules seem to imply that the sun in its daily course should not pass through significant points of the articulation and transition within the houses, but should, so to speak, enter by the right front door and leave by the left back door."

Traditional Spanish-Mexican structures in the southwestern United States tend to be oriented north–south, with the front of the building facing eastward, but it is not the rising sun that is important. Rather, it is the afternoon sun that matters (Figure 4-7). Most houses have a

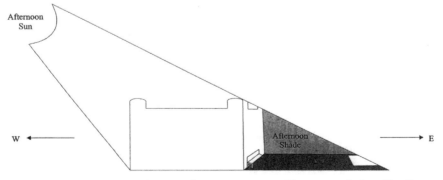

4-7. In the American southwest, afternoons are usually extremely hot. Traditional adobe dwellings are oriented north–south to provide an eastern shade area for relief from the sun's heat (diagram by Iraida Galdon Soler).

masonry or adobe bench placed against the east-facing wall. Here people may sit in the shade out of the heat of the summer afternoon sun (Robinson 1981, 21). The sun was not always welcomed into the house elsewhere either. The well-built structures of the 16th-century English Midlands were oriented to the north (Barley 1987, 84). Presumably the sun provided little additional warmth in the winter, and its exclusion in the summer secured beneficial cooling. A similar situation exists in Greece, where traditional houses face south whenever possible, for maximum sun in winter and shade and airiness in summer (Rider 1965, 232).

Early settlers on the US Great Plains also were guided by celestial observation. The walls of their structures were usually aligned "straight north and south, east and west, with the help of the North Star on a clear night" (Welsch 1967, 337). Of course, the General Land Office rectangular land survey was also useful throughout much of the gently rolling land of the Midwest, where houses are oriented to cardinal compass points as determined by the survey. In this land of prevailing westerly winds, livestock buildings are normally sited east of the house. Robert Riley recognized this in his article "Square to the road, hogs to the east." He liked the idea so much he published two different articles in the same year in two different journals, but with the exact same title, a situation bound to confuse bibliographers! (Riley 1985a; Riley 1985b).

Although a west orientation has a negative connotation in many societies (Mukerji 1962, 32), in many others no such disability pertains. In northern Ghana entrances always faces west. "'Because it is forbidden to build otherwise' was the usual response to the writer's queries on this point" (Hunter 1967, 343). In fact, a westward orientation provides some protection against the frequent rainstorms that move from east to west there. A west orientation is also common in Madagascar (West 1951, 24).

A west or a north orientation in India also has some religious significance, and hence is also generally acceptable, although particular restrictions apply from place to place and in different communities. For example, Nagas avoid the west because this is the direction in which spirits go in death (setting sun?); Nayar caste houses must never face north or south; but in Bengal doors face south to avoid the sharp, cold northerly wind in winter and to get the benefit of soft southerly winds in summer (Crooke 1918, 134). Elsewhere in India, a south orientation is avoided since this is the direction of evil (Chandhoke 1990, 176).

In other parts of the northern hemisphere, especially as latitudes increase, a southerly orientation is quite common, as it provides maximum sun exposure and warmth in winter (Hutslar 1971, 218). However, an early observer of rough dwellings in Texas cautioned prospective settlers to face their dwellings to the south to enable south breezes to pass through the house in the summer months (Robinson 1981, 43; quoting Viktor Bracht, *Texas in 1848*).

A corresponding northerly orientation is not found as often in the southern hemisphere, probably because of the more limited amount of land in its higher latitudes where the need for winter insolation would be most felt. One area where houses "are oriented with surprising rigidity and exactness to the north" is along the East African coast just south of the equator (Garlake 1966, 89). Although by this placement the houses benefit very slightly from winter sunlight, a more important reason for such orientation is the reception of cooling and prevailing winds throughout the year. A world away, in Guyana, an orientation to cooling winds also is common. Here it is to the northeast to catch, as much as possible, the northeast trade winds (Westmaas 1970, 135). In addition to the basic and immediate orientation of Japanese traditional houses to their garden, whenever possible the structures are "open to or face the south, so that they get the full benefit of the south winds of the summer monsoon and of the sun in the cooler season" (Trewartha 1945, 187).

Even such elementary structures as dugouts reflected a conscious orientation. Ann Carpenter (1979, 56) notes that in Texas the dugouts faced generally south, "both to benefit from summer breezes and to avoid north winter winds." A similar southerly orientation is found with early Pennsylvania stone houses, although the orientation is only generally southward to benefit from maximum sunshine and warmth in winter. The German-type barns, with a downslope overhang or forebay, also are oriented toward the south whenever possible. This arrangement permits maximum penetration of sunlight below the overhang and into the basement animal level (Barakat 1972, 11). A further benefit is the more rapid melting in winter of accumulated snow, lodged in front of animal doors, and additional light in dairy areas for milking operations.

In India, whenever possible dwellings faced eastward. The east is considered to be the direction of the gods and "all the religious acts, or acts of religiosity, have taken place in this direction" (Chandhoke 1990, 177). An orientation toward the west is next most popular, although it is difficult to identify the rationale. When necessary, dwellings may face north, but in most parts of India they must never clearly face south, which is the direction of death and evil spirits. A subtle but important point of Hindu geomancy modifies this prohibition. Any obstacle (house, tree, hill, or other) to the south of a house performs the function of negating the prohibition and in such a case the house may indeed face south.

Southerly orientation is encountered in a few areas of India for very different reasons (Noble 2003). In Tamil Nadu cooling southern breezes in summer and cold northern winds in winter override the ancient religious dogma, as does the south-facing warmer winter slopes in the Himalaya, around Dehra Dun (Subramanyam 1938, 174; Dikshit 1965, 43). India is only one of many countries where an elaborate geomancy has been practiced. Throughout Southeast Asia various forms of geomancy are observed; the principles of such divination probably have been refined to its greatest degree in China under the rubric of feng shui, which is briefly discussed above and in Chapter 12.

In the south of the Indonesian island of Bali the question of orientation is more complicated because it involves the entire residential compound rather than a single structure. The "house" in this part of Bali consists of several separate components (structures and spaces) enclosed on three sides by the compound wall. The various parts can be thought of as "rooms" rather than independent buildings or open spaces. Doors may face east, west or south, but just two directions are important. North is toward the central mountains, the abode of the gods, while south is towards the sea, the abode of the evil spirits (Howe 1983, 156). The entire compound is oriented toward the north and is loosely structured to a nine-point system, which some researchers have identified as a model of the Hindu cosmos. What is agreed by all is that the northeast corner is the most sacred space in the compound and the location of the family temple (Howe 1983, 140). Other components, e.g. sleeping rooms, kitchen, and reception area, are more flexible in location.

Muslims, too, are sometimes influenced by religious considerations in the orientation of their dwellings. For example, the elaborate reed huts of the Marsh Arabs in the Tigris-Euphrates delta are constructed to face towards Mecca (Petherbridge 1978, 201). A similar orientation to Mecca is found in Bedouin tents in Sudan, but elsewhere in the Sahara tent openings face west to provide early shade for morning activities (Prussin 1995, 24). Social hierarchy is also expressed by their location:

> The tents of the shaykh's wives, for instance, are placed in a straight line, so that no one wife takes precedence over another; and the important social position of the shaykh's mother is indicated by positioning her tent at the end of the main line and some way forward of it. In Muslim dwellings in Bosnia, in central Yugoslavia, doors are ideally placed

so that the back of the person entering should not be turned to the south-east, that is, towards Mecca. (Petherbridge 1978, 202)

Wind is, of course, an important factor in habitat orientation. Winds of extreme temperature, cold or hot, must be avoided, but cooling winds in summer and warming winds in winter are sought after. When the dwelling is moveable, such as with the tent of the Rabaris of western India (Shah 1980), orientation varies according to season. From December to the beginning of March, winds are from the northeast, but from March to June the winds blow from the southwest. See Chapter 13 for the seasonal movement of the Rabaris.

In the Ganges valley, houses generally face east or north, a fact often attributed to religious influence. However, as R.L. Singh (1957, 56) observes, "the easterly and northerly aspect appears to be related to the cool and rain bearing easterly and northerly winds, while hot and dusty westerly winds of summer are probably the restricting factor to such an aspect of the house".

Location and orientation are both aspects that deal with space and position. Although basically non-structural components of house design, they often influence, and sometimes determine, the other characteristics of a structure. Location is a consideration that usually has economic ramifications, while orientation often speaks to basic symbolic and religious aspects. Both are sensitive to physical and environmental constraints.

~ 5 ~

Building Materials and Construction Methods: Earth Materials

Traditional structures normally reflect their surroundings. Over-whelmingly, they are constructed of locally available building materials (Brown 2004, 23–4) and may vary widely over small distances, especially if altitude changes. Charles Gritzner (1974, 26) found that the altitudinal zonation of traditional dwellings in New Mexico was influenced not only by the easy availability of building materials but also by a number of less recognized factors, including "such fundamental economic laws as comparative advantage, primary resource use, diminishing returns and accessibility."

An excellent example of local geographical variation can be found in the junction zone between the Sierra Madre Occidental and the adjacent Central Plateau of Mexico. "The Sierra region has abundant forests, while often lacking sufficient water to permit easy manufacture of adobes or tiles. The other areas [the plateau] have abundant water, but the forests are distant" (Beals et al. 1944, 7). As a result wooden dwellings predominate in the sierra, while tile-roofed adobe buildings occur on the plateau, especially around Lake Patzcuaro on the plateau. Similarly sharp boundaries exist and are reported by Mason (1973, 24) for quite different buildings and locations in England. Structures made of exotic materials would not fit the definition of traditional buildings (i.e. accepted as a norm in a society), unless, of course, those materials became widely available at low cost and proved to be as efficient, or more so, than the already utilized objects.

Ethiopia offers still a third example of variations based upon availability of materials, but also reflects climatic differences and levels of technology. Naigzy Gebremedhin (1971, 110) suggests that three processes of construction have produced the traditional dwellings of the country. Weaving, using bamboo and grasses, is the building process employed primarily in the lowest altitudes. In the drier northern uplands, piling, the process employing adobe blocks, brick or stone, is encountered, whereas in the somewhat wetter central plateau between Gondar and Addis Ababa the method used is twining or tying, in which woody building materials are tied together by rope or other tying materials.

Sometimes the materials of construction are not natural building items, but rather are easily available and cheaply manufactured ones. Roofs, for example, may even be made of flattened metal oilcans. They are reported from as widely scattered locations as Alaska (Hoagland 1993, 67), India (Cooper and Dawson 1998, 40, 175), South Africa (Weller 1922, 7), and the Rio Grande valley of North America (Newton 1964, 24). Undoubtedly, they occur elsewhere.

Occasionally, the building materials have a close and unique connection to the inhabitants. The Kumbhara are a caste of potters in the Indian state of Orissa, who construct their dwellings out of terracotta pots. "The walls are fully built of stacked pots specially thrown for this purpose and arranged to form one huge thatched room. . . . Inside, this room is partitioned with more vessels into two or three living compartments. The terracotta walls provide remarkably effective insulation during the hot season and, when broken, double as niches" (Huyler 1982, 87). These buildings remind us that "construction techniques do not evolve or emerge in cultural isolation; they reflect and are based upon specific social and economic conditions" (Candee 1976, 55).

Among herders and hunters the use of animal products often makes up a significant component of the traditional dwelling. This is especially noticeable in those environments that offer little else in the way of building materials. Herders in desert, near-desert, and grassland areas use animal hides, as do Eskimos in summer – who in winter employ various parts of whales, walruses and other large Arctic animals.

Some of the earliest inhabited structures were either above or below ground (see Chapter 7). In the main, however, buildings are ground-fast, built from ground level upwards. This, of course, discounts the digging of cellars, often less than half the area of the building floors, and whatever modest excavation was necessary to level the ground; or the raising of a structure a foot or so to avoid the damp ground in humid areas and to facilitate air circulation under the structure to enhance cooling and retard deterioration.

The materials of construction can be divided into two major, basic groupings – *earth materials* and vegetative products. Each of these groupings can be further refined to sod, clay or mud, brick, and stone; and logs, timber, lumber, wattle, bamboo, tree leaves, grasses, and textiles. Each of these sub-divisions might be again ordered on the basis of the technology involved in their preparation and use. A third category, animal hides or skins, are used in a few places, but their use is quite restricted compared to earth materials or vegetative products.

In the middle and higher latitudes as people moved from early pits, dugouts and caves, it was only natural that they turned to materials that could be formed into structures to withstand cold temperatures, as well as keep unfriendly men and animals at bay. One of the most important of these materials was the earth itself. Even today, over a third of the world's population resides in structures made of *mud* (Moughtin 1985, 3). In India, as recently as the 1970s, 60% of all rural dwellings and almost a quarter of urban buildings were estimated to be of mud (Cain et al. 1975, 212).

The use of clay or mud as a building material is popularly believed to be restricted to dry environments, i.e. deserts or near deserts. While it is true that such materials dominate in these locations, mostly because of the scarcity of alternatives, mud and clay are also used in quite humid environments. Clay, earth or mud, in many parts of the world, is referred to as *adobe*, which is a modification of the Arabic word *al-tob* or mud. The use of an Arabic term is understandable because of the prominence of mud-walled and -roofed structures throughout the deserts of the Middle East. Introduced by the Spanish to Latin America, the term diffused to much of the rest of the world.

The principal advantages of adobe as a building material are its high insulation qualities, its extremely low cost because of wide availability, the fact that little skill is required to use it in its simplest forms, and its durability. As a result, adobe also lends itself easily to remodeling efforts (Bunting 1964, 2). Unfortunately, while in other respects a suitable building material, adobe is highly vulnerable to water damage. In humid areas the walls must be plastered and covered by a roof whose eaves extend some distance beyond the wall line in order to prevent back-splash and to guard against rising damp. In dry areas, where even the roof may be partially of adobe, three locations of potential damage are the roof itself, around roof drains where overflow and leakage may damage walls, and the lowest section of wall where back-splash can erode (Bunting 1976, 8). If wood beams are in contact with the adobe roof they are apt not to be watertight. Vigilant maintenance is required with all adobe structures.

In all areas, the walls may be constructed by building layer upon layer of mud in a method widely used in desert environments and sometimes referred to as "puddled adobe." The mud is mixed with a small amount of water and perhaps some binding material such as a little straw. In addition to providing dimensional stability, the straw allows the mud to dry more uniformly, thus minimizing shrinkage cracks (Miller 1949, 6). A ridge or mound of this is laid down as the base of the wall and allowed to dry thoroughly. Then the next layer is applied and allowed to dry. The procedure is repeated until the desired height is reached.

The same process is widely used in drier areas in its simplest mode. The layers of mud are built up with no restraining forms so that a natural, but pronounced, taper of the wall is created. At its base it may be three feet or more in thickness and just a few inches at its top. Such a taper is necessary for stability, but must be constantly monitored and repaired against erosion. Puddled adobe walls have been reported from the Sahara Desert and its margins in Africa, where it often is termed "swish" (Gardi 1973, 57; Rodger 1974, 103; Denyer 1978, 93), in western India on the margins of the Thar desert (Jain 1980), and it was a major method of construction in the dry areas of Mexico and the southwestern US before the arrival of the Spaniards (Bunting 1976, 9), and continuing in use long afterward.

One of the most unusual applications of mud building is practiced by the Musgum (Mousgoum), who reside astride the boundary between Cameroon and Chad. Their roughly conical houses can be as high as 30 feet. The basic structure is formed by strong reeds lashed together, over which the mud is laid. The smokehole opening at the apex is just a few inches in diameter and can be closed easily with a plate or pot when it rains. The single doorway, narrow at knee level and wider at shoulder height, has been described as resembling a keyhole (Gardi 1973, 91). Lumpy projections on the mud cone offer foot and hand holds that permit the owner to climb for repairs or to insert the rain pot.

Humid areas in which puddled mud walls occur today include England, especially in the east Midlands and in the county of Devon where it is identified as *cob*, the Brittany peninsula of France (Figure 5-1) and French-speaking Canada, where the French term *torchi* is used (Rushton 1979, 169; Meirion-Jones 1982, 52). "Cob is made of compacted clay and earth, bound with straw and moulded in various ways to form thick walls finished with lime plaster. It must be kept dry, so cob houses are always built on a stone or brick plinth. When the plaster comes off, the cob deteriorates very quickly" (Penoyre and Penoyre 1978, 54). Several reasons have been advanced for the emphasis on cob building in Devon. Among them are the suitable and abundant clay deposits, the poor timber resources for wood building and also the lack of much wood to be used as fuel for the making of fired brick.

A second method of employing mud, found in both dry and humid regions, utilizes a wooden form or shutter to restrain the mud and its binding elements until dry (Prussin 1970, 17). The form is then removed and raised to confine the next layer (Figure 5-2). Houses with walls made this way occur in many areas. The terms often applied to this method are *tapia* or *pisé*. Because this procedure greatly increases the density of the clay, pisé is stronger than either puddled adobe or even adobe brick (Norton 1986, 35). I have seen this technique being used in places as widely scattered as Morocco, Peru and

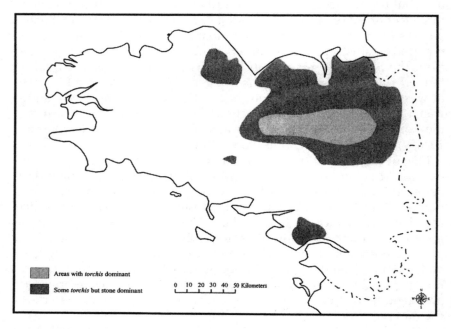

Areas with *torchis* dominant

Some *torchis* but stone dominant

0 10 20 30 40 50 Kilometers

5-1. (above) Map of mud-walled houses in Brittany (drawing by Iraida Galdon Soler, based upon Meirion-Jones 1982, 52).

5-2. (right) Method used in Australia for constructing a pisé wall. Much the same procedure is followed in the rest of the world. The wooden form holds the mud mixture until solidified and the rammer or tamper compacts the material to remove air pockets, cracks and weakly bonded spaces (modified from Irving 1985, 199).

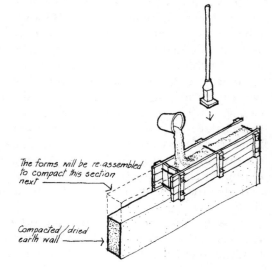

The forms will be re-assembled to compact this section next

Compacted/dried earth wall

5-3. *A wooden tamper used to compact mud in pisé construction in northern Peru (photo by the author, 1985).*

China. It is described by Carver (1981, 98–9) for northern Iberia, by Prussin (1970, 17) for Sudan, by Facey (1997, 90) for Saudi Arabia, for China by Knapp (1989, 70), for Bhutan by Denwood (1971, 26) and for South Africa by Frescura (1981).

The further modification of the pisé by extensive tamping, in which a heavy pounder (Figure 5-3) is used to compact the mud, removing all the air pockets and maximizing the mass, gives this method its other name, *rammed earth*. Occasionally a rammed-earth building is reported even from central or western Canada or the United States (Patty and Minium 1933, 6; Sculle 1989). The construction account in the journal *Manufacturer and Builder* is particularly valuable because it is a contemporary description of the process for 19th-century American farmers (Anonymous 1869a). Lest the technique of rammed earth be considered a new method, Nabokov (1981, 6) reminds us that it was used by 13th- and 14th-century Indians in southern Arizona.

If the earth contained a high lime content, it could be mixed with gravel and poured between the shutters a layer at a time. This variation of pisé construction, which required minimum tamping, is termed "mud concrete" or "poured adobe." It has been reported from Cache valley in northern Utah, and Iron County in southwestern Utah (Goss 1975, 211). One of the traits that make the Mormons of Utah interesting is the rapidity and success with which they adapted to different construction materials as they migrated westward. Coming from a humid, forested environment where frame houses were the norm, they built log cabins in Illinois, sod dugouts in Nebraska, and poured adobe and adobe-block houses in Utah.

Another major, and the most technically sophisticated, method of using mud is in the form of "adobe building blocks." In humid tropical areas the clay soil has a high iron and aluminum content and a reddish or yellowish color. It is referred to as laterite from the Latin word "later" meaning brick (Spence and Cook 1983, 36). This is a recognition of the fact that in a dry period the ground usually becomes extremely hard, and also due to the fact that when a block is cut out, or soft clay is molded into a form, it will dry to a hardness reminiscent of fired brick. The great advantage of adobe blocks is that they can be moved easier than the loose earth (Norton 1986, 30).

Again, two basic techniques are in use. The simplest, called "clay lump" or "toubes," is one in which the clay is formed by hand into a roughly rectangular block (Prussin 1970, 17). No form is used to shape the individual block. In the UK this technique is limited to East Anglia (Sandon 1977, 69: Penoyre and Penoyre 1978, 77; Egeland 1988, 10). Its limitation to that region is the result of two natural conditions: rainfall there is the lowest in all England and drying winds are the strongest (Addison 1986, 34). Clay lump also occurs widely in Africa (Gardi 1973, 53–61; Denyer 1978, 93). In tropical West Africa, the lateritic adobe is formed into cone-shaped lumps and tossed to the builder sitting astride the top of the wall (Blier 1994, 21, has an excellent photograph). The height to which these lumps can be thrown, without the use of scaffolding or ladders, determines the elevation of the wall (Moughtin 1964, 29).

A more sophisticated technique produces "adobe bricks." It requires packing the wet mud into a rectangular form. When partially dry, the mud has hardened sufficiently that the form can be removed. In both cases, clay lump and adobe brick, a thorough drying period of several days is required before the blocks are ready to be used. Even with thorough drying, adobe bricks may be susceptible to water erosion. In Utah a lime stucco may be used as an exterior plaster to combat this problem (Bonar 1983, 217).

As Mormons moved into the drier and less forested west of the US before the middle of the 19th century they came more and more to depend upon adobe brick as a building material (Fairbanks 1975; Jackson 1980). Initially they encountered several problems that they needed to overcome before adobe became their major early building material. First, they needed to find the proper mix of clay and sand. Often they used too much clay, which caused adobe bricks to shrink and crack badly upon drying. Sometimes they used too much sand and the bricks crumbled and failed to bond properly. Second, in their haste to provide shelter they used the bricks before they had thoroughly cured and the adobe would collapse when any weight was placed on it (Pitman 1973, 26).

Other techniques are used elsewhere. In urban areas of Afghanistan, where residents can afford the cost of more durable fired brick, it may be used as facing (Samizay 1974, 149). Fired brick is used in many places in smaller amounts to cap and protect the tops of adobe brick walls (Stanford 1975, 26). In Morocco a layer of reeds may be used instead.

The successful use of mud, of whatever method, requires the addition, or natural presence, of small amounts of binding materials. Straw or other fibers provide longitudinal strength. Lime, gravel, chalk, sand or dung are chemical strengthening agents without which the dried mud may crack and fall apart. In the American Southwest, early Spanish settlers employed a type of adobe bricks called *terrones*. They resembled the sod bricks of the Great Plains in being held together partly by grass roots. They were cut from the ground with a spade in a size larger than the typical sun-dried adobe brick (Motto 1973, 76).

The German-speaking Mennonites who migrated to the Russian areas north of the Black Sea in the 18th century are perhaps unique in having used all three main mud materials – puddled adobe, pisé, and adobe bricks – to construct their dwellings (Sherman 1974, 186). Coming from forest environments, in which timber supplied the basic building materials, the Mennonites were forced to adopt the mud-walling techniques of the Russians and Ukrainians, who were natives of the steppe grasslands where timber was lacking. These experiences stood the community in good stead when it moved to the largely treeless prairies of North America in the 19th century.

Another important earth building material was *sod*, or *turf*, used primarily in grassland areas where timber was scarce. Sod houses and sod dugouts were structures of necessity. Pioneer settlers on the Great Plains of the US found themselves in a vast, largely treeless land, where wood, their familiar building material, was mostly lacking. Because of the known severity of Plains winters they needed shelter, and needed it fast! The urgency was so great that pioneer settlers set about building sod structures even before they had identified that most critical of location elements, a dependable water supply. Often quarters laboriously constructed, had to be subsequently abandoned in order to use a more convenient water supply (Noble 1984, 1:72). Nevertheless, sod was the best solution. It was cheap and readily available. It required little skill to use and had excellent insulating qualities (Figure 5-4). One problem, however, was that about an acre

5-4. Sketch of a sod house, typical of the American Great Plains in the 19th century. Among the immigrant German settlers, the sod blocks were often referred to as kohlstein. The roof of this structure is of wooden boards covered by strips of sod (drawing by M. Margaret Geib).

of sod was needed to build a standard 12 x 14-foot dwelling (Welsh 1968, 41).

Sod houses in North America suffered from the same social stigma that log houses experienced. Although in both instances they were the mark of the pioneer in carving out settlements in what appeared to them to be a forbidding and dangerous wilderness, once the settlement frontier passed by, these structures lost any validity for many of the newcomers, as well as visitors. A traveling architect's account from 1876 is typical of such attitudes. Writing about sod structures in western Nebraska, he says "it is sometimes the result of necessity, but most frequently, we think, especially where allowed long to exist, the result of barbaric laziness" (Hussey 1876, 378).

The sod-house floor plan was usually a simple, one-room rectangle because these structures were normally thought of as temporary dwellings. Nevertheless, some continued to be occupied for more than a quarter century. A few carefully preserved examples can be seen throughout the Great Plains today, and in the 1970s five sod houses in western Kansas were still occupied (Oringderff 1976, 132).

The sod of Nebraska and the Dakotas was sometimes held to be superior by individuals from other regions. Such states "furnished a sod of a peculiarly hard and enduring character; not precisely equaled by anything our informants could discover in our own locality" (Roe 1970, 2). In many areas, a hipped roof of sod over boards or branches was preferred because it permitted all four walls to be built to the same height. In Kansas, however, a gable roof was the overwhelming favorite. Over 76% of all "soddies" there were so roofed (Oringderff 1976, 33).

Although sod was ubiquitous on the Great Plains and provided excellent insulation, sod structures were not without problems. Interiors had poor light and ventilation because of few openings; dirt sifted down from the ceiling in dry periods; on rainy days and for several days thereafter the roof often leaked and dirt floors got muddy (Dick 1937, 114); insects, birds, mice and snakes found shelter in the sod (Drucker 1949, 361); and the heavy weight of sod roofs needed substantial support (Welsch 1968, 49). Despite these difficulties, "soddies" provided short-term shelter for thousands and many were occupied for decades.

In many parts of Europe, especially in western Scotland, Ireland, and Iceland, *turf houses* were constructed using methods similar to those of the North American pioneers. Turf blocks were cut and piled up like bricks or cut stone to form walls, and were also laid on timber frames to serve as roofing. In Ireland a related structure termed a *moss house* was made of turf and peat deposits by cutting and removing peat so that a large block was left at the center. The interior of the block was then scooped away, leaving the remaining turf and peat as free-standing walls into which a door and window were cut (Figure 5-5). Wooden posts were erected to support a roof frame and thatching (Megaw 1962, 90). The early Viking dwellings in Iceland were largely constructed of turf, supplemented by irregular blocks of volcanic rock. Interiors consisted of driftwood framing.

In the coastal southeastern United States, a burnt lime and seashell aggregate called *tabby* became a standard construction material for buildings, walls, and even roadways, under Spanish, French, and British colonial administrations. Its use in the New World derived from

Peat Bog Surface

5-5. Schematic floor plan of a "moss house." The trench and house interior are excavated, leaving the turf/mud wall standing freely in the center (drawing by Iraida Galdon-Soler, based upon Megaw 1962, 90).

African slaves assigned as construction workers, who knew its properties from their earlier residence in the Guinea Coast of West Africa
(Jones 1985, 199). When tabby dries and cures it forms a rock-hard
mass much like cement, so impenetrable that fortresses were sometimes built of the material.

The ultimate rock-hard earth building materials are brick and
stone. If clay, rather than being used after natural drying, is subjected
to baking and fusing temperatures in a closed kiln or oven, *fired brick*
is the result, a much superior building material to mud or adobe. It is
stronger and more durable; not subject to rapid erosion as adobe is;
easier to handle than adobe; and has an equally high thermal insulation value and fire resistance (Rodger 1974, 103). "But brick is not the
most satisfactory of materials in all times and places. In particular its
slow release of heat makes it unsuited to areas where there is little
nocturnal radiation" (Rose 1962, 262). Another major drawback is that
a proper firing temperature is critical. Too high and the brick becomes
brittle; too low and it tends to crumble and be susceptible to water
erosion.

The quality of the soil materials used for the bricks is also important. If the proper balance of clay and sand is not present the brick
will be soft regardless of firing temperature. Exposed to constantly
high humidity, the bricks may prove generally unsatisfactory. This
condition prevails in the lower Mississippi river valley and delta. In
desert areas where brick should be superior to adobe it is not much
used. The problem is lack of wood for fuel and the higher price of
fired bricks because of the cost of fuel when it is available. Brickwork
is usually categorized on the basis of how the individual bricks are
placed in a wall. This is referred to as the brick's "bond." The bricks
themselves are termed "stretchers" if the long side is exposed and
"headers" if the end is exposed.

One large area over which brick became the construction material
of choice for dwellings is the north European plain from the Netherlands to Poland. In this area forests were cleared early on and the
great alluvial flood plains and deltas provided abundant clay deposits for brick making (Jones 1918, 21), as well as the fertile soils to
support stable and prosperous agricultural settlement.

Greater status usually attaches to building in brick rather than in
mud or wood. "In some parts of India and Africa, the proportion of
brick-built homes in a village can be used as some sort of measure
of its level of prosperity" (Spence and Cook 1983, 67). In the case of
wood, this is probably because of the bricks' greater durability and
fire resistance. In the case of mud, a brick structure's elevated status is
perhaps because of its greater cost, more finished appearance, and the
need for more skill in its construction. However, the prestige accorded

to brick buildings in India also may reflect ancient Vedic traditions in which the type and quality of bricks allowed to be used were caste derived. The highest ranking castes (Brahmin and Kshatriya) could use fired bricks and mortar; middle castes (Vaishya and S'udra) were permitted only unfired bricks; and all the lower groups were restricted to wattle and daub and similar materials (Arya 2000, 17).

A danger exists for researchers to overestimate the use of bricks as opposed to wood, for example, because – as years pass – wood structures disappear at a greater rate than brick (Herman 1987). Thus, a researcher may find mostly older brick buildings in areas of study and fewer older wood ones, and come to the erroneous conclusion that brick was the major building material. Studies investigating the disappearance rate of traditional buildings are quite rare. Part of the problem is that many structures, especially of wood or mud, may leave virtually no trace after a short period of decay. A study of the disappearance on the Scioto river floodplain in a single county of Ohio of "agricultural structures" known to exist in 1915 showed fluctuations of the rate of disappearance from one every 24 months to one every 13 months (Noble and King 1989). While these rates may not be typical of the disappearance of all traditional structures even in Ohio, they do suggest that the rural built-landscape is in a constant state of change.

In North America, the dominance of brick is unlikely given the abundance and low cost of wood in earlier periods. The fewer but larger, well-built houses of the wealthy, which tend to be of brick, also are likely to survive at a higher rate (Lounsbury 1983, 186). Nevertheless, fired brick has a long history in the New World. In North America, almost as soon as European settlement began, kilns were constructed to supply fired brick. On Long Island bricks were being produced as early as 1628 (Weslager 1969, 130). By the 19th century, Haverstraw on the Hudson River may have been the largest brick making center in the world (DeNoyelles 1968, 3).

Many writers have commented on "English bricks," presumably brought over to the American continent in the early settlement period as ship ballast if not actual cargo. N.R. Ewan (1938) effectively demolished this idea. He noted that the term "English brick" refers in early documents not to imported bricks but to bricks made to a legal standard in North America as early as 1683. He further noted that

> the possibility of bringing bricks from the mother country becomes remote, if we consider shipping conditions of Colonization days. The ancient sailing ships of but 200 to 300 tons capacity, required many weary weeks in crossing and on their western trips were always overburdened with passengers and freight cargoes made up of goods indispensable to the existence of the new settlers. How improbable it

would be that these vital necessities would be relegated to an embargo in favor of loading the small ships with common brick, which could be and were made here at a fraction of the cost of bringing them overseas. Little credence can be given to the many statements which claim the bricks were brought over "in ballast." The heavily loaded vessels needed no further weight than their own essential cargoes to keep them stable on the ocean voyage. Certainly, if bricks were ever shipped on these primitive boats, their value as ballast could have been used to better advantage on the eastern or "home" sailings, when few exports were being returned to Britain. (Ewan 1938, 12)

Before we reject entirely the idea of bricks imported to the New World as ship ballast, we need to consider the evidence presented by David Cohen (1992, 45–7), who quotes 17th-century documents that indicate that the Dutch in New Amsterdam did, in fact, contract with ship captains for such bricks.

Related to fired brick is the employment of wall cladding employing hung or mathematical tiles. Both of these techniques lie on the periphery of vernacular architecture. Hung tiles, first appearing in the latter part of the 17th century in England, most often occur in the southeastern counties on gable ends and sides exposed to weather to provide more effective protection than the brick and plaster infillings which were not entirely weatherproof. Mathematical tiles, invented late in the 18th century, were specially shaped without an overlapping surface so as to appear as fired bricks (Penoyre and Penoyre 1978, 29). They gave a brick-like appearance but evaded the brick tax in force from 1784 to 1850 (Addison 1986, 100). Used in southern England in the late 18th and first half of the 19th centuries, they were applied mostly to new construction. However, some traditional buildings, to follow fashion as well as to secure better weatherproofing, had these tiles added to earlier wooden frames (Smith, T. 1979).

The most durable earth building material is *stone*. Because of its weight, and hence the difficulty and cost of moving it very far, stone is used for dwellings within a few miles of its origin. Thus, a geological map showing building stone formations such as limestone, sandstone, and slate, is a useful guide to finding traditional stone structures. As Charles McRaven (1980, 11) notes, "stone is expensive if you count your time, cheap if you don't."

Fieldstones were probably the original stone materials used in vernacular construction. Mechanical weathering leaves many earth surfaces cluttered with rock fragments, which with some care can be piled up into walls (Perrin 1963–64, 137). Even without mortar to bind the rocks, walls can successfully be constructed in a technique called *dry walling* in which just the weight of the rocks holds them in place.

Careful fitting of the rocks is required and some kinds of rock are better than others. Angular sedimentary rocks with flat bedding and fault surfaces are best, with some limestones leading the way. The great advantage of dry-wall construction is that, if water penetrates, the effect on the wall is much less than in mortared walls (Denyer 1991, 154).

Because of its weight and the time and skill required for its use, cut or finished stone building reflects regional prosperity. An example is provided by Stell (1965). "From the sixteenth century the Pennines of West Yorkshire, which had previously been sparsely populated, became more prosperous with the development of the woolen industry and new houses were required for the increased population." Not only was stone substituted for timber in building, many existing timber buildings were faced partly or entirely with stone.

Several factors in combination in the Mediterranean basin have worked to promote traditional building in stone in that region. They include a climate in which rainfall does not support extensive forest vegetation to supply timber; bedrock primarily of limestone and sandstone easy to quarry but hard enough to permit use in building; and a population that strained the limits of its resource base under traditional lifestyle levels. Simple stone structures are scattered from Spain and Morocco in the west across the islands and peninsulas of the center to the interiors of Syria, Jordan, and Palestine in the east (Walton 1962; Allen 1969; Ron 1977). The normal mode of stone building in these areas was the erection of circular plan, corbeled, domed or beehive-shaped houses.

The *corbeled stone huts* in Malta have been occupied or used continuously up to the present time. Built of a mixture of rough field boulders and dressed stone, they are huts for temporary shelter of farmers (Fsadni 1992, 9). Although merely temporary field huts, the *girna* exhibit all the basic characteristics of more permanent stone dwellings encountered throughout the Mediterranean basin (Walton 1962, 33). Furthermore, many stone structures, both in Malta and elsewhere, after being used for human shelter continued to serve as housing for smaller livestock such as goats, sheep, and pigs (Fsadni 1992, 83).

Floor plans of stone structures vary from circular to oval, rectangular and square, and in overall form from beehive to barrel vault to pyramid roofed. The corbeled roof is covered by small stones, and even finer gravel. Because corbeled stone huts occur most often in limestone areas, they are frequently associated with, or are in proximity to, extensive cave dwellings. This is true in southern Spain, the Greek islands, and in the heel of southern Italy.

In this latter area, corbeled stone construction reached a high degree of craftsmanship (Allen 1969). In addition to the simple field huts, magnificent dome- and cone-shaped *trulli* were built. The base may be rectangular, oval or circular, and the construction material limestone or the softer volcanic tufa. Several local terms are used to identify these corbeled structures, but trulli is the term most widely applied and known. "The word trullo (sing.) comes from the Greek troullos and its Latin derivative trullus, meaning a building with a conical summit" (Castellano 1964, 7). An alternative term, *chipuro*, is of Greek origin and means "guardian of the cultivated fields," indicating the rural origin of this type of building. Later-built trulli and the bulk of those remaining today are found in villages (Branch 1966, 96).

The method of construction is that of an inner and outer wall with earth and small stone filler between. Until the 1930s, Italian farmers were not wealthy enough to hire builders and they constructed their own trulli. Since then, however, builders have come to the fore and designs have become gradually more sophisticated, but less traditional. The basic form has not changed much, however, indicating local satisfaction and acceptance. In many instances, the later trulli have multiple cones and rectangular stone and masonry additions.

Rectangular stone buildings, in which the domed or vaulted ceiling is encased in a flat stone and masonry roof, are characteristic of Palestine (Amiry and Tamari 1989, 17–25). The walls are thick to support the heavy roof. The two-story structure functions as a housebarn,

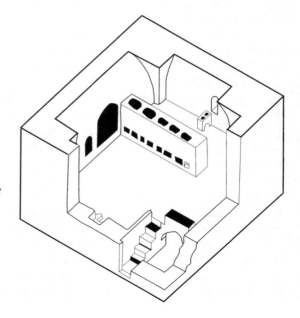

5-6. *An isometric drawing of a Palestinian stone housebarn. The family living space is termed the mastabeh. Mud bins for food storage divide and separate the rooms. A lower level houses live-stock and agricultural equipment (based upon Amiry and Tamari 1989, 22).*

with animals and equipment occupying the lower level and living quarters above (Figure 5-6).

Building with *cobblestone* is an outgrowth and refinement of fieldstone construction. Placing small cobbles in a bed of mortar to create a wall "bears a strong resemblance to the best flintwork and masonry of coursed kidney cobbles" in southeastern England (Perrin 1963–64, 13–14). Cobblestone building reached its apogee in northeastern North America, where the combination of continental glaciation to break up and transport rock fragments, and subsequent stream and lake smoothing, provided an abundant supply of suitable stones (Noble and Coffey 1986) (Figure 5-7). The middle of the 19th century was the period of maximum development of cobblestone architecture (Figure 5-8), which centered on upstate New York (Schmidt 1966, 2). The age and location of cobblestone buildings supports the thesis that surplus "stone masons, thrown out of work by the completion of the Erie Canal, found employment in building cobblestone structures . . . Furthermore, the distribution of these structures reflects those areas in

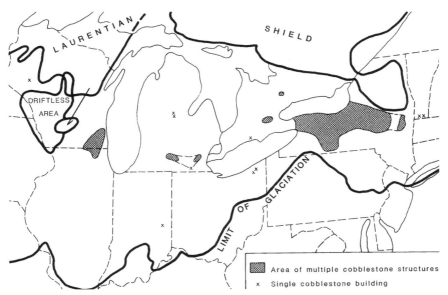

5-7. Cobblestone building in the 19th century was influenced by continental glaciation and by erosional smoothing of stones by lake and river water action. The large area of cobblestone construction in New York State is also related to the number of masons attracted to the area by the building of the Erie Canal and other canals. The Laurentian Shield, an area of old, hard rock, furnished the source area for the cobbles carried south by the glacier (from Noble and Coffey, 1986).

5-8. Cobblestone structures were built in New York State in the 19th century, largely between 1830 and 1855. Only two dwellings are known from after the Civil War, one built in 1872 and the other in 1879.

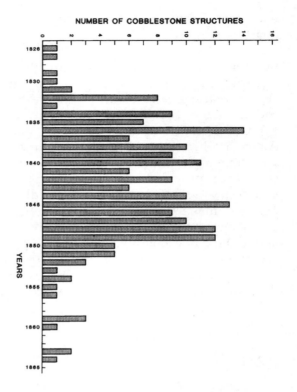

NUMBER OF COBBLESTONE STRUCTURES

which the final phases of canal construction took place in New York State" (Noble and Coffey 1986, 45).

The earliest structures were not actually of cobbles, but of "fieldstones of varying colors, sizes and shapes" (Edward 1978, 33). By general definition, a cobble is a stone that can be held comfortably in one hand (Shelgren et al. 1978, 1). Furthermore, true cobblestone architecture requires the stone to be embedded in a cement mortar primarily in horizontal rows. The natural cement, which makes up almost half the volume of a cobblestone wall, was also directly related to canal construction. The quest for a bonding material, which was needed in enormous quantities for the construction of the canals, resulted in the discovery in 1818 in central New York of vast deposits of natural cement rock (Lesley 1972, 13–14).

Carl Schmidt, the acknowledged authority on cobblestone architecture, proposed a three-period development (1958, 231). The early period was one of mixed stone colors and sizes, and the horizontal courses were somewhat irregular. The middle period brought more standardized sizes and better color matching, and the introduction of water-smoothed stones (Figure 5-9). Finally, the late period saw a con-

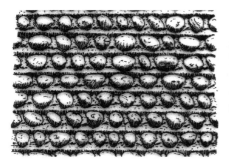

5-9. Examples of cobblestone walling. The regularity in size and shape of the cobbles is typical of the middle period of cobblestone building, when the stones were laid in courses defined by ridges of cement (drawing by M. Margaret Geib).

centration on small stones and almost machine regularity in the horizontal courses.

From a heartland in central New York, cobblestone building advanced westward into Michigan and Wisconsin by the 1840s and 1850s (Frasch 1965, 8). By 1870, census returns listed 25 cobblestone houses in the city of Beloit, the center of Wisconsin cobblestone building (Shedd 1974, 21). Another concentration of cobblestone structures may be found around Paris, Ontario, and a smaller collection at Baldwin, north of Toronto (Rempel 1967, 282). Even before the Civil War brought a cessation of cobblestone building, the popularity of such construction had begun to wane. Perhaps this was a result of a depletion in the availability of the stones, or a lack of young masons to replace the dwindling numbers of the original canal workers, both of which conditions would have resulted in increased costs of construction. The final chapter on cobblestone architecture research has not yet been written.

Another area of stone construction, but of quite different type, occurs in southern Brittany. "Walling formed entirely of orthostats, large flat vertical slabs of stone with their lower ends embedded in the ground, has been recorded in six locations, but only in south Finistère, in the region between Concarneau and Pont-Aven, do large numbers of buildings incorporating this type of walling survive" (Meirion-Jones 1982, 53).

These houses of upright stones are in the same area in which the famous, upright megaliths of Carnac occur. The Carnac monuments undoubtedly served as a model for the use of the stone in house construction. The granite stone slabs are about two and a half meters long and stand upright with the lowest half-meter buried in the ground. Exterior walls are of orthostatic rock, except for the gable wall, which incorporates the heavy granite chimney. Hipped roofs are often encountered since they accommodate the orthostatic stones better than the gable form. Also, the houses are only a single story in elevation because of the difficulty of building upon the upright stones (Meirion-Jones 1982, 54). Cut stone, rubble, and pisé close any gaps in the orthostone walls.

In a few instances, stone in the form of slabs of slate has been used for walling of timber-frame houses (Figure 5-10). In the area around Boppart along the Rhine in Germany, slate, often cut into flat diamond shapes, is a particularly common wall material (Stevenson 1880, 190). Slate as a walling material also occurs in Belgium and in England in Cornwall, Devon, and especially in the Lake District (Brown 1982, 205; Addison 1986, 40). Much later, long after the period of traditional building, slate was used in the early 20th century as wall covering in parts of Pennsylvania and eastern Ohio, and perhaps elsewhere. However, slate walling never reached the popularity of slate roofing.

One quite unusual combination of stone materials is encountered in the Lake District, where wooden lintels are covered first by a course of thin slates projecting from the face of the wall, and then by a

5-10. *Slate-sided houses are found in several districts of Europe. This example is located near Brussels, Belgium. Only the gable wall facing the direction of prevailing wind and storm has been slated. Decorative patterns are formed by using slates of differing color (photo by the author, 1984).*

course of cobblestones holding the slate in place (Denyer 1991, 151). The slate course acts as a deflector of rainwater. Slate also forms a unique structural element in some buildings in this region by forming *crow steps*, stepped slate projections lined up along the roof gable edge (Denyer 1991, 155).

One special kind of earth material used for a seasonal or temporary dwelling is *snow* (Schwatka 1883). The word *igloo* is the general Eskimo word for a dwelling, employed as we might use the word *house* (Ray 1960, 13). However, the term has come to have a more specific application in much of the world outside polar areas, meaning a dome-shaped snow and ice structure. The snow-block dome of the Eskimo igloo "encloses the greatest volume for the smallest surface area of any wide-based structure, so heat losses through wind-chill are minimized." The snow is "cut into rectangular blocks and laid not in horizontal corners, but spirally. This means that the structure is self-supporting throughout, the blocks being trimmed to slope inwards until the key-block is added from outside" (Duly 1979, 54–5).

The igloo was limited in most polar areas for use only as a temporary expedient, and to central North America as a seasonal habitation, but because of its unique use of materials and its attractive and efficient form it is more widely appreciated than its numbers and limited use warrants. Most arctic peoples used partly excavated houses, often with whalebone frames in the winter and animal-skin tents in summer (Cranstone 1980, 488–9). A wide variety of largely non-descript structures served as shelter in spring and autumn transitional periods (Lee and Reinhardt 2003).

Everywhere and at all times, earth materials used in traditional building tend to be employed either in a natural state, such as mud, sod or snow, or after minimal processing, such as brick (both adobe and fired), cut stone, or slate. In societies of lower technological levels, earth materials provide dimensional strength, and because of their lighter weight often dominate a structure's upper areas and roof covering. Because of their more or less ubiquitous nature and low cost, earth materials have been widely employed in all parts of the world, especially in communities that have lower technological levels. However, this circumstance should not be equated with lack of craftsmanship. The mud lump, conical roofs of the Musgum huts; the delicate patterns etched into adobe walls by many tribes in South Africa; and the terracotta pot walls of the Khumbara caste in India, to cite just a few instances, offer examples to refute this negative view of craftsmanship.

~ 6 ~

Building Materials and Construction Methods: Wood and Related Materials

After earth materials, vegetation is the main source of building resources, and wood in various forms and modes is the most important component. Indeed, wood is undoubtedly the most widely used construction material for dwellings around the world (Lazistan and Michalov 1971).

Logs, which in simplest form are nothing more than tree trunks stripped of branches and cut into convenient lengths, are widely used in colder, humid climates throughout the world where appropriate forest resources occur. Log building is not a mode widely found in forested tropical areas for four major reasons. First, although the forest stand is very dense, it is composed of a very large number of disparate species. Second, the forest floor is often waterlogged and covered with a tangle of exposed roots. Third, suitable draft animals have not been available to transport the heavy timbers. Elephants, animals more often of the much drier tropical savanna, have been domesticated and employed in the commercial timber industry only in restricted areas of South and Southeast Asia. Finally, because of the abundance of light forest products and because temperatures are uniformly warm, negating the need for tightly fitted buildings, these lighter materials suffice.

In most of the humid tropical world then, the traditional house is built of *light vegetative materials* (Figure 6-1). The framework is of small wooden or bamboo poles with a thatched roof. In some instances the temperatures are so uniformly warm that walls are entirely dispensed with. This was the case with the *chickee* hut of the Seminole Indians in southern Florida. A similar structure prevailed in the Pacific island of Samoa, where light wall screens, when needed because of cold winds or driving rain, could be lowered into place (Hiroa 1930, 8). Mosquito netting provided protection at night.

6-1. Bamboo structural members, thatch roof, and palm-leaf panels make up this tropical house from Tamilnadu, India. Unless the roof is soon repaired, the house will not be inhabitable for much longer (photo by the author, 1976).

The environmental conditions in most of the tropical world encourage building with easily available light materials. Constantly warm temperatures mean buildings do not have to shield against cold, but constant rainfall means humidity is always high and wood deteriorates quickly, and termites, beetles and woodworms present a constant menace to buildings. Houses, therefore, are utilitarian and functional, not decorative, and not meant to last very long. When the roof, the most critical element, begins to leak, the structure is abandoned if quick repairs cannot be effected (Feeley-Harnik 1980, 566).

Bamboo represents the most widely used structural material of the tropics, while palm fronds and leaves are the most often used surface commodities. As late as the 1980s, housing censuses in the costal lowlands of Colombia and Ecuador showed between a quarter and three-quarters of all rural homes to be of bamboo construction (Parsons 1991, 150).

Not all tropical construction utilized bamboo, however. In the Niger River delta, the common material used in traditional building is the raffia palm, whose use illustrates nicely the ingenuity of builders and the care they take not to waste any part of the plant. The midribs of the fronds are used as poles, or spilt into slats. The leaves "could be folded over two or three of these slats, and pinned into position with smaller *bamboo* skewers to form tile-like roofing mats." The outer bark of the tree is stripped into long sinews for tying material (Jones 1984,

96). When done, other raffia palms could be tapped for palm wine to celebrate the event. More often than not, vines and fibers of various kinds secure the structure rather than nails or pegs (Figure 6-2).

The combination of earth materials in the form of "daub," and vegetation in the form of interwoven light shoots of wood or "wattle," is one of the most common and most successful building modes both in the tropics and the mid-latitudes. Studies of *wattle and daub* are prevalent in the British Isles, where this form of building prevailed for a long time. Bruce Walker (1977, 7) provides a list of terms by which wattle-and-daub building is known in various parts of the British Isles: clay and wattle, clay and mott, stake and rice, clout and clay, clam staff and daub, stab and rice, daub and stower, rice and stower, riddle and daub, keeber and mott, caber and daub, strae and rake, rod and daub, split and daub, and cat and clay. The existence of such a profusion of terms not only emphasizes the former isolation of areas, but how widely practiced the technique was. Still a different term "stud and mud" is widely used in the African tropics (McIntosh 1974, 161).

6-2. *A thatched roof and bamboo dwelling preserved in the Tanzania Village Museum, Dar-es-Salaam. The upper decorative wall screen composed of short lengths of bamboo aids ventilation and structural integrity (photo by the author, 1975).*

6-3. Wattle construction is one of the simplest and cheapest forms of building. The mud daub may be plastered on one or both sides of the wattle. These wattle panels are on a building in the Cloppenburg Open-Air Museum, Germany (photo by the author, 1983).

In a widely used procedure, "the wattle or hurdle work was formed by vertical stakes, each fitted into a hole or slot in one horizontal and sprung into a groove or another hole in the other member of the framework. With these were interwoven pliable material, such as longer rods, osiers, reeds or thin strips of oak" (Wood 1965, 225). The daub consisted of a "marly clay mixed to the right consistency with water" and then augmented and strengthened with the "binding fibrous element of chopped straw, hay, cow hair, and perhaps cow-dung"(Singleton 1952, 77; Wood 1965, 212 & 225). This mixture was then plastered onto each side of the wattle (Figure 6-3), which was then placed as a panel for wall filling. The final step was to provide two or three coats of limewash, "thus adding an egg-shell protection to the rather soft daub. . . . It is due almost entirely to this lime-wash that so much wattle and daub still survives" in the UK (Singleton 1952, 77).

Not only was wattle-and-daub construction common in the UK, it was used across France, Germany (Figure 6-3), and Poland into Russia (Jorre 1967, 82) and to the southeast in the Balkans (Brunvand 1974, 11). Hungarian settlers, familiar with the technique, introduced it to the Canadian Prairie provinces (Stalfelt-Szabo and Szabo 1979, 229).

Wattle-and-daub construction is also reported from the cool highlands of Ethiopia (Brooke 1959, 69), southern Tanzania (McKim 1985) and the High Veld and humid coastal areas of South Africa (Frescura 1981), where a variety of beehive-, cylindrical- and rectangular-plan structures all have this type of wall construction. Wattle-and-daub building is also common both in the rest of tropical Africa and all across tropical Asia. Here, rather than inset wattle-and-daub panels, the entire wall is of unified construction (Norton 1986, 25). Amini Mturi (1984, 185–6) lists wattle-and-daub building as one of the three kinds of construction common to all Africa south of the Sudanic grassland. Because rainfall is high in the humid tropics, decay of wattle-and-daub walls is reasonably rapid, resulting primarily from rain splash and capillary moisture movement. This produces under-cutting and collapse of segments of the clay. Termite inroads are also a serious problem causing decay (McIntosh 1974, 162–3).

Wattle-and-daub construction is also used widely in the Latin American tropics. In the Amazon it is referred to as *torroes* (Sternberg 1984). In Colombia, and less often in Ecuador, the wattle is *guadua*, a type of giant bamboo. The exterior is coated with mud, sometimes mixed with straw and whitewashed (Parsons 1991, 141). The use of laths as an anchor for clay or plaster in later building is an outgrowth of the earlier wattle-and-daub technique. In vernacular structures it can be encountered not only in Latin America but also in such widely dispersed areas as the Indus valley of Pakistan (Lari 1989, 36), and Ukrainian and Hungarian settlements of Alberta and Saskatchewan, Canada (Lehr 1973, 11; Stalfelt-Szabo and Szabo 1979, 229).

A different, but still basically similar, technique is employed on the island of Zanzibar. A frame of strong but lightweight vertical and hor-izontal poles is erected with a roof of coconut leaves. The horizontal members placed both inside and out, form open squares about four inches in size. To this is plastered the mud (Skolle 1962–63, 16).

Light vegetable materials also are used for building in the desert and near-desert area of the American southwest and northern Mexico. The almost universally employed material is the tough stalks of the *ocotillo* shrub, although willow shoots may be used when available (Lehmer 1939, 185). Frequently, adobe may be applied to these in a "wattle-and-daub" technique, but the stalks and shoots, collectively called jacal, is such a significant component of the building that its name is even used to refer to the entire structure itself, as well as the frame poles. The English-language word "jacal" is borrowed from the Spanish, who earlier had modified it from the Aztec word *xacalli*, which means "adobe house or house of straw, a humble dwelling." The English word *shack* is derived from the same origin (Bracken and Redway 1956, 44; Noble 1984, 1:84).

Another light, often poorly and hurriedly-built, structure carries the name *shanty*. This term derives from a French-Canadian phrase used to describe the building where lumberjacks were fed and housed, *une cambuse de chantier* (Mann and Skinulis 1979, 16). These words were anglicized *to camboose shanty*. Camboose means a provi-sion or store room, hence its use in a further changed form to designate the living quarters of the crew on a freight train, the *caboose*.

Chantier, a lumber yard, became the name for the pile of wood thrown together by early French-Canadians as a rough dwelling, or in English a shanty. With a change in spelling and in a further derogatory use, shanty added to Irish was applied in the United States in the 19th century to designate poorly paid Irish laborers who lived in temporary shacks and moved from construction job to job.

One of the world's most unusual building materials is the *baled hay* used in the Sandhills of Nebraska. Here, in an environment without wood, where considerable depths of loose sand are covered by grass, the hay harvested from the grass and compressed into bales proved to be the only available building material in the early days of settlement (Welsch 1970). Today, at least 20 of these dwellings are still occupied, most protected by a stucco covering (Noble 1984, 2:115).

In humid areas of the mid-latitudes, because of the abundance of timber, *log building* became a standard mode of construction. Although the basic technology of log construction is quite simple, great variety exists in the finished product. As Paul Klammer (1963, 13) noted:

> Log cabins are like fingerprints. At first glance they all look alike, but closer study shows that each one differs from all others. The differences are due mainly to the kinds of logs that are used, to the workmanship of the builder, and to his good taste-or possibly that of his wife.

The great coniferous forest zone of Europe, from the Alps and Carpathians in the south, eastward across northern Siberia, and northward across the Baltic Sea to Fenno-Scandinavia, possesses the world's largest concentration of log structures. From this great heartland, log building techniques were exported to North America by the Fenno-Scandinavians and Germanic peoples, and diffused there primarily by the Scots-Irish and Germans (Morgan 1990). Furthermore, John Winberry (1974) holds that German miners were responsible for the introduction of log building into Mexico. From Mexico, it was introduced into the southwestern United States by Hispanic settlers (Gritzner 1971, 54 & 60). Just how important log building was throughout the United States can be gauged from research performed by John Morgan (1986, 41), who found that in Humphreys County, Tennessee, 72% of all houses were of log as were virtually all (96%) barns. Other areas in Appalachia offer similar concentrations (Eller 1979, 96; Langsam and Johnson 1985, 14).

Scholars who spend most of their time investigating structures in areas largely devoid of log buildings seem to have little appreciation of those structures, dismissing them with distaste and scorn. An otherwise excellent article (Carson et al. 1981, 139–40) reveals this orientation:

For those who built them [primitive shelters including log] they were temporary, improvised expedients; for such improvisations are as remote to a study of regional vernacular building traditions in the American colonies as charcoal burners' huts and shepherds' *skali* are to the investigation of vernacular architecture in Great Britain and northern Europe. Much more important – then and now – were the buildings that came immediately afterward.

Even left in their natural round shape, logs can be used for building by laying them horizontally, one atop the other, and securing the corners. Because of the round shape, the logs protrude into the interior and considerable additional material must be added to create flush walls and to fill the "chinks" between logs. This can be small stones, mortar, bark, and narrow pieces of wood, earth or sphagnum moss. Marilyn Brinkman and William Morgan (1982, 45) have expanded the list to include clay mixed with animal manure, animal hair, straw, grass, gunnysacks, and even newspapers. Nailing narrow pieces of scrap lumber to cover the interstices (much like the later and more elegant battens of board-and-batten lumber frame walls, but horizontally rather than vertically) has been reported in Georgia by Wilbur Zelinsky (1953, 174). Gabrille Lanier and Bernard Herman (1997, 74) even mention whole fired bricks as chinking material in the Mid-Atlantic area.

By hewing the logs somewhat, they can be made to fit more tightly, and the amount of chinking, which often needs to be replaced annually, greatly reduced. The savings in both time and effort could be substantial. Roger Welsch (1980, 319) estimated that "the average size log house has approximately ½ mile of linear chinking."

Examining log houses in Alberta, William Wonders and Mark Rasmussen (1980, 202) identified three major methods of weatherproofing a log wall. The commonest method was to use logs in round and to stuff the space between with sphagnum moss covered with lime plaster. Throughout North America, sphagnum moss has been the most widely used material for chinking.

A second method, used in Ukrainian log houses in Alberta, employed square-hewn logs to which thin lath strips were nailed, with a plaster finish applied over the lath (Figure 6-4). Among Scandinavians, logs were so carefully fitted that little chinking was needed, but thin clapboards often covered the exterior. Eventually, the Finns and Scandinavians became so adept at fitting logs that chinking was virtually eliminated (Carter 1984) They did this by scooping out the underside of each log to fit the upper curved profile of the log beneath. The same technique was reported by Ronald Olson (1927, 25) to be practiced by Athabascan Indians around Cook Inlet in northwestern North America.

6-4. *Both vertical and horizontal round logs form the walls of this Ukrainian house near Senkiw, Manitoba. Light willow sticks are attached to the logs to act as an anchor for the mud daub, much of which has already disappeared (photo by the author, 1983).*

Eliminating wide spaces of chinking also made the log houses warmer, since the chinking materials usually had a lower insulation value than the logs. Hewing the log to produce more or less flat sides removed the outer sap wood "which rots easily and is prone to insect damage, it removed excess weight, left flat surfaces to work from, and helped keep rain out by offering a place for the water to drip off at the bottom of each log" (McRaven 1985, 48). Hewing requires only two simple tools, a felling ax and either a broadax or an adze. In southern Indiana and elsewhere, "most frequently the bark was not even removed from the top and the bottom surfaces" (Roberts 1976, 439).

The integrity of log buildings depends upon the method by which the corners are held in place. A wide variety of corner notches accomplish this task (Kniffen 1969). The simplest, oldest and most widely used technique is that of *saddle notching*, in which the logs are left in the round and the notch is cut with an ax in both the top and bottom, or better, just in the bottom to retard decay from the water collecting in a top-cut notch (Figure 6-5). Hungarian settlers on the Canadian prairies, previously unused to log construction, found saddle notching so simple that they used it exclusively (Stalfelt-Szabo and Szabo 1979, 228).

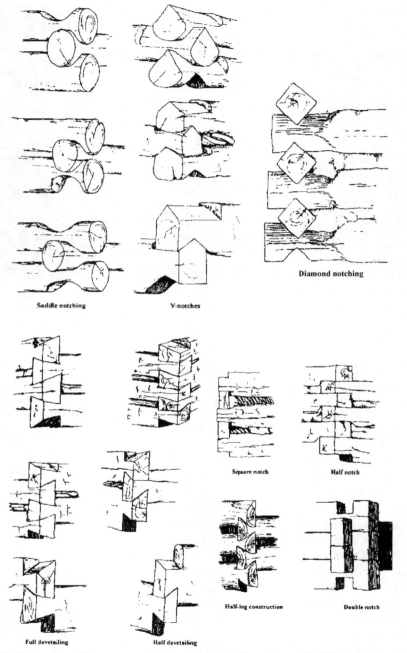

Diamond notching

Saddle notching   V-notches

Square notch   Half notch

Half-log construction   Double notch

Full dovetailing   Half dovetailing

6-5. Examples of log corner notching. Saddle, V-notch, and half dovetail are the most commonly encountered (from Kniffen 1969, 2–5. Courtesy of the Pioneer America Society).

V notches require more careful work: "If the log remains in the round, the visible end of the log is pear-shaped. If the log is squared, the end resembles the gabled end of a house, and the process is often called 'roof topping'" (Figure 6-5). Squared logs have greater aesthetic appeal even in rough, remote areas. Charles Martin (1984, 19) reports that in remote areas of Appalachia "a hewn-log dwelling was called a house, whereas a round-log dwelling was called a cabin."

Dovetail notches are even more complicated, and for ease and speed of construction were often cut in North America by sawing (Roberts 1976, 440). The half dovetail has a flat bottom and the full dovetail a sloping one (Figure 6-5). Dovetail notches drain well because of their outward sloping surfaces, and hence are long lived.

All of these notches were introduced into North America from source areas in Fenno-Scandinavia, the Germanic Alps, and the Bohemia-Carpathian area (Kniffen and Glassie 1966, 63; Jordan and Kilpinen 1990, 11). In addition to the notch types just reviewed, dozens of others of more sophisticated or intricate design exist. The magnificently illustrated volume, *The Craft of Log Building,* by Herman Phleps (1982) contains no less than 45 drawings of different corner notches. They are especially diverse in the countries around the Baltic Sea.

Among the lesser-known notches are the diamond notch, probably derived from the hexagonal notch of Central Sweden (Jordan et al. 1986–87). Square and half notches are originally from the Bohemian-Carpathian highlands and from south-central Sweden (Jordan and Kilpinen 1990). Various tooth notches characterize Fenno-Scandinavia (Erixon 1937; Kaups 1976, 13–14). Such notches also occur in the Carpathians, but are rare in North America. They do appear in the Finnish areas of northern Michigan, Wisconsin and Minnesota, and the mountainous parts of Idaho and Montana. Diamond notches in North America occur primarily in North Carolina and southern Virginia. In contrast, square notches are widely distributed throughout North America (Jordan and Kilpinen 1990, 8).

A major difficulty with horizontal log building is how to fill in the upper gable wall when the structure is capped by a gable roof, the easiest roof to build over a rectangular building. Using logs presents two problems. First, the increasing height makes the heavy logs difficult to handle. Second, the logs do not lock in place with corner notches. To avoid these problems, log builders in North America used hewn planks to close the gable triangle. Germans placed the gable planks vertically (Brumbaugh 1933, 22) and Scots-Irish placed them horizontally.

Most log houses are just one or one-and-a-half stories high and contain one, two or three small rooms. Size limitations were in large part dictated by the length of the timber, its weight – which makes handling onerous (Perrin 1967, 22 & 28) – and the difficulty of joining timbers to accommodate larger floor plans. Michael Ann Williams (1984, 36) notes that the late 19th-century log houses in Cherokee County, North Carolina are smaller than pre-Civil War ones. The explanation is that "as sawn lumber became cheaper and more avail-able, the family desiring a larger house would have preferred frame construction." One of the major reasons for the popularity in Texas of the dogtrot cabin was that it permitted use of shorter lengths of timber in the construction of its two separated enclosed parts. The drier climate of Texas supported only trees of modest growth (Collier 1979, 30).

In other instances where only shorter lengths of log are available, an alternative method of construction is used (Lebreton 1982, 435–6). It has been used, and studied, most widely in French-speaking areas, but also occurs in the Ukraine, Poland, and northern United States around the upper Great Lakes. In Canada, this mode of building spread from French-speaking areas in the east, ultimately all the way to the Pacific coast. Because of its French connection, and the fact that many studies are in English, but by non-French speakers, considera-ble confusion persists in the English definition of the terms (Richardson 1973). Because available logs are short, corner notching is not practical. To solve this difficulty, the horizontal logs are tenoned or pointed at each end to fit into slots cut into the vertical posts (De Julio 1996) (Figure 6-6). This type of construction is generally referred

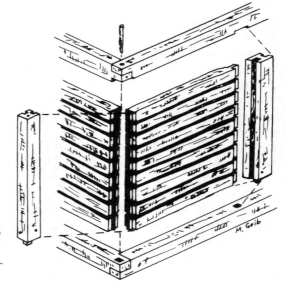

6-6. *Pièce-sur-pièce method of log construction. Cor-ner and side posts are grooved to accept the ten-ons of the horizontal logs. The posts fit into notches and holes in both plate and sill for an extremely tight fit (drawing by M. Marga-ret Geib).*

to as *pièce-sur-pièce*, but in Canada it is also variously called Hudson Bay style, Red River frame, or Manitoba frame.

A variation of French-inspired log building was employed early on in French Canada and throughout the Great Lakes–Mississippi River drainage area. Termed *poteaux-en-terre* or *pieux-en-terre*, depending upon the diameter of the wood, the posts, logs, or poles were used vertically rather than horizontally. In the early period of North American settlement by the French, the posts were driven directly into the ground, as a palisade would be. "When built of rot-resisting cedar, they made a sound and fairly permanent structure" (Peterson 1941, 217). Later on, a wooden sill was introduced to support the base of the vertical members in a mode called *poteaux-sur-sole*. By 1800 houses of these two types comprised more than 97% of the buildings of St. Louis, Missouri (Richardson 1973, 81).

In central and western Europe, when supplies of timber neared exhaustion and cost consequently increased, buildings began to shift to a construction system of half timbering, in which only the major structural members were wood and the walling was of earth materials, most often mud or brick nogging. Even before this happened, a farmstead emphasis on small, special function buildings, rather than large, multipurpose dwellings and barns was the result of depletion of the supply of large logs (Atkinson 1969, 50). Of course, smaller logs were also easier to handle.

An unusual mode of log and mortar wall building involves the stacking of stove-length or *cordwood* pieces of soft wood, usually white cedar, in a bed of mortar. Several obviously appropriate names have been given to this method: stovewood architecture (Tishler 1979, 1982), cordwood construction (Airhart 1976), stackwood house (Anonymous 1977; Anonymous 1978), stackwall building (Alberta OSERP 1976), log end (Roy 1977), and log-butt architecture (Rempel 1967). Examples of *stovewood* buildings occur across northern United States and southern Canada from Minnesota to New Brunswick, and William Tishler has identified examples from Norway and Sweden (1982, 126 & 132–3). The concentration of such buildings in Wisconsin has been particularly well studied (Perrin 1963).

Stovewood building differs from other types of horizontal log construction (Figure 6-7)

> because the walls are made from logs cut into short uniform sections and stacked perpendicular to the length of each wall ... In many instances the logs were split lengthwise into smaller sections. These pieces were then laid in a bed of wet lime mortar that enclosed each chunk of wood but left the cut ends exposed. The resulting wall resembled a pile of neatly stacked firewood. (Tishler 1979, 28)

6-7. *Part of a stovewood wall in a house on the Door Peninsula, Wisconsin. The two-foot-long lengths of wood have been split and placed in a bed of mortar. The timber frame carries numerous ax marks made when hewing occurred (photo by the author, 1980).*

Stovewood construction permits the use of short lengths of wood, which would otherwise be useful only as fuel. Furthermore, lengths of varying diameters can be employed together. The wood must be of the same species and very well seasoned and dry. The insulation value of stackwood is higher than that of brick, masonry or concrete block (Roy 1977, 29–30). Another important advantage is that building a house can be done easily by one person (Airhart 1976, 55). Balancing these advantages somewhat is the great time required to assemble, debark, and lay up the huge number of wood pieces involved (Jenkins 1923, 19). Twice as much wood is needed as in horizontal log construction (Airhart 1976, 56). Also, exposed log ends decay faster than logs with sides exposed (Mann and Skinulis 1979, 153).

Timber-frame structures in the British Isles followed one of two methods of framing – cruck or box. *Cruck framing*, which involved the use of an entire tree trunk, or at least a major branch of a very large tree, was typical of early frame construction in the north and west of the United Kingdom. An enormous amount of research has been done on cruck framing, which survives mostly only in Great Britain. One reason why this and other research on traditional buildings and construction methods has proved so fruitful is that in the British Isles, wars – which are so destructive to traditional buildings – have been largely lacking since the 17th century. Devastation in World War II occurred mainly in the cities.

More than 3,000 cruck buildings can be identified in England and Wales (Alcock 1981, 6). "Over most of western Britain, at all except the highest social levels, the earliest surviving buildings are cruck structures" (Alcock 1981,1), with a particularly high concentration on the North York Moors (Smith, P. 1979, 3). In addition to Great Britain, cruck trusses occur widely in France, reported in Brittany (Meirion-Jones 1981, 39–55), in the Dordogne (Walton 1960–62), and in Limousin (Bans and Bans 1979), as well as elsewhere in the country. Cruck buildings also occur in Northern Ireland (McCourt 1960–62; 1964–65), and Scandinavia (Erixon 1937, 142).

Cruck framing is a very ancient method of building in which a large tree is split in half and the two parts positioned as mirror images opposite one another to form the combined wall and roof supports. In Scotland a pair of crucks cut from the same tree and used to oppose one another is referred to as a "couple" (Walker 1979, 47). A similar terminology appears in Ireland (Evans 1939). At least two cruck pairs are needed and frequently more than that were used.

> In its purest form the cruck truss should support a roof in its entirety, carrying the thrust down to a sill-beam at ground level . . . variations exist in which the walls play a partial load-bearing role. These include buildings in which the crucks are seated in the walls above the ground level. (Alcock 1981, 3)

In the later Middle Ages, as population grew in England and the demand for timber increased, the supply of large trees diminished and their cost rose. Eventually, the shortage of large timbers became so critically short that Henry VIII promulgated an edict to stop the construction of cruck frames in favor of box, in order to preserve the timber for naval shipbuilding. The spread of *box framing* permitted the use of smaller timber than crucks. A consequence of this new emphasis and the innovation of the chimney was the introduction of upper floors, which cruck buildings could not accommodate very well. The box frame dwellings, which already dominated the east and southeast of England, where cruck trusses were virtually unknown, began to spread westward.

The cruck truss and the box frame are two quite different systems of construction. The cruck truss transfers the weight of the entire structure directly to the ground by means of the crucks. Outward thrust is counterbalanced and absorbed by the curve of the cruck. The box frame transfers the weight of the walls, including beams, to the ground by means of its posts. The weight of the roof structure is transferred to the ground by means of a system of rafters, collar beams, girts, king posts or other upper supports, and finally to the house posts. The upper support system works to counteract the outward thrust produced by the roof. An early strategy to assist in countering the roof thrust was to use slanting buttress posts at each house wall and corner post (Chapelot and Fossier 1985, 77). Double rows of holes marking both posts and buttress are a common feature of many archeological sites in northern Europe (Figure 6-8).

One major difference between the cruck truss and the box frame was the roof structure. The cruck truss depended upon a ridgepole for stability. The box frame and rafters, in place of the upper part of the cruck, eliminated the ridge pole and used purlins or horizontally-placed roof boards for stability (Carson 1974, 192). The walls of the cruck frame are not load bearing and thus can be knocked down and rebuilt without damaging the structural framework, which in many houses is effectively hidden behind a later stone or brick shell (Sheppard 1966, 25). The box frame required timbers that were squared off so

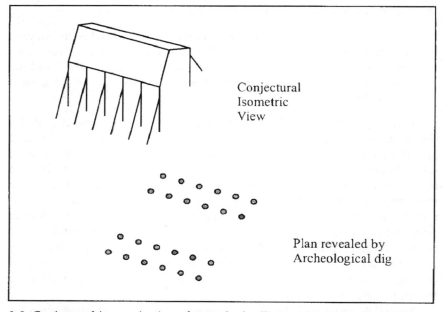

Conjectural
Isometric
View

Plan revealed by
Archeological dig

6-8. *Conjectural isometric view of an early dwelling with buttress posts. The plan as revealed by archeological investigation is also shown. Post-holes may be all that remains of early structures (drawing by the author).*

6-9. Drawing of a pit saw. The man on top is called the sawyer and man below is the pit man (drawing by M. Margaret Geib).

that nogging and cladding could be closely fitted. Hewing of timbers was time consuming and the finished surfaces were irregular.

The early solution was to use the pit saw, which unfortunately was also slow and labor intensive (Figure 6-9). Philip Cox and John Free-land (1969, 16–17) have provided an excellent description of pit sawing in Australia where the saws were copies of European predecessors. Saw pits were:

> About five feet deep, four feet six inches wide and eight to twenty feet long. The logs to be sawn were prepared by first having one or more slabs split from their length to produce a flat surface. The parting was done by driving small iron wedges into the smaller end of the log with heavy mauls to start a small split which was then widened by inserting larger wedges into it down the length of the log until the slab fell away. If necessary, the log was rolled over and wedges driven in from the other side. By means of levers and rollers made of saplings, the log was manoeuvered until it lay lengthwise along the pit supported, with the flat surface downwards, on smaller cross timbers. The sawing was done by two men. Using a steel saw five to six feet long, one sawyer stood below the log in the pit and pulled downwards on a vertical tiller. The other bestraddled the log and pulled the saw upwards with a horizontal handle. The latter, the more skilled of the two, was responsible for guiding the saw, for the straightness of the cut and for starting the saw in a notch axed into the end. He was known as the "top-notcher."

This term, top-notch, has, of course, passed into the English language as an idiom to denote the best or most skillful of anything.

Not until the end of the 17th century did things begin to improve with the perfection of the up-and-down saw, and much later the circular saw. Because pit sawing was so laborious, hewn sides were used whenever a regular surface was not needed (Buchanan 1976, 62). The introduction of power sawing was resisted in England "for more than a century by hand sawyers who felt their craft endangered by this form of automation" (Candee 1976, 133). Once accepted, the life of the pit saw was long indeed. Pit saws were used in the Virginia mountains even after the turn of the 20th century (Bealer 1978, 34). Pit sawing did provide two names, which ultimately became common English family names: Pitman and Sawyer. The practice of vernacular building provided a number of other family names in England – Thatcher, Reeder, Slater, Tyler, Carpenter, Joyner, Bricker, Mason, Pargeter, and Dauber. The situation is similar in other languages.

Half timbering is the term widely used, initially in Europe and later in North America, to describe a timber frame structure in which bricks or other earth materials fill the wall space between the wooden framing members. Half timbering was a technique originally used to reduce the amount of timber in a structure because forest resources were dwindling and wood cost rising. The use of bricks as nogging had certain disadvantages. First, early bricks were somewhat porous, which encouraged dampness. Second, the widely disparate rates of expansion and contraction between timber and bricks caused serious cracking that could loosen the nogging. Finally, the bricks were a heavy strain on the timber frame (Brown 1986, 89). The technique became very popular in Great Britain, especially in Hampshire (Brown 2004, 25), in the Low Countries, and in northern Germany, where it was termed *fachwerk*. As an accepted method of traditional building, fachwerk was brought by emigrating Germans to Missouri, where it still was being used into the 1890s (van Ravenswaay 1977, 20).

The method of timber framing varied from place to place. Even within England three separate approaches can be found. In the east, especially in East Anglia, studs were spaced closely together. In the west, the posts and beams were spaced to produce nearly square, infill panels. In the north, main posts rest on stone foundations. Rows of closely spaced studs and parallel diagonal bracing are prominent, the latter often most prominent on the gable wall (Brown 1986, 46–53).

A variety of materials filled the wall voids between the timber frame members. Initially wattle-and-daub panels were employed, but later these were supplanted by denser materials. This "nogging" was most often of brick whenever it could be afforded, or of mud when brick was too expensive (Figure 6-10). The walls were then covered on

6-10. Layers of mud nogging placed at an angle determined by the cross-brace of the timber frame. The mud was added in rows with each row allowed to dry before the next row was applied. Ruins of a house near Columbia, Missouri (photo by the author, 1980).

the inside by thin wall planks. In cold climates an exterior wooden cladding would also be used for additional insulation. In warmer climates an exterior covering might be applied if "samel brick" had to be used as nogging. Samel bricks were cheap because they were imperfectly fired and disintegrated easily, especially when not protected against the weather (Buchanan 1976, 71 & 73). Thus in North America one finds almost all colonial New England houses to be weather boarded, but in warmer colonial Virginia some structures are half timbered because high-quality bricks had been used. Here, "the primary purpose of nogging was rat proofing instead of insulation" (Buchanan 1976, 71).

The term "box frame" has also been applied to a quite different type of wood construction common in the Appalachian region of the

US (Eller 1979; Williams 1990). In that area, the term refers to a simple house without a structural frame, in which support is provided by vertical planks rather than studs. Because the planks are often rough sawn, small weather strips may be nailed to cover gaps between boards. *Box houses* became the prevailing house type in Appalachia near the turn of the century when sawmills and the developing timber industry made lumber available at a cheap cost (Eller 1979, 98–9). A closely related house, termed a "strip house" by E. Raymond Evans (1976) was built by African-Americans in the eastern Tennessee Valley during the Depression of the 1930s. Using 2 x 4s as a frame, both horizontal and vertical boards were applied to form the dwellings. These box frame and strip houses may be part of a larger and more diverse set of dwellings that are usually included under the rubric of plank framing.

Plank framing, a variation of post and beam timber framing, became more popular in North America than elsewhere because of the abundant forest resources and the diffusion of saw mills to cut logs into more easily handled planks (Cummings 1979; Candee 1976; Koos and Walters 1986). Some of the same confusion which surrounds French log building methods (see above) also attaches to plank construction (Coffey and Noble 1996). In fact, Thomas Ritchie (1971, 66) sees horizontal plank construction as a variant of the French pièce-sur-pièce log construction technique. He proposes diffusion from Denmark in Viking times, to Quebec during French control, to Ontario and ultimately to other parts of Canada. In a later article, Ritchie (1974) identifies a walling system in which grooved corner posts are eliminated and the horizontal planks rather than vertical planks are nailed at the corners. Both of these, with vertical or horizontal planks, he labels "plank wall." Other researchers have proposed a different and more widely used terminology: plank frame, plank wall, plank-on-edge and plank-on-plank.

The earliest form of *plank frame construction* in the United States was employed in colonial New England, where vertical planks were rooted into the ground (Carson et al. 1981, 155). Later on, the vertical planks were rabbetted, tenoned or slotted into a wooden sill. In this form the type spread to other parts of the country (Simons 1982, 69; Brinkman and Morgan 1982, 59–60). Like log structures later, and elsewhere, the thick planks were useful in stopping both arrows and low-velocity firearms (Nelson 1969, 21). The relationship of vertical plank construction to timber frame can be seen in the early New England plank houses (Kevlin 1984, 1).

The later but much more widely used *plank wall* method substituted additional planks for the corner posts. This type, (but unfortunately labeled "plank frame") has been identified in a large number of houses in northeastern Vermont by Jan Leo Lewandoski (1985). In some parts of Vermont, as many as 30–40% of all traditional dwellings were of plank wall construction. A study of traditional dwellings in Independence County, Arkansas revealed that over half of the houses surveyed there were plank wall (Tebbetts 1978). Charles Martin's study (1984) of Hollybush, Kentucky demonstrated widespread use of this construction method in that part of Appalachia. Working in western North Carolina, Michael Ann Williams (1990) found much the same situation, and as a result has suggested that, although not usually recognized as such, plank wall construction is one of the dominant modes of traditional building throughout the entire Upland South of the United States.

Horizontal plank construction is much more rare than vertical, probably because vertical planking eliminates the need for studs and hence is more economical than horizontal (Isham and Brown 1900, 88). The *plank-on-edge* method of horizontal planking is the least often seen, except in eastern Ontario (Ritchie 1974; Kevlin 1984). Unlike in the rest of New England, plank framing in New Hampshire tended to favor the *plank-on-plank* method found also in Ontario and as far west as the Great Lakes (Simons 1982, 69). This method requires the greatest amount of lumber, but provides the thickest wall and hence the greatest degree of insulation.

Alternating planks of slightly wider and narrower width to project into the inside of the wall created a key for fixing plaster (Anonymous 1869b, 175). Plaster might even be needed on the exterior "to make the wall windproof (since such a multitude of horizontal joints would otherwise have provided many opportunities for the wind to penetrate the wall) and partly to protect the wooden wall from moisture" which would have caused not only rotting of the wood, but also dimensional changes in the individual boards due to swelling when damp and shrinking when dry (Fitchen 1957, 27).

German-Russian Mennonites used this technique in housebarns in Manitoba, but with 2 x 4s instead of planks (Noble 1992b). Scarcity of wood probably forced them to use narrower boards, but the method (stacking four-inch side upon four-inch side) is identical to the plank-on-plank method. No clue exists as to where the Mennonites learned this method, or whether it was improvised locally.

In a volume necessarily limited in size, the enormous amount and complexity of detail involved in timber construction, whether of cruck, box frame or plank building, cannot be adequately discussed. Readers will recognize that many of the sources listed in the references to this volume will be more specific and can remedy the omission here.

Advances at the end of the 18th century and the first half of the 19th century brought about an emphasis on *dimension lumber*. The perfection of the circular saw produced wood in standardized sizes and in weights much lighter than timber (Ball 1975). Lumber was easier to handle and cheaper than timber. Changes in nail technology saw hand-wrought iron nails replaced first by cut nails and finally by steel wire nails. Hand-wrought nails, made individually by a blacksmith, were so expensive that in colonial America buildings were burned down to salvage them. In 1645 the Virginia House of Burgesses passed legislation prohibiting the burning of houses for this purpose. Yet "in 1691 the Supervisors of nearby Kent County, Delaware ordered the old county courthouse burned in order to get the nails" (Loveday 1983, 4). Kenneth Lindley (1965, 89) suggests that in some impoverished rural communities of Ireland even the custom of removing coffin nails prior to burial arose because of their value as a building material.

Square-cut nails began to be produced in quantity late in the 18th century. Made by machine, they were cheaper than hand-wrought nails. At least one researcher estimates that "square cut nails are probably the most numerous artifacts one might expect to find in mid-to-late 19th century Anglo-American-occupied sites in the United States" (Fontana and Greenleaf 1962, 44). Finally, steel nails came into widespread use after 1885 (Edwards and Wells 1993, 2). Cheaply produced nails could be used to fasten light lumber pieces firmly together when needed for greater support. The labor involved in nailing a lumber frame was considerably less than that required to cut mortise and tenon joints and the fastening which treenails required (Kevlin 1984, 1). These innovations, together with the perfection of balloon and platform framing, announced the ultimate end of timber framing. Lumber slowly but steadily replaced timber as *the* wooden building material.

Modern construction materials are steadily replacing the traditional. The reasons for such replacement are discussed in Chapter 13. One of the most unfortunate aspects of this process is the gradual diminishing of skill levels of craftsmen. Eventually, a rich component of each group's culture will stand in danger of being lost, and an anchor to the past will be removed from the society's consciousness.

~ 7 ~

Above-Ground and Excavated Structures

Earth materials, and the earth itself, always have been an important source for traditional building. On at least five continents, humans have made use of the earth itself by excavating into the surface. Such structures can be classified under four broad headings: (1) semi-subterranean pit houses on level ground; (2) structures wholly or partially excavated in loosely compacted soil on gently sloping land (dugouts); (3) wholly underground excavations in relatively soft earth materials; and (4) natural hard rock cavities subsequently broadened and deepened by human efforts (caves). Such a classification, although it may help us to understand excavated dwellings, is not entirely satisfactory because the boundaries between one type and others often are not precise, or even completely clear. For example, the differentiation between pit houses and dugouts seems to depend essentially upon whether on not land slopes, and whether the excavation was more or less horizontal or vertical.

The situation is further complicated by the fact that some peoples, German-Russians for example, who settled the Great Plains, constructed pit houses (by our definition), but referred to them as "dugouts." Barbara Oringderff (1976, 46) indicates such structures were referred to in Kansas as " half sods," indicating a partially erected structure. In the other direction, the process of excavation of a dugout is the same basic one involved in creating a loess cave, for example. In a brief discussion of semi-subterranean dwellings in Ireland, Caoimhghin Ua Danachair (1945, 207–8) (later Caoimhim O'Danachair) cites three 19th-century descriptions. One would seem to be a pit structure, while the other two fit the classification type of dugouts, but they are all treated together as a single class of structures.

The absence of a universal *terminology*, which I have briefly noted elsewhere (Noble 1984, 2:165), is a great handicap to extending research. Part of the problem is that researchers work in various geographical areas, in different languages, have dissimilar training, and pursue diverse scholarly objectives. Sometimes researchers make little or no attempt to relate the terms they use or coin to similar terms from elsewhere, often expressed in a different language. Finally, researchers frequently employ locally common terminology, which usually has little application outside the area of its use.

Even within one geographical area, diversity of terminology may exist. As an example, in India the English word "courtyard" has at least 12 major Indian language equivalents, and an even larger supply of locally used words (Noble 2003, 39). Obviously, over a large area, language is the key to appropriate terminology, but it must be related to terms in other languages and areas if material culture study is to be most effective and universally applicable.

Within a single language area, different terms sometimes may be applied to a feature, or different features may have a number of designations to identify them. The widely used term *eyebrow window* is a case in point. The term is often employed to refer to small or half-size windows placed low down in the upper level of a New England one-and-a-half story cottage in the US (Figure 7-1). Perhaps more accu-

7-1. The term "eyebrow window" has been applied to several quite different types of windows. The term fits best for windows let into the roof surface, as illustrated at the top (drawings by Iraida Galdon Soler).

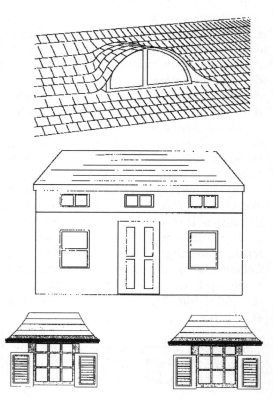

rately descriptive, the term is used over a wider area to identify small half-circular windows let into gable roofs. The structure of the windows and the up-raised roof over the opening do in fact resemble eyes with eyebrows. To extend the confusion of terms further, I have even heard the hooded windows of the English-speaking Caribbean island of Barbados referred to as eyebrow windows. Three windows with entirely different structures are thus identified by the same designation.

The difficulties of classification schemes can be seen by examining dwellings in the plains bordering the lower Danube River in Romania and Bulgaria. These structures, called *bordeis*, have been created by literally burrowing into a slight hillock and then piling the removed sod and earth on top of and around a framework partly made of timber (Figure 7-2). The complex roof includes thatch as well, which may be up to one meter in thickness (Megas 1951, 76). Adjusting to the largely treeless environment of the Danube plain, builders found these semi-subterranean dwellings to be warm in winter and cool in summer, and to offer the additional advantage of being inconspicuous, therefore offering "better protection against the frequent Turkish invasion across the Danube" (Negoita 1986, 23).

Are these pit houses or are they dugouts, or should some other designation be used? The most basic of these houses, which were in use

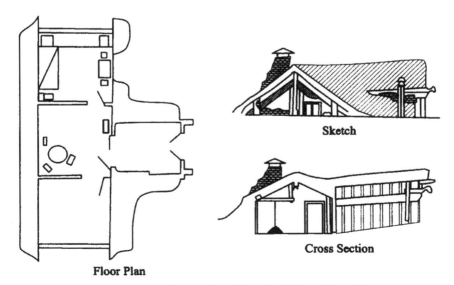

Sketch

Cross Section

Floor Plan

7-2. Sketch, cross-section and floor plan of a typical Danubian subterranean house (drawing by Iraida Galdon-Soler, based upon Stahl 1972, 41).

at least up to the mid-20th century (Focsa 1959, 121), consist of three rooms and a large entrance hallway, the last with a sloping floor. A sill of rock or mud prevents rainwater from flooding the house. The entry hallway lies at right angles to the main dwelling (Megas 1951, 76). An openhearth fire provides heat and is vented in a hood connected to a stone or brick chimney (Stahl 1972, 40–4). More elaborate structures have extensions that house cattle and storerooms for feed and produce, and may even have two entrances as the human housing portions of the structure are expanded.

Another similar dilemma exists with sod or turf houses. Many were excavated some depth into the ground. Some, especially those built by pioneering settlers on the Great Plains of the United States, were entirely erected, not excavated at all. If adobe and fired brick dwellings, both also using somewhat similar earth materials, are treated as erected buildings, should sod and turf structures be treated as erected structures even if some are partially excavated? Again, the boundaries of the standard classification systems may not be appropriate. Perhaps no universal typing system will be satisfactory. In any event, the literature on sod structures, including sod dugouts as well as sod houses, is extensive. This is perhaps not surprising when at least one observer estimates the number of sod dwellings on the Great Plains in the late 19th century to have reached more than one million (Henkes 1976, 30). Another observer looking at just one county in Nebraska estimated that nine-tenths of its citizens in 1876 lived in such earth structures (Dick 1937, 112).

A further difficulty not addressed adequately by the classification system here proposed, is that some structures may be pit dwellings in some instances and erected structures in others. A case in point is the Navajo hogan, which is normally erected above the ground level or very slightly incised into the surface, but which may include a pit four to five feet deep when building timber is scarce (Kluckhohn et al. 1971, 150).

In another part of the world, a similar situation has been documented, but for a different reason. Maori homes in the North Island of New Zealand were basically erected structures sunk just a foot or so into the ground, but in the South Island the same structures were true pit houses excavated several feet into the ground. The rationale for this difference lies in the colder and more stormy and windy climate of the south (Phillipps 1952). These structures would seem to provide a link between excavated and *earth-fast* dwellings (i.e. dwellings that are erected but which are anchored to the ground by embedded posts).

Many dwellings widely scattered across the surface of the world are excavated only a few inches into the earth. In Australia, aboriginal timber, brush and mud huts are built at ground level for summer use and excavated up to 18 inches into the ground for winter occupation (Roth 1909, 49). In other instances the purpose of excavation, rather than to protect against cold weather, seems to be to create a level building surface or to gain more adequate headroom (Edvardsen and Hegdal 1972, 46). Such structures are diverse enough to include the coral block houses of the Red Sea island of Suakin (Greenlaw 1976, 8), an elongated post dwelling from southern Poland (Burcaw 1979, 46), several Native American dwellings from the Great Plains, and many others elsewhere.

The earth lodges of the Indians of central and western North America represent another house type difficult to classify. These structures are constructed following two different modes. Mandan earth lodges were erected buildings of dome shape, utilizing a strong timber frame with a covering of willow branches or mats and prairie grass, and completely encased in sod. Pawnee earth lodges, while resembling closely the Mandan, had important differences. Their lodges were excavated two to three feet, and entrance was via a long, partly underground, tunnel-like ramp.

Somewhat similar to the Pawnee earth lodge in its external form and tunneled entrance was the Thule Eskimo winter house.

> Because building material was extremely scarce across the Arctic, Thule builders framed their winter houses with whatever they could find – rocks, driftwood, chunks of sod, and the ribs, jawbones, skull, and vertebrae of the bowhead whale. The jawbone sometimes served as an arch over the entrance, curved ribs were side posts, bone chunks became wall filling. (Nabokov and Easton 1989, 191)

Scholars have for long surmised that an early circumpolar distribution of *semi-subterranean houses* existed as the forerunner of later occurrences of such structures in parts of Europe, Asia, and North America (Jochelson 1906; Evans 1969, 80; Ghosh 1953, 22). Pit houses show a strong orientation to the northern hemisphere, roughly between 30° and 60° latitude, and a lower concentration in similar latitudes in the southern hemisphere (Gilman 1983, 82–5). In southern South America, pit houses have been identified and studied in Peru, Argentina, Chile, Paraguay and Brazil (Metraux 1929; Gonzalez 1953). Numerous pit dwellings in the northern Argentina province of Cordoba, as well as others in Catamarca Province, have been investigated by Alberto Gonzalez (1943); some of these are communal dwellings and others are single family. The lesser southern hemisphere distribution is likely explained by the much smaller amount of land in the southern hemisphere (Figure 7-3). Pit house occurrences in South America, and some in Africa, are difficult to explain on a circumpolar polar origin basis.

In West Africa, the Bobo-Fing, Gurunsi and Mossi tribes all inhabit semi-subterranean dwellings. Bobo-Fing dwellings are simple circular pits 10 to 12 feet deep, in which a notched log provides access from the narrow entrance (LeMoal 1960). In Gurunsi settlements, excavation serves a defensive purpose. Not only are dwellings partly sunken, but a system of tunnels connects the various structures. Discussing a Gurunsi village, Jean-Paul Bourdier and Trinh T. Minh-ha (1983, 40–1) observe that

> Walls of houses throughout the village have loopholes 15 centimeters wide that are at eye level on the interior, but about knee high on the exterior; a person inside is able to look out and shoot, but it is almost impossible for the invader to send an arrow back and hit the target from a standing position. The dimness of the interiors and their labyrinthian spaces give the inhabitants further advantage: their adversaries, unfamiliar with the place and unable to see when rushing in from the outside, cannot pursue them without incurring high risks.

Elsewhere, semi-subterranean structures were utilized because alternative building materials were not immediately available when a group migrated into an area, or because sufficient time was lacking to construct an above ground dwelling before the onset of the first winter. German-Russian Mennonite settlers entering the largely treeless prairie provinces of Canada in the mid-19th century resorted initially to the old dwelling forms called the *semeljanken* or *semlin*, and the *serai* which they had known in Russia. The semlin which the Mennonites created was a rectangular, excavated pit about three feet deep, with low, above-ground walls of large sods upon which rested a timber and sod roof of gentle pitch. Average dimensions were 24–30 feet long by 12 feet wide. Some reports suggest that farm animals as well as humans occupied the earliest such structures (Goertzen n.d.). The serai was excavated to a depth of one or two feet, but consisted primarily of a thatch roof covering over a gable or hipped wooden frame and extending to ground level. It housed both humans and animals (Francis 1954, 56).

Ukrainian settlers moving into Alberta utilized for their first shelter a quite similar pit house, called a *zemlyanka*, or *staya* in Ukrainian (Lehr 1980, 186). John Lehr described it as follows:

> To construct the dug-out [note choice of term] a rectangular pit was sunk a few feet below ground level, aspen boughs were then placed along the lip of the pit and lashed together to form a low inverted "v" roof framework. Willow and aspen lathes were woven between the

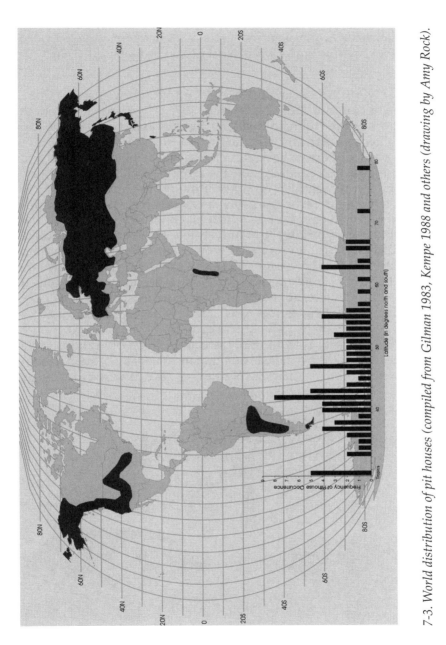

7-3. *World distribution of pit houses (compiled from Gilman 1983, Kempe 1988 and others (drawing by Amy Rock).*

major framework and mud was plastered over the whole. The structure was then covered with a layer of sods placed grass upwards. The interior was lit by a small window opening just large enough to accommodate two small panes of glass while a coarse carpet provided the door covering until a wooden door could be fashioned. (Lehr 1975, 25)

Another North American area of early pit houses was on the Colorado Plateau (Sanford 1950, 23; Bunting 1976, 17). Here, ancestors or predecessors of the later cliff dwelling, adobe-building Indians occupied both rectangular and circular pit houses (Parachek 1967, 11). Ruins of pit houses may be seen in Mesa Verde National Park and other preserves. Built on defensible mesa tops, early habitations were up to three feet in depth. "The sides of the pit formed the walls; the roof was supported by heavy posts and the principal rafters which held a layer of smaller sticks and a final mat of brush capped with wet earth. One entered through the smoke hole by a ladder or down a ramp, which was usually oriented south-southeast" (Nabokov and Easton 1989, 353). The earliest of the Navajo hogans nearby are reported to have been semi-subterranean, but were excavated only a foot or so into the ground. None of these now exist (Page 1937, 47). Hogans in areas where timber was scarce were constructed with a four- to five-foot deep pit (Kluckhohn et al. 1971, 150).

Much more clearly belonging to the classification of pit houses are those dwellings used by the various Indian tribes along the northern Pacific coast of North America (Figure 7-4). Much conjecture exists

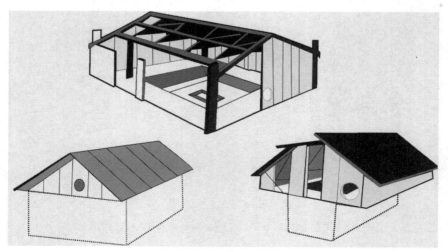

7-4. Sketches of Pacific Coast Indian dwellings, both erected and excavated. Dotted lines indicate excavated parts (based upon Drucker 1965, 26).

regarding the connection of these structures with those in northern Asia. In the Pacific Northwest coast, no circular pits exist and not all the related peoples utilized pit houses. The above-ground structures were impressive, normally accommodating clans with several members each. Built of heavy cedar and fir timbers, the rectangular houses had elevated wooden bench platforms surrounding the excavated center pit, which also contained the fire. More conventional circular pit houses were used by the Salish and other peoples in the nearby Columbia Plateau (Nabokov and Easton 1989, 176–9).

In the westward migration of settlers in North America in the 19th century, many groups espoused the use of *dugouts*. The Mormons resorted to them in the winter of 1846 in Winter Quarters near Omaha, Nebraska (Shumway 1954, 116–17), but largely abandoned such shelters in subsequent winters as they moved westward. Once in Utah, however, the dugout was useful again as a temporary residence during the initial winter of settlement, and subsequently could be used as a root cellar or for storage (Goss 1975, 210). Dugouts in Mormon country are still extant, and at least one has been well documented (Bonar 1983, 213–14).

Other westward-moving groups in North America in the middle of the 19th century also used dugouts as they moved into the Great Plains, where timber for building was largely absent (Barns 1930). Built into the side of a low hill or following the initial depression and contour of a small ravine, the average size of a dugout was a dozen or so feet wide and 15–20 feet in length. Often only one wall was necessary, at the lowest point. The roof of timber and sod, supported by the single wall and the hill slopes, merged almost imperceptibly with surroundings (Figure 7-5). Solomon Butcher (1976, 65) recounts a humorous incident that reflects this:

7-5. Sketch of a Great Plains sod dugout, illustrating the usual location in a small ravine. Such location gave desirable protection from bitter winter winds and cold, but otherwise was damp and soggy (drawing by M. Margaret Geib).

After a time I saw something just ahead of me in the darkness that I took for a post, and believing we had come to a fence, I walked up to it and felt on both sides for the wires but finding none, I put my hand on top of the supposed post and discovered to my dismay that it was a stovepipe, and still warm.

By the time my investigations had resulted in this warm discovery, Morrison had driven the team up quite close to me and demanded a reason for my stop. I explained the nature of my find, and suggested a careful backing up of the team for fear of a tumble through the roof, which would be likely to disturb the sleepers below. I had seen enough of "dugouts" to know that we had discovered one, but just how to get inside I did not yet know. After getting the team out of all possible danger, I started on a voyage of discovery. The problem of the lay of the dugout was soon solved to satisfaction of all concerned. Of course it was dug out of a bank, but just where the bank ended and the house united with it I could not make out in the darkness; but I soon discovered that there was a space of about four feet between the end of the dugout – which had a wall of logs at the end – and the bank which sloped towards the house. The way I discovered this opening was by the happy one of falling into it, and the way I gained admittance into the house was by rolling down the sloping bank and in at the window, and the way I aroused the household was by alighting on a promiscuous collection of tinware, which made noise enough to stampede a bunch of plow horses.

Dugouts had several advantages for the westward-moving pioneer settlers in search of land to own. They could be built quickly – in a few weeks after arrival, and occupied during the three to five years required to secure title to the property. For many settlers, however, the dugout was a very temporary habitation until an erected dwelling could be made. This was especially true for those who arrived early in the spring and had the help of neighbors. Those who arrived late in the year were forced to spend the winter in the dugout, even if outside help was available. The Swedes around Lindsborg, Kansas, and perhaps elsewhere on the prairie, had the advantage of experience with similar dugouts from central and western Sweden (Jaderborg 1981, 68).

Records exist of dugouts built in such a way that land in two adjoining properties could be claimed, and in at least one instance a T-plan dugout in Borden County, Texas occupied space in the corners of three land sections (Carpenter 1979, 53–4). Other advantages of building dugouts included the fact that little construction material was needed and all of it was available locally and at no cost. Dugouts were fire resistant, termite proof, and weather- and storm-tight. They were cool in summer and, most importantly, relatively warm in winter. Balancing these favorable aspects were several disadvantages. Dirt was everywhere and constantly fell from the roof and walls. Roofs always leaked and the interior was dank with an unpleasant smell. Most annoying, and even dangerous, the dugouts attracted mice, lizards, centipedes, tarantula spiders and rattlesnakes.

Even before the great Western migration in North America, pioneering groups settling along the Atlantic coast had used both dugouts and caves for initial shelter (Isham and Brown 1900, 12–13; Downing 1937, 1; Leiby 1964, 85; Bradley 1978, 7; Cummings 1979, 18; Lewis 1981, 70). Charles Carroll (1975, 17–18) provides a useful description of the early shelters, even though he fails to distinguish between pits and dugouts:

> The dugout seems to have been the most common type of shelter built by new arrivals, and even some of the wealthiest settlers lived for a time in these wretched hovels. The dugouts were built by digging a hole in the earth, "cellar fashion," to a depth of six or seven feet, or sometimes by digging into the side of a hill. The breadth of the hole was determined by the needs of the builder's family, and after the digging was completed the excavation was covered over and lined with the trunks of small trees. Cracks were sealed with canvas and mounds of dirt, clay, and turf; but unless a sloped roof was built over the shelter there was little protection from heavy rain. The walls inside the dugout were often covered with bark, and sometimes the floor and ceiling were planked.

Perhaps the best known of all the early immigrant dugouts is that identified as belonging to Johannes Kelpius and located in Philadelphia. It was still extant over 300 years later, largely because it was partly finished inside and had a stone arched doorway (Bucher 1969). Colonists arriving on the Texas Gulf Coast directly from Germany in the mid-1840s also found themselves required to prepare dugouts in order to survive their first winter (Herrmann 1977, 119).

Probably the most unattractive and basic dugouts today are those inhabited by opal miners in central Australia. The settlement at Coober Pedy houses about 100 miners' families in crudely dug shelters (Wells 1968, 164). The dwelling consists of both above-ground and below-ground components and is a response to the great daytime temperatures in the long summer season (Figure 7–6).

Caves carved out of soft rock and vertically cleaved loess deposits are another form of excavated housing. Such structures are extensive and especially notable in three widely separated areas: interior China, the Matmata plateau of Tunisia, and the Cappadocia region of central Turkey. Each of these areas offers a different rock/soil material.

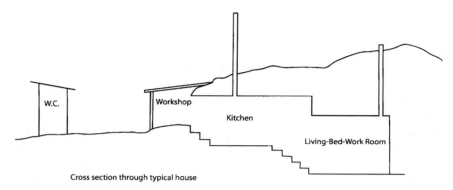

W.C.

Workshop

Kitchen

Living-Bed-Work Room

Cross section through typical house

7-6. Cross-section of a typical opal miner's dugout in Coober Pedy, Australia. The workshop can only be used after dark because of the great daytime heat, but later at night, when it cools, it functions as a children's bedroom (redrawn by Keith Pitts, based on Wells 1968, 165).

Large numbers of people have been housed in these areas and even today a substantial number continue to reside there. In Turkey, although 18th-century estimates of troglodytes reached as high as 200,000 (Kempe 1988, 126), most of the residents today have been evacuated to government housing nearby in order to lessen the considerable danger from earthquake destruction. In Tunisia in 1972,

7-7. The loess cave area of central China.

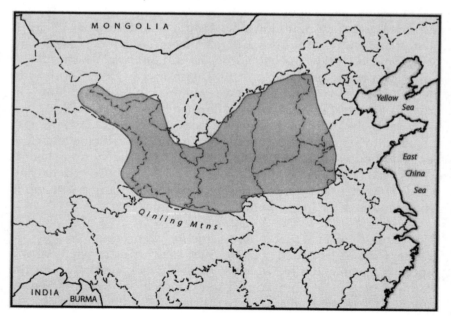

MONGOLIA

Yellow
Sea

East
China
Sea

Qinling Mtns.

INDIA
BURMA

over 500 houses (caves) were occupied (Golany 1988, 48) and more than 5,000 people were estimated to be cave residents in the early part of the 20th century (Kempe 1988, 136). In China, a recent estimate indicated that between 30 and 40 million, or 4% of the entire Chinese population, currently reside in caves (Golany 1990, 26).

Almost all of the Chinese troglodytes inhabit loess caves in provinces just to the north of the Qinling mountains (Figure 7-7). In the loess plateau lands the sites for most of the caves are the valley slopes, and less often along roadways cut down into the loess itself. *Loess* is a loosely cemented but stable soil material which, because it has vertical cleavage, can be cut in vertical planes. Extensive root systems of the surface steppe grasses keep the soil in place. Excavation must be done slowly to allow the soil to lose its moisture and thus to achieve maximum stability (Golany 1992, 75). The excavation is done horizontally, with the walls defined by the vertical root channels. Life takes place in the concealed valleys and along the narrow roadways worn down as much as 100 feet or so below the general surface. On the plateau, the only signs of the dense habitation may be the smoking chimneys that protrude slightly above the surface (Figure 7-8).

The caves, usually measuring about 30 feet long and 12 feet wide, are limited to one or two rooms and plastered to achieve greater stability (Fuller and Clapp 1924, 217–18). Many have vaulted roofs also to help provide stability by transferring load to cave sides (Lung 1991, 47). A single door and window provide light and ventilation (Figure 7-9). The major item of furnishing is a large raised bed called a *kang,*

7-8. *Typical vaulted facade of a loess cave located along a road cut or a vertical cliff. Note the chimney protruding out of the upper ground surface (from Golany 1992, 104. Reprinted with permission of the University of Hawaii Press).*

7-9. *The interior of a loess cave. The adobe or stone bed (kang) occupies much of the space. The ceiling is vaulted and plastered. This cave even has electricity, as witnessed by light bulbs and radio (photo by the author, 1977).*

made of adobe brick, masonry or local soft sandstone (Figure 7-9). It is heated by a very small built-in fireplace, or by heat from the cooking fire. Such heat is necessary during the bitterly cold winters of interior China. Commenting on kangs, both in loess caves and in houses throughout north China, George Cressey (1932, 33–4) noted that

> these bed platforms are ingeniously built up of brick in such a way that the inside is hollow and consists of a series of winding passageways through which smoke of the kitchen stove circulates before going up the chimney. Each kang is thus a furnace which squeezes every bit of heat from the scanty fuel.

Two-story caves are not as common as the one-story and present the problem of easy access to the upper story. Single-story caves normally are entered directly from a roadway or valley floor, but upper-level caves often require an acrobatic climb.

Cave dwelling in China has a history going back several centuries. A number of reasons for the steadily growing concentration of cave houses have been advanced. One suggestion is that the growing rural population and the consequent depletion of forest resources made alternative building materials unavailable (Golany 1992, 7). Other reasons include (1) the heat regulation of caves making them cooler than surroundings in summer and warmer in winter, (2) the saving of precious agricultural land and allowing the use of otherwise unused land such as cliff sides, (3) their ease of construction, and (4) construction costs half those of above ground dwellings (Golany 1989, 17; Golany 1992, 78).

The caves on the Matmata plateau in southern Tunisia (Figure 7-10) are different in several respects from the loess dwellings of China. The earth material here is a deep-bedded, light brown, partially compacted soil with high components of sand and calcium carbonate (Golany 1988, 50). Whereas some caves are situated on steeply sloping land, most occur in clusters around a deeply dug, open-to-the-sky courtyard, which may be square or rectangular (Petherbridge 1978, 202). Generally, however, the central courtyard is circular in shape (Figure 7-11), excavated between five and 10 meters below ground level (Bernard et al. 1931, 7) and accessible only through a sloping tunnel, which leads to the outside at a low spot such as the lower slope of a valley. The central courtyard is surrounded by a series of chambers often excavated on two levels (Norris 1953). The upper level caves are used primarily for storage and usually require climbing a rope for access.

These cave complexes have several advantages in the desert environment of Tunisia. They are, of course, cool in summer and warm in winter, are energy efficient since they do not need to be heated, offer

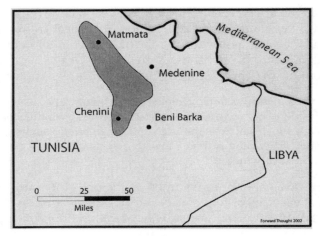

7-10. The Matmata cave area in southern Tunisia.

7-11. An aerial view of open, sunken courtyards in the Matmata plateau. The openings to several caves can be seen appearing obliquely in the courtyards (from a portion of a photograph in Golany 1988, 49. Reprinted with permission of the University of Delaware Press).

protection from dust storms, do not require any water during construction, require very little in the way of maintenance after construction and, perhaps most important of all, are cheaper than above-ground constructions (Golany 1988, 51–2). The Matmata caves, now mostly vacated, have become a center for limited tourist development, with potential for future expansion.

The third great area of excavated structures carved out of soft material occurs on the Anatolian plateau of central Turkey. This region, known generally as Cappadocia, consists of several separate areas, all of which are covered by easily and severely eroded volcanic tuffa, a basically unhardened calcium carbonate that hardens on contact with air (Ozkan and Onur 1977, 96–7). Erosion has produced a heavily dissected, badlands type of topography providing a natural system of defenses with cones rising in some cases over 100 feet in the air (Kempe 1988, 127). The cones of soft rock are easily excavated (Figure 7-12). Because the volcanic rocks are several dozen feet in thickness, many of the caves have easily defended entrances high up the side of a cone, and inside may extend several levels up and down. A network of stairways and winding tunnels connects the various rooms, in some instances on 10 to 12 levels. Initial mass settlement during the 7th and 8th centuries was by Byzantine refugees fleeing the Muslim advance (Harrison 1976, 451). Even better known than the Tunisian cave area, Cappadocia has become a tourist center of international renown.

Another, but much smaller, area of man-made excavations in volcanic tuffa occurs on the Greek island of Santorini in the Aegean Sea. Although now partially abandoned, in the late 19th century roughly half of the island's population inhabited such dwellings (Radford and Clark 1974, 66). Most of the houses consisted of one or two rooms with an unroofed front yard enclosed by such high walls as to function as another room. A major problem of these houses was that the loosely consolidated volcanic rock was hygroscopic. On an island

7-12. Troglodyte dwellings at several levels in Cappadocia, Turkey (photo by the author, 1998).

surrounded by the sea and with a large volcanic caldera filled with
seawater, the house walls were perpetually damp.

The heel of the Italian boot also possesses a number of cave dwellings. The rocks here are also volcanic tuffa, which is easily excavated.
Although some cave dwellings are more complex, most consist of a
single, fan-shaped room with a flat ceiling.

> The fan-shaped plan seems to have offered several advantages to its
> builder-occupants. It was a convenient way to dig a cave, working
> through a single opening and branching off from it radially, pushing
> the rapidly accumulating debris back through the doorway. The fin-
> ished room, with two straight walls, square corners, and a gently
> curving back wall, was in plan a bent rectangle which offered most of
> the advantages of rectangularity while doing away with one of its fre-
> quent problems, dark corners. The simple cave dwelling is evenly
> illuminated from its single opening. The back wall is at all points
> approximately equidistant from the opening, and the dark door-wall is
> kept relatively short. (Allen 1969, 53)

Permanently inhabited *caves derived from natural rock cavities* are a
final type of excavated dwelling, reported from Madagascar, Mexico
(Burleson and Riskind 1986, 95), Egypt (Duly 1979, 32), Sri Lanka,
Pakistan, India (Crooke 1918, 116), and several places in Europe. Cave
dwellers in Britain were documented as recently as 1974 (Kempe
1988, 7). As with the other types of excavations, considerable variety
exists, depending largely on the type of rock in which the cave is
formed. Limestone, because of its basic structural stability and its susceptibility to water solution, accounts for the largest number of
natural cave structures. The ideal situation occurs where water tables
have lowered so that active solution is absent, or at least greatly
reduced, resulting in a dry interior environment for the troglodytes.
In many parts of Europe, Spain and France especially, inhabited limestone caves still exist (Freal 1977, 29). In 1924 Frances Hay claimed
200,000 people in Italy lived in caves (Hay 1924, 229), but this figure
may be excessive, although sandstone caves in Sicily were commonly
inhabited until recently.

In France, David Kempe (1988, 7) estimated that, in the 1980s, limestone cave dwellings with 25,000 inhabitants occurred in three areas:
(1) the valley of the Seine river and to its north in Champagne, (2) the
southeast, back from the Mediterranean coast and east of the Rhone
valley, and (3) the great area of west-central France from the encircling
Loire valley to the Dordogne river. In part of the latter area, the caves
range from simple two- to three-room residence-cum-wine cellars to
extensive communal dwelling networks dating from the Middle Ages
(Fraysse and Fraysse 1963–64). These caves have a history as dwell-

ings that dates back much further, however, to prehistoric times. Cro-Magnon man was discovered in 1868 in one of them, and the paintings of Lascaux, another cave, are world famous.

In Spain, two major concentrations of cave dwellings exist. In Navarra province, in the foothills of the Pyrenees, between a quarter and a third of the populations of various districts lived in caves up to World War II (Ling 1936, 851). The other Spanish area is in the southern province of Andalucia, where standards of living have been higher than in the north. The largest concentration is around Gaudix (Carver 1981, 103). Many of these caves are still occupied, but numbers are steadily declining.

Early on in human history, mankind realized that ground level was a dangerous, and often unhealthy, altitude at which to live. One way to escape its perils was to go underground; another was to seek safety in the opposite direction, initially to the treetops in tropical and subtropical areas. Benoy Ghosh (1953) reported dwellings as high up as 40–60 feet. The Sakai tribe in the Malayan lowland rainforest built flimsy bark and palm frond huts elevated on large tree trunks and branches. Up to 20 feet long, although usually much smaller, the huts were additionally supported by stilts (Forde 1963, 20). That security was a major influence in elevating dwellings is "confirmed by the solitary houses being more elevated than are the village houses" (Ferree 1889, 30).

In Australia, early pioneer settlers were plagued by white ants. In order to secure refuge from these pests, by the 1890s "Queensland houses were raised on tree-trunk stilts seven or eight feet high" (Cox and Freeland 1969, 63). The tubular trails of the ants could be seen immediately on the stilts and broken to cut the vital contacts between ants and ground. Only later were the climatic advantages of the raised stilt position realized (Archer 1987, 103). By 1944 almost 50 valid reasons for elevating houses in Australia had been identified (Irving 1985, 307).

Living well above the ground has several advantages beyond that of security, both from animals and enemies. Cooling breezes are more effective at heights and under-structure ventilation is most effective. In rainy weather one is above the upward splashing rainwater hitting the ground, and secure from the effects of flooding, poor drainage and water-logging. If the elevation was high enough, inhabitants were above the range of most malaria-carrying mosquitoes (Dawson and Gillow 1994, 10). The Urali tribal peoples of south India add still a further reason for utilization of stilt houses, that of "keeping their women in seclusion at adolescence, menstruation and even at childbirth" (Ghosh 1953, 22).

Houses raised up on stilts are widely encountered. Even into the 20th century, tree houses have been inhabited extensively in New Guinea (Bernard et al 1931, 108; Cranstone 1980, 497), central India (Broderick 1954, 110), in Assam in eastern India, to protect against wild elephants (Ghosh 1953, 10), and Sumatra (Ferree 1889, 30). In many areas, such as the lagoon coasts of Vietnam and West Africa (Figure 7-13), lowlands of southern Japan (Earle 1943, 278), the tidal rivers of Brunei, the low-lying coastal areas inhabited by the Mosquito Indians in Nicaragua and eastern Honduras (Salinas 1991, 101–15), the Warraus and Guaranos tribal areas in Guyana (Westmaas 1970, 133), and the lakes of Cambodia and riverine locations in Indonesia, structures are raised primarily to avoid the fluctuating waters, but elsewhere the other advantages predominate. Stilt dwellings in coastal regions, although offering protection against normal hazards, cannot secure safety from atypical catastrophic events. Thus, the December 2004 tsunami in the Indian Ocean saw the destruction of tens of thousands, perhaps hundreds of thousands, of stilt dwellings in coastal areas of Southeast and South Asia.

In the seasonally inundated basins of the Orinoco and Amazon in South America, periodic flooding ranks with protection from insects as advantages of stilt buildings. In drier locations, the space thus developed beneath the elevated floor platform provides a valuable area to pen up animals that might otherwise stray (Westmass 1970, 133; Sternberg 1984).

In the upper reaches of the Peruvian tributaries of the Amazon, communal houses are used by the Yagua peoples. Consisting of little more than a thatched roof and a lower platform raised up on wooden piles four or five feet high, and entirely without walls or partitions,

7-13. *These thatch-roofed stilt houses are well above normal high tide in the coastal lagoon at Ganvie, Benin (photo by the author, 1975).*

they represent the ultimate attempt to capture cross-ventilation breezes (Rapoport 1967). Privacy is attained for individuals simply by turning to face the outside, in which attitude they will not be disturbed by others. As noted by Colin Duly (1979, 69), this "cultural convention directly corresponds to the more familiar material convention of a partition to give privacy."

Throughout the vast monsoon-influenced lands of Southeast Asia, from Assam and the Brahmaputra valley in eastern India to interior southern China, south to the Indonesian islands, and east to the Philippines and New Guinea, *the* house is the stilt house (Figure 7-14). This does not mean, however, that *all* houses within this area are supported on stilts. Many are earth-fast, wattle-and-daub structures. As one moves northward within Southeast Asia, the houses become more sturdy, utilizing heavier timbers and more planks. This shift probably results from two conditions: the greater need for a somewhat more closed structure because of lower temperatures in the low sun period of the year, and fewer light building materials in these regions away from the equator, where growth of vegetation is slower.

In southern China stilt houses occur in the provinces of Yunnan, Guizhou, Guandong and Guangxi, often among minority peoples

7-14. This stilt house in Johore, Malaysia is raised on sturdy cement pillars. Note also the many window openings that provide ventilation in this constantly warm environment (photo by the author, 1980).

(Lung 1991, 48). Built of sturdy timber posts and wall planks, these rectangular-plan dwellings are covered by a wooden shingle roof. The stilt houses of northern Thailand resemble those of southern China in their use of heavier construction materials, but are more elaborate in internal division and often use multiple roofs to cover different rooms and spaces. A kitchen located at the rear takes the place of the open hearth of the Chinese central hall. In China, entry is via a stairway under and toward the center of the dwelling. In northern Thailand the entry is a flight of wooden stairs at the front, leading to a partially open platform where visitors are received and other social functions are performed (Charernsupkul and Temiyabandha 1979, 49). The multiple, independently framed roofs, rear kitchen, reception platform and a space where water is kept in cooling jars for visitors and family, are all features normally shared with stilt houses found further south (Hilton 1956).

A series of floor plans of Malay houses taken from studies by various authors has been compiled by W.B.B. Wan Abidin for comparative purposes. While each floor plan is different, together they illustrate some unifying elements. The main entrance is via the *anjung*, an entrance porch, or directly into the next element, the *serambi* or reception platform. Behind the main room(s) may be a covered verandah with kitchen at the back. The kitchen also often serves as the dining area, and a subsidiary food preparation area called the *dapur* may be the final element (Wan Abidin 1981, 29–30). Physical form and the use of both interior and exterior spaces of the stilt houses vary somewhat as one would expect over such great distances, but a basic unity persists. Jee Yuan Lim (1987), looking at traditional houses in Malaysia, emphasizes the flexibility of the interiors due to moveable partitions, minimal furniture, and a natural willingness to use floors for sitting.

A variant of the normally encountered stilt houses are those structures partially supported by stilts but also built against a slope or cliff. These occur mostly in areas of hilly land and along riverbanks, where the slope would not permit the entire structure to be underpinned by posts, or where the ground would be unstable. "By leaning the house against the cliff, less load is imposed on the stilts, thus making the entire structure more stable" (Lung 1991, 62). Such structures are reported from Sichuan and Guixhou provinces in southeastern China, from King Island in the Bering Sea (Hoagland 1993, 12; Lee and Reinhardt 2003, 101–3) and Chiloe Island, Chile (Shichor 1987, 176).

In tropical areas native houses raised on stilts were so finely attuned to environmental conditions that early officials of colonial governments had their own structures raised up on stilts. They also incorporated the wide verandahs of native structures. Those colonial shelters were built throughout the British, Belgian, Dutch and French colonies in Africa and Asia. Although the colonial structures used native approaches, virtually all of the construction material was imported from the metropolitan country (Jack 1955, 96 & 102).

The history of the verandah in Australia took a somewhat different direction. It traces its introduction in about 1793 from South or South-east Asia, initially to "the southern counties of England where it had been taken by Army men returning from the outposts of the empire" and then ultimately down under.

> Used at first as no more than a covered external passage-way between rooms in one-room thick passage-less houses, it spread, one-storey high, along the face, then around the ends and across the back of the houses widening from three feet to ten on the way to form a cool, shaded and breezy area for sitting in the heat of the day or in the evenings. The verandah became increasingly a living area. A small box of rooms was surrounded by ever-broader verandahs on which, for most of the year, a large part of the normal activities of a country home took place--eating, talking, sewing and reading became out-door activities as people moved out of the stifling conditions indoors. To protect the verandah from the sun, especially in the late afternoon, but to allow the passage of cooling air, screens of open wattling were fixed between the posts. From the late seventies, these first rudimentary efforts were replaced with lattice or trellis work of the thin oregon battens used in the south by the plasterers. The screens first appeared on the western side but by the time battened screens were used, they were hung continuously around all four sides like a skirt. (Cox and Freeland 1969, 63)

Both elevated and excavated dwellings offered enhanced possibilities for habitation. Better security, defense against extreme temperatures, both hot and cold, safety from either rain or flooding and other environmental challenges were some of the advantages to be secured. These came at the price of more difficult accessibility, cramped and often uncomfortable quarters, and dangerous structures subject to earthquakes, rock and soil collapses, wind and rain damage, and uneven subsidence of unstable and water logged shore soils. As time went by, questions of security receded and technological levels improved, with the result that both excavated and elevated dwellings became less attractive and were abandoned because of their recognized disadvantages.

~ 8 ~
Coverings and Climate

The most critical feature of a traditional building is its roof, or whatever else covers the structure. "The roof not only shelters inhabitants and their possessions against sun and rain, and wind and dust, it also makes the space underneath livable in summer heat and winter frost. It protects the walls and holds them together. Few structures can long survive a break in the overhead cover" (Waite 1976, 135).

> Usually, the roof represents the largest single component of the cost of any small building, often as high as 40 percent of the total cost; at the same time, it represents the most complex array of technical problems for solution; and as it tends to dominate the external appearance of the building, its symbolic significance for the owner is commonly of great importance. (Spence and Cook 1983, 263)

In some extreme examples, the walls may be entirely done away with so that the roof rests upon the ground (Carson et al. 1981, 154).

In areas where the ground water table has been penetrated by saltwater, such as the delta and bayous of Louisiana, or on the limited space of small islands, the roof performs the critical function of a rainwater catchment surface, from which the water is led to storage tanks (Raine 1966, 18, 26). In low-lying areas where fresh water is easily polluted by stagnant surface water, the roof also serves to collect necessary supplies of drinking water (Westmaas 1970, 134). In Malta, where rainfall is limited and run-off through porous limestone bedrock is very rapid, the terrace roofs collect rainwater, which is stored in cisterns (Harrison and Hubbard 1949, 80). In the rainless summer these same roofs are used for drying and storing crops and even for sleeping, but in winter they collect vital water.

The roof is so significant that it has even provided the names by which dwellings are popularly known. Hence, we find the hipped-roof house, the pyramid-roof house, the mansard house, and even the "house of seven gables"! In Newfoundland, the earliest European dwelling was a small vertical-walled shanty called the *tilt*, in reference to its shed roof that tilted or sloped in just one direction (Mills

1982, 31). The term today is "used in Newfoundland to describe any temporary or rough shelter and, as most such shelters are or were generally always constructed of vertical logs, to refer particularly to shelters constructed in that manner" (O'Dea 1982, 19).

Because of its importance and high visibility, successful classification systems are built upon roof-form variation (Figure 8-1). Some classifications have almost worldwide applicability, but even those of much more limited scope are highly useful, especially when placed in a geographical context. Roof-form variation is influenced largely by environment, availability of materials, and the evolution of structural systems, which – because they are culturally controlled – are not duplicated elsewhere. The roofs found on Chinese structures do not appear outside East Asia, but some Chinese roofs do have a superficial resemblance to roofs elsewhere. Figure 8-2 presents one interpretation of these artistically pleasing forms (Kostof 1985, 233). Other scholars have proposed somewhat differing classification systems (Knapp 1989).

The reason the roof is so critical is that not only does it provide shelter, it also ensures the integrity of the building itself. Once a roof is breached, admitting water or snow, deterioration begins immediately if a building consists of wood or other vegetative materials. If not quickly corrected, destruction of the structure will follow. The same consequences occur with mud or adobe if precipitation penetrates.

The search for effective materials to block penetration of rainwater has been extensive and exhaustive. The nearly flat mud roof of houses used by the Masai tribe in Tanzania is not always effective in repelling rains, and hides must often be thrown over the structure as added protection during the rainy season (McKim 1985, 66). On the American Great Plains after the Civil War and towards the end of the sod house phase of building, tar paper began to be used as roofing. It was laid down first and sods were placed over it providing an efficient roof. Subsequently, tar-paper roofing without a sod covering spread widely in North America as a cheap, if not very long-lasting, roof material. Tar paper, painted on both sides with petroleum tar, had been developed during the American Civil War to cover ammunition dumps (Kear 1971).

A wide variety of locally available items function as roof coverings. These range from grasses, leaves, straw, and heather, to bamboo, tree bark, branches, timber, logs, and wooden boards, to shingles, shakes, and tiles, to turf, or sod, mud, and stone. Probably the strangest sounding roof coverings to the modern researcher are seaweed – used on the Danish island of Laeso (Faber n.d., 104), on the Aegean island of Santorini (Radford and Clark 1974, 78) and other Greek islands (Wagstaff 1965, 61; Megas 1951, 36) – and fermented animal dung in

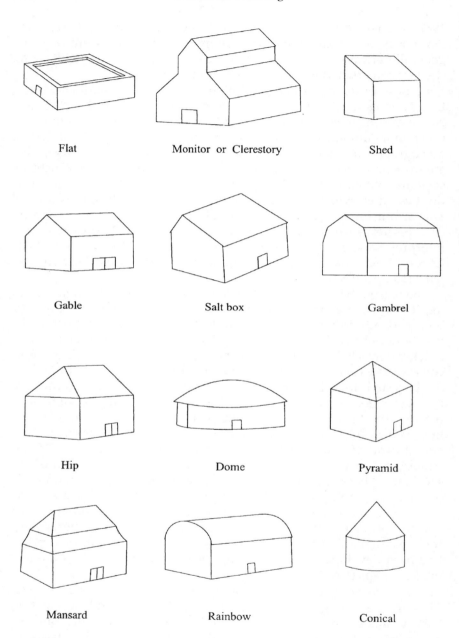

Flat   Monitor or Clerestory   Shed

Gable   Salt box   Gambrel

Hip   Dome   Pyramid

Mansard   Rainbow   Conical

8-1. Chart of roof types illustrating the wide variation of form. (drawings by Ira-ida Galdon Soler).

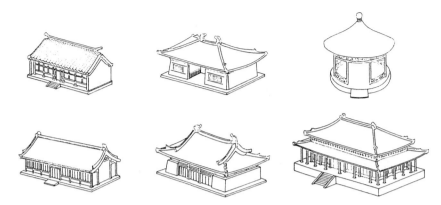

8-2. The most common Chinese roof types (from Kostov 1985, 233. Reprinted with permission of Oxford University Press).

Sudanese villages (Rodger 1974, 103). Both are used in combination with more conventional roofing materials. The seaweed forms an insulating layer much like more conventional thatch elsewhere, and the cow dung an impervious outer plaster to seal the roof better. In each instance, mud, clay, and/or other earth materials make up the bulk of the roof. Incidentally, cow dung is also a widely used material in both Africa and Asia to finish earthen floors, where it forms a hard, durable surface, which when dry is easily cleaned. A similar process and result using sheep dung is reported for Scotland (Beaton 1997, 19).

Turf or sod roofs have been widely used because of their easy availability, low cost and excellent insulating qualities (Erixon 1938, 53; Welsch 1968). At the same time, such roofs suffer from several deficiencies. They do not hold moisture well (Hammer 1968, 59); even if the weather is dry, high winds encourage the sifting down of dirt; they are exceptionally heavy, requiring strong support (Ruede 1966, 207); they harbor a variety of small animals and insects; and when dry they are not fire resistant.

Another earth material, adobe, works well in dry environments. Laid on several layers of wooden beams and poles, with each succeeding upward layer smaller, the entire system is heavy (Figure 8-3). This weight and the scarcity of large timbers in arid areas combine to restrict adobe roofs to rooms of small size. This is the main reason why pueblos, for example, consist of a number of small units built together. A similar approach, followed in Lebanon, consists of log beams supporting the roof weight, succeeded by a layer of twigs, branches or reed matting laid crosswise to the logs, a third layer of thorny brush pressed down into moist mud, and finally a layer of

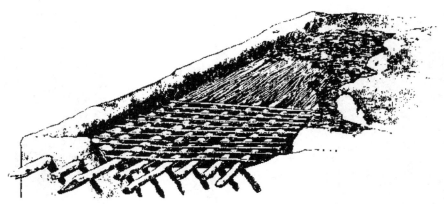

8-3. *Zuni Indian roof construction. The roof consists of several layers, with each succeeding layer denser than the previous one (from V. Mindeleff 1891, 149).*

finely crushed stone, sometimes with a lime-chaff coating on top. The upper layer is rolled periodically by a heavy stone roller to ensure the continued sealing of the material (Ragette 1974, 22–5; El-Khoury 1975, 4).

Today in many places concrete slab roofs are replacing adobe ones. The concrete roof, like the adobe, is subject to rupture by earthquakes, but is more rainproof than the adobe. In a somewhat similar move toward modernity in the Punjab state of India, increased rural prosperity has brought a replacement of the grass thatch layer of adobe roofs with a layer of tiles (Singh 2004, 77 & 85). Not only is the roof made sturdier and more long lasting, but it is also more elegant in appearance, which enhances the local prestige of the dwelling's family.

It might seem at first glance that a *thatch roof* is a simple feature and its construction basic, but nothing could be further from the truth! The material alone encompasses a vast range, from sedges (Sandon 1977, 18) to bracken fern (Sheppard 1966, 22), to grasses of many types (McDaniel 1982, 86), to reeds and rushes (Nash 1991, 32 & 37), to wheat, rye, oat, barley and other types of straw (Fearn 1976, 4), to broom (Meirion-Jones 1982, 65), to heather (Billett 1979, 30), to sunflower, maize and sorghum stalks (Ruede 1966, 28, 29), and a variety of other mid-latitude plants, to palm leaves, banana plants, rice-paddy straw and sugarcane leaves (Singh 1957, 58), to papyrus (Rodger 1974, 104) and other less often used tropical coverings. In Ireland alone the thatching materials include wheat straw, flax, rye straw, oat straw, barley straw, reeds, rushes, tough grasses and heather (O'Danachair 1945, 208–9). The word *thatch* is an Anglo-Saxon version of the German word *Dach* meaning roof (Clifton-Taylor 1972, 336). Both words confirm the widespread nature and importance of such roofs, both in the UK and Germany.

In southern Africa, bundles of reeds form the foundation upon which lighter bundles of grasses are laid (Walton 1948, 144). In other areas as well, thatch roofs consist of bundles of different materials laid in distinct layers. In order to make the roof watertight, the butt ends of the bundles are "dressed" by pounding them upward with a wooden tool called a *leggat*, and inserting additional handfuls of back-fill reed (West 1987, 81). In the UK, where thatch is still placed on some newly built dwellings, earlier thatch roofs

> were constructed so that the thatch projected over the house walls, thereby producing wide eaves so that water was thrown well clear of the walls which were often porous. This feature gave birth to that well-known character the 'eavesdropper', a person who crept under the overhanging edge of the roof to listen clandestinely to what was being said within the house. (West 1987, 11)

In tropical areas, thatched roofs deteriorate rapidly and must be replaced often, although some grass roofs do have exceptionally long lives. In Bali, Indonesia, and Thailand and a few other places, grass roofs may last up to 25 years (Spence and Cook 1983, 274). Members of the Matakam tribe of West Africa, on the other hand, replace millet straw roofs annually just before the rainy season begins (Gardi 1973, 73). Most commonly in tropical areas, a thatched roof lasts several rainy seasons. Colin Duly (1979, 65–6) reports that among the Panare Indians of the Orinoco lowlands, "palm thatching rarely lasts more than four rainy seasons," after which the inhabitants migrate over a short distance and build a new house rather than repair the old one. This practice may also be related to the necessity to eliminate vermin infestation which has built up in the original structure. M.J. Meggitt (1957, 161) comments with reference to New Guinea that "thatch of houses more than three years old is overgrown with weeds, and is no longer rain and wind proof. The houses stink, and are flea-ridden."

One non-tropical area where thatch roofing was renewed annually is the Hebridean Islands of Scotland. Here, the thatch, blackened from the soot of open fires in houses which have no smoke holes, was pulled off and spread on the fields as fertilizer (Sinclair 1953, 27; Fenton 1978, 35). A rather different method of utilizing soot for fertilizer occurs in Shantung Province, China. There, the massive, adobe-brick bed, which has smoke passages passing through it, is broken up every couple of years when the bricks have become impregnated with soot. "In the spring the farmer rebuilds the bed with new bricks and removes the old ones which are broken into powder and either mixed with manure or spread directly on the field" (Yang 1965, 24).

In the middle latitudes, length of life for a thatched roof is considerably longer than in the tropics. Olive Sharkey (1985, 19) suggests a life of 10 to 15 years for Irish thatch roofs, and Edward Ledohowski and David Butterfield (1983, 57) report that a thatched roof on Ukrainian houses in Manitoba could last up to half a century, if properly maintained.

The major climate problem with thatch roofs is not leaking from rains but damage from high winds. Because thatch is so light, it is easily removed in a storm. Although parapets are widely considered a device to retard fire, James Walton (1948, 142) suggests that in southern Africa they are used primarily to prevent the thatch on gable roofs from lifting in strong winds. William Addison (1986, 28) noted that thatchers in England soaked their material in order to make it more pliable and thus easier to work with. At the same time, a solution of alum was added "to reduce the risk of fire." In much of Scandinavia, wind protection is provided by the application of *roof trees* (Figure 8-4), "short pieces of wood pegged together and set along the ridge to

8-4. *Pairs of roof trees hold down the critical thatch over the ridge of a cottage in the Jutland peninsula of Denmark, near Ringsted (photo by the author 1978).*

hold down the top of the thatch" (Donnelly 1992, 215). Throughout northern Europe, heavy stone weights, tarred ropes and wire, and wooden planks are also used to anchor thatch.

Thatch is still the most commonly used covering in the world. In England alone, 50,000 thatched buildings were estimated to still survive as of 1982 (Brown 1982, 252). "In India, some 40 million houses are thatched; in Kerala State over 50% of roofs are made from coconut or palm leaves" (Hall 1981, 7). The rationale for the widespread and persistent use of thatch for roofing in middle latitude regions is not just because of its cheapness, but due also to its superior temperature- and sound-insulating character:

> During the many centuries of its use, no other natural material has ever been found which equals thatch in resistance to both extremes of weather and temperature. It is possible for a variation in temperature within a slate roof to be over four times that under thatch, for similar conditions. This insulating property, which applies equally well to sound and temperature, is due to the cellular nature of the construction caused by the many reeds, each with innumerable cavities in and around them (Singleton 1952, 85).

Wood, in various forms including *bark*, has served as roof covering in a variety of locations. The Iroquois in upstate New York covered their long houses with great slabs of elm bark. In Australia, bark of the "stringy-bark" tree was used for both walls and roof. The bark slabs were heated over a fire to soften the resin and make the material more pliable (Archer 1987, 76–8).

Among the peoples of the Siberian taiga, birch bark conical tents serve as summer dwellings.

> In the spring, the bark is stripped from the trees in pieces sixteen to twenty-five feet in length. Each strip is then rolled to form a tube, filled with moss, and steamed for three days to make it pliable. These strips are dried and then sewn together with spruce root into large sections. Four to six sections are used to cover a tent. (Faegre 1979, 110)

Other Siberian groups construct different forms of bark-roofed dwellings.

"In South China and along the Tibetan border bark roofs are occasionally seen, the slabs placed alternatively concave and convex" (Spencer 1947, 261). Immigrating settlers in both Australia (Cox and Freeland 1969, 27, 43 & 44) and North America (Hudson 1975, 7) used bark for their first dwellings whenever it was available. Everywhere that bark has been employed as a roof covering its use is not only because of availability but also because of its inherent waterproof quality.

Wood in the form of split or sawn boards and planks was an even better roof covering than bark for pioneers in North America. From early times, it was used by the Northwest Coast Indians, who covered their substantial communal houses with long cedar planks. These "were often adzed into a shallow 'U' shape so as to carry water off the house with minimum leakage" (Newman 1974, 23).

Elsewhere, boards and planks did not always form the only roof covering. Usually they provided only a foundation for other weaker or more pliable materials. They were not used by themselves because of the difficulty in many places of securing wood, which could be riven or split into planks of uniform thickness. Also, wood grains, more often than not, were not straight or parallel, so boards were uneven and rough. Many grains produced twisted or bent planks whose irregularities became even more pronounced as they thoroughly dried or, worse, became wet from rain and snow. The best solution was to cover the boards or planks with some other material.

As a final refinement, wood can be split into *shingles* or *shakes*. In Texas, a distinction was made between plank roofing or the use of shingles or shakes. "When a man put a split board roof on his cabin, he 'covered' his house; when he used shakes and purlins he 'roofed' his house" (Connor 1949, 114). Although widely distributed across Europe, shakes/shingles, however they were termed, were rarely the dominant roof covering, even in pre-industrial times. More important was sod and birch bark in the north, thatch in both east and west, sod in the southeast, and tile in central and southern Europe. Perhaps it was the labor and skill required to make the shingles that prevented their widespread adoption. Nevertheless, shingle roofs are fairly common in Scandinavia and in southeastern England (Blake 1925, 34). They were also reasonably common in Ulster as early as the 17th century (Robinson 1985, 22).

Shake roofs occur most often in well-wooded hilly and mountainous terrain, such as the Carpathian Mountains where they are common. Another area where shake roofs have been most carefully studied is the highlands of Mexico. John Winberry (1975) suggests that shake roofs were introduced by Basques from northern Spain. The folk production of shakes, called *tejamanil*, is now largely prohibited in Mexico as a result of government forestry conservation policies.

The use of shingles or shakes is more common in North America than in England, probably because of the greater abundance of wood. White cedar, cypress, oak, and redwood have supplied most of the shingles used in the United States (Blake 1925, 36). Anthony Garvan (1951, 99) noted that in colonial Connecticut shingle roofs "became universal" soon after original British settlement. Because of the shakes' rough and uneven surface, the pitch of shake roofs must be greater than 40° in order to shed water rapidly enough to prevent deterioration of the shakes (Robinson 1985, 22). Also, a steep pitch is necessary since shingles do not lie absolutely flat and rain can easily be blown up under the tails of the shingles (Blake 1925, 35). To reduce warping, shingles often were fashioned with a rounded butt edge (Waite 1976, 138).

Originally, shingles of three-foot length or greater were employed by the Pennsylvania Germans (Bucher 1968). Warren Roberts (1976, 442) also encountered them in southern Indiana, and reports of similar shingles place them in early New England and Long Island. The long shingle, which probably has European antecedents, was replaced by the short shingle when shingle mills began operating around 1800 (Bucher 1968, 54). The key to the long shingle is the lapping both sideways and lengthways to provide watertight cover.

Even *stone* is used as roof covering, although because of its weight its use is restricted to material having relatively thin bedding planes. Of these, *slate*, which can be used effectively in thicknesses of less than one-quarter inch, is most widely employed. The principal difference between slates and most other stones is the natural cleavage of the former, which permits it to be more easily split in one direction (National Slate Association 1926, 6). In England, blue slate was especially prized in the southern areas because it could be split so that its weight was one-third to one-quarter that of slates supplied from sandstone or limestone sources (Jope and Dunning 1954, 209). Nevertheless, roof frames had to be sturdy to support its mass, especially since the roof slope must be only about 35° in order to guard against detachment and falling of individual slates when subjected to strong winds. The other natural hazard for slate is hail. Otherwise, it is a desirable roofing material that can last hundreds of years with minimal maintenance.

Until the development of railroads, slate was limited – because of its weight and relatively fragile nature – to use in domestic structures in areas close to the quarries, along canals or near ports where foreign slates were landed (Robinson 1985). This relationship is well shown in Northern Ireland, where two concentrations of slate quarries exist, one along the Donegal–Londonderry border, and the other in eastern County Down. The plantation surveys of 1611–22 identify an early cluster of slate-roofed dwellings in northern Ulster, and the later Ordinance Survey Memoirs of 1830 reveal a concentration of slate-roofed houses in County Down. Quarries and slate-roofed houses thus clearly coincide spatially. Elsewhere in Ulster, thatch roofing prevailed.

The introduction of railroads, however, made slate economically available over a much wider area. Nevertheless, the cost of shipping a heavy material subject to a significant amount of breakage produced certain ultimate limitations. In the United States, for example, although roofing slate was widely used on structures east of the Mississippi River, the demand west of the Mississippi was quite limited because of high freight rates (Bowles 1939, 284). The most productive quarries were located in northeastern US (Figure 8-5). Although slate roofs are most common in the US and northwestern Europe, they also occur in other parts of the world (Calligas 1974, 121), especially where snow needs to be shed from a roof quickly (Cereghini 1956, 162–4; Bhatt 1986, 26).

Despite the utility of slate, other sedimentary stones have been used for roofing, but in a much more limited scope, both functionally and geographically. One of the most important such stones in Great Britain is limestone, but its use is limited by its weight since thin pieces are difficult to produce. Traditionally, the suitable limestone was quarried in the autumn and then left exposed to weather over the

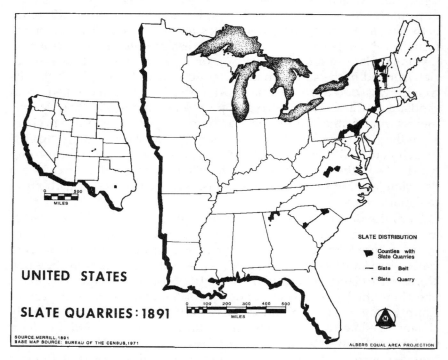

8-5. *Slate-producing areas of the United States in 1891. The slate belt from Ver-mont through New York and Pennsylvania dominated (drawing by M. Margaret Geib).*

winter. "The force of even a single sudden thaw following a hard frost could achieve in a few hours what would take the hand of man many weeks (Clifton-Taylor 1972, 101). Daily watering was necessary, possibly throughout the winter to ensure sufficient splitting.

Another earth material in widespread use as roofing is *tile*, used in a variety of forms, although the material is basically the same in all cases, i.e. baked clay. Chinese tiles consist of a curved tile of smaller radius inverted over a wider radius tile acting as a catchment or trough. Spanish tiles are similar but the radii do not vary, except along the length of each individual tile. They are tapered lengthwise with the smaller radius at the upper end to prevent slipping off the roof (Laws 1995, 34). Greek and Roman tiles, by contrast, have upper curved tiles inverted over a flat trough bottom tile. Much more simple are flat tiles and the better designed, because lighter, *pantiles*, which have a gentle S curve. These originated in the Netherlands but are widely used elsewhere. Mangalore and other recent tiles have interlocking designs that reduce weight significantly (Spence and Cook 1983, 278–81).

Clay destined for roof tiles in the middle latitudes is dug in the autumn, piled into large heaps for curing and allowed to weather over the winter. The process of tile firing has similarities to that of brick making. While a clay tile roof has certain advantages, such as non-conduction of heat, durability and ease of replacement and maintenance, its extreme weight (roughly twice that of slate) requires a heavy supporting frame, and the roof pitch must be steep for stability (Blake 1925, 119–21).

> When pantiles are stripped from cottages for repair or demolition, an underlying layer of hay or straw is sometimes seen, acting as an efficient insulation. No doubt such techniques were introduced at the time when the tiles were substituted for thatch. Tiles, for all their advantages of permanence and incombustibility, must have been desperately uncomfortable compared with cosy thatch – warm in winter, cool in summer. (Penoyre and Penoyre 1978, 112)

Although the Chinese and Japanese were the first to introduce glazed tiles, European use of roofing tile goes back at least to Roman times. In the 13th century, shell-shaped tiles with three furrows or grooves to carry off the water were used in France (Ballard 1934, 27). Widely encountered in Europe, tile roofs were introduced into colonial North America, where they competed with both thatch and wood. A few 18th-century red-tile roofs can still be discovered in the Pennsylvania-Dutch country of southern Pennsylvania (Bucher 1961, 19), the original area with the largest concentration of traditional tile roofs in the United States.

An early method of laying tiles in this area was in vertical and horizontal rows, leaving very narrow vertical joints or gaps. Rain would not penetrate except when driven by exceptionally strong winds, but snow would to a limited extent. As Robert Bucher (1961, 21) notes, "Many are the stories we have read of our forefathers having slept in the loft of the cabin or garret of the house and awaking the morning after a snowfall with an extra blanket of snow covering their bed." A more widely used method of tile placement staggered the vertical joints, the same patterns used for slate and shingle. This provided a tighter seal. The problem with staggering tiles is that the weight of the roof is almost double that of the vertical row roof. In both methods the introduction of furrows reduced the weight substantially. Rounding off the bottom edge of the tile also reduces weight and channels run-off to the center of the next lower tile. Rounded butt tiles are sometimes referred to as "fish scales" (Figure 8-6).

To an extent, the tile roof is a response to climate. This is especially true in Europe, where the drier and warmer southern countries favored tile roofs, whereas the northern, more humid and cooler countries favored thatch and wood. In France the traditional boundary between the types is the Loire valley (Meirion-Jones 1982, 45).

Metal roofs, although they exist, are not commonly used on traditional structures, except as modern replacements. Where they occur, they generally represent the beginning of the decline of traditional approaches to building. Their growing popularity is related in large part to the reduction in labor required for their use. Thatching may

8-6. A "fish scale," flat shingle, tile roof in Holloko, Hungary. Rounding off the butt end of the tiles reduces the danger of wind lifting (photo by the author, 2002).

require days of work because of the skill required, while sheets of thin corrugated iron can be put up quickly and easily. The major drawback to their use is the poor insulation if winters are cold, the great heat in summer and the incessant noise if precipitation is either heavy or prolonged. Otto Koenigsberger and Robert Lynn (1965, 49) report that the drumming of tropical rain on metal roofs without ceilings to baffle the noise disturbs sleep and makes it impossible to understand normal speech.

Combinations of disparate materials are often used to secure the most efficient roofs. In Scandinavia, three layers – wooden boards, birch bark, and sod – form a roof with both high insulating character and impervious nature. The birch bark needs to be replaced only every 15–20 years. A cross-board along the eaves prevents slippage of the sod (Figure 8-7). The sod was laid with the grass side down and grass seed was then sown on top. "The mass of roots and grass blades combined to form a solid covering" (Stewart 1972, 27). A somewhat similar roof consisting of mud mixed with grass and cow dung laid on birch bark has been reported as the usual roof covering in Kashmir (Cooper and Dawson 1998, 23 & 45). In most parts of Ireland and in the highlands of Britain, a layer of sod formed the base upon which thatch was laid. The sods were "usually laid in long strips running up the roof and overlapping at the ridge" (Evans 1957, 56). Because of the windy nature of these areas, the thatch was held fast by various devices – heather ties, ropes, wire or stone weights (Campbell 1935, 71; Sinclair 1953, 19).

8-7. The cross-board helps to keep the upper sod layer of this roof firmly in place. The birch bark layer can be seen clearly above the lowest, sawn board layer, near Trondheim, Norway (photo by the author, 2001).

The three most common *roof types* are the circular cone, gable, and hipped. The circular thatched roof is widely encountered in all tropical and semi-tropical areas. In Basutoland, the circular walled house with a cone-shaped thatch roof, called a *rondavel*, is the basic and earliest house type. After exposure to European construction, some rectangular-plan houses with gable roofs began to appear in place of the earlier rondavels, but they never became as common as oval plan houses combined with hipped roofs. Walton speculates that the difficulty that the Sotho people had with building gable walls (a widespread problem often encountered elsewhere among peoples with an earlier circular-plan tradition of building) encouraged them to adopt a compromise plan. This resulted in the oval plan, which was nothing more than two partial rondavels situated so that two relatively short, straight wall sections could connect them under a single roof. The walls could be built to a uniform height and a modified, hipped roof placed overall (Walton 1948, 141–2).

The *hipped roof* has a short ridgeline from which it slopes in all four directions on a rectangular-plan structure. Although some skill is required in its construction, it has considerable advantages over the gable roof. The triangle of the upper gable wall is not required, eliminating one of the weakest wall parts of a gabled, rectangular structure (Figure 8-8). Also, because the exposed bargeboard edges of the gable roof are replaced by sloping parts of a hipped roof, the tendency for strong winds to lift the roof is greatly reduced. Finally, rainfall run-off is more equally distributed, lessening its erosive potential.

An unusual roof type appeared for a brief time on the northern Great Plains in the last quarter of the 19th century. It was arched in form and had no roof ridge. John Hudson (1975, 7) has suggested that the roof type was derived from the canvas coverings of pioneer settlers' wagons. The earliest versions also had a door on the end, further confirming the wagon-covering origin. The roof type had two advantages – it was light and portable, and it offered less wind resistance than a gable roof, "provided it was oriented at the right angles to the prevailing winds." The arched form of the roof was maintained by a series of light poles under tension. Barbara Oringderff (1976, 33) estimates that about 17% of all Kansas sod houses had "car or rounded roofs," making it the second most popular roof for sod houses, but far behind the gable roof (76%). Somewhat similar in form, but quite different in construction techniques and roofing materials, is the esthetically pleasing curved roof of the peasant huts of Bengal. In these structures it is the crescent line of the eaves that provides the curved appearance of these ridge-and-rafter thatched roofs (King 1977).

8-8. A thatched hipped roof is typical of many structures in the Ganvie lagoon, Benin. Note the extra layers of thatch along the ridge to provide maximum rain protection at the most vulnerable area (photo by the author, 1980.

The simple gable roof form can also include several conspicuous, dramatic or visually satisfying components. In some islands of Indonesia, the end of the ridgeline, for example, may project forward and upward, thus creating a frame for a prominent outward-tilting gable wall, which is colorfully decorated. In central Europe, where the roofline is more restrained and is contained by verge boards parallel to the gable wall, dramatic and intricate gable half-timber decoration is frequently encountered. Traditional designs commonly vary over quite short distances and act as regional identifiers (Radig 1966, 23).

The ridgeline, because it is the highest, and thus most visible, part of the roof, often carries a number of ornamental and symbolic devices. These decorative features, together with the rituals associated with the placement of a ridgepole, are discussed in Chapter 12. The ridgeline is also a potential problem area at a location where providing a watertight covering is essential. Two techniques have been employed with wooden shingle roofs in order to provide the best seal across the ridgepole. One method is to use a double row of overlapping shingles along the ridgeline. In Holland, thatch roofs offered the same challenge, which was met by introducing a course of half-round tiles along the ridge (Jones 1918, 32), and in parts of Japan bundles of thatch placed across the ridge of gable roof *minka* form a protective cap over the ridge seam (Kawashima 2000, 199). Both techniques have the additional advantage of weighting down the thatch to protect against high wind damage.

The second and more widely used method with wooden shingles is to affix the topmost row of shingles on the side facing the prevailing winds, so that they extend a few inches above the ridgeline. This forces wind-driven rain up and over the ridge. Both techniques appear in photographs of African-American settlements in the Arkansas River valley (Gettys and Hughes-Jones 1981) and were also a feature of many pioneer settlements throughout America (Martin 1984, 23). The extension of shingles or shakes above the ridgeline is referred to as *combing* (Buchanan 1976, 69), and it is usually achieved by use of a longer shingle than on the rest of the roof (Figure 8-9).

Another area of the ridged roof combines artistic form with practical functions. French, German and other continental European houses often employ a device called *bell casting* in English or *coyau* in French, which is a change of pitch of the roof at the eaves, to throw the water as far as possible away from the wall to prevent erosion (Figure 8-10). It is called bell casting because in profile the gable roof now resembles a cross section of a bell with a flared rim (Figure 8-11). One technique used in Germany to form the bell cast involves adding a short additional piece to each rafter, placed to create a lower pitch at the eave. The addition to the rafter end is called an *ausshifter* (out thrower) (Stevens 1980/81, 84), and when used in England it bears the name of *sprocket piece* (Clifton-Taylor 1972, 272).

Another strategy to deflect water from the lower parts of a gable-roofed wall and to protect exterior plaster was use of the pent roof. On single-story structures the pent roof was carried across the taller gable walls about halfway up (Lehr 1976, 68). On two-story structures the pent often appeared on all four sides.

A unique variant of the basic gable form of roof was employed along the coast of northern California by the Yurok people. Of rectan-

8-9. *Reconstructed log building at New Salem State Park, Illinois. The ridge combing always slants upward and away from the direction of prevailing winds (photo by the author, 2002).*

gular ground plan and partially excavated, their dwellings were covered by a roof that was a normal gable on one side and a two slope (really a gambrel) on the other (Figure 7-4). No conclusive explanation for this elaboration of the simpler gable form has been advanced (Drucker 1965, 178), but achieving more headroom is a likely answer. Elsewhere on the Northwest Pacific Coast, roofs were either low-pitched gables or of shed type.

8-10. With little or no bell casting, the stucco wall plaster of this cottage near Osieja, Croatia has deteriorated and washed away because of the ground splash of rain. The adobe layers of the wall are exposed, and if not plastered again will begin to erode (photo by the author, 2004).

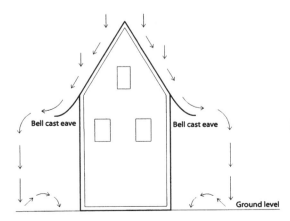

8-11. Diagram of the effect of bell-cast eaves, which direct the roof runoff away from the wall base. Back splash is thus eliminated, or at least greatly reduced (drawing by Amy Rock).

In the Tierra Amarilla area northwest of Santa Fe, New Mexico, traditional Hispanic houses, built of stone or adobe and having flat roofs, frequently support a wooden upper half-story with a gable roof, an Anglo-American introduction (Wilson 1991, 87). First described by A.W. Conway (1951), those that seemed to be the earliest ones offered access to the upper half-story "only by means of a ladder or outside stairway," from which he concluded that the "attico," "alto," or "sobra techo," as they were described in the area, was not an integral part of the building but a later addition to an earlier designed structure.

In other Hispanic buildings in New Mexico, the flat roof had a slight tilt to the east, west, or south to facilitate water drainage. The north was avoided to prevent freezing of water on the roof in winter due to consequent northern exposure (Boyd 1974, 9). Even though rainfall is very low in desert areas, when it does come it often is in short, heavy downpours. Regardless of temperature, such rains are potentially dangerous because of the easily dissolved adobe mud of which most traditional structures are built in desert and near-desert areas.

> Adobe roofs baked under the blazing sun normally provide adequate protection from the widely spaced desert rains. The capillary action that weakens walls also permits adobe roofs to absorb considerable rainwater. During heavy rains, the excess water must be removed from the flat roof by wooden or stone drains projecting through the parapets. Several types of roof drains, or *canales*, [are] used in Indian pueblos. The areas surrounding these drains represent potential trouble spots. Water spilling over or penetrating under the canales can rapidly destroy a large wall section if it is not kept under repair. (Noble 1984, 1:83)

Moisture at the junction of roof and walls is also a problem in more humid areas. In traditional houses with rectangular floor plans the roof is frequently fitted to the walls, that is, it has no overhang at the gables or eaves. Cape Cod cottages are examples of the *fitted roof* type (Figure 8-12), which barely overhangs the walls and is just large enough to protect their tops. This junction is one of the most critical places of the structure because it is so easily damaged by rain (Ghosh 1953, 21). In Scottish houses, "projection at eaves and gable is suppressed and the surface of the wall is continued into that of the roof with the least possible interruption" (quote in Wooley 1974, 292). Many buildings throughout China have similarly fitted roofs (Knapp 1989, 87).

On the Hebridean Islands west of Scotland, longhouses were constructed in such a way that the roof fitted almost *inside* the walls (Gailey 1962, 228). Colin Sinclair has grouped early housebarns of the Scottish highlands into three categories on the basis of roof type and

The Cape Cod cottage

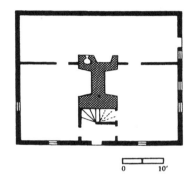

Floor plan of a Cape Cod cottage

roof–wall junction (Figure 8-13). The Hebridean type employs a hipped thatch roof secured to a wide stone and earth wall by ropes anchored to stone projections or corbels in the wall (Walker 1989, 2), or with fieldstones secured by ropes tied across the roof. The wall consisted of outer and inner stone parts with a cavity (*hearting*) filled with earth between. The entire wall system could be six or more feet thick.

> As the rainwater from the roof discharges upon the wall-top it is caught by the hearting, through which it percolates to the soil, thereby providing a damp blanket of earth which very effectively prevents those tempestuous winds to which the Hebridean isles are subject from penetrating the uncemented masonry of the wall.
>
> A nicety of detail is to be observed in the construction of the inner wall, wherein the stones are set with a slight cant upwards towards the inside with a view to preventing the passage of moisture from the hearthing to the interior.
>
> The composite wall of the Hebridean house may indeed be claimed as a forerunner of the system of cavity-wall and vertical damp-course

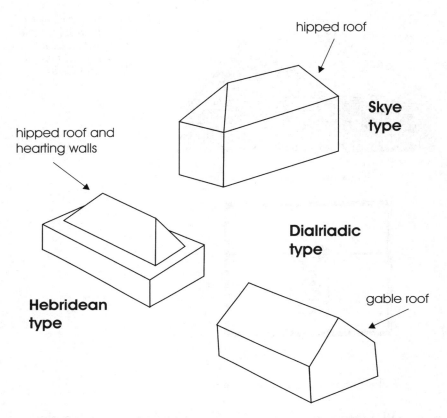

hipped roof

Skye type

hipped roof and hearting walls

Dialriadic type

gable roof

Hebridean type

8-13. Types of early housebarns from the Scottish highlands. The Hebridean type has a hipped roof contained within stone walls; the Skye type is also hipped roofed, but the eaves overhang; and the Dialriadic type is gable roofed (based upon Sinclair 1953, 63).

which features in the construction of modern buildings. (Sinclair 1953, 24)

The roof of the Bernese Middleland housebarn (Figure 2-8), on the other hand, is an excellent example of the *hooded roof* type. In these structures the walls do not *directly* support the roof, as is usually the case with the fitted roof. The hooded roof is particularly appropriate in regions of high rainfall, and especially in high snowfall locations, because moisture is kept well away from the walls and the base of the structure. This is also one of the reasons for the wide roof overhang of the traditional rural Japanese dwelling called a minka, but other considerations are perhaps even more important. In Japan the roof became a status symbol. It is what first catches the eye – massive tile-edged thatch roofs and helmet-shaped roofs. "The history of the Japanese minka is a history of roofs gradually increasing in size and grandeur, encompassing more and more space within their wide overhangs – including space beyond even the walls themselves" (Carver 1984, 138).

Most traditional buildings, however, possess roofs that are intermediate between hooded and fitted. They *are* supported by the walls, but they overhang both eaves and gable. The eave overhang serves two purposes. First, it directs the flow of rainwater from the roof away from the side walls, especially important when the walls are made of daub or a similarly vulnerable material. The larger the overhang, the further away from the wall will be the water when it strikes the ground and splashes back toward the lower part of the wall. A second function of an eave overhang is to cast a shadow upon the side windows and walls, thereby reducing interior temperatures in the hot season. The function is most effectively performed in those areas where strong seasonal contrasts exist in the elevation of the sun (Davis 1982). In Ontario in the 19th century a "second story gable over the front door became an increasingly popular means of improving light in the garret and keeping roof-snow off the doorway" (Cutts 1949, 204). Heavy snowfall also provides a rationale for the pronounced extension of the front gable in Rocky Mountain cabins (Wilson 1984, 34).

A gable overhang is not normally employed to moderate temperatures or to reduce light because relatively few windows occur in gable walls. Furthermore, the gable wall is much higher, and hence the overhang is not as effective in providing shade. In areas of considerable winter snow accumulation, and where the entrance door is located on the gable, the overhang has the function of keeping the door free of snow (Kilpinen 1995, 29), although a pent roof is perhaps more effective.

To a considerable extent, traditional buildings, because they provide shelter, reflect the climate in which they are built. Therefore it is not surprising that structures similar in appearance occur in widely separated locations, although little or no early human connection existed. The bohio – a light cane and thatch, or adobe and thatch, dwelling of the Indians of Panama – has a close physical resemblance to a similar structure built in two areas of Spain: the rugged mountains in Asturias in the extreme north and a similarly rugged area in Andalucia in the extreme south. The structures of the Spanish areas themselves do not seem to be related. With regard to the Panamanian dwellings, although the Spanish house is "almost identical in outward appearance and somewhat similar in floor plan, it differs considerably in construction techniques and materials" (Fuson 1964, 199–200).

Building has a *seasonal rhythm* governed by weather changes. The tipis of the Plains Indians, for example, were made in the spring "in preparation for the summer festivities and tribal gatherings" (Campbell 1915, 687). Immigrants to North America arriving from Europe were urged to arrive in spring so that a dugout could be prepared over the summer (Carson et al. 1981, 140). However, if a sod structure was contemplated, early fall was the optimum season. "If the sodbuster had a choice, he built in the Fall when the prairie grasses were wire-tough and woody, yet at a time when the ground was moist enough to hold the soil firmly to the sod bricks when they were lifted to the wagon box or stoneboat bed" (Welsch 1967, 337).

In western Canada, those who intended to erect log cabins, or even just claim shanties, were advised to peel the bark from cut-down trees during the month of June, when the recent run of the sap made removal an easy task, and before the tree had dried up, when the bark would often adhere tightly. Settlers in French Canada normally cut building timber in the winter, when other work did not supercede and to reduce the accumulation of sap (Moogk 1977, 39). Hewing green logs when the thermometer registered below freezing was also a Canadian custom in order to get "a silky cut" (Roe 1958, 4).

Elsewhere, seasonal conditions were also critical. Builders of "beehive" houses in Syria found themselves governed by two seasonal constraints if they wished to be successful. After the spring rains, adobe bricks had to be made in large quantity. Later, between harvests in mid- and late summer, the dome-shaped structure was built (Copeland 1955, 23). Among the Yoruba in West Africa, mud-wall houses are

> normally erected as the rainy season is giving place to the dry. Mixing the swish-mud, which needs plenty of water, and the drying of the successive layers of mud-wall, which requires spells of dry weather, can be more easily and profitably done at this time of the year. This period also coincides with the slack season on the farm. (Ojo 1967, 17)

Constructing a house in the Indonesian island of Sumbawa is a more complicated task, but still largely seasonally controlled. "The house-building process from beginning to end usually takes several years, since work is only done in the two-or-three month respite between harvesting and planting" (Just 1984, 40). Just how concentrated seasonal activities can be was shown by M.J. Meggitt (1957, 162) in New Guinea. Roughly one-quarter of the dwellings are replaced each year. As the rains begin to ease, building activity increases, giving the impression that the residents are eager to get started. When rain starts again in August building abruptly stops. Generally, in agricultural communities house building is an activity of the downtime, the dry period between rainy seasons close to the equator, the period after harvest (also the dry season) in the balance of the tropics, or the winter time, such as in the lower Himalaya (Bhatt 1986, 24).

Another area where building activities are strongly seasonal is the Thar desert of western India and extending into Pakistan. Roofs are thatched with a grass that grows only during the sparse rains of the monsoon "and is suitably dry by February to April. This is the main building season, following the cold winter and preceding the busiest agricultural season" (Cooper and Dawson 1998, 83).

In some instances elsewhere, however, other considerations are paramount. For low income African-Americans in the Chesapeake Bay area, June was the critical time for harvesting marsh grass for thatching of roofs. Before June the grass growing in marshes and along creeks was not long enough. After June it lost the natural "wax" content, which gave it a waterproofing character, and it also became too brittle to permit the required bending (McDaniel 1982, 86).

In Quebec and other higher latitude locations, the governing climatic feature was temperature.

> The building of a stone house in Eastern Canada was a race against the winter . . . The usual requirement was that the builder begin work just as soon as the weather permitted and, at the latest, by May 15th. The masonry walls and gables were to be ready to receive the woodwork by late June or early July and the house was to be roofed and complete by late September or, at least, in November. The winter weather would have done havoc to unprotected stonework. November 1st, All Saints' Day, was a popular terminal date, for it was then that indentured masonry workers were usually laid off. The choice of religious feast-days to mark off the completion of different stages of the project was a well-used practice . . . (Moogk 1977, 62)

Winters in northern United States and Canada can be extreme. Log buildings, a common traditional building type in these areas, require yearly maintenance to counteract the stresses of frost action. Shoring and leveling were required each spring and lost chinking had to be replaced (Brandt and Braatz 1972, 31). Frost and rainwater together were particularly difficult for masonry construction.

> Lime mortar cures slowly and, in a frost, it will be broken up by the expanding water crystals. At Quebec the mean temperature is above the freezing point from the end of March to mid-November. Rain is another factor, for it will wash away fresh mortar, not to speak of the discomfort for the mason. Masonry work is, therefore, further confined by the need

for dry and warm days. Precipitation in the Quebec region drops off sharply after April and it resumes at a high level in November. (Moogk 1977, 61–2)

Even among nomadic hunters a seasonal rhythm prevailed. Great Plains Indians, for example, prepared buffalo hides to be used as tipi covering in the spring season, although the sewing by women was a fall activity (Lowie 1922, 224). Among the Iroquois, who lived in bark houses, gathering of large bark sheets also was a spring season activity (Lyford 1945, 11) because bark was easier to peel at this time.

In a more indirect way, climate affects nomadic herders by controlling the growth of grasses, which determines the timing of the seasonal migration to new pastures (Ekvall 1968, 33). Some groups are so well attuned to their seasonally changing environment that they have identified otherwise inconspicuous agents of seasonal change. Perhaps the most delightful are the Eskimo, for whom the appearance of the snow bunting in late April or May is the signal to shift from the winter earth house and move to the sealskin tent (Ekblaw 1927, 161). The departure of the bird confirms the Eskimo recognition that a reverse movement of habitation is required.

Where great snow accumulates in the winter, extra care must be taken to prevent the buildup of ice along the eave line of timber-frame dwellings. This condition results when lofts or upper stories are heated, causing snow on the roof to melt. As soon as the meltwater reaches the colder areas of the gutter or the eave overhang it freezes. If enough ice collects, it acts as a dam to the melted snow that then finds its way into the interior of the structure. Traditional builders solved this problem by keeping the loft or attic unheated. In the Engadine of Switzerland a different strategy was employed: the construction of a double-layer roof with an insulating air layer between (Cereghini 1956, 180–1).

In areas where snowfall is heavy, the pitch of a gable roof may be extremely high in some places but quite low in others. A high roof pitch normally occurs where stone and slate are the roofing materials. Snow will slide easily from such surfaces. A secondary advantage is that the steep pitch orients the roof more directly to the sun's rays, thereby increasing insulation and rapid snowmelt. Whenever the roof materials are rougher (e.g. wooden planks, shingles, sod), a low roof pitch allows the snow to accumulate, providing an insulating blanket for the structure against the winter cold (Paulsson 1959, 21; Wilson 1984, 34). The frame of the building must be sturdy. In Scandinavia, Switzerland and Austria an upraised plank along the eaves helps keep the snow from sliding off (Davey 1971, 38). In the snowy mountains of Japan, the timber-frame roofs are provided with metal hooks or long beams to anchor the snow. A permanent roof ladder provides a means of access when the accumulated snow needs to be removed. The increased insulation provided by the snow results in inhabitants moving upstairs during the winter season (Nishi 1967, 243).

While winter and snow require careful planning and sturdy building, the ravages of heavy rain and high winds generally are more serious problems for traditional buildings. Weather and climate exert an important influence on dwelling sites. Exposed sites are avoided, especially in the middle latitudes where gale winds offer periodic hazards. In Ireland, "where there is free choice, shelter from the westerly gales appears to be the first consideration in the selection of a dwelling site." It is said "one method of choosing was to let the wind decide by throwing up a hat on a stormy day and noting its resting place (Evans 1939, 209).

Rainfall is always a factor that influences building activity to a greater or lesser degree. A fine example has been supplied from Australia, where different procedures are employed due to variations in rainfall patterns.

> In New South Wales, where the weather is reasonably reliable, it became the practice to construct and fix the stumps, the bearers, the joists and the flooring-boards before the walls or roof were erected in order to obtain a flat free-working area as quickly as possible. In Victoria with its prolonged wet spells of wind-driven rain, wet floor-boards became badly stained around nail holes so the frame was erected, the walls sheeted and the roof covered before any flooring was laid. In Queensland, where the rain when it comes is a deluge that falls straight down, the practice was to erect the frame, cover the roof, lay the flooring and lastly sheet the walls. (Cox and Freeland 1969, 58)

Christian Kleinert (1976, 200), working in the Himalaya, has offered a general observation that relates house building to variation in both rainfall and temperature. As one moves from east to west, rainfall steadily decreases. The roof pitch, which is quite high in the humid east to shed rain from thatch covering, also decreases until in the western Himalaya only flat mud roofs are encountered. A similar, but much less significant, decline in precipitation occurs from south to north. In this direction, because altitude increases, it is temperature, especially that of winter, which affects buildings the most. The light wood materials of housing give way first to heavier timber and finally to stone at the higher elevations. The form of the house also changes from structures surrounding a courtyard to houses "more closed, showing thick walls and a few openings only."

The combination of cold and wind has always been the nemesis of traditional builders in the middle and higher latitudes. In Japan, "when winter brings cold days, cold winds and snow, the tropical [original Japanese] house with its paper covered walls and matting floors calls for plenty of fortitude" (Earle 1943, 280). Perhaps surprisingly, protection against cold has also been a consideration for builders in tropical areas. In such areas, the constantly warm temperature and high humidity of the tropical environment during the day made the significant drop in temperature with the setting sun not only uncomfortable but unhealthy because of the lingering high humidity. Nevertheless, the stormy combination of precipitation, high wind, and cold temperatures was most troublesome in the abruptly shifting weather of the mid-latitudes.

Traditional builders were alert to the necessity of taking precautions against recurring weather problems. In the St. Lawrence valley, most early French buildings were built of adobe or stone. Generally, only one wall was covered by clapboards in this area of prevailing northeasterly gale winds. The clapboarding protected the mortar against moisture driven into joints by the strong winds (Cameron 1982, 19). Similarly, in Rhode Island, British colonists were forced by the greater severity of New England winters, as opposed to those of Britain, to abandon half-timber construction and to substitute clapboard or shingles for better insulation (Downing 1937, 5).

Perhaps the extreme example of the effect of prevailing winds is given by the hamlet of Cillrialaig in Ireland, where the entire settlement was relocated to avoid their destructive effect. Originally,

> the village lay further to the west and at the other side of the road, but as the prevailing wind rebounded from the precipitous hill overlooking the village a secondary wind-current was formed which proved so destructive to the thatch-roofs that the village was eventually changed to its present more sheltered site. (Campbell 1935, 68)

As well stated by Colin Sinclair (1953, 15), the traditional dwelling in the Gaelic highlands of Scotland "was not the object of domestic luxury and embellishment; it was a house to shut out the storm."

Even where shutting out the storm was not a major consideration the wind could affect building. In Key West, Florida, for example, walls generally lacked plaster, both inside and out, because the shifting of the structure, periodically experienced in high winds, would crack the plaster (Caemmerer 1992, 23). Consideration for prevailing winds also influenced the form of the Plains Indian's tipi, which rose more steeply at the rear, facing the wind, than in the front containing the doorway (Campbell 1915, 691). Such an arrangement had the further important advantage of shifting the apex opening of the tipi away from a position directly over the central fire pit, thereby reducing the potential for rain to fall on the fire.

Wind can be most damaging and dangerous, especially in short, intense bursts. In Ontario, one extreme preventive practice was to chop down all nearby trees so that during a storm log barns, and presumably residences, would not be damaged (Buck 1930, 9). In all areas, strong winds play havoc with roofing materials. Wooden shakes and shingles can be lifted in a violent storm, and thatch easily blown away, a condition that calls for various methods to tie or weight down the thatch. In some valleys of Switzerland roof pitches are extremely low as a defense against the very strong föhn winds blowing downslope (Jacquet 1963, 59).

Northeastern North America and much of Europe were ideally suited for thatch roofing. Not only were reeds, grasses and other suitable plants abundant, the damp climate kept the thatch moist, thus reducing both fire risk and wind damage. Since gable roof edges are the most susceptible to wind lifting, the use of the four-slope hipped roof lowered wind resistance (Fenton 1978, 36). Wind can also be a destructive force with other kinds of roofing. Gable roofs are especially vulnerable. Janice Stewart (1972, 27) notes that in Norway, "boards called *vindskier* were fastened to the edge of the roof to prevent the wind from getting underneath the sod and bark and tearing it loose."

In the Midwest and mid-south of the United States, a high proportion of rural dwellings have an adjacent excavated structure called a *cyclone cellar* (Figure 8-14). In this part of the world, the early vernacular term for a tornado was cyclone. Detached from the house but close enough to be reached quickly in time of need, it provides shelter and emergency supplies. Covered by almost horizontal, heavy, wooden or iron slab doors, from which steep steps lead downward, they are just large enough for the family. "Sometimes they hide their identity by calling them storehouses" (Kniffen 1968, 28), and they do often serve a secondary use as a cold cellar. Charles McRaven (1980, 127) observes that such cellars are often colloquially referred to as "fraidy holes" because snakes and other creatures find them attractive. Michael Roark (1992, 45) suggests that the highest density of storm cellars occurs in the mid-South, where tornado frequency combines with a general lack of house basements. Roark also provides a vivid impression of the childhood experience of taking refuge in such a haven:

> From my childhood experience it can be described as a dark, partially underground cement box with damp concrete walls covered with the slimy tracks of slugs, a floor gritted with dead black roaches and rap-

idly filling with water, an entrance festooned with spidery cobwebs, and a tin-metal door drumming from the pounding rain in symphonic rhythm with the clanging metal chain and the thunder. This ghastly scene was lit by a smoking kerosene lamp and frequent blue arcs of lighting. To be in such a structure was fortunate in comparison to the fate of those who would have fled to the earthen floor and rock-walled folk structure of the storm cellar. It had all the entomological companions previously described, plus the intrusion of other occasional troglodytes, such as the water moccasin or copperhead swimming over ones toes.

In a somewhat similar vein, but much less picturesquely, David Buisseret (1980, 3) mentions that strong vaulted underareas in various Caribbean islands are designed as "hurricane shelters." Carol Jopling (1988) confirms their presence in Puerto Rico. The typhoons of the Pacific also wreak havoc on the light materials of traditional housing. Yap in the Caroline Islands, for example, "had 93% of its homes destroyed by a typhoon in 1925 and many houses destroyed again in 1967. The Yapese, however, are culturally the most conservative of all Micronesians, and it is on Yap, where typhoons strike most frequently, that one finds the greatest proportion of traditional houses" (Webb 1975, 99–100).

The roof is so critical that people will often do away with almost every other constructional element – walls, doors and so on. Early dwellings in New Zealand even dispensed with roof supports and rested the roof snugly on the ground. Today the modern A-frame design follows the same concept. For traditional structures, roofing materials extend over a wide range from light vegetative items to those of heavy earth.

8-14. Drawing of a Midwest "cyclone cellar" and an advancing tornado (from the cover of the journal Material Culture 24:2; sketch by Marylin Mehl. Courtesy of the Pioneer America Society).

Regardless of composition, the main function of the roof is to protect the structure from the weather and climate. The major climatic elements that the roof battles against are rain, snow, and wind. Once any roof of a traditional building is breached, deterioration of the entire building begins.

~ 9 ~

Threats: Man-Made and Natural Hazards

Winds and rains, heavy snowfall and dust storms, the timber rot of humid areas, the frost cracks of winter freezes, and all the other potentially damaging effects of climate and weather are only some of the hazards that affect traditional buildings. The historical record is clearest for cities. It shows well how critical natural and man-made disasters have been. For example, in Charleston, South Carolina in the 18th and 19th centuries, five great fires (1700, 1740, 1778, 1838 and 1861), 10 destructive hurricanes, and earthquakes in 1811 and 1886, all took their toll of traditional buildings (Simons 1927, 19). Nearby, large fires in Savannah, Georgia in 1796 and 1820 wiped out most of that city's 18th-century houses (Stanford 1975, 113). After fires in 1771 and 1775 completely destroyed the wooden buildings of St. George's, Granada, rebuilding was legally restricted to the use of bricks, stone and tile (Groome 1964, 32), totally changing the urbanscape. In Bridgetown, Barbados, disastrous fires virtually leveled the town in 1658/59, 1668 and 1675. The devastation of these fires was augmented by hurricanes and severe earthquakes. "So massive was the destruction on Barbados, and so short of good materials were the settlers, that they felt it necessary to send to Boston for ready-hewn and fitted house frames" (Edwards 1980, 313).

In the countryside, because population densities were lower and civil organization less effective, the record is less clear. Think for a moment of the Great Peshtigo Fire, the greatest fire in North America in the 19th century, which devastated enormous areas, destroyed traditional dwellings on both sides of Green Bay, and killed thousands. As recorded by the simple instruments of the US Weather Bureau, the Peshtigo firestorm was the result of a prolonged drought period followed by a record-setting low-pressure system that generated extremely high winds to fuel the conflagration. The event lies almost forgotten because it was largely ignored at the time since it occurred on the same day as the Chicago Fire. This situation persists, despite the fact that Peshtigo was a much larger conflagration (Gess and Lutz 2002).

Largely overlooked as a continuing problem of man-made hazards is the pressure of steadily growing populations. With cities sprawling out over the surrounding countryside, the demand for more and more facilities requiring ever more space, increases in land costs and value, and the pressure resulting from increasing demand for limited supplies of traditional building materials are all a consequence of growing population pressures. One simple and almost forgotten example of the impact on traditional building is provided by South Africa, where increasing population numbers in the 19th century caused a critical shortage of grasses suitable for building, largely because of increased demand. The result was the gradual introduction of less suitable and inferior wattle-and-daub walling to replace grass thatch (Frescura 1981, 13), thereby entirely changing the character of the settlements.

One of the world's most distinctive areas of vernacular stone buildings is in the Cotswold area of England (Hill and Birch 1994). Here outcrops of limestone, which weathers to a golden hue, supply the principal building materials, used at least since the 14th century. Cottages of original hall and parlor and three-room cross-passage plans now have been extensively altered to provide today's wide variety of

9-1. An excellent example of unsympathetic rehabilitation. The huge buttresses applied to this Cotswold cottage destroy much of the original character of the structure (drawing by Iraida Galdon Soler, based on Hill and Birch 1994, 98).

house types. As happens elsewhere, the original structures are under the threat of unsympathetic restoration as transportation systems improve, permitting affluent urbanites to escape the confines of the city to relocate in this idylic setting. Such *unsympathetic rehabilitation* is not a new phenomenon. Figure 9-1 provides a Cotswold example from the 19th century.

Closely connected to population growth pressures elsewhere are the more subtle (and sometimes not so subtle) actions of colonial administrations to improve the lot of "natives." Many officials were well intentioned, but an equal number viewed native peoples as primitive, unclean, and ignorant. The consequence of both attitudes was pressure on the people to give up their traditional ways of life, including buildings, and adopt a more "modern" approach (Tremblay et al. 1954, 217). Two objectives energized these pressures. One was the desire to control native populations by making them more productive so that taxes could be higher, and more effectively collected. This often meant moving peoples out of hilly, remote areas to lowland sites, where cash crops could be grown. Some administrators in Africa were so zealous that they actually undertook campaigns to burn down traditional dwellings to drive out hill peoples (Denyer 1978, 189).

The other objective was to replace native religions with Christianity. Here the greatest pressure came from missionaries, but if and when disputes arose between the native peoples and the missionaries, colonial administrators invariably sided with their own kind, the missionaries. Not all missionary activity had a negative effect on indigenous populations. Education and public health benefited considerably. Some sympathetic missionaries even helped preserve native culture, usually indirectly by authoring first-hand accounts and observations. Father Berard Haile, working among the Navajo Indians, may be cited as a good example. More often than not, however, the missionary attitude was to eradicate as much of native culture as possible because so much of it was religion based. Only then would Christianity prevail. This activity was especially prevalent in the Pacific Northwest where, for example, *all* native house types were destroyed. Only gradually has Native American culture begun to reassert itself, and structures of traditional design to be built again in small numbers.

In the southwestern United States, similar pressures existed, with only the largest groups, such as the Navajo, able to resist successfully, at least up to a point. "Before the mid-1920s, U.S. Indian administration was committed to transforming Indian communities into variants of the dominant American culture as quickly as possible" (Dozier

1970, 15). The pressures were extreme and the result often devastating to the Native American tribes. The Mescalero Apache were "tamed" by being forced into a reservation to follow sedentary agriculture. There, in the later part of the 19th century, the Indian agent required them to build log cabins rather than to continue use of their tipis and *wickiups* (Henderson 1992, 21). The native people were not allowed any input into the house design. The log structures were built, but the Apache often erected the tipi close by. This continued as their residence while the cabin was used for storage. So much for the subservience of the Apache to alien authority! Remember though, that the Apache were among the most militant of Indian tribes. Father Haile (1954, 10) noted a similar situation among the Navajo, who also frequently continued to live in their hogan while the modern frame house, recently built with the aid of government funding, was used for storage purposes.

The United States and Canada in their dealings with "Indian" groups can be viewed much as colonial powers. The major difference from European countries is that the US and Canada in these instances saw the area where these native populations lived as contiguous extensions of their respective countries, into which their own people would expand. European colonial possessions were distant places that provided economic support to the metropolitan country. Settlement by colonials in most instances was limited or of temporary duration, although long-term impact upon indigenous populations was profound. A 20th-century movement among the Navajo away from Christianity and back toward their traditional religious beliefs (Tremblay et al. 1954 , 216–17) has had as one unplanned result, the preservation of some hogans. Earlier, the hogan (or even the replacement house, if one had been built) was burned down as a matter of course whenever an inhabitant died within it, but this tradition has not yet been revived.

Not all colonial efforts at replacing traditional dwellings had a religious or immediate economic motive. The Japanese administration in the Caroline Islands encouraged modernization and improvement of houses as a public health measure, although admittedly they sought long-term economic benefit (Webb 1975, 99 & 102). Many officials of other colonial powers and their native successors have had similar motivation. Charles Cockburn (1962, 299) remarks about a village in northern Ghana, "the old Gonja tribal village of round houses with thatched roofs has been swept away by new official brooms and replaced by courtyard buildups imitated from Ashanti, Brong – Ahafo and the Accra plain to the south. They are thought by the authorities to be more progressive and hygienic." This southern house-type of lateritic walls and corrugated metal roof "is gradually spreading northwards into more primitive areas and replacing old tribal architecture. Following hard on its trail is the European-style bungalow."

Even such a simple circumstance as the improvement of accessibility usually leads to changes in, or rejection of, traditional dwellings. Across the world in Amazonian Peru, the return of more "advanced" tribal members into the remote Mayo valley has introduced a "modern" house type, which is likely to replace the traditional oval structure (Figure 9-2).

All of the non-traditional houses belong to Aguaruna teachers who immigrated from the Maranon Valley. While the Maranon immigrants bring with them a broader vision of the outside world than that of the traditional Mayo native, they have other reasons for constructing lumber and tin houses. Teachers receive a salary from the Ministry of Education and are also likely cultivate rice, thus giving them additional income to purchase tin roofing material and the labor for making wooden boards. Most of the teachers, and particularly those constructing new houses, have been in the Mayo Valley five to ten years. Only in the last two years have the more acculturated teachers constructed houses that architecturally and symbolically separate them from their native Aguaruna tradition (Works 1985, 12).

Basically similar is the situation occurring in South Asia, providing a more immediate threat to traditional building because the volume of income influx is substantial. In both Kerala state, India and in Bangladesh, workers returning from the oil-rich areas of the Middle

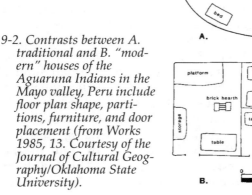

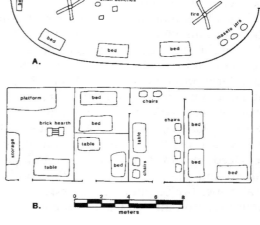

9-2. Contrasts between A. traditional and B. "modern" houses of the Aguaruna Indians in the Mayo valley, Peru include floor plan shape, partitions, furniture, and door placement (from Works 1985, 13. Courtesy of the Journal of Cultural Geography/Oklahoma State University).

East have put a significant proportion of their earnings into rebuilding dwellings with modern materials, form and innovations (Noble 2003, 68–9; Paul 2003, 106).

An array of other factors, which may also be grouped under the heading of "modernization," encourage modifications that change the character of traditional buildings. These factors include the expansion of structures by additions, both horizontally and vertically, by changes in roof type, by addition or repositioning of doors and windows (Figure 9-3), and other structural modifications. In some instances these changes are the result of the introduction of new technology, often accompanying colonial administration. Gillian Feeley-Harnik (1980, 567–8) cites the example of the introduction of the sawmill to Madagascar as promoting the change from sliding light-material panel doors to European-type plank doors set in wooden frames and held by hinges and locks.

Not all technological changes are detrimental or inappropriate. In the American Southwest, puddled adobe, a technique used by Native Americans, gave way to the use of adobe brick introduced by Spaniards. The walling method changed, but adobe continued to be used and the structures were not greatly altered in appearance. The replacement of puddled adobe by rammed earth in other parts of the world provides other closely related examples. Figure 9-4 offers a dif-

9-3. New construction with modern window openings will gradually change the appearance of the Taos Pueblo, New Mexico (photo by the author, 1967).

9-4. *Stilt house in Brunei in which modern concrete pillars are replacing traditional wooden ones. Nevertheless, the character of the structure is not much
altered because the posts, although different in material, are quite similar in
form (from Hansen 1995, 34. Courtesy of Eric Hansen/Saudi Aramco World/
PADIA).*

ferent type of acceptable modification, in this case of a stilt house.
This well-maintained structure in the middle bend of the Brunei River
is in the process of having its posts of iron wood and mangrove timber gradually replaced by concrete piers. The appearance is altered
somewhat, but the basic traditional aspect and condition of the house
is not violated (Hansen 1995). At the beginning of the 20th century,
sheets of corrugated iron began to cover wooden walls in coastal Iceland to combat frigid temperatures, unusually brisk winds, and the
absence of other economical walling materials (Abrecht 2000, 9 & 21).

Although these changes were technical improvements, other
changes may be motivated by social pressures that manifest themselves in a desire of the inhabitants not to be regarded as primitive,
out-of-date or old-fashioned. These pressures grow as generations
succeed one another. Charlotte Wilcoxen (1984, 87) calls this "the van-
dalism of progress" and John Milbauer (2004, 2) refers to it as "the
juggernaut of popular culture." Navajo children, taken away from the
Reservation and forced to live in a government Indian school, ultimately were among the strongest pressure groups influencing the
adoption of White housing to replace the traditional hogans (Tremblay et al. 1954, 217–18).

Henry Glassie (1999, 273) offers an example of how violent the reactions can be when a younger generation rejects the objects and values of the older. He cites a situation in Ireland: "when Dick Cutler moved his family into Ellen Cutler's house after her death, her dresser of Delft displayed to him, as it had to her, communal connections and an old-fashioned taste. The difference was that he hated what she loved. He took an axe, smashed the china to bits, and threw it out in the street."

Social status is also a factor operating to modify traditional architecture. In Nigeria,

> the two-storeyed house locally called an "upstairs" made its appearance earlier first in the Delta and then on the Cross River and was built in his home village by every really wealthy trader as a monument to his power and financial prowess. . . . The idea of a house with an upper storey raised off the ground derived from a Victorian invention which, when first introduced into the Delta and the Cross River, was called an "iron house". This was a prefabricated timber-framed bungalow, roofed with corrugated iron and raised above the ground on cast-iron piles or in some cases brick columns. Most of the house consisted of an open verandah, which completely surrounded two small rooms. There was no kitchen and no servants' quarters; these were expected to be constructed locally and to be separate from the house. This type of bungalow seems to have been made in considerable quantity in Britain during the nineteenth century for export to the tropics. (Jones 1984, 100–1)

Partially related to these ideas is the gradual substitution of modern materials for traditional (O'Danachair 1957, 61). Sometimes the new materials are cheaper or more durable, and their use, therefore, not surprising, but as Roland Rees and Carl J. Tracie (1978) suggest, modernization has a leveling effect. Speaking of the settlement by immigrant groups of the Canadian Prairies, but in terms that have widespread application, they note that

> time replaces the distinctive with the common currency of the host culture . . . Homogenization of the region's housing inevitably has stripped the landscape of much of its interest and culture . . . Gone, too, from many of the more recent farmsteads is the traditional shelterbelt, as familiar an icon of prairie settlement as the grain elevator. Wantonly exposed to wind, sun, and drifting snow, new houses on the prairie are the epitome of technological arrogance.

In the Brunei example cited above, concrete pillars, which are more durable, unobtrusively replace mangrove and ironwood piles (Figure 9-4). In many other instances, however, modern materials are less environmentally suitable. Building with "tightly fitted milled lumber" for walls, and flooring, with a corrugated-metal roof and louvered glass windows, greatly hinders the "easy movement of air through the building" in other Brunei stilt houses, thus negating one of the most important aspects of the traditional nipa palm structure (Hansen 1995, 36–7). The popularization of corrugated iron, the so-called tin roofs, in tropical areas is an excellent example of the introduction of environmentally unsuited materials. These metal surfaces conduct great amounts of heat into the dwelling, much more than do traditional roof materials. See Chapter 8 for additional problems with tin roofs.

Early colonial settlers in Australia also faced the problem of heat buildup with galvanized roofs. Several strategies were employed to minimize the heat problem, but none was entirely effective:

> Straw thatching could be laid as an insulation before fixing the iron sheets; the bulk of the roof space could be augmented by increasing the pitch, thus giving a larger volume of insulating air; the hot air in it could be kept moving out in numerous ways – ventilators in gables, perforations or inlets in the eaves lining, outlets near the ridge or, best of all, a combination of eaves inlet and small ventilating gables at the apex of hipped roofs. (Cox and Freeland 1969, 59)

Walls, also made of sheets of iron, were a more difficult problem.

The preservation of an adequate number and variety of basically unaltered buildings is certainly necessary to show that the material cultural landscape of an area changed with the passage of time. "But the implication is that change occurred by discrete steps, and that entire units were constructed all at once, never again to be altered by more than a different coat of paint" (McIlwraith 1983, 111). Nothing could be farther removed from the truth! Almost all buildings, especially traditional ones, are in a state of continual, albeit often gradual, change. This process is one of the most difficult problems facing the historic preservationist. What should be preserved and emphasized?

Another almost irresistible source of pressure to modify traditional housing comes from the insurance industry. Rates for the use of "modern" materials are usually lower than for traditional. This is certainly the case in Europe with roofing. Gwyn Meirion-Jones (1982, 47) cites the pressure of French insurers to have thatch roofs replaced by slate. In Canada, disused log cabins, replaced by frame houses, are often torched to reduce insurance, as well as to lower taxes.

Finally, there is the exploitation of local resources by non-local interests. In northern Thailand, for example, in recent years, teak – which was a standard building material for traditional buildings –

has become a very expensive commodity, mainly because of the heavy exploitation of the Thai teak forests by foreign companies and their local affiliates. This exploitation has led to nationalization of all forests in an attempt to re-establish forestry as a source of national income. Consequently, the peasants have no longer been allowed to cut timber for their own use. (Haagensen 1982, 113).

The traditional building material, wood, has thus become prohibitively expensive, and recourse to concrete and brick much more common for ordinary housing (Chaichongrak et al. 2002, 155).

A quite differently, and almost diametrically oriented force, that of wildlife conservation and the establishment of natural resource reserves and parks, also often works against the preservation of traditional dwellings. In Nepal,

> native lowlanders often find themselves resettled in villages shared with other ethnic groups, many of whom originate in the hills and mountains. This mixture often results in villages lacking social structure and unity, as well as any singular pattern of housing styles associated with a specific ethnic group or environmental condition. Resettlement villages are designed mainly for expediency, often with little concern about vernacular architecture, ethnic cohesiveness, or traditional adherence to housing styles. (Zurick and Shrestha 2003, 26)

The establishment of the Great Smoky Mountains National Park in the US in 1926 also required the displacing of several thousand residents of that area. "After an early policy change that halted the wholesale elimination of the cultural landscape, the National Park Service used the preservation of traditional culture as an implicit justification for the park's creation." But so many traditional structures had been destroyed by then that the cultural landscape created for park visitors was no longer a faithful representation of the original (Williams 2001).

Destruction of habitat sites also occurs throughout the world in the name of economic development. One of the better documented cases involves the destruction of early settlement sites on the Black Mesa in northeastern Arizona by open pit mining operations of the Peabody Mining Company (Warburton 1985, 70). Such destruction is not an isolated or unique situation. I remember walking behind a bulldozer in Guatemala City in 1963 as it leveled prehistoric settlement mounds. Shards littered the ground and I was able to collect several obsidian knives unearthed by the machines. No thought was given by the developers to preserving any of the objects.

The drive for development in underdeveloped countries, while commendable as an economic strategy, often neglects to understand the importance and value of traditional culture (Knapp 2003, 7).

"When tradition is lost, not only are settlement patterns and house forms lost but the very relationships on which cultural identity and survival are based are lost" (Henderson 1992, 16). Traditional buildings are usually sacrificed on the altar of development.

Even in developed countries the drive for additional development goes on inexorably. However, those who pay the highest price are often those who benefit least from such "improvement" or whose lives are disrupted. The building of the Falcon dam in Texas and the filling of its reservoir created an emotional trauma for those displaced by it:

> Places that tied the former occupants to the scenes of their own memories existed no longer. The sites where one could relate the continuity of his own personal existence to the fruitful contributions of those who preceded him were gone forever. Former residents were physically and emotionally disoriented because they had lost the feeling of comfort attached to a stable environmental image ... Growth and change are normal functions of life during time. The concern is with how and where growth will happen as well as with the quality of life resulting from this interaction. (George 1975, 80)

To cite another example, beautifully decorated houses in southern Egypt and northern Sudan were inundated by the rising waters of the Aswan Dam and the Nubian villagers were compelled to relocate at a great distance in new houses of corrugated metal and cement (Wenzel 1972, 6). Thirty-five thousand Nubians in Sudan were moved. The new dwellings were considered by the relocated inhabitants to have poorly ventilated kitchens, to be too small, and so closely crowded as to have privacy invaded. The government-employed builders of the houses "defend those designs by pointing out that the small compact units are the fastest and cheapest to build. Such arguments are lost on the proud Nubians who have long been famous in Sudan for their spacious living quarters" (Lee 1969b, 38–9).

A different situation, but ultimately similar in result, is taking place in the outer islands of Indonesia.

> More and more often, traditional houses are being replaced by houses on the modern Javanese model, built of brick and cement with galvanized iron roofs. Often this is simply because modern houses are more comfortable, cheaper to build, and require less maintenance than traditional houses. In other cases modern houses are built by wealthy or important figures in the community as a conscious denial of the traditional ethnic past and as a means of identifying with the Javanese-dominated national culture of the present. (Just 1984, 31)

The danger to traditional structures from population pressures and the attractiveness of modernization are on-going problems that, although significant, attract little attention. After all of the above has been said, it must be remembered that one of the impelling reasons for abandoning traditional practices and patterns so readily today is "that modern technology and materials offer vast improvements in physical comfort and convenience" (Carver 1981, 27).

Often more noticeable than the human responses are natural hazards because of their catastrophic nature. These include storms, volcanic eruptions, earthquakes, and fire, but structures are not immune to other kinds of devastation. Wars and revolutions take their toll (Morse 1886, 45). Few log cabins earlier than 1862 can be found in southern Minnesota because the Sioux Indian uprising in that year destroyed almost all of them (Klammer 1960, 72). In England, few dwellings were built in the 1640s and 1650 as a consequence of the Civil War (Barley 1987, 183), and on the Continent centuries of land warfare have played havoc with traditional buildings.

The power to resist the government and the military is difficult in periods of emergency. Christopher Weeks (1996, 17–18) reports on the destruction of traditional colonial period buildings in Harford County, Maryland in World War I when "the U.S. Army condemned virtually all Harford's bay-frontage in 1917 and turned productive tomato patches and peach orchards into weapons-testing sites." Finally, in World War II, the last standing 200-year-old house was experimentally fire-bombed by the army. Sic transit gloria mundi!

The scale of wars and the devastation caused by larger armies and greater fire power in the 20th century increases the chances of traditional buildings being destroyed, even though cities now bear the brunt of warfare. Consider for a moment the scenes of destruction from Normandy and Russia in World War II, or the eradication of entire villages of bamboo, palm and other light materials during the Vietnam War. In northern Norway, prefabricated dwellings almost entirely replaced traditional log structures, as a result of German scorched-earth practices in World War II (Hegstad 1997, 53).

Civil unrest and disturbances may also result in changes in traditional buildings. For example, after the Indian Mutiny in 1857, during which many houses were destroyed by incendiaries, thatching was outlawed in British cantonment settlements (Kipling 1911, 308), and it rapidly fell out of favor in other Indian urban settlements. In another example,

> The absence of timber construction in Ireland can, perhaps, best be explained by the disappearance of the essential material as a result of the leveling of the woods for which the country was famous in the past.

This was coupled with the widespread destruction of the houses of the people, particularly of the better placed, in the wars, revolts and clearances which followed each other in unending succession in the sixteenth, seventeenth and eighteenth centuries. (O'Danachair 1957, 71)

In Sudan early in the 20th century, civil unrest, combined with famine and plague, "were manifested by the abandonment of permanent mud structures and the construction of temporary grass dwellings. After the 1920s, however, prosperity blessed the Sudan, and the grass huts were abandoned for the more substantial and prestigious earth houses" (Lee 1969, 396). Current problems in Sudan, however, have undoubtedly erased much of the advances experienced after the 1920s as reported by David Lee.

Also acting as threats to traditional buildings are a range of *natural hazards* over which mankind has very limited control, although some technologies and strategies have been evolved over time to lessen their impact and destructiveness. Probably the most significant hazards have been fire, earthquakes and violent storms. At the same time, degradation by termites and other wood-consuming insects and fungal growth, although gradual, is a continuing menace in all humid environments. The threat is especially severe where both temperatures and humidity are constantly high (McIntosh 1974, 163). Even as far poleward as such diverse locations as the United States and Australia, termite destruction is a major problem: "Termites are formidable, capable of eating through several layers of sheet lead in order to reach their goal – wood of any kind, preferably softwood" (Archer 1987, 101). Other vermin also may be a problem. One of the reasons given for the 18th-century substitution by brick of timber and wattle and daub as the generally accepted building material in Lancashire and Cheshire was better protection against rats and other vermin (Singleton 1952, 81).

Mention also must be made of volcanic eruptions as catastrophic forces of destruction (Krissdottir 1982, 8). Most people will recall stories of the destruction of Pompeii. More graphic television images of peasants fleeing from erupting cones in the Philippines, the Caribbean, the Andes of South America and throughout the Mediterranean area are fixed in our minds. The paradox is that these same volcanoes produce exceptionally fertile soils and the areas clustered around them support high density rural populations, most of whom use traditional methods in securing shelter. The volcanoes even provide some of the building materials. In the Teotihuacán valley, wall plaster is actually made from crushed volcanic ash (Charlton 1969, 286–7); easily cut volcanic rock provides a basic building material in many parts of the world.

The destructive force of the wind has been mentioned in the previous chapter. In particularly destructive storms such as hurricanes and tornadoes, devastation can be of great magnitude as any viewer of modern-day television can attest. The middle sections of North America are the places most vulnerable to tornado destruction. Here tornado winds probably rival fire as a destroyer of traditional structures. Rebuilding is rarely with construction materials or building forms that approximate the original.

Hurricanes, variously termed cyclones, typhoons or some other local designation, primarily affect islands and continental coastal areas in both tropical and mid-latitudes. These storms devastate much wider areas than do tornadoes. Just how destructive can hurricanes be? Remember that the typhoon of 1925 is estimated to have destroyed 93% of all houses in Yap Island of the Carolines (Webb 1975, 99).

Hurricanes are such an ever-present potential danger in Bermuda that they have influenced the form of dwelling roofs. Early eave projections were limited to just eight inches or so beyond the line of the wall because anything longer presented a danger of wind lifting during a hurricane (Raine 1966, 25). The walls themselves were strengthened against the hurricanes by placing the hearth and chimney stack to the south, the usual direction of the storms.

The effect of earthquakes on traditional building has been largely neglected, although Frederick Aalen (1984, 62) did report that in the Greek Ionian Islands, rebuilding after earthquakes changes the composition of the cultural landscape. After the event, traditional buildings of gable roof and rectangular plan were replaced by hipped roof, squarish-plan houses, dramatically altering the appearance of the villages. The violence of such earthquakes is profound. The quake of 1953 was so destructive that in the village of Vasilikades in Cephallenia, Greece all houses save one were destroyed (Vryonis 1975, 401). Despite such significant impact, the effect of earthquakes on traditional structures has been little explored by researchers beyond the recording of the scope and severity of destruction, and this is often limited to urban areas, probably because population density there provides greater visual impact (Figure 9-5). One unusual effect associated with earthquakes in mountainous areas where traditional buildings predominate is the great danger that exists from rockfalls and tumbling boulders, often of enormous size (Ambrasseys et al. 1975).

With regard to traditional building, Clarence Cullimore (1948) has noted the damage to adobe houses in Santa Barbara, California, and Dimitri Philippides (1983) to stone structures on the island of Lesbos, Greece. Arnold Smith (1962, 30) merely states that the great majority

9-5. Damage to a compound wall, resulting from a severe earthquake in the 1970s in Sian, China (photo by the author, 1977).

of vernacular houses were partially ruined by an earthquake in 1881 in the island of Chios in the Dodecanese. Other references are usually even more fragmentary.

Because of frequent earthquakes of strong intensity, on both the Greek mainland and islands, the damage to traditional buildings has received considerably more attention there than elsewhere. Demetrius Porphyrios (1971, 31) reports that "destructiveness was so widespread and so devastating that it forced the inhabitants to evolve special building methods." These include stone foundations, timber frames with brick nogging in small independently framed panels, wooden corner elbows dovetailed into the frame for rigidity, and a "hanging roof" independently framed so its movements will not be transferred to the walls.

Buildings constructed of all types of materials are vulnerable, although those of lightest structure, and/or loosely joined seem to resist earthquakes best (Munro 1963, 56). Various techniques such as horizontal timber braces in stone or brick walls (Petherbridge 1978, 204; Doumas 1983, 50), wooden frames with panels of bamboo matting and plaster (Kanvinde 1971, 373), or other structural or design defensive strategies (Carver 1984, 139–40; ud-Din 1984, 276) are also helpful. James Parsons (1991, 142) reports that bamboo frame structures in Ecuador have excellent earthquake resistance. "Although the structures may appear woefully unstable, they generally survive

without damage from the frequent strong earthquakes that characterize this part of the continent."

Similarly, in the Philippines a series of strong earthquakes in the
middle of the 17th century destroyed large numbers of houses of
stone, built following the Spanish colonial architectural pattern. At
the same time the native houses had lighter construction with multiple, flexible connections and jointing, and because their roofs rested
on firmly planted wooden pillars that swayed with each shock,
instead of being rigid, they generally survived earthquakes intact
(Zialcita 1997, 50). The same difference between wooden and stone
buildings was observed in the Danish West Indies (Chapman 1991,
quoting an 18th-century report).

Cave dwellings excavated in loose material (see Chapter 7) are particularly vulnerable. In China, hundreds of thousands of people have
succumbed in cave houses when earthquakes have struck (Cressey
1932, 35). For a long period of time after a quake, tiny huts of mud are
erected on the streets of villages and cities – even in urban neighborhoods of well-built houses – and resorted to as temporary refuges
(Figure 9-6).

In coastal areas, destruction to traditional housing often comes not
from the earthquake itself but from tsunamis generated by the quake.
In recent memory, the enormous damage associated with the great
Indian Ocean tsunami of December 2004 remains vivid, although as

*9-6. Temporary earthquake shelters on the streets of Beijing, China. These huts
shelter people afraid to go back into destroyed, or even still standing, structures for fear of aftershocks or new earthquakes (photo by the author, 1977).*

yet little has been written of the impact on traditional dwellings and the long-term consequences of their destruction.

In the final analysis, however, over the long pull of history it is fires that have been the greatest threat to traditional building. A survey of early log houses in Saskatchewan indicated fire as the most common agent of destruction (Taggart 1958, 85). Sometimes the destruction was intentional. Old wooden structures were often burned down in order to lower insurance costs and to reduce taxes by removing a building from the tax rolls (Mann and Skinulis 1979, 27). In urban areas a great threat arises from the closely packed nature of structures so that, once established, the fire can create devastation over a wide area.

Even in relatively small agricultural villages, fire has periodically wreaked its vengeance on bamboo frame, thatched-roof huts. One neighborhood of the village of Bhotpotty, Bengal took its local name of Chhobari (neighborhood of ashes) from the regular occurrence of fires that gutted its lightly built houses (Sen and Dhar 1997, 254). The settlement is located along the western part of a former rail line, which explains the source of the igniting sparks. A reconstructed thatched-roof black house in the Highland Folk Museum in King-ussie, Scotland suffered the same fate from sparks from a passing steam locomotive early in the 20th century.

In Skansen-type open-air museums, the risk of fire, because so many of their structures are wooden, is extraordinarily high. Also, the destruction can spread quickly to great numbers of buildings, destroying centuries-old structures, which have been carefully and painstakingly preserved. The great fire of July 2, 1994 in the Polish open-air museum at Sanok is perhaps an extreme example. The con-flagration burnt down 13 buildings, two wells, and 1,384 exhibits (furniture, textiles, papers, and so on), and caused damage estimated at US$400,000 (Czajkowski 1994, 8).

Builders of traditional structures in both town and countryside have employed various strategies to combat fire. In the Cape Province of South Africa, where traditional houses have distinctive curving gables and whitewashed walls, an ancient tradition of fire protection persists in the *brandzolder* (DeBosdari 1953, 21). Because roofs of Cape Dutch houses are of thatch, fire is an ever-present danger. The brand-zolder is a loft floor in which tiles or bricks are embedded in a layer of puddled clay, producing a fireproof floor on to which burning thatch can fall. In Connecticut in the earlier colonial period and later, one of the most important elected officials was the *chimney viewer*, whose responsibility was to examine the chimneys for structural soundness every six weeks in winter and every three months in summer (Kelly 1924, 58).

Recognizing that bakeovens, in which high temperatures were achieved and maintained for long periods, were the culprits in many kitchen fires, the Portuguese in Barroso adopted the strategy of building a free-standing communal oven entirely of granite slabs, or alternatively of moving the oven to a remote site. Central or removed from the village, with rotating days fixed for each family, the fire is kept burning permanently, except on Sundays. "This allows the oven to be a meeting place for inhabitants of the village, offering them free shelter and always open to those in need" (Associacao dos Arquitectos Portugueses 1988, 273).

In Key West, Florida a disastrous fire in 1886 destroyed approximately one-half of all structures in the settlement. Rebuilding saw the popularization of fire-resistant metal roofs in place of the earlier wooden shingles. The metal roof had the additional advantage of being a better collector of rainwater to fill cisterns, the most common source of water supply in the near-sea-level settlement (Caemmerer 1992, 23).

A more complex situation resulting from natural hazards occurred in the Philippines late in the 19th century. Because heavy roofs introduced by the Spanish, formed of three layers of curved tile sometimes fell in during earthquakes, many dwellings retained thatch roofs. Unfortunately these were often consumed by fire, creating a danger to all of the other houses, which were at least partially built of wood. The government in 1880 decreed that either flat tiles or galvanized metal was to replace both curved tile and thatch. Because galvanized iron was cheaper it became more widely employed and continues to raise the temperature in many Philippine homes (Zialcita 1997, 52).

In the towns of French Canada, house design in the 17th and 18th centuries broke with the earlier steeply pitched, gable roofs common in the countryside. In the town dwellings, parapets projected "not only above the shingled roof but also carried forward beyond the line of the eaves, on massive corbels to retard the spread of fire if one should break out" (Figure 9-7). "A lower pitch in the roof (to allow firefighters to walk on it) was also obligatory" (Cameron 1982, 12–13). These design features continued to be followed in the countryside, even though the original need produced by close spacing did not apply, confirming the often-reiterated observation that architectural leadership proceeded from the towns (Carless 1925, 142). A similar design feature of parapets to retard fire-spread exists on many village houses in China (Lung 1991, 26).

Throughout the world, a range of legal measures has been adopted to combat fire. In the Middle Ages the town of Bergen, Norway

9-7. The Montreal house, with its stone construction, gentle roof pitch and the gable parapet, which permitted better fire defense (drawing by M. Margaret Geib).

prohibited the use of wooden hoods and chimneys suspended above an open-hearth fire (Stewart 1972, 39). However, not until the 18th century were wooden chimneys outlawed in colonial Georgia (Corry 1930, 193). Even later in Brisbane, Australia an act was passed that prohibited "undue subdivision of land" to reduce fire risk from overcrowded building in a timber-built city (Irving 1985, 14). In the UK, thatch roofs in medieval times were required by law to be covered with a coat of limewash to retard fire (Innocent 1916, 211–12; Briggs 1953, 103). Even earlier, in 1212, London had prohibited the use of thatching (Salzman 1952, 223). Nevertheless, such prohibition was ineffective in controlling London fires, which, of course, culminated in the Great Fire of 1666. In New Amsterdam and subsequently in New York City, fire and building codes from 1656 to 1849 promoted the use of tile over thatch because of the latter's fire susceptibility (Waite 1976, 136).

Traditional building must of necessity wage an unremitting struggle against both man-made and natural hazards just to maintain itself. It is unlikely that traditional building will expand in future because of the scale of modern development, the desire of people for increased standards of living, and the persistence and unpredictability of natural hazards. The great danger is that replacement of the traditional will occur with such rapidity that societies become disoriented and lose the stability which contact with the past and tradition provides.

~ 10 ~
Openings:
Doors and Windows

In early prehistoric pit dwellings entry was through a smoke hole in the roof and down a ladder inside. At an early date, entry was made easier by a curving, side-located ramp way and an opening through a wall. No door was used, the opening being covered merely by an animal skin. This kind of doorway covering has continued right up to the present in some areas. Elsewhere, a bundle of reeds that is easily shifted may serve to close the entry way (Patel 1987, 279). Both reeds and hides are in use in southern Africa (Walton 1948, 144). In Scotland, early doorways were also covered at night, during storms, and in the winter, with simple woven hurdles (Beaton 1997, 46). Similarly, in Ireland, doors of woven wattles and straw mats were employed (Lucas 1956, 18; Patterson 1960, 15). Originally the common dwellings of the Ainu in Hokkaido had no doors, "but in the doorways of the well-to-do a specially strong mat was suspended" (Munro 1963, 56). Clearly, access through openings was more important than the material to close and secure the opening.

Security was provided by keeping the doorway size as small as was reasonable. In parts of South Africa, corbeled stone huts were built with doorway openings generally less than two feet high and only 18 inches wide, necessitating the inhabitants' crawling in and out. The rationale for such a small opening was to keep out large wild animals and to place hostile intruders at a distinct disadvantage. The entry was closed "by a flat stone with a hole in the center through which a finger could be inserted to pull the stone in place from inside the hut" (Walton 1951, 46). In other areas of southern Africa, Bantu grass huts also have small door openings closed by grass mats and reed mats, and secured with simple but ingenious locking devices (Figure 10-1) (Knuffel 1973, 42–3).

Normally, door size is kept small in traditional dwellings, not only to ensure security, but also to keep the door, which has to be swung, lifted, pushed, pulled, or pivoted, to a manageable weight. Furthermore, in cooler climates smaller doorway size helps to conserve

interior warmth. In some cases, however, above-average size doors
are required to serve special needs. Inett Homes (1978, 12) reminds us
that many dwellings in Herefordshire, UK needed back doors four
feet wide in order to permit passage of barrels for cider, an important
cottage agricultural product of the area. Wider than average doors
also are found on many longhouses in Scotland to accommodate
entry to the byre of long-horned Highland cattle (Naismith 1985, 30).
Among the Batammaliba in Togo, doorways normally coincide
roughly with body width, but when the family has cattle the door
may be constructed in a trapezoidal shape to allow the long-horned
animals to pass (Blier 1994, 237, footnote 18).

Another unusual, but very practical, doorway design can be found
in the early pueblos of the American Southwest. Blankets and skins
were used to block the doors for privacy and protection against cold

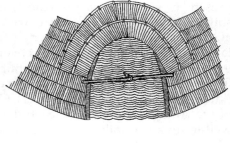

*(above) 10-1. Sketches of both exte-
rior and interior sides of a Bantu
grass hut doorway closing, showing methods of securing (from
Knuffel 1973, 42–3. Reprinted
with permission of ADEVA
(Akademische Druck-u. Verlag-
sanstalt), Graz, Austria).*

*(right) 10-2. Sketch of a notched
pueblo doorway from Canyon de
Chelly, Arizona. The wider upper
part permits loads to be taken
directly through the opening
(from V. Mindeleff 1891, 190).*

weather, but it is the form of the doorway that is unusual (Figure 10-2). The lower part of the opening is narrow, just wide enough for legs to pass through, while the upper part is considerably wider. "The stepping of the doorway, while diminishing its exposed area, does not interfere with its use in bringing in large bundles" (Mindeleff 1891, 190–1).

Because of their small size, most early dwellings needed only a single entry point. In the sod dugouts of South Dakota, the door was arranged to swing inward so that occupants would not be trapped by heavily drifted snow, which in blizzards could accumulate rapidly in the hollow before the door (Sands 1980, 31). In Louisiana an opposite arrangement of outward-swinging doors was used in order to conserve limited space inside the early, small Cajun house (Kane 1944, 180).

Solid wooden or other similar doors are a relatively late invention in traditional buildings, and even today many structures throughout the world are built without solid doors. In areas where timber was not readily available in the earliest periods of settlement, substitutes were frequently employed. Mildred Sharp (1921, 20) calls attention to at least one instance from early western settlement in Iowa in which a table served as a door, "being taken down and used as a table, and rehung as a door after meals."

In Europe, as the wooden door became more popular, various strategies were used to make it more sturdy. One was to employ heavy planks in place of light, woven panels. In order to attach the planks in the strongest way possible, heavy nails were driven through the plank and the door framework. The nails were clinched so they could not be pulled out. They were permanent! This gave rise to the expression of a finished matter as "dead as a doornail" (Salzman 1952, 309). In the Viking period in Scandinavia, the door was placed on a pivoting post and dropped into a groove in the doorsill when closed (Shetelig and Falk 1937, 323). In Slavic areas of Eastern Europe, the wooden door often assumes an irregular hexagonal shape by the cutting off of the top corners (Kuzela 1963, 306). This may be an attempt to replicate the arch form, but in wood and without having scroll saws and similar sophisticated tools. The doorway frame was a bit more complex and somewhat more difficult to fit, but that was balanced by the lesser weight of the door, whose upper corners were cut off. The lighter door would swing more easily and utility of the door was not affected.

The Cape Dutch houses in South Africa possess an entrance door that at one and the same time is ancient in form as well as innovative. Derived from the early divided door of the Netherlands, it allows the upper part to be opened while the lower stays shut. The door also has a sliding sash window that can be lowered to replace the upper door half in windy or cool weather. This allows light to enter while keeping out draughts (DeBosdari 1953, 22).

Even later than the invention of the solid door is the practice in Europe of providing more than one entry. As buildings became larger, a second door offered convenience and also provided for the possibility of cross-ventilation, especially if positioned directly across from the first door. The desirability of cross-ventilation was universally recognized at an early time (Kipling 1911, 308 for India; King 1976, 28 for Saudi Arabia; Evans 1939, 216 for Europe; Noble 1984, 1:42 for the United States). The draft provided by opposing doors was also useful in ridding a dwelling of smoke from open fires. The problem in Europe, especially in the British Isles, was that of cold winter winds at just the season when accumulated smoke was most bothersome. In Ireland also, such a situation was not very desirable in the long winter season, but two opposed doors did have an important advantage. "Either door is used as occasion requires in order to prevent the changeable winds from entering the kitchen" (Campbell 1935, 70).

Over time, the use of the kitchen back door declined along with the practice of milking cows in the kitchen. In order to do the milking, the animals had been led in through the front door and out through the back. The decline in the use of the back door by visitors or strangers is locally given as due to the fact that strangers "might leave the house by a different door from the one which they entered and so take the luck of the house with them." As E. Estyn Evans further notes, it is more probable "that the back door has outlived its functions, which were connected with wind protection and smoke disposal and also with the care of the animals" (Evans 1939, 216).

Doors not only provide access but perform a variety of other functions as well. They are especially important symbolically. In Africa, "thresholds were everywhere imbued with profound ritual connotations as spiritual boundary points" (Denyer 1978, 117).

> Any enclosed space, whether physical or conceptual, requires an opening: the corollary to the meaningful spatial definition of an "enclosed" space is an entrance into it. The entrance is the mediator; it marks the point where man makes the transition between exterior and interior, between the unknown and the known . . . Throughout West Africa, all rites and rituals relating to change or transition in man's existence occur at the entrance. "Outdooring" or naming ceremonies announcing the birth of a child, hence its entry into life, are performed at the entrance to the compound. Funerary rites take place at the compound entrance and strangers are received in the antechamber located at the entrance to the compound. (Prussin 1974, 199)

Throughout India, the doorway, together with the prayer room or prayer niche, and the hearth, represent the three most symbolically important components of the house, regardless of the social position of the inhabitants. It is often the only external part of the structure given any decoration or embellishment. Confirming its symbolic function is the fact that it is the doorway frame of wood or stone, rather than the door itself, that receives most decoration, usually in the form of elaborate carving (Noble 2003, 49–50).

Another indication of the symbolic significance of the doorway can be found in Myanmar (Burma) houses where floor boards must run *across* the space just inside the doorway. Otherwise whatever energy, good fortune or positive effect comes in the front door simply goes out, or flows out of the house through the back door (Nwe 2003, 232). Here is an example of a modification of the Chinese feng shui principle.

In many dwellings located in the Himalaya, in which the upper story provides the residence and a lower story shelters animals, entry to the living level is by means of ladders and an open trapdoor. Such an arrangement obviates the need for an external stairway, which could be a feature weakening household security. It also allows heat from the animal quarters to flow upward, supplementing the poor heating facilities of the upper story, a desirable feature during the long, bitterly cold winters of the mountain altitudes (Denwood 1971, 26).

Another significant function of doors is to restrict passage, thereby ensuring or enhancing privacy (Carson 1976, 24). The question of privacy is two-edged. A closed door enhances privacy by restricting access, but an open door invites entry – visual if not physical. Many courtyard houses in India provide access via an entrance room with offset doors, so that the courtyard and interior of the dwelling cannot be seen from the street (Singh 1965, 12–13). A further strategy to ensure privacy is to offset outer doors of houses situated across a lane or village street (Chandhoke 1990, 172).

Doors not only assure privacy, they provide security and protection (Connor 1949, 114), but the doorway offering entry into a dwelling is a point of potential weakness and danger. This may explain why so much symbolism can be attached to it. A strongly built and fastened door can be a powerful deterrent to a hostile or thieving invader. In the American desert Southwest, after ground-level doorways were introduced, Indian residents had no timber to fashion heavy doors in order to secure their dwellings when they were away for extended periods. Their solution was to wall up the doorway with heavy adobe bricks to keep unauthorized visitors out (Bunting 1976, 38).

In many parts of the world where dwellings occur in small, scattered and apparently unordered clusters, the position of the entry door to one-room huts is a most rigidly and carefully controlled feature, often planned in such a way that entrances to neighboring huts never face one another directly. The practice is reported from the edges of the Thar desert in western India (Jain 1980, 27), but in northern Tanzania and among the pygmies of the eastern Congo a more complex system operates. Hut entrances face one another when inhabitants are on good terms, but away when animosity prevails (Turnbull 1965, 102–5). Because the huts are lightly built, repositioning is a relatively easy task. Elsewhere, the orientation of doors also may be a function of kinship (Woodburn 1972, 196–7).

In a large number of European and European-derived dwellings with gable or hipped roofs, the doors usually occupy a position on an eave side of the structure. Around Tabor, South Dakota, a large collection of traditional houses with L-shaped floor plans were built by Czech settlers. Here, the entry door(s) are located on the inside of the "L"s (Rau 1992, 295). Presumably, such positioning provides shelter from the cold and often strong prairie winds.

Throughout Appalachia, and even somewhat beyond in the US, dwellings frequently have two front doors, each one providing entry into a different room. Such structures are especially common in southern Missouri, Arkansas, Mississippi, and middle Tennessee (Tebbets 1978, 45; Sizemore 1994, 58), although they may be found as far away as eastern Pennsylvania, and Kansas and Texas in the opposite direction (Domer 1994, 1). The rationale for two front doors close to each other has long puzzled scholars (Kauffman 1954/55, 27). The various explanations given are not convincing. It is hardly a product of Victorian refinement (Kauffman 1954/55), nor it is likely that such a costly feature was meant to provide "extra cross ventilation, for easy escape in case of fire, and for additional privacy in making essential trips outside during the night, since both front rooms were often used as bedrooms" (Sizemore 1994, 59). A much more likely explanation is that the building of double pen dwellings, necessary and desirable as families grew, continued an earlier tradition by simply moving or building single pen cabins together, each with its own door. Later on, the double pen house was built in its entirety from scratch but retained the front entry to each room, thereby permitting a modicum of privacy when visitors came. Such a retention is an illustration of *architectural inertia,* a situation where a design feature is retained long after its original purpose or rationale has been met or satisfied.

A similar process has been described for extensions of early houses in what has been termed the New Mexican Hispanic modular building tradition:

> As the growth of the family required, and as resources allowed, additional rooms were added. Each new room was essentially like the first, a separate module with its own exterior door ... While each room typically had a door to the outside, there were not always interior connecting doors. Movement from room to room often occurred, instead, outside the house. The narrow porches frequently added after 1880 sheltered this exterior circulation (Wilson 1991, 88).

Having the door on an eave side of a gable-roofed building could create considerable inconvenience in areas of high rainfall, and especially in areas of high snowfall. Porches were expensive to build. The pent roof, a device worked out in Europe, helped, but it was awkward and also expensive to build, and only partially effective. Wooden door hoods also were tried, and helped to an extent, but suffered from the same problems. In eastern Canada, with its long winters and heavy snowfall, the answer in the 1830s was to redesign the roof by adding a large central gable-side dormer. Not only did this expand headroom in the attic and provide better lighting there, it shed snow to either side of the dwelling entryway (Arthur 1938, 15).

Log houses in eastern North America almost always had the door(s) on the eave side of the structure, continuing the long tradition of such door placement inherited from Europe. However, on the Great Plains, the Rocky Mountains and throughout western North America, the door is located on the shorter gable-end wall. The door in these cabins is universally off-center, probably to accommodate the iron stove that in the 19th century had supplanted the wood-burning fireplace as the source of heat. Placing the stove adjacent to the door served two purposes. First, this allowed the source of heat to be where heat was most needed, near the site of the greatest potential loss of heat, the door. Second, placing the stove near the door reduced the distance required to carry heavy fire wood (Wilson 1984, 34).

The most carefully studied western log cabin is the one that has been given the designation of Rocky Mountain cabin (Figure 10-3). Four chief characteristics or features differentiate it from eastern log cabins: a roof pitch lower than 45°; heating by means of a stove rather than from a fireplace; an extended, front-facing gable roof; and an off-centered door on the gable-end wall (Wilson 1984, 33). The forward extension of the roof provides additional sheltered living space and results in a seasonal alteration of room uses.

Several reasons have been advanced to explain the shift of the door from the side in eastern structures to the end wall in western log houses, and specifically in the Rocky Mountain cabin. For this latter structure the possibility has been advanced that it may represent a simplification of the southern dogtrot house (Wilson 1984, 64). This seems unlikely. Mary Wilson also suggests that the shift of the door

10-3. *Isometric view of a*
   Rocky Mountain cabin.
   The door on the gable wall
   and the extension of the
   roof are diagnostic features
   (from Wilson 1984, 2).

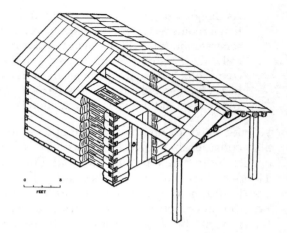

and the design of the Rocky Mountain cabin may be a local innovation. This does seem likely in the case of this particular design, although the door shift probably occurred in earlier types. Roger Welsch (1980, 319), for example, notes that some early log builders on the Great Plains solved the problem of scarcity of logs by shifting the door to the gable. He says,

> logs were scarce on the Plains and the walls were usually low – 5 to 7 feet high – and a door in the eave end would either have been very small and low or would have had to cut through the sill and plate logs, introducing structural instability. So, the main door was often in the middle of the gable end, thus taking advantage of a slightly higher wall.

Only about 10% of sod houses that Welsch (1968, 85) was able to study closely had doors on the gable, however.

Terry Jordan (1978, 111–13) suggested that the scarcity of suitable wood for logs, and the wide-spread use of sod dugouts where the door, of necessity, was located on the gable wall, may have been the inspiration for placement of doors on the gable wall of log structures. Finally, a Finnish-Scandinavian origin for the door position has been proposed by Jordan and Matti Kaups (1989) and Jon Kilpinen (1995).

Throughout the Muslim world, entrance doors are arranged to guard privacy and shield the house's womenfolk. In Iraq, double entry doors lead into a small lobby with a blank wall facing the doors. Entry to the house itself requires a right-angle turn. Thus, gaze from the street and casual entry are blocked and controlled (Bennett 1968, 86). On a different conceptual level, in China the entrance door is often accompanied by a decorated "spirit wall" either outside or immediately inside across the entry, forcing those who enter to turn either to the right or left (Cressey 1932, 31–2; Lin 1975, 54). "This spirit wall not only prevented strangers from observing the family's activities, but also prevented the evil spirits that lurked outside from entering as they could not turn corners" (Sullivan 1972, 133).

In addition to its other functions, the door frequently performs an important symbolic function:

> The symbolic importance of the house entrance – the vulnerable threshold between the household and the public – is often emphasized by the construction of a monumental and sometimes highly decorated doorway, frequently utilizing symbols and colors of an apotropiac or auspicious nature. For example, the doorways of those who have returned from the *hajj*, the pilgrimage to Mecca, are brightly decorated with an abundance of inscriptions, folk motifs and images of places and things seen on the journey. In Muslim East Africa, the elaborate wooden doors of Swahili houses, with their heavy brass locks and chains, are considered such an important feature that the construction of a new house begins with the door. (Petherbridge 1978, 197)

Perhaps it was early Muslim contacts and influence which prompted Hindu builders of extended family houses (*haveli*) in Gujarat and Rajasthan states in India to surmount their entrance door and doorframes with extremely intricate and elaborate carved wood. "A family too poor to afford much wood carving would have, nevertheless, a carved door" (Pramar 1983, 26).

A world away, on the eastern margin of the Pacific Ocean, evolved one of the most elaborate and symbolic doorways found on any traditional structure. Here, in Alaska and Canada, houses had intricately carved clan totem poles attached to the facade. The lowest totem, a symbolic representation of the clan animal, contained an oval hole, which was the entrance to the dwelling. Passing through the pole opening, one symbolically entered the clan by passing through the representation of the clan animal. What could be more dramatic or carry such a powerful message? After contact with explorers and missionaries, the totem door was first supplemented and then replaced by a European-style door.

Severe climatic conditions, whether iregularity of tropical downpours (Figure 10-4) or continual cold of Arctic winters, prompt a response in traditional as well as modern building. Such adaptations often involve the entryway. In the Caribbean, where rainfall is frequent and heavy, a unique traditional building feature was the development of *sedan porches* (Crain 1994, 81). In early British colonial times, transport of the colonials was by sedan chair (Buisseret 1980, 7). The porch was a small, elevated structure completely walled and roofed to permit the sedan chair to be drawn up tightly. The porches were immediately

10-4. The oversized projection of the corrugated iron roof helps to deflect the heavy tropical downpours from the doorway of this dwelling in Johore, Malaysia (photo by the author, 1980).

adjacent to the dwelling's front entry. J.R. Groome (1964, 33) calls attention to the fact that similar roadside porches are documented from England. He also suggests that the Caribbean sedan porch may additionally have been a device to deflect tradewind-driven rain from the dwelling entrance. At the same time, its lateral doors could provide a "reasonable form of air conditioning."

By contrast, in polar igloos air conditioning is certainly no problem, but the bitter and constantly cold temperatures in winter must be addressed. This is effectively solved by building an entrance tunnel at a lower level than the floor of the igloo. This serves as a cold air trap. A similar device is used in areas where the winter season dwelling is a partially excavated structure.

Windows also offer an illustration of the differing responses of diverse groups to what are similar environmental challenges. The intense Mediterranean sun is met with by placing few and narrow windows in the outside walls of traditional North African houses, with wide windows framed with dark shutters in Italy or Spain, or "with wide surfaces of glass lined with light shades as in the Californian ranch houses" (Gottmann 1957, 19). Generally speaking, the number of windows in a dwelling of the middle or higher latitudes is related to the size of the structure and the number of its rooms. "A source of light was required in each room" (Lebreton 1982, 440).

The word *window* is derived from an Old Norse term, *vindauga*, which meant "wind eye" (Stewart 1972, 29). The Greek word for window is *parathyron*, which translated literally means "beside the door." In this position the opening let light into the dwelling when the door was closed. It also provided security for the householder, who could see who was at the door (Doumas 1983, 50). A window thus has a strong European orientation, even more so because the use of glass was essentially a Western characteristic. Elsewhere, and even early on in Europe, windows were unglazed and closed only by shutters, which of course negated one of the most important functions of the window, the transmission of light into the interior.

The Dutch, both at home in Europe and in the New Netherlands in America, typically kept shutters closed night and day, so that "light was admitted as sparingly as possible." This practice was related to the tradition of lightly sanding wooden floors to "absorb moisture that might otherwise remain as incidental spills." When the shutters were opened, "dust particles were observed in every ray of sunlight that was allowed to penetrate. The belief grew that light carried the dust or stirred it up" (Funk 1987, 86–7).

Individuals sleeping in upper stories or enclosed lofts of dwellings everywhere frequently suffered because no windows had been provided for ventilation, smoke exhaustion, and light entry. These problems were solved in at least one early Norwegian house in Wisconsin by building a *skyveluke*, "a small hatch in the roof, with a sliding cover" (Perrin 1967, 4).

Shutters, almost always of wood, were hinged to permit them not only to close the window opening, but also to swing out of the way during the day. In most locations shutters were placed on the outside of the wall, initially in order to conserve interior space, and later to protect the easily shattered, expensive glass of the windows, which usually opened inward (Laws 1995, 107). Occasionally in early California houses the shutters were inside (Hannaford and Edwards 1931, v). When glass first began to be used, the window was the casement type that opened inward, and the outside placement of the shutters was continued. Later, when glass became widely available and sash windows replaced casement, the functions of shutters shifted to control both ventilation and light.

Window openings may have several functions in addition to those of providing light and ventilation, especially the expelling of smoke.

In Guyana, a window-shutter–shelf combination (Figure 10-5) not only performed privacy and ventilation functions, it also offered a place to hold blocks of ice. Air from the trade winds thus could be easily cooled. "Ice was brought from the American lakes to Guyana and stored in sawdust or sand until sold. It is easy to imagine that only the richer house owners could afford such luxury: the cooler however was built into the fabric of quite poor houses" (Westmaas 1970, 149). The shutter was louvered to permit airflow, the shelf was slotted to allow drainage, and the triangular sides were pierced by decorative cut-outs, which was desirable because the windows faced the street. An earthen pot placed in the enclosure provided cool drinking water. This arrangement, called a *Demerara window* was also a convenient place to dry small items of clothing and for other household use. The term Demerara window is also found in neighboring Surinam (Volders 1966, 30) and in the Caribbean islands formally belonging to Great Britain. In these areas, however, the name is often applied to any window that opens outward from hinges along the top, whether or not it incorporates a shelf or has sides.

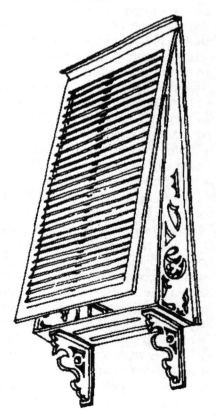

10-5. Sketch of a partially open Demerara window typical of Guyana (from Westmaas 1970).

The standard classification of glass window types is based on the method of their opening, referring mostly to Western usage and as much to formal structures as to traditional buildings (Harrison 1973, 266). The earliest glass windows usually consisted of very small, diamond-shaped panes and were entirely fixed in place. The slanting edges of the diamond shape permitted rain water to run off more quickly than from horizontal mullions (Addison 1986, 21), and the diamond-shaped panes allowed even the smallest pieces of the expensive glass to be used along the window opening edges (Brown 1982, 272). These early windows were gradually replaced by casement types, in their turn replaced by sash windows (Wilson 1976), which were invented in continental Europe, probably in the Netherlands or Belgium.

The word *sash* is derived from the French *chassis*, meaning frame (Briggs 1932, 88). In the earliest ones the upper sash was fixed. Not until the late 17th century did both upper and lower parts move (Cook 1971, 44). Sliding sash windows normally move vertically. However, in the UK, in an area including Humberside and Lancashire but centered in Yorkshire, those called "Yorkshire windows" slide horizontally. Another unusual window treatment occurs to the west in Cumbria. Most windows are large, squarish, and usually with vertical sliding sashes, but some houses have an ingenious variation in which the top half pivots horizontally and the bottom half is fixed (Penoyre and Penoyre 1978, 134 & 143).

In Cape Province, South Africa, the Boers in the 18th century adopted sash windows in which only the lower half moved. The outside shutters were slatted so that when the window was open and the shutter closed, air could move freely in and out, but at a reduced velocity and volume. When the window was closed the half shutter could be fixed open to allow maximum light inside. "Hence the characteristic daytime silhouette of window-frame with open shutters on a Cape Dutch house, the lower half of the silhouette being twice as wide as the upper half" (DeBosdari 1953, 22).

Although window openings provide desirable interior light and offer attractive ventilation, they do have some difficulties. First, they require some skill and care in construction in areas of lower temperature, to ensure that precipitation, winds and cold do not penetrate. Second, they weaken the wall if not properly made and can endanger the stability of the entire structure. Third, windows diminish security by offering a means of penetration into the interior for both individuals and weaponry. Finally, construction of window openings involves additional expense. These last two problems especially have worked to restrict window openings in many parts of the world. Eugene

George (1975, 47) notes that in south Texas *no* windows existed in dwellings until after the departure of Indians from the frontier.

It was not until well into the 18th century that small amounts of glass began to be used in ordinary vernacular buildings (Cook 1971, 33). It was even later before windows became a standard feature on traditional structures in remote regions. In Appalachia, for example, it was almost the 20th century before windows commonly appeared in log cabins (Eller 1979, 96). This was also the case in southern Serbia, where window paper began to be replaced by glass only after the first decade of the 20th century (Lodge 1936, 97).

Before glass, a variety of other materials were pressed into service with generally unsuccessful results. Paper, often oiled to make it more translucent, was widely employed in the Orient (Yang 1965, 40), and in eastern Europe (Lodge 1936, 97), as well as in frontier America. Oiled linen cloth tacked to a light wooden frame was also used (Brown 1986, 132). In the Arctic and among the Indians of the Northwest Pacific coast, fish gut membranes were used in small windows (Olson 1927, 25). W. Elmer Ekblaw (1927, 168) noted also that a thin section of sealskin was used in windows above igloo doors. "This window lets the light in, but because it is translucent only, a peep-hole in the center is necessary to look through." In Galicia in northwestern Spain, the early circular huts of granite often had no windows at all. When they did, they were covered with translucent pigskin (Laws 1995, 28).

Many early structures had window openings reduced to glass-less slits in order to reduce rain penetration and to discourage birds and other animals from entering. Splayed window openings in houses built with stone walls allowed more light to enter the dwelling than square-cut openings. The inside horizontal dimension of the window opening was significantly larger than in the square cut version (Lay 1982, 24). Later, the Great Plains sod houses used the same technique (Welsch 1968, 79). Interiors of early dwellings were usually quite dark and gloomy because of the lack and small size of openings to the outside. One technique employed on the southern Great Plains to improve lighting was to cover the interior with cheap whitewash (George 1975, 48).

The "black houses" of the Hebrides and the closely related dwellings of Skye are characterized by a general lack of windows and even smoke holes (Walton 1957, 155). What little light is admitted comes through one or two small openings located toward the base of the thatch roof. F.L.W. Thomas (1869) commented that "only a dim religious light pervades the place on the brightest day."

Not only do some windows let in rain from outside, as noted above, others, especially in adobe houses in hot desert environments, can admit heat. To avoid this, openings may be tightly closed from just after sunrise to almost dusk. "As soon as it becomes cooler outside than in, the windows and doors are opened and the air allowed to blow through. . . . Ventilation is continued until an hour or two after sunrise. Then all openings are sealed up in defense against outside temperatures" (Rodger 1974, 104).

The presence or absence of windows can be an important indicator of the ethnic group associated with the dwelling. For example, in Canada, traditional houses of the Ukrainian settlers can be further identified by the presence or absence of roof-placed eyebrow windows. If present, the Ukrainians originated in Bukovyna; if not, they came from Galicia (Lehr 1980, 193).

In many instances it is not the character of the opening, nor the arrangement of the glass that fills the opening that is most interesting, but rather the peculiar features accompanying the window. Decorative window surrounds (Figure 10-6) occur in many societies and are especially common in Russia (Dmitrieva 1982–83, 43–7). E. Estyn Evans (1939, 220) reports on the Donegal custom of keeping three

10-6 An elaborately carved wooden window frame, emphasized by contrasting paint, Kostroma, Russia (photo by the author, 1997).

smooth stones on the window sill "for luck." On a more practical note, Clarence Lebreton (1982, 434) quotes a Father Chiasson writing about houses in Acadia as having notches in the window sash that were used to tell the time by the position of the shadow of the sun's rays. In Quebec Province, Canada, simple wooden shields on the windward-facing windows help to deflect precipitation and reduce the need for more frequent maintenance and repair of windows and window openings (Figure 10-7).

Window openings have several functions: they admit outside, natural light; they provide ventilation; they permit smoke to escape; they allow those inside a structure to observe what is outside, which may be critical to the inhabitants' safety and survival; and they "control glare that results from the brightness of the exterior light" (Cain et al. 1975, 221; Doumas 1983, 50). The dormer window, which M. Barley (1987, 106) notes was invented as early as the Middle Ages, and whose main function is to admit light, also performs the secondary function of helping to create more headroom in a loft or attic.

Window openings in traditional Chinese houses perform a further function: that of admitting and conducting beneficial cosmic forces (*ch'i*) in a desirable path through a dwelling. At the same time, though, windows may allow intrusion of negative cosmic forces. Hence, a series of rules incorporated under the rubric feng shui must be adhered to (Walters 1988, 46–9), which explains much of Chinese traditional dwelling architecture.

10-7. *Simple wooden shields deflect the strong winter winds away from the windows of this old French-built cottage on the Ile d'Orleans, Quebec (photo by the author, 1976).*

Among the Ainu of the northern island of Hokkaido in Japan, orientation of a sacred window in the house is more important than that of the entry door, which faces west so that the sacred window in the back wall of the house may face toward the east. This is the direction of life and west is that of death (Munro 1963, 78). Perhaps it is also symbolic that residents and visitors entering an Ainu house are moving toward the east (i.e. away from death). The sacred window is the entry and exit for most of the items used during religious ceremonies held within the house.

Another window of particular religious significance is the "soul or spirit window." Found on early houses in parts of Switzerland (Weiss 1959, 141), Germany, where they often were "located inside the flue of a large walk-in fireplace" (van den Hurk 2005, 2), and in some early Mennonite houses in Pennsylvania (Godshall 1983, 25), it is always of tiny size, smaller than all the other windows of the house. It is a relic from the days when it was supposed to allow a deceased person's soul to escape after death (Weaver 1986, 259–61). James Walton (1962, 33) reports a similar opening in corbeled stone huts on the Ligurian coast. F.J. Trisch (1943, 113) also reports that "Swedish and Russian peasant huts in remote districts had a smallish gable-window; it was usually kept shut, but whenever anybody died, it was opened immediately and left open for a certain number of days (i.e. 3, 7, 9) and the peasants explained it was for letting the spirit go in and out unhindered."

A different traditional window device with religious associations is the German window cross. In many traditional houses in Central Europe, windows have four panes, moveable or not, separated by rigid mullions fixed permanently in place to form a cross. In folklore this cross serves as a barrier against the devil, "for even when the four windows have been thrown open, the wooden cross stands fast in its frame" (Taut 1958, 12–13).

The small size of many windows often was a significant indicator of other considerations. Early windows of Irish houses were "always very small and few in number, a tradition born of necessity. Prior to 1800 window taxes were levied on the number and sizes of windows, and those who couldn't see their way to paying very much made sure they allowed only the minimum amount of daylight and fresh air into the home" (Sharkey 1985, 13).

William Weaver (1986, 259) indicates that windows in the Kammer room of Pennsylvania Dutch houses are also of quite small size. Their size ensured security since money was kept in this room and daylight was not important in a room used primarily at night.

Reduction in size is also especially noticeable in regions of bright daylight, bare earth and building surfaces, and high temperatures.

Because of the latter, window openings are necessary to provide ventilation, but the combination of the other factors produces extremely high glare, bringing both psychological and physical discomfort (Cain et al. 1975, 221). An alternative to reducing window size is to use decorative wooden lattice screens as a baffle. This strategy has the further benefit of allowing women inside the house to view the street unobserved. Hence, these window screens are widely found in the Muslim Middle Eastern countries. In many areas, however, reduction in both number and size of window openings is desirable. This strategy reduces the accumulation of dust and sand (Jain 1980, 19), and regulates temperature by restricting intake of hot air.

Japanese traditional dwellings are often constructed primarily to emphasize aspects of the adjoining garden.

> The designing of the garden and the locating of openings in the house are undertaken simultaneously. Numerous irregularities in the exterior walls of Japanese dwellings have no other aim than to give a room the benefit of a particularly interesting glimpse. In the same manner the amazing variety of windows is to be accounted for by the fact that their size or shape or location is intended to bring out some detail or some specific ensemble in the garden. (Villeminot 1958, 16)

One door and one window are about the minimum in a structure. On the American prairies, a dwelling, whether a dugout, sod house, log house or claim shanty, had to have such in order to meet the requirements of the Homestead Act (Sands 1980, 31). The winter house of the Thule Eskimo also has just one entrance and one small window located just above the entrance (Ekblaw 1927, 168). Elsewhere around the world other examples of minimal fenestration can be found.

In some instances, openings resemble windows but are really apertures that have special functions. One of these is the *vent hole* found in the cellar of stone farmhouses in the French *département* of Quercy. Here the cellars are used for wine making and the oval opening is needed to permit toxic gases of fermenting wine to escape. "These openings sometimes have a shutter on the inside, which can be closed when ventilation is not required" (Mollison 1978, 35). Small apertures called *dung holes* are also a feature of the byre walls of house-and-byre structures in Ireland (Patterson 1960, 16). These, of course, are openings to permit dung to be thrown out into piles or pits. Similarly, the barn space of housebarns in western islands of Scotland usually has a *winnowing hole* to facilitate the required draft for processing grain (Fenton 1978, 20), although these are often blocked up today.

Traditional houses in Denmark often have apertures called "corpse doors" that are specifically for the passage of a coffin and are bricked up soon after its departure (Raglan 1964, 32). A somewhat similar, but much larger, opening occurs in one-and-a-half-story New England cottages in the eastern Midwest of the United States. Here it is a full size door, widely called the "funeral door," used to allow coffins to be removed horizontally from the house after funeral services, and directly into hearses. These doors were not otherwise used, except for cross-ventilation in unusually hot summers. Normally, steps were not even provided to permit easy entry or exit (Noble 1984, 1:106).

The problem of removing coffins from small houses without adopting the indecorous method of standing the coffin (with body inside) up on end necessitated the provision of "coffin niches on tight staircase landings," reported from Kingston, New York and Nantucket Island, Massachusetts, and of coffin doors, similar to those discussed in the preceding paragraph, in Utah, New Hampshire, and North Carolina in the United States (Sinclair 2005, 1–2), and in North Holland (Janse 1970).

Jeroen van den Hurk (2005) provides the following description of the North Holland practice. In North Holland, with examples dating back to the 17th century, what is referred to as a *death door* is

> A single door, with a transom light, giving access into the best room of the house. You only entered through this door on your wedding day and spent your wedding night in the room. The room usually held the family's most prized possessions, but was afterwards only used for the funeral wake. The funeral bier was then carried out through this door, which would only be the second time it was opened. The room was usually several feet above grade and so was the death door. It would not have a permanent set of steps leading up to the door, but a removable set of wooden steps would be put in place for these two occasions.

Among the Haida Indians of the Pacific Northwest coast, the removal of a corpse was simple, yet highly symbolic, so as not to pollute the doorway. A plank from the house side was removed and the coffin passed through (Blackman 1973, 48). Similarly, polar Eskimos avoided entrance/exit pollution by unceremoniously dragging the corpse through a hole punched in the back wall, or by removing it through a window or smoke hole (Lee and Reinhardt 2003, 31; Garber 1934, 207). Eskimos in southwestern Alaska removed the dead through the skylight. Lifting the skin cover of the skylight also allowed the spirit to exit the dwelling (Lee and Reinhardt 2003, 154–5).

Windows and doors are necessary features of all domestic structures – at least the openings are. The higher the standard of living, the larger and greater the number of openings, and the more these openings can be blocked and closed easily at required times. Both doors and windows are apt to have symbolic importance. As a result they are frequently highly decorated and elaborately adorned. The door is especially important. It serves not only as the entrance for household-ers to the outside world, but also at the same time it admits non-family members into the confined sanctum of the dwelling. A critical function of reception and acceptance is thus fulfilled.

~ 11 ~
Heating and Cooling

Traditional structures exist in all temperature environments. Ideally, the structures must permit some adjustment for heating and/or cooling. However, the strategies to attain this adaptation vary from place to place. In the Bahamas, heating and cooling both exerted an influence on form. Because kitchens were sources of uncomfortably high temperatures in summer, they were always separately constructed and located a slight distance away from the house (fire was also, of course, a consideration). Dwelling walls could be of wattle and daub, clapboards, or tabby, with the latter material much preferred because it was fireproof and most effectively blocked the cold winds of winter (Otterbein 1975, 15–24).

In a very different way, heat and cold influenced the form and use of the Turkish house. Because of significant temperature differences there between summer and winter, approaches to housing have to be flexible. In many parts of Anatolia people live in different structures at different times of the year, but many houses are constructed to accommodate the temperatures of both seasons. In these houses, to capitalize on cooling ventilation, summer-use rooms were located at structure corners and in single files with large windows, had thin partitions, were high ceilinged and of large dimensions. In the same dwellings, to combat winter winds and low temperatures, some rooms were interior, on upper floors, had thick, insulating construction, and low ceilings (Kucukerman 1988, 39–40).

In some areas, however, the temperature of just one season drove the design of the structure. In most early and low technological societies in Europe, *heating* was the critical necessity, and hence an open hearth occupied a central position. From this location, warmth, however small, spread throughout the structure, and the fire was away from the flammable constructional materials of the building. Flames had to be kept low to ensure against the roof thatch igniting. One way to keep them low was to dampen the fire with wet leafy vegetation, producing considerable smoke. Unfortunately, that smoke had no ready outlet. It escaped through small, narrow smoke slits in the upper parts of the walls (Atkinson 1969, 56), or through the thatch roof itself. Houses with hipped roofs often had small openings called *gablets* located just below the ends of the ridge, through which smoke could escape (Barley 1987, 17). Being closer to the central fire, they worked better than holes at gable peaks in those structures that had a gable roof.

In southernmost Europe, heating was necessary only in the middle of the brief winter period. A brazier of charcoal was all that was needed (Wace and Dawkins 1914–15, 100) to provide heat in whichever room was occupied. In southern Japan (Trewartha 1945, 191) and in Spanish Florida (Manucy 1962, 33), the same strategy was employed. Of course, in much of the tropics no heating was required at all.

Respiratory diseases and chronic eye infection contributed to poor health and the short life expectancies common in traditional societies. Smoke holes, chimneys, and other exits for smoke eventually alleviated much of the problem. Nevertheless, smoky features had remarkable tenacity. An open central fire could be found in the UK as late as 1850 (Stevenson 1880, 9).

The problems of removing smoke from a dwelling, even with a chimney, have been humorously related by Australian observers. The chimney:

> was not more than two feet square, and left quite open in the fond hope of persuading or enticing the smoke to go out there instead of continually struggling for passage through the crevices of the bark roof or pouring out in volumes at the ever open doors and windows. But such was the perversity of this obstinate element that it too generally preferred any illicit vent to the legal one and very frequently asserted its supremacy in such a manner as effectually to drive the inmates out of doors altogether, for sheer lack of breath to continue the contest any longer. As this generally took place in very wet weather, when fire could not be maintained out of doors, as was the usual summer custom, and besides, the chilliness rendering it acceptable in the house for its warmth, it may be conceived that the piety of the inmates, at no time very conspicuous, was not vastly enhanced by their having to stand in the rain, perforce, in order to escape suffocation, until it pleased the vaporous enemy to allow them a short respite by retiring to the loft or any other part of the premises, *except* the chimney of course, which it appeared most of all places to shun. (Cox and Freeland 1969, 45)

The improvements that accompanied attempts to control smoke can be followed in Europe and elsewhere. The widely used open hearth in the middle of the dwelling persisted in Ireland and the Hebrides of Scotland well into the 19th century (Fenton 1978, 31). In these "black houses," so termed because soot covered the walls, rafters and thatch, smoke could be ineffectually controlled, and then only if two doors were present to create a draft (Evans 1939, 219).

The initial successful attempt to control smoke was the use of the *smoke hole*, an opening in the roof to permit the rising smoke to exit quickly (Figure 11-1a). Moving the smoke hole off-center, so the fire was not extinguished by rain, was an early improvement (Lay 1982, 6). Without a chimney to create a draft, however, the smoke hole was not totally effective. Vertically placed thin planks around the top of the smoke hole to improve draft and screen against wind was a simple technique employed by Indians in parts of Alaska (Olson 1927, 25). Elsewhere, all sorts of handy objects were used to improve the draft. William Hance (1951, 83) mentions the use of surplus herring barrels stuck into thatch roofs in the Outer Hebrides. Other devices, including stacks of broken pots (Noble 1984, 1:81), were used elsewhere.

Gradual recovery from the Black Death brought minimal improvements in heating throughout Europe. In Norway the fire was moved into the corner closest to the doorway and raised upon a stone hearth. Surrounded on three sides by rough stone walling, its proximity to the door helped a little in smoke abatement. This arrangement was called a *rokovn* or smoke-stove. One of its main advantages was that it used less wood than the central hearth, an important consideration in wood-poor western Norway (Stewart 1972, 30–1). Also, the surrounding stones radiated heat back into the room.

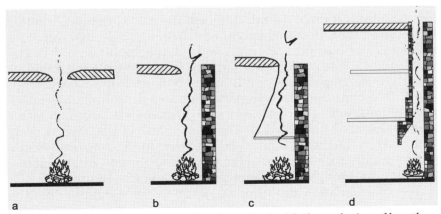

a   b   c   d

11-1. *Stages in the improvement of smoke control with the evolution of hearth and chimney in northwest Europe: (a) smoke hole located in the center of a room, (b) smoke hole moved to brick or stone wall, (c) wooden hood collects smoke better, (d) taller flue removes smoke more effectively (drawings by Kevin Butler, based upon Gailey 1984, 113).*

In villages in England, where two-story structures were desirable because of land costs, and in the Weald of southern England, where prosperity encouraged the building everywhere of substantial two-story houses (Harding 1990), a high smoke bay was often incorporated within the dwelling (Harris 1987, 20). Smoke from the adjacent open fire could be contained in the smoke bay and dissipated little by little through gablets in the roof thatch or small openings in the upper part of the gable-end wall (Brown 1986, 124). Even the single-story cottages of Eastern European villages, such as in Holloko, Hungary, often had small rooms or spaces adjacent to open, corner stoves to collect and dissipate the smoke (Mendele 1991, 8 & 11).

In order to make the smoke hole more effective, a wattle-and-mud hood (Figure 11-1c) was evolved to collect the smoke closer to the ground (Haslova and Vajdio 1974, 38). The suspended smoke hood persisted in some places up to the 17th century and in remote areas even later (Frolec 1966, 88). In Dutch houses in New York, this feature was called the Dutch jambless fireplace (Wilcoxen 1984, 93), and it continued to be built well into the 18th century. Because of the ever-present danger of fire in houses roofed with thatch, the external opening might be contained in a rough, sod structure, the forerunner of the true chimney (Gailey 1984, 113). In the poorer houses a cask or barrel with the ends knocked out was placed over the smoke hole to improve the draft (Wood 1965, 277). In the pueblos of the American Southwest, stacks of burned-through clay pots served the same purpose (Noble 1984, 1:81).

Movement of the hearth to the gable and the construction of that wall in brick or stone (Figure 11-1b) was the intermediate step allowing the introduction of the full chimney. The gable location permitted the support for a higher chimney, thus helping somewhat to reduce the danger of roof fires (Figure 11-1d). According to Sigurd Erixon (1937, 148), it was probably in northern Italy that the gable fireplace was originally popularized, diffusing from there northward and westward. Moving the chimneystack outside the structure, which occurred first in England, placed it even further away from flammable materials (Forman 1948, 121). This innovation was enthusiastically embraced by English and Scots-Irish settlers in the American South, where the displacement provided the further benefit of eliminating interior heat throughout the long and hot summers (Figure 11-2).

Several other strategies were employed in the American South to facilitate ventilation. Doors became both longer, and wider and wider. In the 19th century, in plantation residences, the so-called French doors reaching from near the ceiling to the floor took the place of the smaller standard windows used elsewhere. Hall passageways also were enlarged to encourage through movement of breezes. House

11-2. Good example of an exterior stone chimney attached to a log house. A variety of boulders and flat fieldstones have been used. A lime mortar binds the stone. Note also the large boulders upon which the sills of the house rest. Located in Cades Cove, TN (photo by the author, 1972).

plans, referred to as letter plans (T, L, H, U) by Thomas Waterman (1950, 17), were one room wide rather than the two found in double file houses, which helped improve cross-ventilation. The detached kitchen was probably the most effective feature of all (Gamble 1990, 16–18).

In African-American communities in southern Maryland, log chimneys were built and deliberately made to lean away from the house for fire protection. If a fire did start, the chimney could be quickly toppled. Some of these chimneys leaned so far they had to be propped with poles (McDaniel 1982, 78). The practice of building outward-tilting stick chimneys was common with all groups throughout Appalachia (Eller 1979, 96).

The perfection of the chimney in Europe had wide-reaching consequences for traditional building. Referring to housing in Essex, Harry Forrester (1959, 7) observed, "a brick chimney against a wall in place of a central hearth made it practicable to carry the first floor across the whole of the house, thus converting the upper part of the hall into an extra chamber." The modification also changed the external appearance of the structure by permitting jetties to be continuous across the entire facade. A shift to houses of two stories, easier to heat through openings or grates in the upper floor, and thus more habitable, occurred all across Europe (Hansen 1971, 49; Holan 1990, 72).

Another consequence of the popularization of the brick chimney was to encourage the development of the *black kitchen* dwelling in east and central Europe (Haslova and Vadjio 1974, 38). The name comes from the fact that the centrally located kitchen is really a walk-in hearth surrounded by massive brick and mud walls, and provided with a tall tapering chimney on which soot collects (Figure 11-3). Cooking is done within this room, although other food preparation and cleanup may be done in an adjoining room. Heat is provided to the rest of the house both by radiation from the walls and from low vents, which open into surrounding rooms (Ionescu 1957, 32). The upper reaches of the chimney are used for smoking and curing meats. The black kitchen house was introduced into North America by German-Russian Mennonites in Manitoba (Noble 1992b) and by Pomeranian Germans in Wisconsin (Perrin 1961), but it was always a rare type in the latter area. Some other German-Russians had abandoned the black kitchen in their long residence in the Volga River valley settlements. Upon their resettlement in Kansas, they constructed dwellings that had the Slavic adobe and brick hearth and oven in the center of the structure (Petersen 1976, 25), rather than the walk-in black kitchen. This substitution of a Slavic feature with a German one is a fine example of *cultural borrowing*. William Sherman (1974, 188–9) has noted other examples of the Russian and German exchange of ideas and culture.

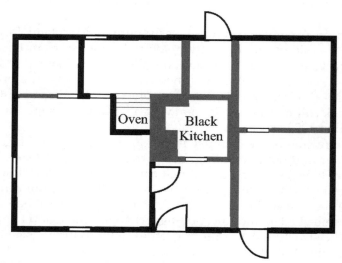

11-3. *Plan of a black kitchen house from Furstenwald, Germany (drawn by Iraida Galdon Soler, based on Radig 1966, 56).*

Within the structure, in addition to the adoption in places of the black kitchen, the effect of heating decided the placement of rooms. Kitchens, or other rooms in which cooking is done or fires kept, tend to be on the north side of buildings in the northern hemisphere (Bemis and Burchard 1933, 264), and on the south side in the southern hemisphere (Metson 1945, 359). In the adobe houses of the early Hispanic settlers in New Mexico, the problem of excess heat from the kitchen was solved by seasonal relocation. The kitchen had a northern location in the summer and a southern position in the winter. The rooms seasonally vacated were used for storage in the interim (Boyd 1974, 12). In other communities – the German-Russian Mennonites in Saskatchewan, for example – women took advantage of warm summer temperatures to cook and bake on oven stoves "made of bricks that stood outside in the farmyard away from the farmhouse" (Brednich 1977, 25).

An even more widespread strategy for combating the heat of summer was found from the Appalachian uplands all the way to the Rocky Mountains. Here, in an area where seasonal contrasts of temperature are extreme, the preparation of food was also undertaken in seasonally differentiated locations (Noble 1984, 2:97–8). The fireplace or stove inside the dwellings was used in the cooler weather when the warmth generated was welcome. In the hot season, cooking at first was done outside in the open, and later in the summer kitchen, a small (12–14 x 20–22 feet), one- or two-room rectangular building standing several feet away from the dwelling, and having its own stove or fireplace (Figure 11-4). This practice had the additional

11-4. The gable window of the summer kitchen indicates a loft used for storage and perhaps earlier for sleeping during harvest, when additional hands were needed. The off-center location of the window probably indicates an interior-positioned gable chimney. The farm is located near Findlay, OH (photo by the author, 1982).

11-5. This small frame-and-log summer kitchen in northeastern Ohio is now very close to the house because the house wing is a later addition to the original structure (photo by the author, 1982).

benefits, beyond the ensuring of cooler temperatures in the house, of reducing fire risk for part of the year, removing cooking and other food preparation odors, and litter and clutter from the main structure, and reducing flies and bug infestation there. After summer cooking and fall butchering, "the summer kitchen served as a walk-in refrigerator until Spring" (Bobbitt 1989, 233).

The summer kitchen seems to be a Germanic feature (van Ravenswaay 1977, 137; Williams 1916, 150; Long 1965). Nevertheless, they proved so useful that, as an excellent illustration of *cultural borrowing*, the idea of the summer kitchen (Figure 11-5) was adopted in America by many non-Germanic settlers. Hattie Williams quotes a German source to the effect that "in the German colonies in Russia, this structure was the chief means of protection against fire, which proves so destructive given thatched roofs. In summer, when the buildings were not protected by snow, no fires were allowed built in the main dwelling but all cooking had to be done in these Sommerkuechen." Amos Long Jr. offers a different explanation for the development of summer kitchens among the Germans in Pennsylvania. He suggests that use as a summer kitchen was a stage in the life of original small dwellings, evolved as families grew, and not purpose-built buildings.

> As the size of the family increased and as the dwellings of the early pioneers or the facilities of the kitchen became inadequate to perform the increased domestic chores associated with farm and home, succeeding generations, during the latter part of the 18th and 19th centuries erected a separate or attached building; or, a completely new and larger main

dwelling was erected separate from or against the original structure. The original structure was then frequently used as the summer house or work kitchen. (Long 1965, 11)

Although strongly associated in North America with settlers of Germanic origin, the summer kitchen is not well documented among Germans in Europe, except for those with a Russian connection. Timothy Kloberdanz (1980) indicates that the German Mennonites borrowed both the centrally positioned adobe brick oven and the summer kitchen from their Russian neighbors, which would make the latter facility a Slavic feature rather than German. The structure has been mentioned as a feature of traditional Magyar cottages in a village near Budapest (Mendele 1991, 8), which suggests another possibility for the origins of the building. Furthermore, the summer kitchen is a feature of traditional farmsteads in Estonia, as witnessed by their inclusion in the Estonian open-air museum (Lange 1995, 62).

In North America, detached or "summer" kitchens are also reported among Norwegian settlers in Texas, although the feature apparently is not found in Norway (Breisch 1994, 99). The greatly increased heat of a long Texas summer probably explains their adoption in that state by Norwegians, who may have borrowed the idea from nearby Germans.

To a certain extent, the design of the hearth and its efficiency when needed for warmth rather than just food preparation, depended upon the fuel being consumed. The Dutch in Pella, Iowa, who migrated there directly from the Netherlands, "discovered that shallow hearths designed for peat fuel provided insufficient warmth against the harsh Iowa cold and could not accommodate logs adequately" (Long 1981, 17). They quickly switched to fireplaces of American size.

In tropical areas, as much cooking as possible is done outdoors because of the heat generated, the ease of smoke dissipation, and the lower risk of fire. At the same time, outdoor cooking must deal with frequent, and often heavy, rainfall. In West Africa, many foods require pulverizing as an initial step in cooking. In Ghana, "the nature of the preparation of certain meals, like *fufu* which requires pounding with pestles which are unusually long in Ashanti, would require ceiling heights that are not attainable in the average kitchen; it therefore has to be done outside" (Faculty of Architecture 1978, 458) whenever there is a respite from the rain.

For traditional buildings, the height of the ceiling, or even its existence at all, often provides an explanation of its temperature-regulating function. If it is lacking or very high, the feature allows hot air to rise until collected near the roof. If it is lower, its function is to conserve heat. G.J. Afolabi Ojo (1976, 17) observed that the Yoruba constructed a lower ceiling in order to deal with the lower temperatures of nighttime, particularly during *harmattan* season. Russian settlers in Alaska were faced with a different situation. To combat long cold periods they needed to insulate dwellings, which they did by placing a filling of sand between ground-floor ceilings and the floor of the upper story of log houses. Only a log or stone house could bear such weight.

In northern China, the kitchen tends to be centrally located. This was the most economical location for fuel conservation and maximum heat production in the winter for the entire house. In the south, the kitchen is usually situated in the northern part of the dwelling, which accords with feng shui principles that the preferred orientation of houses is to the south, and the kitchen should be as far away as possible from the entrance (Walters 1988, 48–9). Another problem in northern Chinese traditional dwellings is that the large bed built of sun-dried bricks is often connected by smoke passages to the kitchen stove and at the other end to a chimney. "When a fire is lighted in the stove the smoke passes through the tunnels into the chimney and then into the air" (Yang 1965, 24). This arrangement tends to overheat the rooms in summer, resulting in recourse to a temporary or make-shift kitchen in the open. A similar heating system connects kitchen and master bedroom in traditional Korean houses (Choi 1987, 18; Lee 1991, 66). Two contrasting heat surfaces are produced, the *ondol*, a clay hypocaust-heated floor, and the *maru*, a wood-floored area with an empty space beneath for ventilation (Choi 1999, 99–100).

Similar in principle is the *gloria*, used in Castile in northern Spain for heating during the long winters (Carver 1981, 102). The fuel is straw, which is burned "at the mouth of a furnace," located outside but adjacent to the entrance.

> The hot air that is produced circulates in a space between the real floor of the dwelling and the raised floor of the rooms that are to be heated. This space contains a series of ducts which channel the hot air from the fireplace across the width of the building and over to a vertical chimney on the other side. (Feduchi 1974, 121)

The kitchen of the Irish longhouse stood in the center of the structure between the byre and the bedroom. In western Ireland, both a front and a back door gave direct access to the kitchen. By using only the lee-side door, depending on the direction of the wind, warmth in the kitchen could be regulated. "A stranger coming to the closed door instead of the open one may be greeted with the remark 'You'd make a bad sailor,' in other words, 'you do not appear to know from which direction the wind is blowing'" (O'Danachair 1964, 70).

In colonial New England dwellings, the central location of the kitchen or cooking place maximized heat generation within the entire house during the winter season. The location of the buttery and dairy rooms followed the reverse process. They needed to be in the coolest parts of the structure, which was normally in the north or east corner of the rear of the house (Cummings 1979, 31).

Ultimately, the chimney became one of the most distinctive elements of the house both in northwestern Europe and eastern and southern United States (Figure 11-2). Chimneys were considered so significant that they sometimes became the basis for house classification systems (Bemis and Burchard 1933, 264–5), or at least critical elements of the system (Figure 11-6) (Noble 1984, 1:52–5).

A significant improvement in space heating was the perfection of fireplaces in upper-story rooms. They typically were smaller than the hearths of the ground floor because less heat was needed in the upper rooms. The flue diameter could be smaller, and its reduced size "permitted offsets at floor level to support the hearth of only a small fireplace" (Kauffman 1972, 40). In the Channel Island of Guernsey, second-story fireplaces began to be built after 1720.

> It was only then that the Guernsey builders discovered that building a brick partition inside a wide chimney provided two flues, enabling one chimney to serve two fireplaces; previous to that date, they had to choose between a downstairs or upstairs fireplace; they could not have both, with a one-flue chimney. It was definitely the most important house improvement in the first of the 18th century. (Guernsey Society 1963, 22)

Although the hot-air furnace had been invented as early as 1815 (Allen 1930, 62), heating by means of open fireplaces remained common in parts of the US well into the 20th century. In the Cotton Belt, almost half (46.5%) of farmhouses surveyed at the beginning of the 1930s Depression were heated only by a fireplace. The percentages in the Tobacco–Bluegrass area (21%) and the Appalachian–Ozark highlands (15.5%) were lower, but still significant (Melvin 1932, 11). In other parts of the world, open fires persist to the present day in the Himalaya (ud-Din 1984, 270, 283) and other mountain areas, and many, many other rural locations.

An unforeseen consequence of house improvement with the spread of chimneys was the imposition of hearth taxes introduced in England and Ireland in the 17th century. The tax was initially favored by taxing authorities (see Chapter 2). However, popular pressure eventually forced officials to agree that only actively working hearths would be taxed.

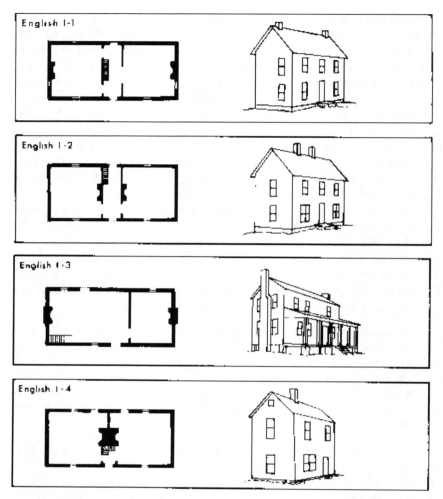

English I-1

English I-2

English I-3

English I-4

11-6. *The number and position of chimneys can be a key element in classifying houses. These are all I-houses but are sub-types because they have interior gable, interior paired, external gable or central stack chimneys (drawing by M. Margaret Geib).*

Fire also has a symbolic or mystical aspect, in addition to simply providing warmth. The domestication of fire proved to be one of mankind's greatest achievements. In the process, fire gained an aura of sanctity not entirely lost today in many societies (witness Parsee fire temples in India), and its symbolism remains strong (witness the Olympic Games' torch bearing and national eternal flame memorials). The power of fire to intimidate wild animals was not lost on early tribes. Even up to the present century, among Australian aborigines fires were "built and kept going on nights when temperatures are 100 °F and no cooking is done – it keeps spirits away" (Rapoport 1977, 41).

In areas with long cold winters, conserving heat within a structure is as important as creating the heat in the first place. The insulating property of construction materials is the key. Earth materials, including ice, generally prove superior to wood or metal. American Plains Indians recognized the value of the earth, and in winter customarily piled earth and stones all round the base of their tipis to block cold drafts. The practice had the additional advantage of helping to anchor the structure against winter winds (Jeancon and Douglas 1931, 2). Regardless of the particular materials used for insulation, effective construction must attempt to block any openings, even wall cracks and crevices.

A related strategy to conserve warmth is to pile up a low barrier to cold temperatures along the lowest parts of the walls, especially the wall facing the prevailing wind. In the colonial period, Connecticut houses were often banked with turf, piles of leaves or, near the coast, with seaweed (Isham and Brown 1900, 202). Even today, in rural areas of the northern United States, low bales of hay can be seen in the wintertime piled up around the foundations of frame houses. Traditional farmhouses in the Jaeren area of extreme southern Norway often had high stone walls erected only about three feet to the windward of the house as a buffer in order to break the force of strong prevailing winds. The barrier also significantly reduced the effects of penetrating moisture-laden wind, which contributed to wood rot (Norsk Folkemuseum 1996, 71 & 76).

In the middle latitudes, the challenge is not just conserving heat in winter, but also dissipating it in summer to ensure maximum *cooling*. Structures built into the earth (see Chapter 7) and those made of sod or turf work well (Barns 1930, 61). Adobe, which is one of the most efficient insulating materials, also functions well in desert areas, where days may be extremely hot with nighttimes significantly cooler (Rodger 1974). The thickness of walls of adobe ensures cooler daytime temperatures, while "the solar heat trapped by the roof slab in the daytime keeps the interior warm through the chill night" (Fitch and Branch 1960, 139). Another quite effective material used to retain heat is the black tent found in Afghanistan and surrounding areas. Made of woven goat hair, the dark material absorbs heat as well as providing shade so that the interiors are up to 10–15° Centigrade cooler than the surrounding atmosphere (Szabo and Barfield 1991, 29).

In humid areas such as the eastern Midwest of the United States, structures were often built with ventilation tunnels. These were not for the comfort of residents, but rather to keep storage cellars cool or to keep the wooden understructure of a building cool and dry in order to prevent rot (Bronner 1980, 14–15). Elsewhere, the widespread use of decorative screens and fretwork was another technique widely employed to promote air circulation. It had the additional important advantage of filtering sunlight and reducing glare (Crain 1994, 5).

In the warm deserts or near-deserts, where humidity is low, windows are small, and may even be replaced by "small air holes" in order to reduce the nuisance of dirt and dust (Harrison and Hubbard 1949, 3). The process demonstrates sound principles of aerodynamics:

> If you perforate the back wall of the building with a few ventilation holes, placed high up to minimize dust, [and keep a large opening opposite to the prevailing wind] the low pressure inside the room will actively suck air in through the holes, creating a steady breeze. The larger the opening facing downwind, the stronger will be the breeze coming through the holes. (Facey 1997, 77)

A few desert areas, however, experience high humidity. One such is the Red Sea coast of Saudi Arabia (Talib 1984, 67–72). Here, and in other similar climatic areas, elaborately carved wooden window screens called *mashrabiyas* or *rowshans* not only provide privacy but, because they project out from the wall, encourage desirable cross-ventilation. These windows, which can be highly decorative, are also a feature of dwellings in Pakistan and western India (Noble 2003, 48).

Constructing buildings around a restricted courtyard is a widely employed strategy to reduce the effects of heating by utilizing convectional methods, but this works best in regions where clouds (especially at night) are not common (Facey 1997, 74). Also, the courtyard must be small enough so that the walls of a two-story house will shade the area during the day. "The courtyard floor and earth beneath acts as a combined radiating and storage unit" (Durham 1960, 666). Optimal cooling occurs where the building surrounding the courtyard or atrium is two, or even three, stories high. The ground floor in such instances is used mostly for storage and for resting in the hottest season. The upper floor is the main living floor and the third floor or terrace provides accommodation for sleeping in the hottest season (Talib 1984, 50). The small courtyard or atrium acts as a ventilator shaft, permitting hot air to be expelled as it is warmed by the sun during the day, and to allow cooler night air to sink and pass into surrounding rooms after dark.

Frequently, the courtyard of a dwelling in dry climates will contain a pool or fountain and plantings of some sort.

The evaporation of water and the presence of plants both raises the humidity in unpleasantly dry climates and helps to keep the air cool. In moderately humid climates such as in Algiers, on the other hand, houses do not contain courtyard pools because any increase in the already high relative humidity would cause discomfort. (Petherbridge 1978, 200)

In northern Syria, a rough but ingenious attempt to provide ventilation in the adobe beehive dwellings is accomplished "by building in lengths of tree trunk about 4 inches in diameter and longer than the thickness of the dome. These are twisted to keep them free while the dome is drying and later can be pulled out in summer for a better circulation of air" (Copeland 1955, 23). Even in polar areas, ventilation devices were sometimes required to keep the interiors habitable regardless of outside temperature. One of the most unusual was that employed by Siberian and St. Lawrence Island Eskimos, who used a hollowed-out whale vertebra as a vent passage in the roof of their semi-subterranean winter houses (Lee and Reinhardt 2003, 132).

In the Middle East, several related devices have been evolved to use the wind as an effective cooling agent. The most important of these are the wind tower, the wind catcher, the wind sail, and the *porous water jar system*. This latter device, called the *maziara* in rural areas of Upper Egypt, is employed at many other locations in the Middle East. It consists of a large porous water jar placed in a windward opening. Testing equipment has shown that even though the outside temperature ranged from 19° to 36 °Centigrade, the temperature of the maziara water remained constant at about 20 °Centigrade. This constancy is explained by the fact that, as outside air temperature rises, relative humidity decreases, and as the air becomes drier more water evaporates and the cooling rate increases. "One feels comfortable in Egypt only between the narrow ranges of 21 °C to 26 °C" (Cain et al. 1976, 61). Combined with a wind catcher, the cooling efficiency is even better. A loosely woven, thick mat placed across a door or window opening and regularly doused with water is a cruder variation of the same idea. It can be found from northern India to Iran (Bourgeois 1980, 75).

The *wind catcher* is probably the most widely distributed technique for cooling in the Middle East. The term "wind catcher" refers to a group of devices consisting of a fixed hood or scoop just above the roofline of a dwelling (Figure 11-7) and attached to an open shaft, which in its turn leads to openings into various rooms. The direction of the wind catchers is fixed, to the north in Egypt and to the northwest in Sind, Pakistan to catch the prevailing wind. The height is usually above roof level, where wind velocity is greatest (Lari 1989, 134).

A variation of the wind catcher can be found in the eastern province of Saudi Arabia. A row of openings, called *badgirs*, is placed along the second-floor wall of the dwelling. "The wall panel above the opening is recessed and acts as a wind catcher. The indirect passage of air prevents dust from entering and provides privacy" (Talib 1984, 89). The top of the device consists of another wooden panel, which can be lowered to reduce airflow or dropped entirely to close off the intake during sandstorms.

A simpler form called a *wind sail* occurs throughout the Persian Gulf and Gulf of Oman areas. These consist of four vanes of huge cloth sails erected within a wooden frame and placed atop the dwelling. The moveable vanes permit the device to trap the frequently shifting winds (Cain et al. 1975, 218), and to deflect them into the dwellings.

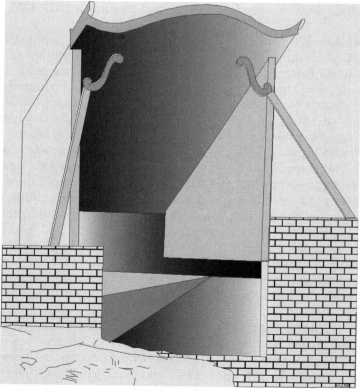

11-7. *A wind catcher of the type used in Cairo, Egypt. The device faces the normal direction of prevailing winds. Its direction cannot be adjusted (drawn by Iraida Galdon Soler, based upon Lari 1989, 133).*

Finally, in Iran and the United Arab Emirates, one encounters the *wind tower* (Figure 11-8). These are variations of the wind catcher, but in a much more elaborate and sophisticated form. The tower is quite tall to catch maximum wind movement, to be above the dust and pollution level, and to avoid flies and mosquitoes. Built of stone and mortar, the height of the wind tower has the additional advantage of thermal mass. The tower itself cools off at night and remains cool through much of the next day. Air entering the tower is cooled, and because cool air is heavier than warm, it falls through the tower and into the dwelling (Johnson 1995, 14). One great advantage of the wind tower over the catcher is that it is multidirectional (Jackson and Coles 1975, 52).

The cooling efficiency of both wind towers and wind catchers is enhanced if the captured breezes can be directed across a pool or fountain. In the winter season, both wind catchers and wind towers must be covered to exclude wind that is too cold. Covers are also necessary when sand or dust storms blow.

In lower latitudes generally, and especially in humid ones, dissipating heat is more important than conserving it. Even just the slight movement of air in warmer latitudes provides a cooling effect. Houses of the colonial period in Lagos, Nigeria show several strategies to promote ventilation. Initially built on stilts, the elevated position allowed inhabitants maximum benefit from cooling breezes. Multiple windows accompanied by slatted jalousies near the floor level permit intake of air (Jack 1955, 101–2). Ventilation at or near floor level is much more effective in cooling in tropical areas (Yuan 1981, 22).

Extremes of heat are rarely encountered in humid tropical regions, but humidity is uncomfortably high. The Panare of the Orinoco plain, Venezuela construct a densely thatched, conical, communal dwelling with a roof that reaches the ground. Only a single, small door opening and a tiny smoke hole break the roof/wall surface. Admirably suited to provide protection against rain in the somewhat cooler part of the year, the structure, which has no cross-ventilation, is uninhabitable in

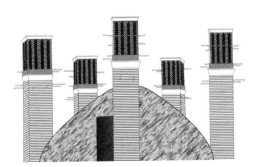

11-8. Wind towers of the type found in Yazd, Iran. The top of the tower can be turned to face any wind direction (drawn by Iraida Galdon Soler, based on Lari, 1989, 126).

the hotter, longer dry season. The solution is for the group to break into small parties, seek temporary places for hunting and fishing, and to sleep in the open in hammocks (Duly 1979, 66).

A checklist for optimal climatic control in the tropics has been compiled by Jee Yuan Lim (1987, 71):

> allowing adequate ventilation for cooling and reduction of humidity; use building materials with low thermal capacity so that little heat is transmitted into the house; control desert solar radiation; control glare from the open skies and surroundings; protection against rain; and ensure adequate natural vegetation in the surroundings to provide for a cooler micro climate.

Careful adjustment to climatic requirements characterized the *bahay kubo*, the traditional rural house of the Philippines. Built on stilts to encourage air circulation, the construction is light and porous.

> Light and air enter the house through large windows which are opened by pushing out bamboo panels covered with thatch shingles, through the floors and, occasionally through gaps in the woven walls. Air flows through the house continuously even on a hot day, while light suffuses the interior in a unique, soothing, diffused manner. (Zialcita 1997, 47)

A traditional feature of houses in both Southeast and South Asia is the open, but roofed, verandah. Often almost surrounding the dwelling, the verandah protects it from most rain, even in the monsoon. Hence household activities can be carried on in the cooler verandah rather than in the interior of the house. It is also here that visitors are received (Hilton 1956, 135; Charpentier 1982, 54; Dall 1982; Dumarcay 1987, 30) and offered a drink of water kept cool in clay jars (Charern-supkul and Tamiyabandha 1979, 49; Thomsen 1982, 86).

Traditional structures are not always carefully adapted to fluctuations in seasonal temperature. For example:

> The prevailing type of Japanese house was designed for the never-ending summer of the tropics. This would appear to be one of the cultural features that the Japanese inherited from that branch of their stock which moved northward from the tropical islands of southeastern Asia. In its present-day modified form it is perfectly adjusted to the long, hot, humid summer of subtropical Japan, which is, to be sure, the dominant season in the populous southwestern part of the country. It is less well adapted, on the other hand, to the chilly, raw winters of the same section, and still less so to northern Honshu and Hokkaido with their continental winter climates. (Trewartha 1945, 185)

"The structure of a Japanese house is completely adapted to the requirements of summer. Indeed, it seems to be only a summer house" (Taut 1958, 79). What more could it be, with only paper walls which slide to create wide openings, and with heat only from a charcoal brazier?

> Apparently the philosophy of the Japanese is to endure the discomfort of winter in anticipation of obtaining the fullest enjoyment of the long summer to come. Genuine fortitude is required, however, to carry on normal living throughout the winter in a drafty tropical house in which little or no provision is made for heating the rooms, but only the occupants. It is true that in the mountains and in northern Japan, where winter temperatures are much lower and the summer period cooler and shorter, the subtropical house has been modified to some extent, but the amazing thing is that so many of its tropical features have been retained. (Trewartha 1945, 185–6)

The emergence of mankind from excavated dwellings raised the critical question of how to deal with greater seasonal temperature variations. In higher latitudes the problem was the extremely cold temperatures of long winters, while in the tropics it was the heat of long summers. In the middle latitudes both conditions were the challenge. A variety of techniques, slowly perfected because of the low levels of technology in traditional societies, was the result.

~ 12 ~

Ceremony and Decoration

In traditional societies, "the act of constructing a house goes beyond simply providing protection against the elements. It also requires assuring spiritual protection for those who will live in the house. Supernatural powers are focused on a site in advance of any actual construction as well as upon the completed building" (Pavlides and Hesser 1989, 290).

In Chapter 4 we noted the influence of environment, especially climate, on building form and features, but social custom and social pressure may also determine architectural features. One example out of many is the popularization of the use of weatherboarding over exposed log or plank walls in the coastal districts of Norway in the 18th century. "It was not the necessity of insolation against cold," but rather the desire to form a stronger affinity with the fashionable wall covering popular in much of the rest of Europe at that time (Alnaes 1950, 150). Likewise, the construction of a verandah on even average traditional houses in Madagascar ensures social distinction and prestige (Block 1971, 12).

But fashions and social pressures do shift. Throughout almost the first three-quarters of the 20th century, log houses in the United States, as in Norway, were considered to be rough, primitive, and low-class housing. As a consequence, weatherboards were widely used to mask earlier log construction (Gavin 1997, 13 & 21). However, in the affluent 1960s, when many individuals were seeking a challenge to the status quo, fashions changed and social pressure relaxed. These changes encouraged persons who wished to ride the changing fashion crest, to seek out hidden log buildings, to rip off the siding, and to bask in the glow of their visual confirmation of society's rediscovery of its heritage. Needless to say, this was not a widely pursued innovation, but enough affluent people did do so in their quest to maintain their position as societal leaders. As a result, the log house reasserted its position as an American icon, regardless of the ethnic background of its original builders.

Another instance of social pressure to adopt a currently popular fashion can be seen in the replacement of hipped roof-ends by gables in western Ireland. "It is most likely that the adoption of gable ends was essentially the spread of a fashion, emanating perhaps from the towns or copied from the superior dwellings of the landowning class, which had the advantage of being more convenient when any expansion of the house was undertaken" (Aalen 1966, 53). In both these cases, modification propelled by social pressure had a quite practical benefit – in Norway with better insulation and in Ireland much greater ease of expansion.

The perceived reasons for *rituals* associated with building were "to ensure good fortune, a comfortable and happy life and a progressive increase in wealth and reputation" (Charernsupkul and Temiyabandha 1979, 57). Lord Raglan (1964) identifies five types of rites: (1) to ensure the building site finds favor with the gods; (2) to consecrate it after divine approval has been secured; (3) rites when the foundations are laid; (4) rites performed during the building; and (5) rites performed when building is completed, but before the structure is occupied. Selection of a suitable building site initiates the process of construction and hence in most traditional societies must be given appropriate ceremonial attention. One important consideration in Ireland was to ensure that fairy pathways not be encroached upon or blocked, and in Sweden permission had to be asked of fairies before building.

A more widely held concern was to ensure that no malevolent forces could influence the proposed house site. This was done in Ireland by placing "two large stones in the positions where the corners of a gable would be. On top of these stones lamps were placed and lighted. If they were not interfered with after a few nights, it was considered safe enough to proceed with building on the site, but otherwise the site was not considered lucky" (Gailey 1984, 28).

Similarly, among certain tribes in central India the prospective householder

> places three stones, one on top of the other, at the four corners of the plot chosen. He also places three stones at the point where he wants to set the three middle posts in support of the ridge of the roof. Then he ties a string round the four corners of the chosen site. This is done in the evening. The next morning he returns to the site and if he finds the stones still undisturbed, he believes this to be a sign that he should build his house there. But if the stones have been disturbed and scattered by some animal stumbling over them during the night, the man goes in search of another site, believing that his family would come to harm if he were to build on that particular site. (Fuchs 1960, 26)

A somewhat similar divination ceremony is reported from Malaysia (Lim 1987, 98–9). Although identified as a ceremony to locate the site of a house, it appears in reality more a ceremony to confirm an already chosen site. The rites are performed in early evening by the carpenter or someone else familiar with ceremonial rituals. Incense is burned and prayers are offered, but the critical part of the rituals involves the woman of the house using her out-stretched arms to measure both a stick and a length of rattan, which is subsequently tied to the stick. The stick is driven into the ground to mark the exact center of the proposed house and a brim-full pail of water on a plate is placed beside it. The next morning the rattan and stick are measured again to see if they have lengthened. The small pail of water is checked to see if it has overflowed into the plate. If any of these actions have occurred, the site is suitable. The water is the key element since birds and small animals attracted to the water for a drink are likely to ensure the overflow.

"In Thailand, rituals start with a real attempt at divination." Eight opaque jars, each containing a different totem, are assembled on site. One jar is chosen at random. "If it contains rice, the future of the house will be assured and happy, if it is charcoal, it might burn down, if it is a white hair, its life will be short, if it is a stone, its occupant will be rich, and so on" (Dumarcay 1987, 15).

The commencement of building represents one of the most important occasions in which ritual was centered. The ceremonies associated with choice of location have already been discussed above and in Chapter 4. India offers a wide variety of rituals. In Haryana state, Fridays and Sundays are considered the most auspicious days to begin building (Chandhoke 1990, 183). In former times, Muslims wishing to construct a house would often seek out a Hindu Brahmin priest to fix the best day (Clarke 1883, 738).

At the very beginning, even before any construction activity, the earth that would be disturbed, symbolically injured, or violated, had to be propitiated to atone for these subsequent acts. "In Gujarat the owner pours water into the first pit which is dug, sprinkles lac and red powder, puts in a betel nut and coins and digs a clod himself to share in the risk." In Kandesh, the owner pours melted butter on the main post "till it trickles into the soil, ties a yellow cloth filled with rice and millet round the pole, and lays holy grass on the top." In South Karnataka, a large square is marked out with lines of whitewash on the ground and magical symbols in the corners. A roughly drawn humanoid figure in the center represents the earth spirit dwelling in the ground. It is surrounded with flowers and boiled rice. This practice, and other similar ones throughout South India, derives from ancient Indian rituals collectively called *vaastu shastra*, which in simple terms may be viewed as "the creation of forms that are in harmony with the natural laws of the cosmos" (Arya 2000, 2).

In central India, "an astrologer calculates the direction in which the world serpent is lying and plants the first brick or stone to the left of that direction." The explanation is that snakes and elephants are believed always to turn to the right. The house is thus protected from earthquakes or destruction caused by movement of those powerful creatures (Crooke 1918, 132–3).

In many societies, a dwelling is considered to be alive and therefore rituals must be addressed to the house itself, and not to impersonal forces or spirits, however evil or potent they may be (Howe 1983, 139). Among the Savunese the cosmology of the house extends to providing the individual constructional components with names of human body parts. Thus a careful listener can identify neck, head, tail, chest, ribs, snout, and cheeks in the layout of the house. Perhaps the most interesting place is the gap that exists on the thatching framework. "Its ends do not quite meet and the opening is considered the path of the 'breath' of the house" (Kana 1980, 228), thus confirming the living state of the dwelling. Elsewhere in Indonesia, similar attempts to humanize dwellings are encountered. In Bali "a house, like a human being, has a head – the family shrine; arms – the sleeping quarters and the social parlour; a navel – the courtyard; sexual organs – the gate; legs and feet – the kitchen and the granary; and anus – the pit in the backyard where the refuse is disposed of" (Covarrubias 1942, 88).

A less descriptive, but no less symbolic, approach was employed by the Pueblo peoples, who "baptized the homes with offerings after construction just as they did their children after birth" (Nabokov 1981, 4). Similarly, in societies where timber is felled for house construction, prayers and offerings must be made to the tree. In Myanmar (Burma), "before a tree is cut, a Wa villager must first ask permission and give the tree the reason for felling it" (Nwe 2003, 227).

When used as posts for house building in eastern Sumba, Indonesia, the felled trees must be erected in the same manner in which they grew, with root end down and the crown end upward. The word used to describe the erection of the post is *pamula*, meaning "to plant." Dire consequences would attend those posts improperly planted – early rot, illness of inhabitants and even death (Forth 1981, 32).

In Southeast Asia, measurements based on the human body are used to plan house construction. This gives the structure a close human connection and helps establish the idea that the house is alive. In Bali, "when the size of any particular part has been so determined a small, additional length known as the 'soul of the measure' is tacked onto the end" (Howe 1983, 139). Elsewhere in Southeast Asia, an offering may be made to appease the *naga* (snake spirit), who is the spiritual owner of the land and who lives beneath the site (Charpentier 1982, 58; Dumarcay 1987, 15). This ceremony undoubtedly is an attempt to placate the very real venomous snakes that abound in the countryside. Placing snakes, usually vipers, in the foundations or thresholds of housebarns in Scandinavian countries was also formerly a widespread practice (Sandklef 1949, 53), and for the same reason.

It must not be thought that all traditional house-building rituals are based upon superstition. The Temne of Guinea rely on measurements provided by "the outstretched arms of any adult man," which is then transferred to a convenient stick (Littlejohn 1960, 64–5). As a result, dimensions vary from house to house over a short range. Similar techniques are known from Bali (Soebadio 1975) and it is likely that they have been employed in most lower technology societies because of the simplicity of the technique. Vivat Temiyabandha offers an example of the very practical matters that gave rise to timber cutting and transport taboos:

> Forest logs could only be transported either by river during the month or so of high water or, beginning some two months later, by ox-cart during the months of the cool dry season after the paddy had been planted in the fields. Because cutting timber in the forest and transporting it back to the villages was impractical during the other months of the year it was also regarded, and declared, inauspicious to do this work in the other months. (Charernsupkul and Temiyabandha 1979, 57)

Other taboos and rituals surround the actual construction processes. Even the position of posts laid out on the ground before their use is determined according to a set of rules. Such orientation may vary according to the month of construction, but their pointing to the southwest is never allowed in certain parts of Southeast Asia (Dumarcay 1987, 16). The erection of the posts may follow a religiously prescribed uniformity. In Bali, pillars must be erected in a clockwise order with the initial post located in the northeastern corner. In Laos, the posts' orientation depends on the naga's position at the time of building (Charpentier 1982, 58).

Among the Sotho of South Africa, two parts of a circular hut under construction are especially important ritually. These are a raised ledge of mud, which functions as a stand for the household's pots, and the entrance doorway. The medicine man of the group places forked sticks of *mofifi* wood at these places. "These protect the inmates from evil influences for they shroud the interior of the hut in darkness . . . and evil spirits are unable to see the objects inside. A third mofifi prong is placed in the apex of the thatch when the hut is completed to ward off lightning" (Walton 1948, 140).

Placing symbolic and/or sacred objects within the structure so that they become a permanent part of the building is practiced in many different parts of the world (Pavlides and Hesser 1989, 282). The ancient custom of embedding a cock's head and a few coins in the cornerstone of a dwelling continues to the present day in parts of Fenno-Scandinavia (Sandklef 1949, 52–4) and in the island of Cephalonia, Greece, where the balance of the rooster is stewed with rice and egg-lemon sauce and consumed by those helping to build the house. The rooster's spirit is thought to enter the building "and consequently no other spirit can enter . . . If this is not done the house will be haunted" (Vryonis 1975, 401). As a further protection, an Orthodox priest is employed to read prayers and swing incense fumes from a censer to drive away evil spirits.

Elsewhere, a number of ceremonies are observed when a new dwelling is about to be occupied. The new Navajo owner "strews pollen on the poles of the cardinal points when he is ready to occupy a new hogan" (Haile 1942, 45). Among the Tarascans of the Sierra Madre Occidental of Mexico, as the frames and lintels of every door and window are completed, several small bunches of flowers are hung. Another more elaborate ceremony occurs with the final roofing of the dwelling. Cigarettes are offered to friends and relatives, who then are obligated to participate in the nailing of the wooden roof shakes. After the completion of the roof, a celebration with food and liquor finishes the rituals (Beals et al. 1944, 30).

In addition to rituals that initiate a new dwelling, other ceremonies are performed periodically to ensure continued good luck and prosperity (Figure 12-1). Among many peoples a yearly repainting of the structure is an accepted custom. Among Slavic people, such repainting often coincides with Easter. An association with spring-time rebirth and renewal is likely. Lord Raglan (1964, 43) suggests that the annual rite of house purification, common in many societies, is the origin of the modern, widely practiced routine of "spring cleaning." In some other societies there is a connection with individual celebrations, such as a wedding. Throughout India graceful geometric symbols called *alponas* (Figure 12-2), or *kolam* or *rangavalli* in the south, are carefully marked out in rice flour just in front of entrances to ensure good fortune on festive occasions (Hakansson 1977, 84).

Women have an especially close and symbolic association with the house in many traditional societies. Not only do they spend most of their life within the dwelling, or very nearby outside, and often have been the builders of the structure, but the dwellings "are known by the name of their leading and most active woman." The affinity of women and their dwellings is further affirmed by the custom of burying the afterbirth of babies on the east side of the house in Toraja, *(right) 12-1. A small palm-frond shelter woven to provide protection for a lamp displayed at Buddhist New Year in many houses in Kandy, Sri Lanka (photo by the author, 1980).*

(below) 12-2. Geometric rice flour designs called alponas are placed in front of Indian shops or dwellings to ensure good luck (photos by the author, 1959 and 1973).

Indonesia, or even within the structure itself in Botswana (Larsson 1989, 519–20; Waterson 1989, 490), or at the threshold in central Java (Raglan 1964, 28).

In many communities, the dwelling threshold has particular symbolic significance and entrance must be by the right foot first. In some cases the threshold must not be stepped upon at all. This taboo is supposed to be the origin of the modern custom of carrying the bride across the threshold of her new home. "Among the Frisians, the 'bride-lifter' is a regular wedding official" (Raglan 1964 28). The symbolic significance of the doorway in some societies is nicely illustrated by practices prevailing among the Eskimos of St. Lawrence Island in the Bering Sea. Here, a pregnant woman must move through a doorway opening so that her head passes before her feet. This is to ensure that her baby will come out head first at birth (Carius 1979, 8).

Spirit houses found in Thailand are miniature dwellings carefully crafted and placed in a conspicuous or auspicious location within a house compound. They often are exact models of the larger traditional structures and contain images that represent the spirits who had to be displaced in the building of the dwelling. The spirit house represents the new abode of these spirits, who are given periodic offerings of flowers, food and other desirable objects (Chaichongrak et al. 2002, 23).

Not all house initiation ceremonies are observed to combat magical, symbolic or mystical forces. A few have a quite practical objective. The Mae Enga of New Guinea light a small fire inside a newly constructed dwelling before the residents move in. The warmth of the smoldering fire, which burns for two to three days, dries out both the ground and the wood of the structure, as well as driving out evil spirits. Casting leaves or fronds on the fire to create smoke has the additional benefit of expelling insects from thatching (Meggitt 1957, 175).

In the Far East, an elaborate, complex, and all-embracing geomancy casts its influence not only over traditional building in China but even among the sophisticated urban populations of Hong Kong and Singapore. Lillian Too (1996, 31) observes, "much of Feng Shui practice is based on symbolism. This often involves descriptions of mythical beasts peculiar to that culture. This creates a cultural barrier between Eastern and Western scientific understanding." You bet it does!

Although feng shui is couched in mystical expression and promises security from evil, unhappiness and misfortune by following Taoist tenets, it can also be valued on a different level as a clever and effective device to create artistically harmonious landscapes and structures. An early missionary, E.J. Eitel, (1873, 5), alert to the teleological orientation of feng shui, provided a perceptive and sensitive analysis:

> Natural science has never been cultivated in China in that technical, dry and matter-of-fact fashion, which seems to us inseparable from true science. Chinese naturalists did not take much pains in studying nature and ferreting out her hidden secrets by minute and practical tests and experiments. They invented no instruments to aid them in the observation of the heavenly bodies, they never took to hunting beetles and

stuffing birds, they shrank from the idea of dissecting animal bodies, nor did they chemically analyse inorganic substances, but with very little actual knowledge of nature they evolved a whole system of natural science from their own inner consciousness and expounded it according to the dogmatic formulae of ancient tradition. Deplorable, however, as this absence of practical and experimental investigation is, which opened the door to all sorts of conjectural theories, it preserved in Chinese natural science a spirit of sacred reverence for the divine powers of nature.

Presenting the rules and aspects of feng shui in the guise of powerful and threatening forces secures their widespread acceptance among a receptive population. What is surprising to Western observers is the strength of the acceptance of feng shui among present-day urban dwellers in Hong Kong, Taiwan, Singapore, China and elsewhere. The Japanese seek a similar harmony, balance and beauty, but in a more secular fashion (Taut 1958, 35).

The rules of carpentry are intertwined with geomancy in mainland China, and even more strongly in Taiwan. Measurements are based upon the orientation of components of the structure (e.g. doors and windows) and vary according to the direction each faces. Therefore, the width of different doors and windows will not be exactly the same, since according to geomancy measurements in some directions are favorable and others unfavorable (Ruitenbeek 1986, 20). "Before houses were 'designed' they evolved, with a sensitivity towards their environment that may be seen as truly organic" (Ayers 1981, 17). Part of this environment was the world of the supernatural, over which man had little control. Out of this belief arose the practice of placing symbols on, and offerings to, the structure to placate the spirits. James Ayers relates the 1963 discovery in London of items bricked up in a dwelling wall about 1600. These "offerings" included "a basket containing two shoes, a candlestick, a goblet, two strangled chickens and two chickens that had been walled up alive."

The roof ridge in many cultures offers the possibility for display of symbolic *decoration*. The Tarascans in Mexico affix a cross with an arch over it, decorated with paper flowers, in the middle of the ridge of the roof. "It is said to protect the house against violent storms and the devil" (Beals et al. 1944, 30). Once construction is completed, if the roof is of thatch a row of flowering plant roots or seeds may be sown along the ridge to mark the event and as a more or less permanent decorative device. Gwyn Meirion-Jones (1982, 48) comments on the procedure as followed in Brittany:

the first peg to be placed in the roof timber was driven home by the owner, who, when the roofing was complete, provided a celebration meal. Building tradesmen, masons, and carpenters, usually received nourishment in part-payment of their work. The thatcher . . . was also fed during the course of his work . . . If the food was good, he planted seeds of flowers in the clay capping of the ridge. If it had been poor, then weeds were sown instead.

I have seen the same roof ridge flowers in Normandy, and Trewartha (1945, 188) commented on the "bright-colored flowers growing on the ridge of the thatch roofs" in Japan.

In other parts of the world where sod, grass, mud, cow dung and other combinations of organic and earth materials are used as roofing, abundant floral displays can be encountered (Myrthe 1967, 96–7). These, however, have little symbolic significance. Among these are numbered the sod roofs of the American Great Plains, the early spring-flowered roofs of Scandinavia, and the garden-like displays of Kashmir (Cooper and Dawson 1998, 45). In Korea, India and Bangladesh various gourds are allowed to climb onto roofs using space otherwise wasted, and in the process keeping the vegetables away from excess moisture on the ground (Choi et al. 1999, 67).

Crossed verge boards culminating in carved animal head finials are a frequent technique, which places symbols in a highly visible location. In the Mezen river basin of northern Russia, horse heads are carved into the ends of the ridgepole rather than on the verge board extensions (Dmitrieva 1982–83, 37). In Norway, verge boards called *"vindskier* usually ended in dragon heads or some such design and were a carry-over from heathen times and Viking ships. Originally they were thought to be a protection from evil spirits" (Stewart 1972, 27–8). Decorative crossed verge boards were supplemented in the Netherlands by ornately carved single-spike wooden finials of a wide variety of design (Jans 1969, 51–7). Similar in form are the crossed verge boards noted by Marvin Mikesell (1985, 75) in the Ktama region of northern Morocco. The ends of the boards are carved in the shape of a crescent moon, "crowned with a carved model of a charcoal brazier and a teapot, thus uniting the symbols of hospitality and good luck."

The practice of decorating verge boards and finials is also widespread in Southeast Asia, but in both Japan and Madagascar crossed horn finials were restricted to religious buildings and royal structures (Feeley-Harnik 1980, 567; Waterson 1990, 11). Elsewhere, a variety of animal images and symbolic devices occur on houses, but a common theme is animal horns, which are supposed to provide protection for dwelling inhabitants.

Not only can the verge board be decorated, the entire gable wall may also be embellished The gable end walls of central Germany offered one such possibility by varying the combinations of half-timber and brick infill of the impressive Hallenhauser. The Japanese place large, decorated openings high up in the apex of gable walls of their minka (traditional farmhouses). These often contain elaborately fashioned lattice openings, decorated carvings, "artful arrangements of bundled straw," and other devices. In addition to decoration and adornment, the openings serve the very practical purpose of admitting light and ventilation to the loft, where silkworm cultivation takes place (Kawashima 2000, 20 & 194–9).

In Taiwan, it is not only the gable wall that offers decorative space but also the line and form of the verge (Figure 12-3). These decorative devices "usually express symbolic meanings related to the five elements (wood, fire, metal, water and the earth) and the yin-yang concept." On some other dwellings, which have the graceful swallow-tail ridgelines, representations in carefully molded mortar may be seen of "spirits animals, auspicious fruits, and other symbolic items placed along the ridge line or along the sweep of the swallow tail" verge boards (Knapp 1986, 106).

Southern Italy, on the east side of the Italian "boot," offers a wide variety of decorative finials that surmount the stone trulli (Branch 1966, 116–19). Circles, swastika, celestial bodies, crosses and more complex symbols are included and strongly suggest a mystical protective original function rather than mere decoration.

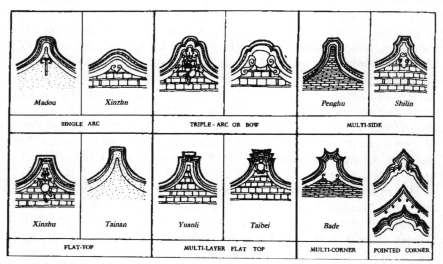

12-3. *Variation in the gable profiles on dwellings in Taiwan (from Knapp 1986, 106. Reprinted with permission of the University of Hawaii Press).*

Although many traditional structures remain the products of necessity, with little or no attempt at decoration (Mindeleff, C. 1898a, 487), others are attractively decorated, often with careful attention to the simplest elements. Wood carving is one of the most satisfying types of structural embellishment, especially when carefully done, and it usually far outlasts painting. The *havelli* of western India are well known for such ornamentation (Noble 2003, 48–9). The wooden cottages of the central Volga river valley offer another example (Figure 12-4).

Unity of color and lack of decoration from house to house is usually related to the economy and may be an index of poverty. In the late 1930s toward the end of the Great Depression, a traverse of houses in the United States from the Great Lakes to the Gulf of Mexico found almost 40% of the dwellings to be unpainted. Undoubtedly, such a high percentage there at that time was related in large part to the depression economy. When painted, white was the overwhelmingly preferred color, more than five times the incidence of any other color (Finley and Scott 1940, 418).

When it can just be afforded, the cheapest material, such as whitewash, is applied. Outside, the whitewash protects the walls from the elements. Internally, the whitewash obliterates grime and dust and

12-4 An unpainted, but elaborately carved, izba in Uglich, Russia. Note the matching eave dentils and the carving under the windows (photo by the author, 1997).

12-5. *On this cottage in Kostroma, Russia the elaborately carved window surrounds are supplemented by other decorative wooden carvings (photo by the author, 1997).*

increases available light by reflection. If a bit more expenditure can be justified, window and door surrounds are covered with a contrasting color. Usually this color has some mystical, cultural or political symbolism connected to it. Window and door surrounds in Russia, especially along the Volga, are particularly attractive (Figure 12-5).

The attachment of a particular color to an ethnic group may be so strong that it permits group identification. John Lehr (1981, 204) observed that in Alberta, Ukrainian settlers from Bukovyna used green trim, whereas those from Galicia employed blue. But color is only one aspect of decoration. Even in the arrangement of basic huts within a compound an effective artistic approach may be evident.

> Since the house is the most dominant part of his environment, man decorates it, taking pride in his worldly possessions. Often, many of these decorations are put on the house for their own sake; at other times they carry a symbolic meaning implying auspiciousness and good fortune for the inhabitants. Certain symbolic images in house decoration are related to rituals that have to be performed on different festive occasions. Absence of decorations can also indicate the misfortune experienced by a household. (Jain 1983, 46–7)

Painting in bright colors is a technique widely encountered around the world (Lee 1969b; Brunvand 1974; Duly 1979; Arreola 1988, 299).

In dry areas, adobe walls, which would otherwise be rather dull and drab, are often decorated with paints derived from locally available plant dyes or soil deposits (Mahapatra and Patnaik 1986). To provide a contrast, doors and window shutters are invariably painted green throughout the Sudan portion of the Nile valley (Lee 1974, 245). Highlighting window frames for emphasis is a technique widely employed in the Netherlands. Moldings and surrounds to openings are usually painted in contrasting colors to the prevailing color of the structure (Jones 1918, 28).

In northern and northeastern Ghana, wall paintings consist mostly of non-figurative, rectilinear, symmetrical designs (Smith 1980, 26) rendered in three colors: red, black and white. On the other hand, "in many Caribbean countries, blue is believed to ward off evil spirits" (Jopling 1988, 205 & 267). Carol Jopling further observes that in Puerto Rican areas "where people of African descent are concentrated, deep blue is prevalent." Is it only coincidental that in West Africa, from which a high percentage of Caribbean peoples originated, the color associated with Shango, the most powerful god figure, is a dynamic blue?

In the Hausa area of northern Nigeria, house decoration is a combination of structural design, adobe sculpture and bright painting. Substantial rectangular adobe dwellings carry projections that are reminiscent of battlements. They appear at building corners and frame doorways. H.P. Elliot (1940, 276) speculates that these features may originally have had a functional purpose but have evolved into a conspicuous but totally decorative element. Colin Duly (1979, 49) terms these projections above the eave line "rabbit ears" and offers the possibility that they may represent swords or phallic symbols. Regardless of their symbolic purpose, they combine with other decorative devices to present striking examples of Hausa house decoration.

Michael Crowder (1956, 9) observes, "in the patterns there is a boldness of color and a simplicity of design that distinguishes them from the often fussy and over elaborated decorations of most Moslem cultures." Arabesques with emphasis on arcs and circles increasingly are augmented with low reliefs of bicycles, motorcars and other modern status symbols. The bas-reliefs modeled in adobe increasingly are covered in a thin coating of cement, making the facade decoration much more permanent. In areas where adobe makes up the major wall material, decoration may be enhanced by bits of broken pottery, entire small plates, mirrors or the bottoms of glass bottles embedded firmly into the clay or laterite while still soft. Such practices are reported from the Ibo area of Nigeria (Talbot 1916), in Nubia along the

Nile valley (Lee 1969b), and for the Thar desert of India. The practice undoubtedly occurs elsewhere.

Hausa interiors also are decorated with painted forms, and ceilings and walls sport decorative china plates. "Doors are often decorated with beer-bottle caps, showing the extreme adaptability of the Hausas to new acquisitions, and their subjugation of them to their own use" (Crowder 1956, 10). Doorways often support a projecting canopy of mud around deleb palm trunks, which has a decorative effect as well as sheltering the entry from the occasional downpour (Elliott 1940, 277).

Non-Arab Nubians who inhabited the Nile valley straddling the border between Egypt and Sudan evolved an elaborately decorated house. It included intricately painted designs, pottery, including embedded dinner plates, and a variety of forms sculpted in mud (Lee 1969b, 37), even automobile headlights, "which gleamed like pearls against the dark ground" (Wenzel 1972, 4). Designs of geometric form were painted on the walls or were incised by "etching a whitewashed surface so as to reveal the brown mud beneath." The building of the Aswan Dam and the flooding of Lake Nasser obliterated all of these structures (see Chapter 9).

Religious symbolism also provides a source for some domestic dwellings, although not as often or prominently displayed as might be expected. Anywhere in the world, an interior wall or corner can be dedicated as a sacred center, but little in the way of exterior decoration exists. A few crosses and small saint shrine niches can be found as external features in Latin America and parts of Europe, and crescent moons exist in the Middle East. In south India, the more affluent dwellings employ wide vertical bands of alternating red and white color. The design is popular because it has a Hindu religious connotation, since it appears also on temples and temple compound walls (Hirt 1982, 129–36).

Anthony Kirk-Greene (1963, 15) observed that many of the Hausa mud and soft concrete wall decorations on the houses of the prosperous merchant class are the same as found on the leather covers for the portable Koran carried by pilgrims on the *hajj* to Mecca. At the same time, however, he also noted similar decorations on the houses of more affluent prostitutes. Although a religious connection may have been the original impetus for the decoration, it is clearly wealth that sustains and spreads the practice.

To return to Europe, one benefit of the introduction of chimneys in dwellings was that they "emptied the rooms of smoke, so that it was possible to paint and decorate them without the risk of soot obliterating the paint" (Faber n.d., 101). Even with chimneys, interior religious decoration is limited in most traditional houses everywhere. An exception in European structures was the "holy corner," a small area where sacred relicts were kept (Lodge 1936, 98). Jeffrey Godshall (1983, 25) traces this custom back to early folk beliefs that each house had its own god. In the Ukraine the feature has been termed the "corner of honor" by Z. Kuzela (1963, 307). John Lehr (1973, 13) describes "The Holy Wall" found in Ukrainian dwellings in Alberta, Canada as being the easternmost and "traditionally hung with icons, religious calendars, family photographs and decorated with embroidered linens and dried flowers, etc."

In Greece the holy corner or holy wall shrine is called the *iconostassi*, and in addition to icons often houses dried flowers or laurel leaves, marital wreaths, small vessels containing holy water, a votive oil lamp, incense burner, candles, and a wooden stamp with the monogram of Christ, used to decorate bread baked at home to be brought to church (Pavlides and Hesser 1989, 284–6). A similar custom of sacred or venerated corners and walls still prevails in many Asian and African communities.

The Sotho of South Africa employ two techniques of decoration. Geometric patterns in bright colors are painted on adobe walls, forming a striking contrast with the dun-colored mud. The second technique is to embed small stones of contrasting colors, usually brown and white, in graceful leaf-like patterns (Walton 1948, 141). The stones have the additional value of reducing rainfall erosion of the walls. House builders in southwestern Saudi Arabia used downward sloping bands of inlaid small stones to channel rainwater away (King 1976, 27). A different technique is used by the Lela in Upper Volta. Their house walls are of adobe mixed with a thin layer of cow dung, "on which nested-V motifs are imprinted by repeatedly pressing two segments of corn cobs to form regular vertical patterns . . . Besides being decorative, they function to break up the flow of rain into smaller streamlets, thus preventing a localized erosion of the walls" (Bourdier and Minh-ha 1982, 72).

In northwest Syria, where mud brick, beehive houses are white-washed both inside and out, "the wooden door, if painted, will be a bright blue as protection against evil spirits" (Copeland 1955, 24). Such protective decoration occurs, or occurred, in every society. Among the Pennsylvania Dutch, an outgrowth of European societies, "hex signs, crosses, amulets, magic formulae, and the like, for the protection of animals and men and the premises from evil spirits . . . are usually cut or placed inside a barn or house as prophylaxes against harmful spirits or, possibly over doorways or windows on the outside" (Barakat 1972, 4–5).

One of the most unusual and effective approaches to interior decoration occurs in many rural villages of Gujarat state, India. Here, although the simple dwellings are constructed of stone and/or concrete blocks, the interiors are adorned with an intricate set of textile coverings,

> A whole reconstruction of major architectural parts in textiles was done to create a parallel superstructure in a soft material expression of love for drapery, hangings, coverlets and canopies . . . The encasing in textiles of the entire living rooms of these communities is so complete that while sitting inside a concrete building, for example, there is the distinct impression of being inside a tent. (Jain-Neubauer and Jain 1983, 42)

Such elaborate decoration appears to be an effective attempt to recall earlier nomadic days.

Protection of a building's inhabitants against the "evil eye" is another characteristic found in India. The danger arises from the covetous glance at the structure of a demonic spirit or evil eye. South Asia is the center of this idea, but it may be encountered in locations as wide afield as the Nubian desert (Wenzel 1972, 39), Greece (Pavlides and Hesser 1989, 290) and Malta (Tonna 1989, 166). Furthermore, August Mahr (1945) also traces Pennsylvania Dutch hex signs back to earlier devices in Europe employed to deflect or neutralize the evil eye. The concept of the evil eye is an ancient and widespread one (Elworthy 1895), but its association with construction of buildings is more restricted.

Throughout India and Sri Lanka a variety of devices and techniques are employed against the evil eye (Figure 12-6). W. Crooke (1918, 123) suggests that "a bit of the house is left unfinished to avoid the Evil Eye," while C. Purdon Clarke (1883, 739) notes that a water vessel is placed in front of the house as "a sovereign charm to avert the evil eye of envious folk" (note that the evil eye has taken on a totally different aspect), and Ilay Cooper and Barry Dawson (1998, 23) remark that "handprints deflect the evil eye and discourage destructive spirits." Anand (1974, 16) offers a differing explanation of the open hand decoration, a device encountered so often in India. He suggests that in the Punjab it is a symbol of generosity. Kulbshan Jain's interpretation is somewhat different: he views the open hand as an auspicious symbol of good fortune (Jain 1983, 49 & 54).

Anthony King (1984, 21) offers still a different explanation. He cites a British engineer, Capt. Thomas Williamson, who in 1810 reported that hand prints in red ocher were "to typify the infinite powers of the Creator whose hands are supposed to be innumerable and perpetually in motion." All of these interpretations, while diverse, are basically compatible. Images of powerful, but protective, god figures

12-6. Gourds are decorated to counter the influence of the "evil eye." These are placed on or near the structure during construction throughout South Asia. Other devices to accomplish the same object are also used (photo by the author, 1973).

are also used to guard against the evil eye. Today, paper or cardboard images of powerful and terrifying figures are nailed or pinned to the frame of the dwelling under construction. Other devices have also been employed (Noble 2003, 46), including the stringing together of seven green chillies and a lime over the doorway. "So pervasive is this belief that ready-made evil-eye-warder kits such as the above are sold at traffic junctions in metropolises" (Arya 2000, 76).

One method of obtaining modest decoration at fairly minimal cost is the use of *patterned brick* and *brick diaper*, the latter also variously known as Dutch cross-bond, zig-zag, and Flemish checker (Trindell 1968, 485). Examples of these techniques are known from Flanders (Sickler 1949, 6) and Normandy in France (Brier and Brunet 1984, 49), Norfolk, England, where bricks are intermixed with flints (Briggs 1953, 73), to Connecticut (Watson 1984), New Jersey (Eberlein 1921; Sickler 1949; Gowans 1964, 14), Maryland (Trindell 1968, 486), and Michigan (Noble 1996, 14–15). The decorative element is achieved by widening the mortar between key bricks to emphasize natural diagonal lines, creating geometric figures, and by using bricks of slightly

12-7. This house near Hol-
land, MI offers an example
of decorative brick pattern-
ing. Only prosperous
farmers could afford this
kind of structure (photo by
the author, 1982).

different colors or hues. Variation in hues is achieved according to how and where in the kiln a newly molded brick is placed. Those in the hottest part of the kiln will have a darker, bluish hue (Watson 1984, 4). Placing the end of a brick toward the hot center of the kiln results in headers being darker than stretchers when they are later placed in a wall. Considerable skill is required to use these methods effectively both in the kiln and in bricklaying.

In New Jersey, Richard Pillsbury (1976, 104–6) identifies two centers of patterned brickwork, an early one in Salem County and a later one in Burlington County. This 18th-century patterned brickwork, which has been termed "the most elaborate, community-derived brick building tradition in colonial or post-Revolutionary America," had a strong Quaker connection. The brick makers and bricklayers were mostly Quakers, and the prosperous homeowners for whom the dwellings were built were also Quakers (Chiarappa 1991, 31).

Another method of achieving decorative effects is to employ different clays, which results in bricks of different colors. This technique is known as *dichromatic brickwork* if bricks of two different colors are used, and *polychromatic brickwork* if more than two. In southern Ontario red and yellow bricks were used to great effect late in the 19th century (Ritchie 1979, 60). Most often the design is concentrated on the building's corners and around windows and doors, although some diamond and zig-zag patterns exist (Figure 12-7). A smaller area of distinctive brickwork occurs in the Dutch-settled area of southwest Michigan (Noble 1996).

Even in areas where traditional housing is able to maintain itself in the face of competition from "modern" building, a steady decline in ornamentation is perceptible (Feeley-Harnik 1980, 568–9). Machine-made materials are used primarily because of their lower cost, immediate or eventual. Decorative devices are mostly handmade and therefore expensive. The tyranny of economy works constantly to eliminate all but the most regular (i.e. machine-made) decoration.

~ 13 ~

Communal Dwellings and Seasonal Shelters

Over much of the world, a house is the domain of a single family, either nuclear or extended. In some places, however, dwellings are communal, sheltering a large number of individuals, most of whom are at least distantly related and thus have a common ethnic identity. The relatedness of the dwelling's inhabitants, and to a lesser extent their ethnic unity, are what defines the structure as a traditional communal dwelling, and what distinguished it from the modern apartment building or condominium development, for instance.

At the other end of this fixed accommodation scale are those families who regularly, but usually seasonally, occupy at least two dwellings, either in the same physical location or in geographically separated places. This latter may involve the tending of domesticated animals that must move to secure food or water, or to escape extreme weather. Nomadic peoples often continue to reside in the same dwelling rather than two separate ones, but two or more locations always are used. The Rabaris of western India may have the record for residence shifting. They are reported by Mayank Shah (1980), to move their encampment about 50 feet or so *every day*. This is to ensure that fields on which local farmers permit them to graze their animals will receive manure from the animals that spend each night in the immediate vicinity of the encampment. At the other extreme of distance, some Eskimos are reported to have moved seasonally a distance of up to 250 kilometers (Dumond 1987, 83). Geographers and anthropologists refer to longer-distance periodic movement as *transhumance*. Tibetan nomads normally shift place of residence between three and eight times each year as herds require pasture. These peoples and others have solved the problem of shelter and periodic migration by evolving structures that are portable (Figure 13-1). By contrast, "one tribe in southern Tibet, moves once every three years and builds half-cave, half-sod houses at each move" (Ekvall 1968, 33).

13-1. *An encampment of Berber nomads in the Atlas Mountains of Morocco. Once the forage for their animals nears exhaustion they must strike their tents and move to a new site (photo by the author, 1990).*

Communal dwellings have a worldwide distribution ranging from the semi-subterranean dwellings of southern Russia to the pueblos of the southwestern United States, the clan homes of the Northwest Pacific Coast in Canada and Alaska, bamboo and thatch structures of the Amazon and Orinoco basins, tropical longhouses of Southeast Asia, the circular strongholds of the Hakka people in southern China, bark-clad shelters of the Iroquois of the eastern United States, the multi-structures within a compound in Africa south of the Sahara, and to hundreds of other types elsewhere.

The earliest communal dwellings were very early indeed, from Paleolithic time. Although most early pit dwellings were for single families, a few locations in southern Russia appear to have housed several families together (Daifuku 1952, 1), and the Aleuts of the Aleutian Islands and the Alaska peninsula constructed communal, semi-subterranean dwellings in which a central common area was surrounded by individual family cubicles, or even private family rooms (Hoagland 1993, 12–13). This approach to dwelling was further elaborated on Nunivak Island, where a linear series of pit houses were each connected by a short entry tunnel only to a single, larger main sub-surface passageway. "For an entire community, then, there might be only one entryway into this complex" (Lee and Reinhardt 2003, 123).

Given the scarcity of communal housing and the abundance of single-family structures, it seems likely that, for whatever reason, the communal was only an occasional outgrowth of the individual at this early time. A similar process was identified by Cosmos Mindeleff (1898b, 114) as the origin of pueblos in the southwestern United States. However, in the 20th century a reverse process in the pueblo appears to be taking place, the former apartment-like family homes are beginning to give way to separated single-family dwellings (Dozier 1970, 11).

Although the word *pueblo* is Spanish for village, town or inhabited place, for many it has come to refer especially to the Amerindian adobe buildings of the southwestern US. These pueblos include both cliff dwellings and those located on valley bottoms or mesa tops. Fully elaborated pueblos evolved from about 1000 AD up to the present day (Sanford 1950, 21). The US National Park Service preserves and protects many of the ancient and abandoned pueblo settlements, but others are still occupied. Of these, probably the best known is Taos Pueblo, north of Santa Fe, New Mexico, where two communal buildings (one six stories high and a quarter-mile long) (Jackson 1953, 22) make up the entire settlement. The most dramatic pueblo site is that of Acoma, west of Albuquerque. Perched high atop a steep-sided mesa, it dominates the countryside for miles around, but many of its residents have shifted to more accessible housing on the lower plateau level. Ironically, this move, the growing interest of tourists to visit the original dramatic settlement, and strong control and protection by tribal authorities to thwart undesirable commercial exploitation, together seems likely to be sufficient to secure preservation of the ancient settlement.

Adobe pueblos consist of numerous single-cell components. The pueblo was not conceived of in its entirety; it grew by the accretion of single-cell units. It is, therefore, a structure of simple construction. Furthermore,

> the Pueblo Indians were not concerned with building for posterity. They built their houses to satisfy an immediate need, the need of a lifetime or perhaps two. They never intended to erect lasting monuments and consequently never learned how. They never thought of buildings as works of art and therefore made no effort to adorn them. (Jackson 1953, 21–4)

Even further,

> the Hopis (Pueblo Indians) have no architectural terminology that classifies buildings into types, and no word for room or interior. Instead they use the term "the place where" – a certain action takes place or a certain object is to be found. In other words, if an action ceases or if the object is removed, the house no longer has any identity; it is simply a solid, a man-made lump of adobe.

When building stone was readily available it was used for pueblo construction. Cosmos Mindeleff (1898b, 113) notes that the edges of mesas and the walls of canyons furnished a plentiful supply of building stone for cliff dwellings. But often such stone was not readily available so that recourse to adobe was necessary. The earlier pueblos were constructed of puddled adobe, but after contact with Spaniards a switch to adobe bricks occurred (Nabokov and Easton 1989, 367).

The most critical item of construction was the wooden beams required to support mud roofs. Since timber was scarce in the desert environment of the southwest, roof beams often had to be brought from some distance, requiring great effort. Not surprisingly, these valuable lengths of wood were frequently cycled through several subsequent buildings, even when their lengths were not entirely appropriate. Ends of the beams thus at times projected beyond the walls, creating one of the most characteristic and attractive visual features of the pueblo.

The pueblo, which is entirely above ground, contains one or more *kivas*, circular pits used for ceremonial purposes. These probably reflect the original pit dwellings, which were given a later symbolic religious aura. Indeed, the word *kiva* in the Hopi language means "old house" (Sanford 1950, 24). For a recent, more extensive discussion of pueblo adobe construction based upon the original research of Victor Mindeleff (1891) see Noble (1984, 1: 78–83).

Communal Amerindian dwellings are found in other parts of North America. Great buildings of timber were built among the tribes of the Northwest Pacific Coast. "Newcomers to their land were always impressed by the massive size and construction of the cedar dwellings they came upon. Their journals and diaries made frequent mention of the structures, giving measurements and descriptions that often captured the sense of wonder experienced by the writers" (Stewart 1984, 60–1). Among the coast-dwelling Salish people, one clan house was estimated by an early visitor to measure 650 feet long by 60 feet wide and with a height of 18 feet (Stewart 1984, 65). The interior was divided into individual family spaces, each complete with its own hearth. Most Salish and other tribes' dwellings were somewhat smaller. Houses erected by the Tsimshian were considerably smaller and roughly square in plan, 50 x 55 feet being average size (Drucker 1965, 119). Their interiors were also partitioned into open cubicles occupied by the different families.

The Tlingit lived northward of both the Tsimshian and the Salish. Perhaps because of this more northerly location and the consequently colder winters, their homes were smaller, averaging about 45 x 40 feet. Form and construction methods were similar to those of more southerly tribes. Spruce became the major wood for structural members,

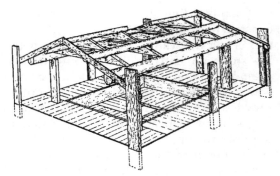

13-2. Sketch of the framework of a Tlingit house (from Shotridge and Shotridge 1913, 86–7. Courtesy of the University of Pennsylvania Museum of Archeology and Anthropology).

with the easy-splitting hemlock for boards and plank. Red cedar, the major wood employed further south, had to be imported by canoe and hence was not much used. Figure 13-2 shows the structural framework of a house of the Chilkat, a sub-tribe of the Tlingit. Families occupied screened-off sections of the uppermost level (Krause 1956, 88). The lower level, below ground, was the warmest work and social area. The central fire pit was even lower. Outside steps and corresponding inside steps led to and from the raised threshold necessary because of periodic high snowfall in riverside locations. The walls consisted of horizontal planks, except across the front, where planks were vertical (Shotridge and Shotridge 1913, 86–8).

Everywhere along the coastal zone the houses were of post and beam construction, sometimes with the beams mortised into the posts. The more southern peoples preferred horizontal wall planking, while vertical planking predominated in the north. "The house walls were often lined with cedar-bark mats against winter winds that whistled through the cracks between the planks" (Drucker 1965, 120). Smoke from the fires exited through a central rectangular smoke hole covered by moveable boards, except in Kwakiutl houses, where the formal smoke hole was dispensed with and loose roof planks were simply pushed aside as necessary (Vastokas, 1967, 46).

The other major area of Amerindian communal dwellings was amongst the Iroquois, who styled themselves the "People of the Longhouse." The dimensions of the longhouses varied from 30 to 200 feet in length and 15 to 25 feet in width, with the average length about 60 feet and the width about 18. A framework of light timber was covered with slabs of bark, elm being preferred. A central aisle about six feet wide ran from one end to the other (Lyford 1945). Roofs of the single-story structure were reported to be continuously curved from side to side (earlier) or of gable type (later), and were composed of large bark slabs (Figure 13-3). According to Lewis Morgan (1965), the Iroquois longhouse disappeared before the beginning of the 19th century, but

13-3. Sketch of an Iroquois longhouse. Unlike the illustration, these houses normally had multiple hearths and accompanying smoke holes (modified from Lyford 1905, 12).

archeological remains persist and modern-day reconstructions have been attempted. The interior of the structure was divided into small family spaces or cubicles of about six feet wide on either side of the main aisle. The longhouse was heated in winter by fires in small hearths along the central corridor at every other place between units (Duly 1979, 62). The great advantage of the longhouse was that it could be extended easily if additional units were needed. In exceptional cases, longhouses may have sheltered up to 200 persons.

Communal longhouses exist in other parts of the world and have some similarities to Iroquois longhouses. They are single story, much longer than wide and contain numerous hearths, but they are usually elevated on piles, thus creating a ground space sometimes used for animals and storage, and, of course, their materials of construction and covering are different.

Communal dwellings are scattered across the length and breadth of Southeast Asia from Assam, India, to northern Myanmar (Burma) and the southern highlands of Vietnam, to Sumatra, the Mentawai Islands, Borneo, northern Sulawesi and Flores in Indonesia. Most of these structures are referred to as longhouses and some of them are long indeed! Roxana Waterson (1990, 84) reports a Sea Dyak longhouse of 771-foot length, although most are considerably shorter. B.A.L. Cranstone (1980, 494) reports even longer structures in Borneo; up to a quarter-mile long and housing 600 people. Albert Bemis and John Burchard (1933, 41), however, cited average occupance of just 200–300 persons in Borneo longhouses. The basic structural problems of large houses is the outward thrust of the roof. The problem is solved in the longhouse by using a gable roof, keeping the roof low and the width of the building relatively narrow.

Raised up on wooden piles, the longhouses of the Garo, Kachin, and Palaung in Myanmar (Burma) and northeastern India have split-

13-4. Stilt-supported longhouse from northern Myanmar (Burma). This particular structure, built on a slope, uses poles of unequal length to support horizontal floors (from Scherman 1915, tafel 8).

13-5. Stilt-supported longhouse from Assam, India. Note the cattle tethered on the ground below the house platform (from Scherman 1915, tafel 10).

bamboo floors and a bamboo or light wood frame (Figure 13-4) supporting a thatched roof and often wattle walling. The area under the structure (Figure 13-5) is used for animal shelter and general storage (Scherman 1915). Similar in form but much heavier is the longhouse of the Miri, who live in the Brahmaputra valley. With dimensions of about 55 x 15 feet, the structure possesses a sturdy timber frame. The raised floor is supported by several additional wooden posts. At each end is a balcony where much of the daily household work is done (Payne 1980, 68). As in most longhouses, a number of hearths exist, each one serving a small part of the group, who live in partitioned-off cubicles opening on to the open, longitudinal hallway part of the building.

A quite different form of communal dwelling has evolved in southern China, where the Hakka people reside. Both rectangular and square plan, three- and four-story structures resembling fortresses have been built, but the most impressive are those of circular plan (Figure 13-6), which are unlike any other structures in China (Knapp 1986, 45–9). The history of the Hakka, an often-repressed minority people, who are referred to as "the Guest People" – although they have resided in south China from the fourth century – undoubtedly explains the severity of their construction (Sullivan 1972, 139–40). Up to 180 feet in diameter, with as many as 120 individual compartments, each entered from a common interior balcony, the building accommodates separate families. Up to 300 to 500 individuals may live in a single structure (Lung 1991, 37–8, 42). The compartments form a ring around the open courtyard, which contains communal kitchens, privies, pens for small livestock, and a temple (Figure 13-7). The rammed earth walls, which reflect the earlier necessity for defense, can be over 30 feet thick. The dun and dark yellow hues of the unpainted walls, complemented by the grayish black color of roof tiles, are completely without exterior, or much interior, decoration or embellishment, further contributing to the somber character of these dwellings.

13-6. Sketch of a large, doughnut-shaped, Hakka communal dwelling (drawing by Iraida Galdon Soler).

*13-7. Diagram of a Hakka
house showing cubicles,
balconies, circular hall-
ways, and center temple
structures (from Knapp
1986, 49. Reprinted with
permission of the Univer-
sity of Hawaii Press).*

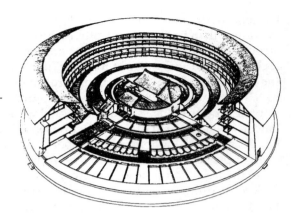

Another important area of communal dwellings occurs in the Amazon and Orinoco lowlands, extending to surrounding higher country.
Here, the structures of the Yanamamo and other tribes are circular,
but quite different in form, materials, and construction from those of
the Hakka. Just one story in elevation, the light wood or bamboo
frame is entirely covered in palm leaves (Nash 1923, 329). Strictly
speaking, the building is not a communal house because each adult
male builds and maintains only that part of the structure that his
immediate family will occupy (Smole 1976, 55). Nevertheless, the
occupants of the building are all kinfolk and they do shelter under a
common roof. The inhabitants of these structures number on average
between 65 and 85 people.

The largest of the dwellings are well over 200 feet in diameter with
average diameters half that size; they rise up to 25 feet high. The largest are those that have a ring-like plan, with the covered dwellings
surrounding an open central area. Others cover the central area with a
closed form and build to greater height. Only a small smoke hole is
left open at the center of these structures, which may rise almost to 75
feet. These taller, more closed communal dwellings have a wide distribution across the Amazon lowland. The roof has a circular, tent-like
form in contrast to the ring model, which has cubicles with lean-to
roofs.

The term *maloca* can be used to refer to all Amazonian and Orinoco
communal houses. In addition to the circular forms just mentioned,
some tribes build structures of rectangular or oval plan. Each tribe has
its own variations in form and details of construction, but "many of
these architectural differences can be shown to be variations on a
common theme." The maloca represents a response to social adjust-
ments within the tribe. Residence in a new maloca is voluntary and its
size will depend upon the charisma of a newly emerging leader. The

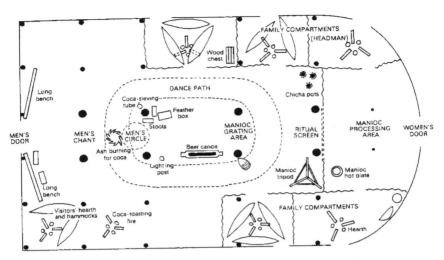

13-8. Floor plan of a maloca showing functional areas. The black dots represent the position of roof support poles (from Hugh-Jones 1985, 83. Courtesy of the Trustees of the British Museum).

dimensions of the structures, which in rectangular versions can be over 130 feet long and 40 feet high, reflect this charisma (Hugh-Jones 1985, 79–80). While the individual families live in separate interior compartments, the structure also has male- and female-dominated and recognized areas (Figure 13-8). Nevertheless, movement of both males and females is relatively unregulated, unlike the practice in many other societies.

Similar communal houses are built by the Waiwai in southern Guyana. These circular-plan dwellings constructed of light wood and leaves have two unusual features. One is a small conical leaf-covered canopy attached to the central pole near its apex and above the structure. Because it is over the smoke hole, "it prevents the rain from entering the house from above, and the spirits too at night" (Yde 1965, 152). The center pole itself is the other unusual feature. It does not rest on the ground, but rather is suspended from the framework at the top of the structure.

In New Guinea and some parts of Southern Asia, dwellings are organized along gender lines. The Mae Enga of the western highlands of New Guinea erect communal houses for men and individual houses for women. A study conducted in 1955 indicated just under 30% of all structures were male houses and just over 70% were female (Meggitt 1957, 161). Construction methods and floor plans are similar, but size varies. "Women's houses vary comparatively little in their overall dimensions; men's houses vary markedly," depending upon how many males are accommodated in each structure. Any variation in size in a woman's hut depends upon the number of pig pens included within the structure. Although the separation of males may have several reasons, the concentration of fighting men with weapons handy in case of surprise attack must not be discounted (Cranstone 1980, 500).

Terminology and social relationships can be quite confusing in Haryana state, India. Here, segregation of women, men and animals is practiced up to a point, usually depending upon income and wealth. The ideal is to have three structures: a *ghar* in which women of the family sleep, work and socialize; a *baithak* in which males sleep and socialize; and a *gher* in which animals are sheltered (Chandhoke 1990, 223). The baithak and ghar occupy one compound or plot of land, and the gher a separate one. If the farmer lacks sufficient land or resources, all functions will be accommodated in a single compartmented building, in which case it will be termed a ghar. If the separate gher is large enough to have an entrance through which a tractor can be driven, the structure is called a *darwaja*. Men may enter the ghar for meals and after dark, but women do not visit the baithak. Every built-up space is referred to as *chhawa*, or more rarely *makan*. Is it any wonder that students of traditional structures often lose their way in the tangle of terminology?

Change of permanent dwelling or shift of geographical location is a basic feature of many traditional societies. The move occurs for a variety of reasons. Decline in fertility of surrounding fields may necessitate a shift of up to several miles (Dunham 1987). Deterioration of the structures, especially those of light construction in the tropics, also requires the building of a replacement. Intra-group conflict, changes of group leadership, and other stressful situations may each result in a move of some members to new dwellings in different locations. Natural disasters, changes in environmental conditions, improvements in economic levels, and other circumstances also may trigger habitation changes. L. Carl Brandhorst (1981, 73) suggests that a common housing change among pioneer settlers in Kansas was from dugout, to crude stone cabin, to "big" house. Elsewhere in the United States the shift from log cabin to timber-frame house was a standard theme in the 19th century.

A death occurring in a structure was often a sufficient reason to abandon the building and erect a new one (Murdock 1934, 40; Page 1937, 47; Brugge 1983, 186). Lack of space caused by the enlargement of the family, on the other hand, rarely resulted in shifts to new quarters. The original dwelling was expanded if at all possible, or increased crowding was accepted.

Many peoples regularly had more than one residence, which they occupied seasonally. Generally, such *seasonal dwellings* were a response to temperature changes, but other environmental conditions could also cause seasonal movement. In England, the county of Somerset received its name, which may be translated as "land of the summer dwellers," because of seasonal, severe flooding in winter, which prevented year round early settlement (Addison 1986, 47).

Perhaps the most unusual seasonal shift anywhere was that employed by the Kamtscatdales in the Kamchatka Peninsula of Siberia, who employed summer houses elevated on stilts and winter dwellings sunk into the ground (Ferree 1890, 150–1). Among the nearby Ostyaks, communal and seasonal houses converged, but in an unusual way. Winter houses are occupied by several families, while the summer ones are used by one only. The pattern is probably related to seasonal availability of food resources, the greater labor involved in building winter shelter, and the winter need for the greater heat produced by larger numbers of inhabitants.

The Iglulik Eskimos living on Southampton Island in northern Canada regularly occupied three quite different dwellings in response to seasonal changes of weather (Mathiassen 1928). During the long winter, the igloo of snow and ice provided surprisingly warm shelter, although if inside temperatures rose too high meltwater become an annoyance. From May to October, seal or caribou skin tents were occupied. A large number of sizeable stones anchored the tent, keeping its wooden poles from blowing over in the frequently strong winds. In the fall, and less often in spring, a rough, partly excavated, dwelling covered by a tent roof and anchored by stones, earth, and whale skulls was used. However, throughout most of polar Eskimo country from Bering to Greenland, people used semi-subterranean earth and stone winter houses and skin-covered tents in summer. During the brief transitional periods in spring and fall, "when it was too cold to live comfortably in a summer tent but too warm or wet to occupy the usual winter house," a small crude non-descript shelter was resorted to (Lee and Reinhardt 2003). Elsewhere in North America, where climatic extremes were more moderate, a number of interior-dwelling tribes built both summer and winter houses.

The Pomo Indians of northern California were not exactly seasonal migrants, but moved periodically among three quite different environments. They usually wintered in communal structures in the valleys of several rivers. There they constructed houses consisting of a framework of poles in a circular or rectangular plan, over which a thick thatch of grasses was laid. Several low fires were kept in the interior and the structures were warm and watertight. Dwellings in the two other environments were less carefully built and housed families that were primarily nuclear. In the coastal forest zone, small houses of redwood bark and split slabs, resembling the form of a tipi, were thrown up. A small opening at the top allowed smoke to escape. The narrow doorway closed by pulling one or two slabs across it. In the drier interior, especially around Clear Lake, the houses were usually elliptical or roughly circular in plan. The framework was light poles covered by thule (rushes). Each one sheltered a single family (Barrett 1916).

A seasonally occupied dwelling is often a much rougher structure than a permanent one. In Newfoundland, a basic building consisting of walls of vertical wooden slabs or poles covered with a single-slope roof is called the Labrador Tilt. Such a structure may be erected by woodsmen for winter logging, as well as by fishermen in the summer fishing season (O'Dea 1982, 4). By contrast, some seasonally migrating peoples expend considerable energy in building their dwellings (Figure 13-9). The Gujar herders in the western Himalaya of India spend the summers at high altitudes, where alpine meadows offer ample pasture. Here, because even summer season temperatures are cold at night, dwellings are hewn out of the rock of a hill slope, and the men sleep, cook and seek shelter for the summer (Cooper and Dawson 1998, 60).

For some peoples, the seasonal shift involves merely a movement from one part of the house to another.

13-9. *Summer shelter of sheep herders in the Carpathian Mountains, southern Poland (photo by the author, 1988).*

In many Turkish houses the winters are spent on the ground floor, which is built of stone, while summers are spent on the upper floors, which are of wood . . . Alternatively, in many areas, the winter and the summer rooms may be on the same floor, but are situated, respectively on the south and north sides of the house. (Petherbridge 1978, 204)

Among the Kickapoo Indians, who migrated in the 19th century from Wisconsin to Coahuila, Mexico, separate summer and winter dwellings occupy the same compound. The rectangular-plan summer structure with vertical walls of juniper or willow frame supporting *sotal* siding is covered with a hipped roof of sotal cane. Adjacent is a *ramada*, a wall-less shade structure used as a summer work area. The winter house consists of a bent sapling frame placed to form an oval floor plan. Mats of light wood and plant stalks cover the frame tightly. The winter house, in contrast to the summer, has a fireplace for heat. The Kickapoo compound also normally has a separate cookhouse and a menstrual hut (Nabokov 1978, 50–3).

German settlers around Fredericksburg, Texas in the latter half of the 19th century erected small dwellings that, rather than seasonal houses, reasonably could be called weekly houses; in fact, however, they are termed *Sunday houses*. Built by or for ranchers and farmers who lived in the countryside, the Sunday houses provided shelter for the farm family coming to town for Sunday church services. In Fredericksburg and a few other nearby towns, Sunday houses often cluster near churches, confirming their rationale of origin (Mueller 1972, 56).

Sunday houses are very small, befitting their limited use (Figure 13-10). One or two ground-floor rooms, and a loft, where children or young males slept, are connected by an outside staircase. The gable-roofed structures are usually of wood construction, although an occasional stone building can be found. The weekly visit to town over rough roads and across hilly terrain included Saturday marketing as well as Sunday church services (Giovannini 1984).

> Each builder considered his needs. If his family lived near town and used a Sunday house only for Sunday dinner, a one-room lumber house sufficed. . . . Large families who traveled fifteen or twenty miles to town in a wagon or hack, liked the two-story, lumber house that had two rooms downstairs and a large room or two above. (Mueller 1972, 56)

The Sunday house could be called into service at times other than the weekends. Visits to the doctor and the county fair, wakes and funerals, and long-term stays by children in town for school could be accommodated. Finally, the Sunday house could be a retirement home when sons succeeded to farm ownership (Herrmann 1977, 131).

13-10. *A Sunday house in Fredericksburg, TX. Note both the small size of the structure and the outside stairway. These are now often being turned into weekend vacation houses for the urban dwellers of San Antonio and Austin (photo by the author, 1982).*

The pattern of alternative residences was somewhat different among the German-Russian Catholics in western Kansas. "Since field cultivation was a family matter on the Kansas scene, permanent summer dwellings were established on the distant family farmstead. The entire family would move to the farmstead during the planting and harvesting seasons." On Saturday the family shifted to its village dwelling, returning to the farmstead late Sunday or early Monday. "After the planting of the winter wheat the family returned to the village and daily village life was resumed" (Petersen 1970, 44).

A similar pattern governed the harvest season. Between 1925 and 1935 farmers began to shift permanently to country places, as automobiles providing swifter transport came into general use. Still, some farm families continued to follow the two-house system at least up to the 1970s. Those who had shifted often kept the village house as a retirement residence.

Northwest Pacific Coast Indians had a strong seasonal regime only indirectly related to temperature changes. Occupying their winter, coastal-situated plank houses from October to May, they shifted to interior locations where the males participated in freshwater fishing and hunting, while women gathered berries, roots and other foodstuffs. These inland structures were usually tents or similar light structures. In some instances, both the winter and summer residences were plank houses. This was true of the Wakashan who inhabited Vancouver Island. "When families moved from summer village to winter village or vice versa, they took down most of the wall and roof planks, loaded them across two canoes lashed together, and set them up again around the bare frameworks at the other village" (Stewart 1984, 68). Even though the planks were heavy, the labor of moving them was still less than moving the heavier framework, or building two separate structures.

Some desert edge nomads frequently follow the same rationale, moving the skins or cloth of their tents but leaving the framework behind to be used at some future time (Faegre 1979, 55, 61 & 67). Such a strategy enables them to move quickly and lightens the burden on pack animals but, of course, it can only be utilized in country where some wood is available for a new frame or where their old frame will not be disturbed.

The Rabaris, a semi-nomadic group in the desert of Kutch in western India, occupy permanent houses during the monsoon, and for a time thereafter while the grass can sustain their flocks (Shah 1980, 51). Beginning in November, however, they take to their tents to roam over Kutch and the adjacent wetter area of Saurashtra. The changeable orientation of the tents was reviewed above in Chapter 4.

Seasonally occupied sets of dwellings are referred to as "camps" among the Navajo in the southwestern United States. The camp may consist of hogans and houses, ramadas and other shade structures, and livestock pens and corrals (Jett 1980, 102–3). Ramadas, windbreaks, tents, and other shade structures are primarily associated with summer camps (Spencer and Jett 1971, 166–8). The seasonal shift of the Navajo was a response to several considerations: location of grazing ranges; location of cultivated fields; temperature differences; availability of fuel; water sources; availability of peach orchards and pinon forests to supply fruit and nuts for food; location of forage along migration routes; and social considerations (Hoover 1931, 432). Each of these carried a different weight, depending upon natural conditions and the agricultural orientation of various Navajo groups. Those Navajo who were more farmers than herders spent summers in the villages and moved to the lower highlands, where firewood for heat is plentiful, in the winters. "Where grazing has an importance equal to or greater than that of farming, the seasonal migration pattern may be the reverse" (Jett 1978, 70) in order to take advantage of summer pastures.

Seasonal shift of residences everywhere requires that either permanent structures be located in each place, or that the structures be portable. The moveable tents and yurts of nomadic peoples are well known:

> The requirements of a Bedouin shelter are that it should provide a space in which it is cool and protected yet able to catch and trap any cooling breeze. It should provide a modicum of privacy for a man and his wife from the eyes of strangers and also be large enough for the entertaining of visitors. It must protect from the rains and keep a man's few possessions partially dry. But primarily, it must be easy to erect, dismantle and transport. (Verity 1971, 30)

Both tents and yurts are used by nomads in Afghanistan, but the tent is much more transportable than the yurt. The tent can be carried by a single camel, whereas the yurt requires two or three. Consequently, the yurt is confined to better-watered steppe grass areas that require the animals to shift less often. The yurt dominates in and north of the Hindu Kush, and is most closely associated with Uzbek and Turkmen nomads. The tent also has a wider distribution because of the widespread availability of both goat hair and cotton fiber (Szabo and Barfield 1991, 30–1 & 60).

Herders in Ireland in 1690 were reported to have dwellings "built so conveniently of hurdles and long turfs that they can remove them in summer towards the mountains, and bring them back to the valleys in winter" (Evans 1969, 81). More common and widespread in Ireland were simple, rough stone or local sod huts called *booleys*. These were occupied only in the summer season, when cattle moved to summer hill pasture. In parts of counties Mayo and Kerry, beehive huts were still used as milk houses and for storing turf at least to the time of World War II (Evans 1939, 221). Herders in southeastern Poland along the Carpathian Mountains follow a pattern closer to that followed by other transhumance peoples. A permanent winter home in a lowland village alternates with another summer habitation. A similar pattern was followed from at least the 10th to the 18th centuries in Wales. The summer house (*hafod*) was a primitive structure, which sometimes became "the permanent home of a new branch of the family" (Smith 1967, 772).

In southern Scotland, the tenant commonly "owned the roof and the roofing timbers, and these he removed with him when he departed to another house and holding" (Sinclair 1953, 27; Gailey 1962, 238). In Newfoundland, on a different level, it was not the roof that migrated but the wooden house frame, imported from the Maritimes and finished with local wood siding (Pocius 1983, 14). In the tropics, the use of light materials such as palm fronds and grasses facilitates the periodic shifting of dwellings (Nwafor 1979; Kuper 1946, 22). In Indonesia, when labor is available from relatives and clansmen, these structures are light enough to be moved intact (Dawson and Gillow 1994, 12).

The more normal technique for moving a structure is to dismantle it. In Thailand pre-fabricated sidewall panels and gables made moving easy, but dismantling and re-erection were not undertaken on the same day because of religious strictures (Chaichongrak et al. 2002, 11 & 182). Among the Tonga in southern Africa, entire villages are periodically moved. When this happens, the mud walls are constructed on site but the roofs are carried from the old to the new location (Oliver 1977, 7). On the American Great Plains, the Homestead Act of 1862 provided for eventual private ownership of the government land if a settler met certain conditions, one of which was residence on the property for five years, and another was "improvement" of the claim. These requirements were often met by quickly constructing a flimsy, small, frame dwelling, universally called a *claim shanty*. Every five years these could legally be moved quickly and easily to another claim (and sooner illegally) to gain more land (Straight and Mustoe 1996, 77–8).

The movement of entire houses was usually limited to lighter structures. Nonetheless, even heavy timber buildings could be moved. In Denmark, the abolition of serfdom and feudal service, together with land redistribution in the 18th century, allowed some farmers to take their dwellings apart, move from the village to their new holdings and reassemble them on the new site (Faber n.d., 101–2). The somewhat similar situation with the chattel houses of Barbados was discussed in Chapter 2. Portable wooden houses are also reported from early times in Russia (Jorre 1967, 80) and in North America. Heavy wooden structures are usually moved by disassembly rather than intact (Burris 1934, 48). The simple but solidly built *troje* of the Tarascan Indians of the Mexican Sierra Madre Occidental can be disassembled, moved and re-erected in as little as a day and a half (Beals et al. 1944, 14).

A quite different but also easily moved dwelling is the *wanigan*, a rectangular, one-room building, with a very gently pitched gable roof and tar-paper walls, anchored by vertical wooden battens (Hoagland 1993, 50 & 228). They were used in the 1930s and later to house itinerant workers. The structure was mounted on skids to enable its relocation on frozen ground or snow during the winter season.

An exception to the general rule that heavier houses were disassembled prior to relocation is the practice that has been identified among the Cajuns of Louisiana during the early part of the 20th century:

> When a man bought a house, . . . he called his neighbors and organized a hauling bee, or *halerie*. With a dozen yoke of oxen and three wagons they soon had the house underway with no difficulty. First they took the beds off two wagons, and in place of the rectangular coupling poles they used long logs perhaps thirty feet long. They jacked up the house, then ran the poles under it. Next they chained them up to the two front pair of wheels, thus supporting the house, and it was ready to roll. They hitched five to six yoke of oxen to each of the wagons, and away they went across the open prairie. With no fields, ditches, or fences to hinder them, they could make twelve or fifteen miles per day. (Post 1962, 90)

Everywhere that colonials penetrated, so too did their ideas of housing. This helps to explain why, over time, in Africa the native circular hut gradually has given way to rectangular structures. Requiring immediate housing and not wishing to be perceived as "going native," colonial administrators, missionaries and traders ordered prefabricated housing units from their home country. In those places, such as New Zealand and Australia, where colonists intended to be permanent residents, early shelter was overwhelmingly by prefabricated units imported from the UK (Metson 1945, 359; Boyd 1952, 29; Stacpoole 1976, 23).

To stand the rough usage on the journey out and to permit them to be advertised as permanent prefabricated and portable dwellings, houses consisted of iron slabs for walls and roof and were lined only with canvas (Archer 1987, 60). You can image how unbearably hot they were in summer! The very first colonial building erected in Australia was a prefab shipped out from England (Cox and Freeland 1969, 16).

The situation of New Zealand is particularly interesting because by the middle of the 19th century things had turned around and New Zealand was one of the leading suppliers of prefabricated houses to California to meet the shortages created by the gold rush (Peterson 1948, 43). The impetus for shipment of prefabricated buildings to Iceland arose from the virtual lack of suitable building materials there. Thus, Norwegian and Danish whalers, merchants, and traders had such structures imported, beginning in the late 18th century and continuing through the 19th (Abrecht 2000, 21, 63 & 201).

The shipment of prefabricated buildings from industrial countries to overseas destinations is a phenomenon that developed mostly after the introduction of steam navigation and the perfection of railway systems (Peterson 1965; Darnall 1972; Mills and Holdsworth 1975; Dennis 1986; Liphschitz and Biger 1994), although there are a few much earlier examples (Ennals and Holdsworth 1998, 55; Bridenbaugh and Bridenbaugh 1972, 134). The design of exported portable houses sent to Africa, Southeast Asia and elsewhere in the tropics in the early 19th century "seems to have made little concession to the different climate, let alone lifestyle, or social conditions of their inhabitants. After the 1850s, however, they became increasingly adapted to tropical requirements" (King 1984, 197–8).

In the 19th and 20th centuries, communication facilities had become so perfected that, in most instances, it was ideas that moved rather than the physical objects themselves. Modern materials, forms and techniques grew steadily more acceptable in replacing the traditional. The process was most clearly seen in the rapidly expanding urban areas. For most peoples, the future lay in the cities.

~ 14 ~
Change versus Constancy

The study of architecture, whether vernacular or formal, allows us, in the memorable words of Professor William Carless (1925), "to steal a glance down the vista of time." We see in the case of traditional building the constancy of approaches and concepts, and at the same time, the modifications reflecting changes in culture, environment, economy, and lifestyles.

Unfortunately, the everyday houses of ordinary people rarely enjoy the attention that showplaces and the dwellings of the well-known receive. Jean Sizemore (1994, 1), writing about houses in the Ozarks, correctly perceives the problem against which all traditional structures struggle:

> Time is running out for the ordinary and unpretentious houses that people in the rural Arkansas Ozarks built for themselves in the period from 1830 to 1930 and for our opportunities to observe them. Since the structures are overwhelmingly constructed of wood, they are deteriorating rapidly. Many are vacant; the simplicity and practicality that are their essence are also their undoing, for they are largely unappreciated both by the families whose forebears built them and by most preservationists who are accustomed to prizing buildings that are imposing and unusual, rather than ordinary.

Because of the constantly high humidity and the use of light, biodegradable materials or easily eroded earth, few structures in tropical Africa are recognizable for more than about a generation (McKim 1985, 14). Recognizing a similar situation of rapid deterioration in a different climate, but on the flood plain of a major river, John Warren and Ihsan Fethi (1982, 22) suggest that traditional buildings in Baghdad, Iraq are naturally following "an architectural pattern based upon the acceptance of decay." Nevertheless, the concepts that gave rise to the buildings have an obstinate tenacity. It is not the house itself that has such a hold on human intellect, but rather the ideas intimately associated with it – the materials of which it is built, the form it assumes, the location and orientation of the building, and the mystical and symbolic significance of each of these elements.

The preceding chapters have shown several examples of the tenacity with which groups hold to traditional methods, materials and forms, even when their utility has declined or disappeared altogether. In part it is this *constancy* that helps maintain stability in societies by providing continuity (Scofield 1936, 230). It helps a society to maintain integrity and identity, especially in those instances where the group has migrated into alien territory. Speaking of tribal societies, Colin Duly (1979, 6) observes:

> When the economy is just about at subsistence level, and the tribe has little contact with other cultures, we generally find that, unlike our own society, it rarely values innovation and novelty, rather regarding them as undesirable or even dangerous. The force of tradition provides the stabilizing element binding one generation to another.

We must bear in mind, however, that "while discouragement of innovation insured continuity and order in the community by avoiding the arbitrary or merely fashionable, it also prevented needed improvement" (Carver 1981, 27).

The hold which tradition exerts is profound. Anthony Kriesis (1948, 268) compared two Greek houses, one from 432–348 BC and the other of AD 1690, and found their form concepts to be exactly the same, despite the approximately 2000 years separating the two buildings. He concluded:

> although building materials and structural features changed, the basic arrangement of the vernacular Hellenic house has been preserved by an unseen undercurrent of precious tradition. Such changes as there were, were due to the builder's open-mindedness in adopting functional improvements, while the survival of the ancient type is testimony, not to the builder's conservatism, but to the functional suitability of that form.

Lest this constancy over such a long period of time be taken as an isolated example linked to classical building, consider the perseverance of the passage house in Iceland (Krissdottir 1982). This dwelling consists of a series of three to five free-standing, one-room units connected by a subterranean cross-passage at their rear (Figure 14-1). Originally all the units were semi-subterranean dugouts, but in the prosperity of the 19th and very early 20th centuries above-ground wooden units emerged to replace the dugouts, although the cross-passage remained underground (Sigurdsson 1971). At least one unit of the complex was heated by hot springs, which abound in Iceland and are still widely used today for winter heating. The passage house was built in Iceland for approximately 800 years, from the 12th to the

14-1. *Sketch and schematic floor plan of an Icelandic passage house. The partly erected and partly excavated complex evolved from much earlier totally excavated structures (drawn by Linda Bussey).*

20th centuries. A common variant of the cross-passage dwelling utilizes a plan (Figure 14-2), in which some rooms open on either side off a passage at right angles, and some rooms, not connected to either the passage or other rooms, open directly to the outside. The free-standing units were usually partially encased in a turf roof and thick turf walls to increase insulation.

An even longer connection exists between present-day circular thatched huts in Gujarat State, India and virtually identical Harappan-age structures there that may date from 2000–1500 BC. "There is a close link in the design, shape, size, material and the techniques of construction" (Patel 1987, 279). John Corbett (1940, 100) notes a similar, if shorter, continuity of design among Navajo hogans. As a final example, a present-day Ethiopian traditional house can be shown to be almost identical in form to a recently discovered model in clay of a

14-2. *Floor plan of a variant of the Icelandic passage house. The passage does not cross behind the erected units, but lies at right angles to them (sketch by Kevin Butler).*

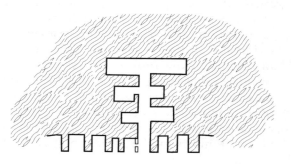

dwelling "believed to be about fifteen hundred years old" (Gebreme-dhin 1971, 109). Such widely spread examples confirm the importance of constancy of form as a defining characteristic of traditional building.

The tenacity of tradition is expressed nicely in another dimension by the continued adherence by many communities to thatched roofing. However, in the tropics thatch fights a losing battle with corrugated metal, and in the middle latitudes, once dominant over vast areas, it survives today in rural Japan (Nishi 1967, 249) and in widely scattered pockets in Europe, especially in France (Brier and Brunet 1984; Meirion-Jones 1982), in England (Sandon 1977; Billett 1984), in the Scottish islands and highlands (Fenton 1978; Gailey 1984), in Wales (Smith 1989), in the Ukraine (Kuzela 1963), in Ireland (Evans 1969), in the Czech Republic (Haslova and Vajdio 1974), and in Slovakia (Lazistan and Michalov 1971). In all these areas it also fights a losing battle with metal sheets and asbestos shingles. Gerard Moris-set (1958, 192) also records barns with thatched roofs as recently as the mid-20th century in the Yamachiche region of Quebec.

An important facet of constancy is the surprising permanence of some individual traditional structures. Time and time again, writers have stressed – as I have done in the beginning of the chapter – the impermanence of vernacular or traditional building. Albert Manucy (1962, 10) astutely observes that "the home of the common man seems to have a special kind of impermanence, as any homeowner can tell you." The construction was often hurried, the materials subject by their nature to rapid deterioration, and the skill of building often meager. Nevertheless, almost everywhere a few buildings survive for two or three centuries, and in exceptional cases even longer and often in unexpected locations. To cite just one example, Kevin Stayton (1990, 10) observes, "at least fourteen old Dutch farmhouses still exist in the borough of Brooklyn." Dutch residences from the 17th century in the middle of New York City, a city notable for its periodic whole-sale rebuilding!

Where urban places are smaller and pressures for redevelopment less, a surprising number of traditional dwellings may still exist. In a 30-square-mile area of northeastern County Dublin, over 600 traditional structures were recorded in 1993, with about two-thirds located in towns and the rest in the countryside (Dublin Heritage Group 1993, 2). This was despite a dramatic loss between 1964 and 1993 of thatched-roofed houses.

One of the most significant agents in the process of preservation of these cultural links is the *Skansen* or open-air museum. Most widely spread and successful in Europe, they now operate to some degree on every continent. In 1986 one source estimated the worldwide number at over 400 (Negoita 1986, 7). The earliest and perhaps still the best of these museums is that of the original Skansen in Stockholm, established in 1891. "Beginning with seven or eight acres, the site expanded to seventy-five acres with 150 buildings by 1982" (Donnelly 1992, 212).

Other open-air museums exist in Sweden, but they do not reach the level, or have the support, that Skansen has. A similar situation exists in many other European countries. The list of leading museums would include Norsk Folkemuseum in Oslo, Norway; Seurasaari in Helsinki, Finland; Dansk Frilandsmuseet, near Copenhagen; Arbaer Folk Museum near Reykjavik, Iceland; the Swiss Open-Air Museum of Rural Life at Ballenberg; Bokrijk in Belguim; Openluchtmuseum, Arnhem in the Netherlands; the Museum of Folk Architecture, Sanok in Poland; Welsh Folkmuseum St. Fagan in Wales; and Muzeul Satului (Museum of the Romanian Village) in Bucharest, to mention only the best-known examples representing the traditional buildings of an entire country.

In Germany, a different system operates, with each province having its own museum and no single museum operating as the national facility. Similarly, in Russia – because of its vast territory – regional or provincial museums operate. The best known is probably the Kizhi Open-Air Museum on the shore of Lake Onega in Karelia, although the largest such museum in Russia is Malye Korely, near Arkhangel (Sewan 1995, 86). Even small European countries such as Estonia and Iceland have well-established open-air museums. Iceland, for example, has no fewer than seven (Bartoszek 1990, 268).

Two important perils exist in the operation of open-air museums. First is the danger that attractive, rather than typical, structures will be selected for the museum. In fact the directives for setting up the Romanian museum, as quoted by Jana Negoita (1986, 10), included the following criteria: "[The house] should be handsome. The museum is set up to be seen by many people, from Romania and abroad. It is not fit that houses that are not perfect models of beauty should be accounted characteristic."

This is, of course, related to a second pitfall, that of such selective choice, so that national propaganda and political objectives are furthered more than architectural preservation and interpretation. This is sometimes done by entirely omitting a minority group's structures. I noticed in an open-air museum in the Silesian region of Poland that no ethnic German structures were included, despite the well-known presence and political control over the region by Germans over long periods. Perhaps this is understandable in an area where borders have shifted and severe ethnic conflicts have matured over time. Still, one cannot help feeling that one objective of the museum is to buttress the Polish claim to this region.

The visitor guides that the European open-air museums publish are excellent quick-reference documents, enabling students to interpret the structures. They also raise the intellectual curiosity of a larger population to appreciate traditional buildings. The value of these facilities lies in the faithfulness with which they preserve structures in their original form and context as far as possible (Figure 14-3). At the same time, important modifications that were widespread, or which illustrate important changes in the society, should not be overlooked. Optimally, a mix of the two approaches is desirable.

Old World Wisconsin, perhaps the premier open-air museum in the United States, has approached this challenge by creating ethnic groupings typical of different time periods. Among the most successful of these are the groupings of Finnish structures. One set of these buildings consists of structures from the end of the 19th century. A separate and more extensive grouping of Finnish structures from 1915–19 illustrates later building techniques. All of the museum's structures are buildings originally erected by immigrants within the state of Wisconsin. The museum is situated in a landform called the

14-3. Entrance to the Opole Open-Air Museum in Poland. The clean and neat character of the entrance is maintained throughout the grounds and structures and is a common characteristic of virtually all Skansen museums. In this respect they differ from the true environment of most traditional structures (photo by the author, 1985).

Kettle moraine, where the naturally undulating topography separates each group of buildings, so that each time period and each ethnic group is not seen from others nearby. The innovative arrangement is a tribute to the imaginative design and skill of landscape architect, William Tishler.

A quite different approach has been taken by the Museum of American Frontier Culture, located near Staunton, in the Valley of Virginia. Here, three clusters of European buildings – a German farm, a Scots-Irish farm, and an English farm – have been brought from Europe and augmented by an American pioneer farm typical of the Shenandoah valley. The idea is to show how various European structures and agricultural practices together gave rise to the American buildings and patterns. To my knowledge, no other open-air museum attempts this kind of large-scale interpretative presentation.

A differing philosophy energized the creation of Upper Canada Village, north of Toronto (Cochrane 1976, 31–4). Established to memorialize the early settlement of the upper St. Lawrence valley by the United Empire Loyalists who fled there from the United States after the American Revolution, its scope has continued to broaden as an inclusive open-air museum for Ontario. Its initial momentum was the preservation of early traditional structures from destruction by the flooding of land resulting from the construction of the St. Lawrence Seaway project. Today, it represents the leading open-air museum of eastern Canada. Other open-air museums focus upon individual ethnic groups and include the Ukrainian Cultural Heritage Village near Edmonton, Alberta, and the German-Russian Village Museum south of Winnipeg, Manitoba.

Open-air museums in Africa and Asia represent only the beginning stage of this type of preservation effort. The best examples in Africa are the Tanzania Village Museum near Dar-es-Salaam; the Bomas of Kenya near Nairobi; the Zambian Village Museum near Livingstone; and the Museum of Traditional Nigerian Architecture in Jos. Most of these were established or significantly extended in the 1960s, in the realization that such complexes could serve as important tourist centers, primarily to attract North American and West European tourists. The major difference between the African museums and those of Europe is that "while vernacular architecture in Europe is, generally speaking, a phenomenon of the past, in Africa it is still a living reality, providing housing for the majority of the rural inhabitants" (Mturi 1984, 276). Often planners and developers, who favor replacement of the traditional with the modern, take a dim view of such museums, which they feel compete with their projects for limited government resources.

The establishment of open-air museums in Asia is even less well developed, but notable examples such as Meiji Mura and the Hida Minzoku Mura Folk Village in Japan and the Korean Folk Village near Seoul have a growing impact. The Museum of Isaan Houses at the Maha Sarakham University in northeastern Thailand is the most notable open-air museum in all of Southeast Asia, despite its remote location. It deserves to be more widely known. In all of these facilities the principal idea is to interpret earlier folklife primarily to local populations who are increasingly affluent and urban, and hence largely divorced from traditional life (Knapp 2003, 78).

The concept of open-air museums as a strategy to preserve traditional architecture has not yet taken firm hold in Latin American countries or the Caribbean. In 2003 I was able to visit a facility in Barbados called Tyrol Cot. Attached to the home of the first prime minister, Sir Grantly Adams, is a small collection of chattel houses and an old plantation slave cottage. In order to preserve these buildings, they have been turned into craft shops by the Barbados National Trust. The collection is praiseworthy, but not extensive. At least the idea of historic preservation has been raised here, which is more than has happened in most of the rest of Latin America.

Change, and constant, even if slow, modification, is another basic characteristic with which traditional building must contend. "It can be argued that there can be no change without tradition, that tradition provides the matrix within which any changes may be introduced." Even so, the rate of change may be virtually imperceptible, as small innovations are tried, repeated and proved to be effective and gradually incorporated into customary practice, or are found wanting and dropped (Oliver 1989, 58).

On occasion, however, change may occur rapidly as the result of military conquest, imperial edict, mass movements of people, abrupt changes in the environment or other situations requiring rapid adjustment. Immigrants, for example, had to adjust both to the changed character of the environment and to the cultural milieu into which they came. A natural tendency was, of course, to build as they had been used to, but such was not always possible or even desirable. Further, the immigrants often existed on the edge of poverty, and change was inevitable.

As an illustration of adjustment to change, Reidar Bakken (1994, 78) calls our attention to several differences in traditional building techniques between the migrant source region of western Norway and Coon Valley, Wisconsin, the area into which the migrants moved. In Coon Valley, settlers abandoned many common Norwegian techniques. Instead they built small houses of one-and-a-half stories, with high pitched roofs, wooden roofs instead of turf, interior as well as exterior whitewashing, changes in type of log corner notching, use of rafters rather than purlins, frame instead of log construction in upper gable walls, and additions made at right angles to the original house. These modifications were so widely used by Norwegian settlers in Coon Valley that they came to represent their architectural signature, recognizable to others.

Dwelling patterns in Yemen offer another clear example of change that is taking place not only there but also in many other parts of the globe. The tower house, or, more exactly, the tower housebarn mentioned in Chapter 2, is being replaced by a single-story home of quite different design.

> A large entrance forms the axis of the house, with rooms on both sides. These houses, surrounded by an enclosed garden, lack the stables and stores associated with the traditional tower-house, and all the rooms have large windows. It is the home of a different kind of society, where the living style is no longer patriarchal: the stables have been replaced by garages, the stores are unnecessary because liquid gas has take the place of firewood; supplies are bought daily according to need, and there are no more grindstones. The latticed box for keeping water and hanging the meat has been replaced by the refrigerator. (Costa and Vicario 1977, 16–17)

Although the emphasis in traditional building is on constancy, and change is often viewed with suspicion, if not actual alarm, innovations are steadily experimented with and modifications are regularly adopted (Bergengren 1991). "We cannot stop the clock," or as Albert Manucy (1962, 44) puts it in different terms, "homeowners have always been notorious property-improvers." Usually this process operates slowly, but in some instances the pace of change is swift. Friedrich Schwerdtfeger (1972, 553) reports the virtually complete substitution of circular-plan huts by rectangular ones in a Hausa compound in northern Nigeria in the timespan of a single generation.

Often modifications in traditional building are the result of contact between two different ethnic communities. When one group has a higher technological level than the other or is more powerful, new techniques of construction may be borrowed by the other group (Shufeldt 1892). Sometimes mere proximity is sufficient to promote exchange of material culture forms and processes. John Lehr (1973, 10) notes that Ukrainian traditional building was influenced by Germans and Poles in Galicia, while Romanians affected the Ukrainian building practices and structures in the neighboring province of Bukowina, although they did not intermix with the Ukrainians.

When the Navajo migrated to what later became the American Southwest, "they borrowed new construction techniques from the Pueblo culture." Their hogans became more complex structures covered with a layer of earth (Lee 1983; Brugge 1968; Jett 1987). The situation was complicated when the Spaniards arrived at a much later date. Elizabeth Boyd (1974, 2) notes that the Spaniards introduced to Indian communities metal hoes, wooden construction forms, metal tools to cut and shape timber, and crowbars and pulleys to raise heavy wooden beams. The Pueblo Indians readily adopted these innovations.

In other instances, the innovations arise within the group itself. The loosening of ties to a distant homeland enables migrating peoples to experiment with new forms, to try new materials, and to define more clearly their new status. Speaking of the colonization of North America, Peter Ennals and Deryck Holdsworth (1998, 53) comment:

> Initially, the pressure to establish a toehold on the continent made older methods expedient and reassuring. But this conservative instinct to reproduce the comfortable ordered timelessness of the home parish or village must also have been challenged by the very act of emigration. Assaulted by new pressures and possibilities, the newcomer's instinct for the familiar must surely have been tempered by a willingness to experiment and to find in material expression such as housing, a symbol of a new beginning.

Innovation also arises from inventions and new techniques. The introduction of nail-cutting machines about 1800, the circular saw in 1814, prefabricated cast iron around 1850, and a number of other perfected tools revolutionized building practices in America and hastened the demise of traditional building there (Hanson and Hubby 1983, 8).

The negative impact on traditional buildings from colonial administration has been raised above in Chapter 9, but even more casual interaction with non-local contacts is often detrimental for tradition. Paul Dunham (1987, 18) reports that in New Guinea in routine periodic visits, the Australian police patrols recommend use of the rectangular frame "as superior in construction to their traditional round frame." As a result the more traditional conical frame hut is fast disappearing.

A similar pattern of replacement of circular-and oval-plan structures by rectangular has been proceeding elsewhere throughout the 20th century. In northeastern Tanzania in the second half of the 19th century, rectangular-plan huts were found only in islands and small coastal areas (Figure 14-4). By the period 1910–20, rectangular-plan buildings had spread across most of southern Tanzania, presumably resulting from the influence of Arab and Indian traders who

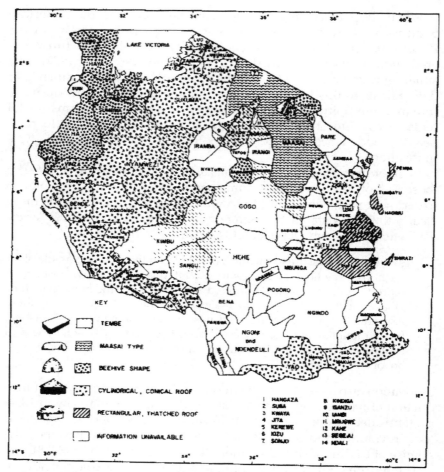

14-4. *Distribution of house types in Tanzania, 1860–90. Compare with the next figure (from Works 1985, 68. Courtesy of the Journal of Cultural Geography/ Oklahoma State University).*

possessed power, wealth and prestige (McKim 1985, 72). The 1950s and 1960s saw further spread to all but the remotest parts of the country (Figure 14-5).

The cross-passage found in longhouses in Monmouthshire offers examples of both evolutionary development and of design inertia. Originally the front and back doors were of the same size and directly opposite one another. Later the doors were shifted somewhat to a staggered position, but they still opened into the cross-passage.

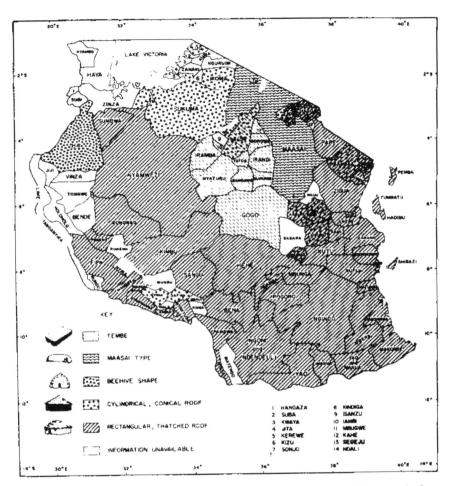

14-5. *Distribution of house types in Tanzania, after 1950. Note the spread of rectangular-plan house types at the expense of more traditional houses (from Works 1985, 71. Courtesy of the Journal of Cultural Geography/Oklahoma State University).*

Presumably the animals always entered from the farmyard side, while the door at the other side was used solely by people. The fact that those entering the house through the latter door walked by the chimney-stack and passed its full width before reaching the door into the hall, gave the inhabitants a sense of privacy, while the door meant primarily for animals, being close to the byre wall, may have helped to keep the human side of the passage as free of mud and dung as possible.

On other longhouses, even where later building gave the animals a separate and direct entrance into the byre, the staggered doors remain. "Here as so often in architectural history, a feature of planning or construction survives long after the conditions that brought it into being have vanished; it is a cultural relic, not a necessity" (Smith, J.T. 1963, 393).

The under-valuation of traditional building by Western-oriented investigators has been noted by Anita and Viera Larsson (1984) working in Botswana. Traditional and modern buildings are often seen as opposites, with the former associated with simple, undeveloped building methods that result in poor houses with a short lifetime. Modern housing, on the other hand, means houses built in durable materials with modern conveniences such as piped water, sewage disposal and electricity. The concept of traditional housing in reality is more complex. Tswana housing provides the necessary structures for different activities linked to farming and herding and social life.

During the winter the households remain in the village settlement of the community. During the growing season, however, people move out to their fields, where they stay for the whole growing season. If there are cattle, they are kept the whole year at a third place, generally referred to as the *cattlepost*, where adequate water and forage is available. Each location has a dwelling unit consisting of a fenced yard with some houses, different simple structures, and often a walled courtyard.

Tswana housing is adapted for traditional farming and herding activities performed regularly over the year. To provide a suitable dwelling is a part of the self-subsistent economy; traditional building methods require no capital expenditure at all. Materials (soil, timber, and grass) are collected from communal tribal land. The householders themselves construct the dwelling in such a way that no advanced tools are needed. The strength and capacity of human labor is sufficient (Larsson and Larsson 1984, 18–19).

Numerous agents for change exist. Often prosperity and innovations in technology, especially in transportation, which affects accessibility or availability of materials, result in modifications to traditional building practices. In Iceland, societal prosperity in the 19th and 20th centuries meant that the cost of imported timber to this largely treeless island could be borne. Steadily throughout this period, as noted above, gable-roofed extensions to cross-passage houses (Figure 14-1) replaced the existing subterranean units (Sigurdsson 1971). Icelandic settlers, arriving in Manitoba near the end of the 19th century, built houses that in form were close to the erected parts of houses they had left in Iceland (Ledohowski and Butterfield 1983, 20–1). Constructed in the early period of log, and later of timber or lumber frame, they were of one-and-a-half stories, one room wide, two or three rooms in all, and usually completely devoid of decoration or even protective paint (Ledohowski and Butterfield 1983).

The introduction of new techniques, even though not directly in construction, affects traditional building. The development of railroads had a significant impact because new construction materials, which often were sturdier, longer lasting and cheaper, became available from non-local sources. As William Facey (1997, 13) dramatically states for Saudi Arabia, in connection with the completion of the railroad across the country to the capital of Riyadh in 1951 – "that day sounded the death knell for an ancient tradition of building." Similarly, in the UK, the coming of railroads in the middle of the 19th century in Cumberland presaged the demise of clay wall construction (Brunskill 1962, 59). L. Carl Brandhorst (1981) also reported that the coming of the railroad to Kansas made lumber costs competitive with stone, which had been the principal building material for erected houses up to that time. Even when materials do not change, technological innovations may cause shifts in usage. Again, the introduction of the railroad had a profound impact, by decimating the market for heavier Scottish roofing slates in favor of cheaper, lighter Welsh slate brought by rail (Beaton 1997, 23).

Changes in the environment may also lead to changes in traditional building approaches. Such shifts are often quite rapid and almost always are the consequence of man's activities. The removal of forest cover usually means a move from wood as the dominant building material to alternative materials. When the cutting is accompanied by an increase in technology, such as the introduction of saw mills, the first step may be to use a more sophisticated wood mode. Both in northern North America and in northern and central Europe, log building gave way to timber frame initially, to dimension lumber later on, and finally to other materials.

The environment may be altered in other ways, too. Henderson et al. (1978, 23) note that Plains Indians were forced to abandon skin tipis and use canvas when buffalo herds were decimated by White hunters in the 19th century. In another example from South Africa, increasing population in the 19th century reduced the supply of range grasses suitable for construction uses, with a resulting shift to inferior wattle-and-daub construction for tribal huts (Frescura 1981, 13).

The change in environment experienced by migrating groups as they enter a new area also may function as an agent of change. The experience of European-derived settlers encountering the largely treeless mid-section of North America and the need to shift quickly to sod houses and dugouts has been extensively documented. Less widely known is the shift among French colonists in Canada away from the thatch and slate used in France for roofing and the acceptance of wooden boards, shingles and hollowed out half-logs, which were easily and abundantly available in Canada (Ennals and Holdsworth 1998, 62).

Although the substitution by new materials for traditionally used ones can be linked to the environment, it is always related to other factors as well. Perhaps the most important of these is cost. Even the most conservative and tradition-bound house builder eventually may be forced to accept substitute materials. The corrugated metal roofs, now engulfing the tropics to replace the traditional materials, is an example, when labor is included as a cost of construction. In mid-latitude regions such as Ireland, thatched roofs are giving way to slate and tile, which are two to three times less expensive (Dublin Heritage Group 1993, 16).

Long-accepted ways of doing things migrate with the individuals themselves. This *cultural baggage*, as noted earlier, enables the migrant to feel comfortable in an alien environment (Rees and Tracie 1978, 3). Thus, the commonplace colonial dwellings of New England were distinct from those of Virginia and the Chesapeake Bay region because the initial English settlers came from quite different parts of England. A similar example is offered by Lin Heng-tao (1975, 26), who notes that the earliest Chinese houses in Taiwan are in the south and match those of Ming and Ching times in southern Fukien from which the immigrants originated. Later colonizers settled primarily in the north of Taiwan, where they preserved the housing characteristics of northern China.

Norman Steward (1965) provides still other examples from Paraguay illustrating this phenomenon. Japanese immigrants clung to a heavy thatched roof with "pyramid yosemune [square-hipped] forms with pronounced bulges of thatch protecting the ridge" despite its unsuitability in the humid, hot climate of Paraguay. Polish-Ukrainian settlers raised carved wooden finials of no other purpose than decorative, above the ridge at gable ends. A third group, Canadian Mennonite colonists, built gigantic barns although "collection and storage of winter feed for livestock is not a climatic imperative." Also among Canadian Mennonites in Paraguay, "basements for storage of produce from the inevitable kitchen garden and the attached 'summer kitchen' reflect experience hard-won from the extreme seasonality of mid-latitude continental climates" in Canada.

Nevertheless, new settlers will invariably come into contact with other ethnic communities, with a likely result of *cultural borrowing*. The change may be as seemingly simple as happened with the

Tuareg, who changed the orientation of their tents from west to south to follow the practice of a numerically superior Arab population (Faegre 1979, 70), or it may involve a change of construction materials, or even form. However, cultural borrowing does not operate in all situations of close proximity. Harold Shurtleff (1939, 170) noted the lack of it in the Delaware Valley between the English – who built timber-frame dwellings – and the Swedes, who constructed log buildings. In contrast, Wilbur Zelinsky (1953, 186) observed that a shift from log building to frame construction did occur among a colony of Swiss in North and South Carolina under the influence of contact with the numerically larger English colonists.

In the opening pages of this work I called attention to the example of the Scots-Irish adoption of log building techniques after contact with Fenno-Scandinavians and Germans in eastern North America. In New Zealand another example of cultural borrowing has been identified. After contact with British colonists, Maori dwellings took on changes both in form and decoration (Stacpoole 1976, 196). Wooden panel doors and a glazed window or two were the most visible alterations. A somewhat different example has been provided by Clifford Zink (1987, 280), who observes that as time passed, Dutch settlers in early New York and New Jersey came under the influence of English building practices with the result that their buildings began to acquire a distinctly hybrid character.

In these examples, the transfer of technology is clear, but it is not always so. William Sherman (1974, 194) asks the question, "Who borrowed from whom?" pointing out that cultural borrowing is a complex process, often operating in both directions. Robert Fuson (1964) has provided an example of the problem from central Panama. The bohio, a light material shelter of the Amerindians, occurs in an area where post-conquest Spanish homes also exist in numbers. Each house type evidences changes over time. The earliest Spanish houses possess internal kitchens. Over time the kitchen became semi-detached and then entirely separate from the main building (Figure 14-6). This process of separation used a structure similar to the bohio with a thatched hipped roof and ultimately with cane walls.

The kitchen of the bohio followed a similar pattern. In the earliest homes the kitchen was internal, but the location appears to be a holdover from the bohio's place of origin in Ecuador. A tile-roofed shed addition permitted a move of the kitchen to a peripheral location. This appears to be a response, given its adobe walls and tile roof, to Spanish influences. Eventually the kitchen became totally separate. Although precise confirming information is not available, it appears that the borrowing was going on in both directions, and was also strongly climate related.

The transfer of technology also may operate entirely within a single culture as economic levels rise and social customs change. We have already noted above the early disappearance in Europe of the "mixed" house providing shelter to both humans and animals (Chapelot and Fossier 1985), but many other changes are underway. As people become more urbanized and exposed to "modern" concepts of housing, traditional building is steadily altered in form, materials, and even function. The almost irresistible pressure to keep up with changing fashion was noted in Chapter 9. Admittedly such pressures frequently improve housing conditions, but often the "improvements" are little more than cosmetic alterations. James

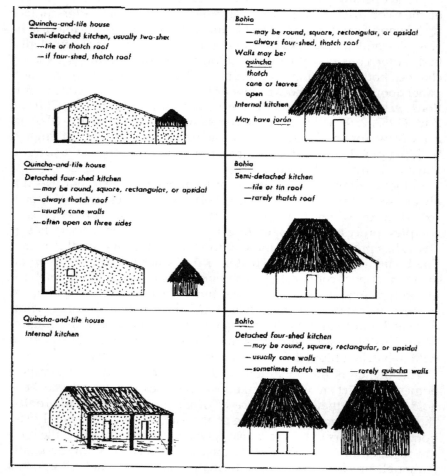

14-6. *Evolutionary changes in Spanish and Indian traditional houses in central Panama (redrawn by Linda Bussey, based upon Fuson 1964, 206).*

Deetz (1996, 160) calls our attention to the shift from vernacular building to the Georgian style in 19th-century US: "commonly, older house
facades were styled by replacing the old casement windows with new
sliding sashes, adding a more classical door, and otherwise adding
details that did not alter the basic form of the house."

A final consideration is the natural disappearance of structures. All
buildings decay (see Chapter 6), especially rapidly in the case of those
made of mud or wood. Searching for Dutch houses in the mid-
Hudson valley, Sophia Hinshalwood (1981, 56) noted, "in the 1970s,
41.5% of houses on the 1850s county map had disappeared or were
replaced by a more recent house. A further 36.4% had been altered to
such an extent that the original form was difficult to identify." Nevertheless, 680 houses built before 1850 were extant in the mid-Hudson
valley from the highlands to the Mohawk River.

In Morocco, Darryl Baker (1986, 153–4) has cataloged several significant shifts. These included: reduction of the size and number of
rooms; increasing popularity of overhanging second stories; reduction in size or even disappearance of the courtyard; disappearance of
the L-shaped entryway and its replacement by a hallway; greater regularity in the form of the dwelling; shift of the kitchen from the upper
floors and the terrace to the ground level; and increasing specializa-
tion of function of spaces. Major social changes, including the
increasing number of nuclear families, the decline of polygamy, and
the reduction in number of children per couple in higher income families, have also affected domestic architecture, primarily in the
decreasing size of dwellings (Petherbridge 1978, 208).

Traditional buildings function – although often only imperfectly,
and always only partially – to preserve a society's way of life (Bell
1973, 107). The struggle is difficult and often ultimately a losing one.
As Jan Brunvand (1989, 196) observes in viewing the countryside in
Romania, "Most houses, in fact, combine traditional and innovative
aspects, perhaps having adobe walls decorated with contemporary
realistic murals, or metal roof trim (plus a television antenna) placed
atop a hand-hewn log house."

The traditional dwelling also very frequently has a symbolic character, which although known to its inhabitants is unrecognized by
many researchers. The maloca of the Amazon tribes offers an example
(Figure 14-7):

> It is in the context of rituals that the maloca assumes its major signifi-
> cance as a cosmic symbol for at such times the house becomes one with
> the universe and spirit world it represents. The roof is the sky sup-
> ported by the posts, which are mountains, with the walls representing
> the hills at the edge of the world. Malocas are oriented on an east–west
> axis with the men's door to the east and the women's door to the west.

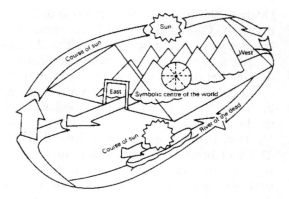

> The ridgepole along the top is the path of the sun across the sky and a post above the centre of the house and centre of the world is his seat at midday. An imaginary river, flowing down the middle of the house from west to east represents the rivers of the earth that flow in this direction and below the floor runs the river of the dead, where the dead go after burial in canoes, flowing from east to west to complete the circuit. By day, the sun travels across the sky to set in the west where it travels up the underworld river in a canoe to rise again in the east. In this way space and time are brought together in one symbolic complex. (Hugh-Jones 1985, 93)

Similarly, the plank houses of the Pacific Northwest Coast Indians also replicated the world in a symbolic way.

> The world was seen as a large plank house supported at the corners by huge poles; the sky was a roof, through the holes of which sunlight shines as stars. On another level, the house could be seen as the body of an ancestor: the ridgepole a spine from which descend the rafter ribs, supported by the limbs of house posts, the face a painting on the housefront or the carved gable end of the ridgepole. (McGhee 1984, 14)

A symbolic aura, nicely illustrated by Peter Nabokov and Robert Easton (1989), also surrounds the location and orientation of their structures. The coastline dwellings of the Northwest Pacific Coast peoples are oriented to the water but situated at the junction of ocean and earth, adjacent to the forest. Smoke rises towards the sky world; the hearth is upon or embedded in the underworld.

The idea that the traditional dwelling is a microcosm prevails in many societies (Marh 2004, 65), even though the concept may not be recognized entirely by the group's members. The structure, explained by its ceremonial aspects, its traditionally accepted components, and its symbolic rules of usage, expresses categories and principles with the widest application in the society's thought and action, and "so provides a comprehensive representation of orderly, universal forms and relations" (Forth 1981, 23). Functioning as a microcosm, a dwelling "expresses fundamental ideas about the world, the proper place of human beings in the world, and their proper relations with one another" (Feely-Harnik 1980, 583).

It is fitting to close this work with three insightful quotations. The first by Michael Levin (1971, 143) refers to Africa but could be applied to all traditional societies throughout the world:

> Every man in an African society is an architect. His orientation is towards the balance of model, materials and user, the latter usually himself. In a closed, traditional society he acts unselfconsciously, regarding design within the cultural system of which he is part. With the transformation of his society under the pressures of modernization, the stable equilibrium within the system is lost and the design process becomes one of selfconscious manipulation of new models, materials and new concepts of use. Each man is an architect for an uncertain future.

The second quotation is an excellent brief summary of the value of traditional building by the historian Charles van Ravenswaay (1977, 112):

> People everywhere seek to live in the kind of housing with which they are familiar as part of their cultural tradition. Consequently, the shape of a house and the arrangement and type of rooms and passageways are all keys to the cultural history of the people who build and live in them.

Finally, Geographer David Lowenthal (1975, 24) has this to say about the traditional landscape:

> Through awareness of the past, we learn to remake ourselves ... The continuous accretion of the tangible past is counterbalanced by its continuous loss, both physical and symbolic. Our immediate past landscapes will be less consequential to our descendants, for whom *our* immediate future will have become an important element of *their* past.

References Cited

A note about form. In this list of references cited I have taken some minor liberties with the standard method of bibliographical citation. First of all, in titles of articles or chapters in books all words are presented in lower case except the first word and proper names. Second, titles of books and names of journals are presented with initial capitals except for small articles or otherwise ordinary connecting words. This I do without regard to how they appear in the original in each case. Chapters in books have the inclusive pages immediately following the chapter title. The names of the editor(s) of the book precede the book title.

Aalen, Frederick H.A. 1966. "The evolution of the traditional house in western Ireland," *Journal of the Royal Society of Antiquaries of Ireland* 96:47–58.

Aalen, Frederick H.A. 1973. "Vernacular architecture of the British Isles," *Yearbook of the Association of Pacific Coast Geographers* 35:27–48.

Aalen, Frederick H.A. 1984. "Vernacular buildings in Cephalonia, Ionian islands, Greece," *Journal of Cultural Geography* 4:2:56–72.

Aalen, Frederick H.A. 1997. "Buildings," pp. 149–152 in Aalen, F.H.A., Kevin Whelan and Matthew Stout (eds.), *Atlas of the Irish Rural Landscape.* Toronto: University of Toronto Press.

Abrecht, Birgit. 2000. *Architectural Guide to Iceland.* Reykjavik: Mal og menning.

Acworth, A.W. 1949. *Treasure in the Caribbean.* London: Pleiades Books.

Addison, William. 1986. *Farmhouses in the English Landscape.* London: Robert Hale.

Addyman, P.V. 1972. "The Anglo-Saxon house: A new review," pp. 273–307, vol. 1, in Clemoes, Peter (ed.), *Anglo-Saxon England.* Cambridge: Cambridge University Press.

Agorsah, E. Kofi. 1985. "Archeological implications of traditional house construction among the Nchumuru of northern Ghana," *Current Anthropology* 26:1:103–15.

Aguirre Beltran, Gonzalo. 1958. *Cuijla:Esbozo etnografico de un pueblo Negro.* Mexico City: Fondo de Cultura Economica.

Ainsley, W. Frank. 1996. "Evolution of the chattel house: Folk housing in Barbados," *PAST – Pioneer America Society Transactions* 19:31–9.

Ainsley, W. Frank. 2003. "The Waldensian housebarns of western North Carolina," *PAST – Pioneer America Society Transactions* 26:1–8.

Airhart, Sharon. 1976. "Cord wood house," *Arrowsmith* 4:54–7.

Alanen, Arnold R. and William H. Tishler. 1980. "Finish farmstead organization in Old and New World settings," *Journal of Cultural Geography* 1:1:66–81.

Alberta, Oil Sands Environmental Research Program. 1976. *Housing for the North: The Stackwall System*. Edmonton: Alberta Environment and Environment Canada.

Alcock, N.W. 1981. *Cruck Construction: An Introduction and Catalogue*. London: Council for Archaeology.

Allen, Edith. 1930. *American Housing : As Affected by Social and Economic Conditions*. Peoria, IL: Manual Arts Press.

Allen, Edward. 1969. *Stone Shelters*. Cambridge, MA: MIT Press.

Alnaes, Eyvind et al. 1950. *Norwegian Architecture Throughout the Ages*. Oslo: H. Aschehoug.

Al-Sabbagh, Jihad D. 1992. "The courtyard house in the hot zones: the French Quarter in New Orleans as a case study," unpublished MSc thesis, Louisiana State University, Baton Rouge.

Ambraseys, N.G. Lensen and A. Moinfar. 1975. *The Pattan Earthquake of 28 December 1974*. Paris: UNESCO, Technical Report.

Amiry, Suad and Vera Tamari. 1989. *The Palestinian Village Home*. London: British Museum Publications.

Anand. 1974. "The house of the Punjab village," *Marg* 28:15–19.

Andersen, Kaj B. 1978. *African Traditional Architecture*. Nairobi: Oxford University Press.

Anderson, Cardwell Ross. 1961. "Primitive shelter," *American Institute of Architects Journal* 36:33–9, 46–54.

Anonymous. 1869a. "Cheap houses – building en pisé," *Manufacturer and Builder* 1:4:110–11.

Anonymous. 1869b. "Plank walls for cottages,"*Manufacturer and Builder* 1:6:175.

Anonymous. 1977. "The return of the cordwood house," *Mother Earth News* 47:29–34.

Anonymous. 1978. "A century (or more) of stackwood homes," *Mother Earth News* 54:106–7.

Archer, John. 1987. *Building a Nation: A History of the Australian House*. Sydney: William Collins.

Arreola, Daniel D. 1988. "Mexican American housescapes," *Geographical Review* 78:3:299–315.

Arthur, Eric R. 1938. *The Early Buildings of Ontario*. Toronto: University of Toronto Press.

Arya, Rohit. 2000. *Vaastu: The Indian Art of Placement*. Rochester, VT: Destiny Books.

Associacao dos Arquitectos Portugueses. 1988. *Arquitectura Popular em Portugal*. Lisbon: Associacao dos Arquitectos Portugueses.

Atkinson, Adrian. 1969. "Bernese Middle Land farmhouses," pp. 49–65 in Oliver, Paul (ed.), *Shelter and Society*. New York: Frederick A. Praeger.

Attebery, J.L., K.J. Swanson, J. Toluse and F.L. Walters. 1985. "The Montgomery house: Adobe in Idaho's folk architecture," pp. 46–55 in Attebery, Louie W. and Wayland D. Hand (eds.), *Idaho Folklife*. Salt Lake City: University of Utah Press.

Attebery, Jennifer. 1976. "Log construction in the Sawtooth Valley of Idaho," *Pioneer America* 8:1:36–46.

Attebery, Jennifer. 1982. "The square cabin: a folk house type in Idaho," *Idaho Yesterdays* 26:3:25–31.

Attebery, Jennifer. 1998. *Building with Logs: Western Log Construction in Context*. Moscow: University of Idaho Press.

Ayres, James. 1981. *The Shell Book of the Home in Britain*. London: Faber and Faber.

Baker, Darryl. 1986. "The traditional house and new middle class housing, T. Ling in Morocco," *Ekistics* 319:149–56.

Bakerdsay. 1979. "Silesian Polish folk architecture in Texas," pp. 130–5 in Abernethy, Francis E. (ed.), *Built in Texas*. Waco: E-heart Press.

Bakken, Reidar. 1994. "Acculturation in buildings and farmsteads in Coon Valley, Wisconsin, from 1850 to 1930," pp. 73–91 in Nelson, Marion John (ed.), *Material Culture and People's Art Among the Norwegians in America*. Northfield, MN: Norwegian-American Historical Association.

Ball, Norman. 1975. "Circular saws and the history of technology," *Bulletin of the Association for Preservation Technology* 7:3:79–89.

Ballard, George. 1934. "Early slate and tile roofing," *Sheet Metal Worker* 25:27.

Bans, Jean-Christian and Patricia Bans. 1979. "Notes on the cruck-truss in Limousin," *Vernacular Architecture* 10:22–9.

Barakat, Robert A. 1972. "The Herr and Zeller houses," *Pennsylvania Folklife* 21:4:2–22.

Barke, Michael. 1979. "Weavers' cottages in the Huddersfield area: A preliminary survey," *Folk Life* 17:49–59.

Barley, M.W. 1967. "Rural housing in England," pp. 696–766 in Finberg, H.P.R. (ed.), *The Agrarian History of England and Wales, Volume IV, 1500–1640*. Cambridge: Cambridge University Press.

Barley, M.W. 1987. *The English Farmhouse and Cottage*. Gloucester: Alan Sutton.

Barns, Cass G. 1930. *The Sod House*. Lincoln: University of Nebraska Press (reprinted 1970).

Barrett, S.A. 1916. "Pomo Buildings," pp. 1–17 in Hodge, F.W. (ed.), *Holmes Anniversary Volume, Anthropological Essays*. Washington: privately printed (reprinted by AMS Press for Peabody Museum of Archeology and Ethnology, Harvard University).

Bartoszek, Stanislaw. 1990. "The Icelandic museums of folk culture," *Acta Scansenologica* 6:268–9 (Sanok: Muzeum Budownictna Ludowego w Sanoku).

Bealer, Alex W. 1978. *The Log Cabin: Homes of the North American Wilderness*. Barre, MA: Barre Publications.

Beals, Ralph L., Pedro Carrasco and Thomas McCorkle. 1944. *Houses and House Use of the Sierra Tarascans*. Washington: Government Printing Office (Smithsonian Institute, Institute of Social Anthropology, Publication #1).

Beaton, Elizabeth. 1997. *Scotland's Traditional Houses*. Edinburgh: Stationery Office.

Bedal, Konrad. 1980. *Hallenhauser und Langsscheunen des 18. und 19. Jahrhunderts im ostlichen Holstein*. Neumunster: Karl Wachholtz Verlag.

Beecher, Kenneth H., Jr. 1991. "Culturally persistent characteristics in rural houses of peripheral Europe," unpublished PhD dissertation, Texas A&M University, College Station.

Bell, Timothy A. 1973. "The metamorphosis of Tahiti: change and tradition in a transforming landscape," *Yearbook of the Pacific Coast Geographers* 35:103–13.

Bemis, Albert F. and John Burchard. 1933. *The Evolving House: A History of the Home*. Cambridge, MA: MIT Press.

Bennett, Keith. 1968. "Iraqi courtyard houses," *Architectural Review* 144:86–8.

Bergengren, Charles. 1991. "The cycle of transformation in Schaefferstown, Pennsylvania houses," pp. 98–107 in Carter, Thomas and Bernard L. Herman (eds.), *Perspectives in Vernacular Architecture IV*. Columbia: University of Missouri Press.

Bernard, Augustin et al. 1931. *L'habitation indigene dans les possessions francaises*. Paris: Societé d'Editions Geographiques, Maritimes et Coloniales.

Bhatt, H.P. 1986. "Rural houses in Tehri Garhwal (Uttar Pradesh)," *Geographical Review of India* 48:2:20–7.

Biermann, Barrie. 1971. "Indlu: The domed dwelling of the Zulu," pp. 96–105 in Oliver, Paul (ed.), *Shelter in Africa*. London: Barrie and Jenkins.

Billett, Michael. 1979. *Thatching and Thatched Buildings*. London: Robert Hale.

Billett, Michael. 1984. *Thatched Buildings of Dorset*. London: Robert Hale.

Bisher, Catherine W. 1983. *The "Unpainted Aristocracy": The Beach Cottages of Old Nags Head*. Raleigh: Division of Archives and History, North Carolina Department of Cultural Resources.

Blackman, Margaret. 1973. "Totems to tombstones: Culture change as viewed through the Haida mortuary complex, 1877–1971," *Ethnology* 12:1:47–56.

Blake, Ernest. G. 1925. *Roof Coverings: Their Manufacture and Application*. London: Chapman and Hall.

Blake, Vershoyle and Ralph Greenhill. 1969. *Rural Ontario*. Toronto: University of Toronto Press.

Blier, Suzanne. 1994. *The Anatomy of Architecture: Ontology and Metaphor in Batammaliba Architectural Expression*. Chicago: University of Chicago Press.

Block, Maurice. 1971. *Placing the Dead: Tombs, Ancestral Villages, and Kinship Organization in Madagascar*. London: Seminar Press.

Bobbitt, Christopher K. 1989. "Summer kitchens of Harrison County, Indiana," pp. 228–40 in Walls, Robert E. and George H. Shoemaker (eds.), *The Old Traditional Way of Life: Essays in Honor of Warren E. Roberts*. Bloomington, IN: Trickster Press.

Bonar, Linda L. 1983. "Historic houses in Beaver: An introduction to materials, styles, and craftsmen," *Utah Historical Quarterly* 51:3:212–28.

Bourdier, Jean-Paul and Trinh T. Minh-ha. 1982. "The architecture of a Lela compound," *African Arts* 16:1:68–72 & 96.

Bourdier, Jean-Paul and Trinh T. Minh-ha. 1983. "Koumboli: Semi-sunken dwellings in Upper Volta," *African Arts* 16:4:40–5 & 88.

Bourdieu, P. 1973. "The Berber house," pp. 98–110 in Douglas, M. (ed.), *Rules and Meanings*. Harmondsworth: Penguin.

Bourgeois, Jean-Louis. 1980. "Welcoming the wind," *Natural History* (November) 70–5.

Bowles, Oliver. 1939. *The Stone Industries*. New York: McGraw Hill.

Boyd, Elizabeth 1974. *Popular Arts of Spanish New Mexico*. Santa Fe: Museum of New Mexico Press.

Boyd, Robin. 1952. *Australia's Home: Its Origins, Builders and Occupiers*. Melbourne: Melbourne University Press.

Bracken, Dorothy K. and Maurine Redway. 1956. *Early Texas Homes*. Dallas: Southern Methodist University Press.

Bradley, Robert L. 1978. *Maine's First Buildings: The Architecture of Settlement, 1604–1700*. Augusta: Maine Historic Preservation Commission.

Branch, Daniel P. 1966. *Folk Architecture of the East Mediterranean*. New York: Columbia University Press.

Brandhorst, L. Carl. 1981. "Limestone houses in central Kansas," *Journal of Cultural Geography* 2:1:70–81.

Brandt, Lawrence R. and Ned E. Braatz. 1972. "Log buildings in Portage County, Wisconsin: Some cultural implications," *Pioneer America* 4:1:29–39.

Brasseur, Gerard. 1968. *Les Etablissements Humains au Mali*. Dakar: IFAN (l'Institut Fondamental d'Afrique Noire).

Brednich, Rolf W. 1977. *Mennonite Folklife and Folklore: A Preliminary Report*. Ottawa: Museum of Man (Canadian Centre for Folk Culture Series #22).

Breisch, Kenneth A. 1994. "Good building stone and a 'lay of the land' that makes for 'Hominess': Norwegian-American settlement patterns and architecture in Bosque county, Texas," pp. 92–117 in Nelson, Marion John (ed.), *Material Culture and People's Art Among the Norwegians in America*. Northfield, MN: Norwegian-American Historical Association.

Bridenbaugh, Carl and Roberta Bridenbaugh. 1972. *No Peace Beyond the Line: The English in the Caribbean, 1624–1690*. New York: Oxford University Press.

Brier, Max-Andre and Pierre Brunet. 1984. *L'architecture rurale française: Normandie* Paris: Musee national des arts et traditions populaires.

Briggs, Martin S. 1932. *The Homes of the Pilgrim Fathers in England and America*. London: Oxford University Press.

Briggs, Martin S. 1953. *The English Farmhouse*. London: B.T. Batsford.

Brinkman, Marilyn Salzl and William Towner Morgan. 1982. *Light From the Hearth*. Saint Cloud, MN: North Star Press.

Brodrick, Alan Houghton. 1954. "Grass roots: Huts, igloos, wigwams and other sources of the functional tradition," *Architectural Review* 115:100–11.

Bronner, Simon. 1980. "The Harris house and related structures in south-central Indiana," *Pioneer America* 12:1:9–30.

Bronner, Simon J. and Stephen P. Poyser. 1979. "Approaches to the study of material aspects of American folk culture" *Folklore Forum* 12:2 & 3:118–31.

Brooke, Clarke. 1959. "The rural village in the Ethiopian highlands," *Geographical Review* 49:1:58–75.

Brown, R.J. 1979. *English Country Cottage*. London: Robert Hale.

Brown, R.J. 1982. *English Farmhouses*. London: Robert Hale.

Brown, R.J. 1986. *Timber-Framed Buildings of England*. London: Robert Hale.

Brown, R.J. 2004. *English Village Architecture*. London: Robert Hale.

Brugge, David M. 1968. "Pueblo influence on Navajo architecture," *El Palacio* 75:3:14–20.

Brugge, David M. 1983. "Navajo activity areas," pp. 185–91 in Ward, Albert E. (ed.), *Forgotten Places and Things*. Albuquerque: Center for Anthropological Studies.

Brumbaugh, G. Edwin. 1933. *Colonial Architecture of the Pennsylvania Germans*. Lancaster: Pennsylvania German Society.

Brunskill, Ronald W. 1954. "The development of the small house in the Eden Valley from 1650 to 1840," *Transactions of the Cumberland and Westmoreland Antiquarian Society* 53:160–89.

Brunskill, R.W. 1962. "The clay houses of Cumberland," *Transactions of the Ancient Monuments Society,* new series 10:57–80.

Brunskill, R.W. 1988. *Traditional Buildings of Britain.* London: Victor Gollancz.

Brunvand, Jan H. 1972. "The study of Romanian folklore," *Journal of the Folklore Institute* 9:133–61.

Brunvand, Jan H. 1974. "Traditional house decoration in Romania," *Utah Architect* 56:9–13.

Brunvand, Jan. 1989. "Casa Frumoasa: An introduction to the house beautiful in rural Romania," pp. 191–207 in Walls, Robert E. and George H. Schoemaker (eds.), *The Old Traditional Way of Life: Essays in Honor of Warren E. Roberts.* Bloomington, IN: Trickster Press.

Buchanan, Paul E. 1976. "The eighteenth-century frame houses of tidewater Virginia," pp. 54–73 in Peterson, Charles E. (ed.), *Building Early America.* Radnor, PA: Chilton Book Co.

Buchanan, Ronald H. 1963. "Geography and folklife," *Folk Life* 1:5–15.

Bucher, Robert C. 1961. "Steep roofs and red tiles," *Pennsylvania Folklife* 12:2:18–26.

Bucher, Robert C. 1962. "The continental log house," *Pennsylvania Folklife* 12:4:14–19.

Bucher, Robert C. 1963/64. "Grain in the attic," *Pennsylvania Folklife* 13:2:7–15.

Bucher, Robert C. 1968. "The long shingle," *Pennsylvania Folklife* 18:4:51–6.

Bucher, Robert C. 1969. "The first shelters of our pioneer ancestors," *Pioneer America* 1:2:7–12.

Buck, Charles S. 1930. "The origin and character of the early architecture and practical arts of Ontario to 1850," unpublished MA thesis, University of Western Ontario, London.

Buck, P.H. (see Hiroa).

Buisseret, David. 1980. *Historical Architecture of the Carribbean.* London: Heinemann.

Bunting, Bainbridge. 1964. *Taos Adobes.* Santa Fe: Museum of New Mexico Press.

Bunting, Bainbridge. 1976. *Early Architecture in New Mexico.* Albuquerque: University of New Mexico Press.

Burcaw, George Ellis. 1979. *The Saxon House.* Moscow: University Press of Idaho.

Burleson, Bob and David H. Riskind. 1986. *Backcountry Mexico.* Austin: University of Texas Press.

Burley, David V. and Gayel A. Horsfall. 1989. "Vernacular houses and farmsteads of the Canadian Metis," *Journal of Cultural Geography* 10:1:19–33.

Burris, Evadene A. 1934. "Building the frontier home," *Minnesota History* 15:43–55.

Butcher, Solomon. 1976. *Pioneer History of Custer County, Nebraska and Sod Houses of the Great American Plains.* Broken Bow, NE: Purcell.

Caemmerer, Alex. 1992. *The Houses of Key West.* Sarasota: Pineapple Press.

Cain, Allan, Farroukh Afshar and John Norton. 1975. "Indigenous building and the Third World," *Architectural Design* 45:4:207–24.

Cain, Allan, Farroukh Afshar, John Norton and Mohammad-Reza Daraie. 1976. "Traditional cooling system in the Third World," *Ecologist* 6:2:60–4.

Calligas, Harris A. 1974. "The evolution of settlements in Mani," pp. 115–37 in Doumanis, Orestis B. and Paul Oliver (eds.), *Shelter in Greece.* Athens: Architecture in Greece Press.

Cameron, Christina. 1982. "Housing in Quebec before Confederation," *Journal of Canadian Art History* 6:1:1–34.

Camesasca, Ettore (ed.), 1971. *History of the House*. New York: G.P. Putnam Sons.

Campbell, Ake. 1935. "Irish fields and houses," *Baealoideas: Journal of the Folklore of Ireland Society* 5:57–74.

Campbell, Walter S. 1915. "The Cheyenne tipi," *American Anthropologist* 17:4:685–94.

Campbell, Walter S. 1927. "The tipis of the Crow Indians," *American Anthropologist* 29:1:87–104.

Candee, Richard M. 1969. "A documentary history of Plymouth Colony architecture, 1620–1700," *Old Time New England* 60:2:37–53.

Candee, Richard M. 1976. "Wooden buildings in early Maine and New Hampshire: A technological and cultural history, 1600–1720," unpublished PhD dissertation, University of Pennsylvania, Philadelphia.

Carius, Helen Slwooko. 1979. *Sevukakmet: Ways of Life on St. Lawrence Island.* Anchorage: Alaska Pacific University Press.

Carless, William. 1925. "The architecture of French Canada," *Journal of the Royal Architectural Institute of Canada.* 11:2:141–5.

Carpenter, Ann. 1979. "Texas dugouts," pp. 53–9 in Abernethy, Francis Edward (ed.), *Built in Texas*. Waco: E-heart Press.

Carroll, Charles F. 1975. "The forest society of New England," pp. 13–36 in Hindle, Brooke (ed.), *America's Wooden Age: Aspects of its Early Technology.* Tarrytown, NY: Sleepy Hollow Restorations.

Carson, Cary. 1974. "The 'Virginia House' in Maryland," *Maryland Historical Magazine* 69:2:185–96.

Carson, Cary. 1976. "Segregation in vernacular buildings," *Vernacular Architecture* 7:24–9.

Carson, Cary, Norman F. Barka, William M. Kelso, Garry Wheeler Stone and Dell Upton. 1981. "Impermanent architecture in the southern colonies," *Winterthur Portfolio* 16:3:135–96.

Carter, Thomas. 1975. "The Joel Cock house: 1885, Meadows of Dan, Patrick County, Virginia," *Southern Folklore Quarterly* 39:329–40.

Carter, Thomas. 1984. "North European horizontal log construction in the Sanpete-Sevier valleys," *Utah Historical Quarterly* 52:1:50–71.

Carver, Norman F., Jr. 1981. *Iberian Villages: Portugal and Spain.* Kalamazoo, MI: Documan Press.

Carver, Norman F., Jr. 1984. *Japanese Folkhouses*. Kalamazoo, MI: Documan Press.

Castaneda, Luis. 1995. "Festival de las Mascaras," *Revista Geo Mundo* 114–23.

Cereghini, Mario. 1956. *Building in the Mountains*. Milan: Edizioni del Milione.

Chaichongrak, Ruethai, Somchai Nil-athi, Ornsiri Panin and Saowalak Posayananda. 2002. *The Thai House: History and Evolution*. Trumbull, CT: Weatherhill.

Chandhoke, S.K. 1990. *Nature and Structure of Rural Habitations*. New Delhi: Concept Publishing.

Chapelot, Jean and Robert Fossier. 1985. *The Village and House in the Middle Ages*. Berkeley: University of California Press.

Chapman, William. 1991. "Slave villages in the Danish West Indies: Changes of the late eighteenth and early nineteenth centuries," pp. 108–20 in Carter,

Thomas and Bernard L. Herman (eds.), *Perspectives in Vernacular Architecture IV*. Columbia: University of Missouri Press.

Chappell, Edward A. 1980. "Acculturation in the Shenandoah Valley: Rhenish houses of the Massanutten settlement," *Proceedings of the American Philosophical Society* 124:1:55–89.

Charernsupkul, Anuvit and Vivat Temiyabandha. 1979. *Northern Thai Domestic Architecture and Rituals in House Building*. Bangkok: Fine Arts Commission of the Association of Siamese Architects.

Charlton, Thomas. H. 1969. "Sociocultural implications of house types in the Teotihuacan Valley Mexico," *Journal of the Society of Architectural Historians* 28:284–90.

Charpentier, Sophie. 1982. "The Lao house: Vientiane and Luang Prabang," pp. 49–61 in Izkowitz, K.G. and P. Sorensen (eds.), *The House in East and Southeast Asia*. London: Curzon Press.

Chelvadurai-Proctor, R. 1927. "Some rules and precepts among Tamils for construction of houses, villages, towns and cities during the mediaeval age," *Journal of the Ceylon Branch of the Royal Asiatic Society* 30:80:337–60.

Chiarappa, Michael J. 1991. "The social context of eighteenth-century West New Jersey brick artisanry," pp. 31–43 in Carter, Thomas and Bernard L. Herman (eds.), *Perspectives in Vernacular Archicture IV*. Columbia: University of Missouri Press.

Choi, Jae-pil. 1987. "Modernization and its impacts on the internal spatial organization of the traditional Korean house," unpublished PhD dissertation, Georgia Institute of Technology, Atlanta.

Choi, Jae-Soon et al. 1999. *Hanoak: Traditional Korean Homes*. Elizabeth, NJ: Hollym International.

Clarke, C. Purdon. 1883. "Some notes upon the domestic architecture of India," *Journal of the Society of Arts* 31:731–46.

Clifton-Taylor, Alec. 1972. *The Pattern of English Building*. London: Faber and Faber.

Cochrane, Donald. 1976. "The history and development of the Loyalist farm at Upper Canada Village," *Proceedings of the Annual Meeting of the Association for Living Historical Farms and Agricultural Museums* 2:31–4.

Cockburn, Charles. 1962. "Fra-Fra house, Damongo, Ghana," *Architecture Design* 32: 299–300.

Coffey, Brian. 1985. "Factors affecting the use of construction materials in early Ontario," *Ontario History* 77:4:301–18.

Coffey, Brian and Allen G. Noble. 1996. "Mid-nineteenth century housing in Buffalo, New York," *Material Culture*. 28:3:1–16.

Cohen, David Steven. 1992. *The Dutch-American Farm*. New York: New York University Press.

Collier, G. Loyd. 1979. "The cultural geography of folk building forms in Texas," pp. 20–43 in Abernethy, Francis E. (ed.), *Built in Texas*. Waco, E-Heart Press.

Collins, Charles O. 1989. "Great Plains privies: A micro-geography," *North American Culture* 5:1:3–30

Connor, Seymour V. 1949. "Log cabins in Texas," *Southwestern Historical Quarterly* 53:2:105–16.

Conway, A.W. 1951. " A northern New Mexico house type," *Landscape* 1:2:20–1.

Cook, F. Palmer. 1971. *Talk to Me of Windows*. South Brunswick, NJ: A.S. Barnes.

Cooper, Ilay and Barry Dawson. 1998. *Traditional Buildings of India*. London: Thames and Hudson.

Copeland, Paul W. 1955. "'Beehive' villages of north Syria," *Antiquity* 29:21–4.

Corbett, John M. 1940. "Navajo house types," *El Palacio* 47:5:97–107.

Corry, John. P. 1930. "The houses of colonial Georgia," *Georgia Historical Quarterly* 14:3:181–201.

Costa, Frank J. and Allen G. Noble. 1986. "Planning Arabic towns," *Geographical Review* 76:2:160–72.

Costa, Paolo and Ennio Vicario. 1977. *Yeman: Land of Builders*. London: Academy Editions.

Covarrubias, Miguel. 1942. *Island of Bali*. New York: Alfred A. Knopf.

Cox, Philip and John Freeland. 1969. *Rude Timber Buildings in Australia*. London: Thames and Hudson.

Crain, Edward E. 1994. *Historic Architecture in the Caribbean Islands*. Gainesville: University Press of Florida.

Cranstone, B.A.L. 1980. "Environment and choice of dwelling and settlement: an ethnographic survey," pp. 488–503 in Ucko, Peter J., Ruth Tringham and G.W. Dimbleby (eds.), *Man, Settlement and Urbanism*. Cambridge, MA: Schenkman.

Cressey, George. 1932. "Chinese homes and home sites," *Home Geographic Monthly* 2:31–6.

Crooke, W. 1918. "The house in India from the point of view of sociology and folklore," *Folklore* 27:113–45.

Crouch, Dora P. and June G. Johnson. 2001. *Traditions in Architecture: Africa, America, Asia, and Oceania*. Oxford: Oxford University Press.

Crowder, Michael. 1956. "The decorative architecture of northern Nigeria," *African World* (February) 9–10.

Crumbie, Peggy D. 1987. "The I house in Oklahoma: A geographic study in folk housing typology," unpublished MSc thesis, Oklahoma State University, Stillwater.

Cullimore, Clarence. 1948. *Santa Barbara Adobes*. Santa Barbara, CA: Santa Barbara Book Publishing Company.

Cummings, Abbott Lowell. 1979. *The Framed Houses of Massachusetts Bay, 1625–1725*. Cambridge, MA: Harvard University Press.

Curtis, Nathaniel. 1933. *New Orleans: its Old Houses, Shops, and Public Buildings*. Philadelphia: J.B. Lippincott.

Cutts, Anson B. 1949. "The old Scottish architecture of Ontario," *Canadian Geographical Journal* 39:5:202–17.

Czajkowski, Jerzy. 1981. "An outline of Skansen Museology in Europe," pp. 12–31 in Czajkowski, Jerzy (ed.), *Open-Air Museum in Poland*. Poznan: Panstwowe Wydawnictwo Rolnicze i Lesne.

Czajkowski, Jerzy. 1994. *Park Etnograficzny w Sanoku w Ogniu*. Sanok: Sierpien.

Daifuku, Hiroshi. 1952. "The pit house in the old world and in native North America," *American Antiquity* 18:1:1–7.

Dall, Greg. 1982. "The traditional Acehnese house," pp. 34–61 in Maxwell, John (ed.), *The Malay-Islamic World of Sumatra*. Clayton, Victoria: Monash University.

Darnall, Margaretta Jean. 1972. "Innovations in American prefabricated housing, 1860–1890," *Journal of the Society of Architectural Historians* 31:1:51–5.

Davey, Norman. 1971. *A History of Building Materials*. New York: Drake Publishers.

Davis, Neil. 1982. *Alaska Science Nuggets*. Fairbanks: University of Alaska Geophysical Institute.

Dawson, Barry and John Gillow. 1994. *The Traditional Architecture of Indonesia*. London: Thames and Hudson.

Dawson, G.M. 1880. "Report on the Queen Charlotte Islands," in *Report of Progress for 1878–79*. Montreal: Geological Survey of Canada.

DeBosdari, C. 1953. *Cape Dutch Houses and Farms*, Capetown: A.A. Balkema.

Deetz, James. 1977. "Material culture and archeology – What's the difference?" pp. 9–12 in Ferguson, Leland (ed.), *Historical Archeology and the Importance of Material Things*, Lansing, MI: Society for Historical Archeology, Special Publication, no. 2.

Deetz, James. 1996. *In Small Things Forgotten*, New York : Doubleday.

De Julio, Mary Antoine. 1996. "The Vertefeuille house of Prairie du Chien: A survivor from the era of French Wisconsin," *Wisconsin Magazine of History* 80:1:36–56

DeKay, Charles. 1908. "Primitive homes," *American Architect and Building News* 104:1710:105–11.

Dennis, Thelma B. 1986. "'Ready-made' houses in Alberta, 1900–1920," *Alberta History* 34:2:1–8.

De Noyelles, Daniel. 1968. "Bricks without straw at Haverstraw," *New York Folklore Quarterly* 24:1:3–15.

Denwood, Philip. 1971. "Bhutanese architecture," *Asian Affairs* 58:24–33.

Denyer, Susan. 1978. *African Traditional Architecture*. New York: Africana Publications.

Denyer, Susan. 1991. *Traditional Buildings and Life in the Lake District*. London: Victor Gollancz/Peter Crawley.

Dick, Everett. 1937. *The Sod-House Frontier*. New York: D. Appleton-Century.

Dickinson, W. Calvin. 1990. "Log houses in Overton County, Tennessee," *Tennessee Anthropologist* 15:1:1–12.

Diddee, Jaymala. 2004. "Evolution of folk house types in Maharashtra," pp. 51–9 in Grover, Neelam and Kashi Nath Singh (eds.), *Cultural Geography: Form and Process*. New Delhi: Concept.

Dikshit, Ramesh D. 1965. "Rural house types in Dehra Dun Valley," *Deccan Geographer*, 3:43–50.

Dillingham, Reed and Chang-lin Dillingham. 1971. *A Survey of Traditional Architecture of Taiwan*. Taichung: Center for Housing and Urban Research, Tunghai University.

Dmitrieva, S.I. 1982–83. "Architectural and decorative features of the traditional dwellings of the Mezen river Russians," *Soviet Anthropology and Archaeology* 21:3:29–54.

Domenig, Gaudenz. 1980. *Tektonik im Primitiven Dachbau*. Zurich: ETH.

Domer, Dennis. 1994. "Genesis theories of the German-American two-door house," *Material Culture* 26:1:1–35.

Donnelly, Marian C. 1992. *Architecture in the Scandinavian Countries*. Cambridge, MA: MIT Press.

Doumas, Christos G. 1983. *Thera: Pompeii of the Ancient Aegean*. London: Thames and Hudson.

Downing, Antoinette F. 1937. *Early Homes of Rhode Island*. Richmond: Garrett and Massie.

Dozier, Edward P. 1970. *The Pueblo Indians of North America*. New York: Rinehart and Winston.

Drew, Philip. 1979. *Tensile Architecture*. Boulder, CO: Westview Press.

Drucker, Flora. 1949. "A sod house," *Journal of Geography* 48:9:353–62.

Drucker, Philip. 1965. *Cultures of the North Pacific Coast*. Scranton, PA: Chandler.

Dublin Heritage Group. 1993. *Vernacular Buildings of East Fingal*. Dublin: Dublin Public Libraries.

Duff, Wilson and Michael Kew. 1958. "Anthony Island, A home of the Haidas," *Provincial Museum of Natural History and Anthropology, Report for the Year 1957*, C37–C64.

Duke, Philip and Gary Matlock. 1999. *Points, Pithouses, and Pioneers*. Niwot, CO: University Press of Colorado.

Duly, Colin. 1979. *The Houses of Mankind*. London: Thames and Hudson.

Dumarcay, Jacques. 1987. *The House in South-East Asia*. Singapore: Oxford University Press.

Dumond, Don E. 1987. *The Eskimos and Aluets*. London: Thames and Hudson.

Dunham, Paul, Jr. 1987. "House types of Papua New Guinea's Kasakana," *Journal of Cultural Geography* 8:1:15–23.

Durham, Daniel. 1960. The courtyard house as a temperature regulator," *New Scientist* (September 8) 663–6.

Dyer, Christopher. 1986. "English peasant building in the later Middle Ages (1200–1500)," *Medieval Archaeology* 30:19–45.

Earle, Frances. M. 1943. "The Japanese house," *Education* 63:277–81.

Eberlein, Harold D. 1915. *Architecture of Colonial America*. Boston, MA: Little, Brown.

Eberlein, Harold D. 1921. "Early brick houses of Salem county, New Jersey," *Architectural Review* 70:2375:139–48.

Edvardsen, K.I. and B. Hegdal. 1972. *Rural Housing in Tanzania*. Dar-es-Salaam: Ministry of Lands, Housing and Urban Development.

Edward, Susan. 1978. "Cobblestone houses: a part of the land," *Historic Preservation* 30:3:31–6.

Edwards, Jay. 1976–80. "Cultural syncretism in the Louisiana creole cottage," *Louisiana Folklore Miscellany* 4:9–40.

Edwards, Jay D. 1980. "The evolution of vernacular architecture in the western Caribbean," pp. 291–339 in Wilkerson, S. Jeffery K. (ed.), *Cultural Traditions and Caribbean Identity: The Question of Patrimony*. Gainesville: University of Florida.

Edwards, Jay D. 1993. "Cultural identifications in architecture: The case of the New Orleans townhouse," *Traditional Dwellings and Settlement Review* 5:1:17–32.

Edwards, Jay. D. and Tom Wells. 1993. *Historic Louisiana Nails: Aids to the Dating of Old Buildings*. Baton Rouge: Department of Geography and Anthropology, Louisiana State University.

Egeland, Pamela. 1988. *Cob and Thatch*. Exeter: Devon Books.

Eighmy, Jeffrey Lynn. 1977. "Mennonite architecture: Diachronic evidence for rapid diffusion in rural communities," unpublished PhD dissertation, University of Arizona, Tucson.

Eitel, E.J. 1873. *Feng Shui*. Hong Kong: Lane, Crawford (reprinted 1979 by Pantacle Books, Bristol).

Ekblaw, W. Elmer. 1927. "The material response of the polar Eskimo to their far Arctic environment," *Annals of the Association of American Geographers* 17:4:150–98.

Ekvall, Robert B. 1968. *Fields on the Hoof: Nexus of Tibetan Nomadic Pastoralism*. New York: Holt, Rinehart & Winston.

El-Khoury, Fouad. 1975. *Domestic Architecture in the Lebanon*. London: Art and Architecture Research Papers.

Eller, Ronald D. 1979. "Land and family: an historic view of pre-industrial Appalachia," *Appalachian Journal* 6:83–109.

Elliott, H.P. 1940. "Mud building in Kano," *Nigeria Magazine* 20:275–8.

Elworthy, Frederick. 1895. *The Evil Eye*. London: John Murray.

Ennals, Peter and Deryck W. Holdsworth. 1998. *Homeplace: The Making of the Canadian Dwelling over Three Centuries*. Toronto: University of Toronto Press.

Erixon, Sigurd. 1937. "Some primitive constructions and types of layout, with their relation to European rural building practice," *Folkliv* 1:124–55.

Erixon, Sigurd. 1938. "Some notice on connections and differences in the rural buildings of Europe," *Travaux du Premier Congres International de Folklore*, Paris.

Evans, E. Estyn. 1939. "Donegal survivals," *Antiquity* 13:207–22.

Evans, E. Estyn. 1940. "The Irish peasant house," *Ulster Journal of Archaeology* 3:3:165–9.

Evans, E. Estyn. 1957. *Irish Folk Ways*. London: Routledge and Kegan Paul.

Evans, E. Estyn. 1965. "Cultural relicts of the Ulster-Scots in the Old West of North America," *Ulster Folklife* 11:33–8.

Evans, E. Estyn. 1969. "Sod and turf houses in Ireland," pp. 79–90 in Jenkins, Geraint (ed.), *Studies in Folk Life*. London: Routledge and Kegan Paul.

Evans, E. Raymond. 1976. "The strip house in Tennessee folk-architecture," *Tennessee Folklore Society Bulletin* 42:5:163–6.

Everest, Allan S. 1966. *Pioneer Homes of Clinton County, 1790–1820*. Plattsburgh, NY: Clinton County Historical Association.

Ewan, N.R. 1938. *Early Brickmaking in the Colonies*. Camden, NJ: Camden County Historical Society.

Faber, Tobias. n.d. *A History of Danish Architecture*. Copenhagen: Det Danske Selskab.

Facey, William. 1997. *Back to Earth: Adobe Building in Saudi Arabia*. Riyadh: Al-Turath.

Faculty of Architecture, University of Science and Technology. 1978. "Traditional forms of architecture in Ghana," *International Social Science Journal* (Paris) 30:449–76.

Faegre, Torvald. 1979. *Tents: Architecture of the Nomads*. Garden City, NY: Anchor Books.

Fairbanks, Jonathan L. 1975. "Shelter on the frontier: Adobe housing in nineteenth century Utah," pp. 197–209 in Boston Museum of Fine Arts, *Frontier America: The Far West*. Boston: Museum of the Arts.

Fearn, Jacqueline. 1976. *Thatch and Thatching*. Aylesbury: Shire Publications.

Feduchi, Luis. 1974. *Spanish Folk Architecture: The Northern Plateau*. Barcelona: Editorial Blume.

Feeley-Harnik, Gillian. 1980. "The Sakalava house (Madagascar)," *Anthropos* 75:559–85.

Fenton, Alexander. 1978. *The Island Blackhouse*. Edinburgh: HMSO.

Ferree, Barr. 1889. "Primitive architecture," *American Naturalist* 23:24–32.

Ferree, Barr. 1890. "Climatic influences in primitive architecture," *American Anthropologist* 3:1:147–58.

Ferris, William R., Jr. 1973. "Mississippi folk architecture: Two examples," *Mississippi Folklore Register* 7 (Winter): 101–14.

Finley, Robert and E.M. Scott. 1940. "A Great Lakes-to-Gulf profile of dispersed dwelling types," *Geographical Review* 30:3:412–19.

Fitch, James Marston and Daniel P. Branch. 1960. "Primitive architecture and climate," *Scientific American* 203:6:134–44.

Fitchen, John. F., III. 1957. "A house of laminated walls," *Journal of the Society of Architectural Historians*. 15:2:27–8.

Flannery, Kent V. 1980. "The village as a settlement type in Mesoamerica and Near East," pp. 23–53 in Ucko, Peter J., Ruth Tringham and G.W. Dimbleby (eds.), *Man, Settlement and Urbanism*. Cambridge, MA: Schenkman Publishing Co.

Focsa, Gheorghe. 1959. *The Village Museum in Bucharest*. Bucharest: Foreign Languages Publishing House.

Folkers, Johann Ulrich. 1954. "Stand und Aufgaben der Gulfhausforschung," *Zeitschrift für Volkskunde* 51:17–36.

Folkers, Johann Ulrich. 1961. *Haus und Hofdeutscher Bauern, Mecklenburg*. Münster: Aschendorff.

Fontana, Bernard L. and Cameron J. Greenleaf. 1962. "Johnny Ward's ranch: A study in historic archaeology," *The Kiva* 28:1–2:44–66.

Forde, C. Daryll. 1963. *Habitat, Economy and Society*. New York: E.P. Dutton.

Forman, Henry C. 1948. *The Architecture of the Old South: The Medieval Style, 1585–1850*. Cambridge, MA: Harvard University Press.

Forman, Henry C. 1966. *Early Nantucket and its Whale Houses*. New York: Hastings House.

Forrester, Harry. 1959. *The Timber-Framed Houses of Essex*. Chelmsford: J.H. Clarke.

Forth, Gregory L. 1981. *Rindi: An Ethnographic Study of a Traditional Domain in Eastern Sumba*. The Hague: Martinus Nijhoff.

Fox, Cyril and Aileen Fox. 1934. "Forts and farms on Margam mountain, Glamorgan," *Antiquity* 395–413.

Francis, E.K. 1954. "The Mennonite farmhouse in Manitoba," *Mennonite Quarterly Review* 28:56–9.

Frasch, Robert W. 1965. "New York's cobblestone buildings," *New York State Tradition* 19:2:5–9.

Fraser, Henry. S. 1990. *Treasures of Barbados*. London: Macmillan Caribbean.

Fraysse, J. and C. Fraysse. 1963–64. *Les troglodytes en Anjou a travers les ages* (3 vols.). Cholet: Impr. Farre.

Freal, Jacques. 1977. *L'architecture paysanne en France: La maison*. Paris: Editions SERG.

Frescura, Franco. 1981. *Rural Shelter in Southern Africa*. Johannesburg: Ravan Press.

Frolec, Vaclav. 1966. *Die Volksarchitektur in Westbulgarien im 19 und zu beginn des 20 Jahrhunderts*. Brno: Universita J.E. Purkyne.

Fsadni, Michael. 1992. *The Girna: The Maltese Corbelled Stone Hut*. Malta: Dominican Publication.

Fuchs, Stephen. 1960. *The Gond and Bhumia of Eastern Mandla*. Bombay: Asia Publishing House.

Fuller, Myron L. and Frederick G. Clapp. 1924. "Loess and rock dwellings of Shensi, China," *Geographical Review* 14:215–26.

Funk, Elisabeth Paling. 1987. "Netherlands' popular culture in the Knicker-bocker works of Washington Irving," pp. 83–93 in Blackburn, Roderic H. and Nancy A. Kelley (eds.), *New World Dutch Studies: Dutch arts and culture in colonial America, 1609–1776*. Albany, NY: Albany Institute of History and Art.

Fuson, Robert H. 1964. "House types of central Panama," *Annals of Association of American Geographers* 54:2:190–208.

Gailey, Alan. 1962. "The peasant houses of the south-west highlands of Scot-land: distribution, parallels and evolution," *Gwerin* 3:5:227–42.

Gailey, Alan. 1984. *Rural Houses of the North of Ireland*. Edinburgh: John Donald.

Gamble, Robert. 1990. *Historic Architecture in Alabama: A Primer of Styles and Types, 1810–1930*. Tuscaloosa: University of Alabama Press.

Ganju, Ashish. 1983. "Desert dwellings," *India Magazine* (December) 66–77.

Garber, Clark M. 1934. "Some mortuary customs of the western Alaska Eski-mos," *Scientific Monthly* (September) 203–20.

Gardi René. 1973. *Indigenous African Architecture*. New York: Van Nostrand Reinhold.

Gardner, George W. 1935. "Some early 'single room houses' of Lincoln, Rhode Island," *Pencil Points* 21:1:93–108.

Garlake, Peter S. 1966. *The Early Islamic Architecture of the East African Coast*. Nairobi: Oxford University Press.

Garvan, Anthony N.B. 1951. *Architecture and Town Planning in Colonial Con-necticut*. New Haven, CT: Yale University Press.

Gates, Donald S. 1933. "The sod house," *Journal of Geography* 32:353–9.

Gavin, Michael. 1997. "The diamond notch in middle Tennessee," *Material Culture* 29:1:13–23.

Gebhard, David. 1963. "The traditional wood house of Turkey," *American Institute of Architects Journal* 39:36–9.

Gebremedhin, Naigzy. 1971. "Some traditional types of housing in Ethiopia," pp. 106–23 in Oliver, Paul (ed.), *Shelter in Africa*. London: Barrie and Jenkins.

George, Eugene. 1975. *Historic Architecture of Texas: The Falcon Reservior*. Aus-tin: Texas Historical Commission and Texas Historical Foundation.

Gess, Denise and William Lutz. 2002. *Firestorm at Peshtigo*, New York: Henry Holt.

Gettys, Norman and Alicia Hughes-Jones. 1981. "Log pens and lifestyles: the Aylesworth photographic collection," *Bulletin of the Oklahoma Anthropologi-cal Society* 30:51–66.

Ghosh, Benoy. 1953. "Primitive Indian architecture," *Journal of the Indian Society of Oriental Art* 17:1–55.

Gilman, Patricia. 1983. "Changing architectural forms in the prehistoric Southwest," unpublished PhD dissertation, University of New Mexico, Albuquerque.

Gimbutas, Marija. 1971. *The Slavs*. New York: Praeger.

Giovannini, Joseph. 1984. "The Sunday houses of central Texas," *New York Times*. (February 9) 19 & 21.

Glassie, Henry. 1963. "The Appalachian log cabin," *Mountain Life and Work* 39:5–14.

Glassie, Henry. 1968. "Types of the southern mountain cabin," pp. 338–70 in Brunvand, J.H. (ed.), *The Study of American Folklore*. New York: W.W. Norton

Glassie, Henry. 1968–69. "A central chimney continental log house," *Pennsylvania Folklife* 18:2:33–9.

Glassie, Henry. 1972. "Eighteenth-century cultural process in Delaware valley folk building," *Winterthur Portfolio* 7:29–57.

Glassie, Henry. 1999. *Material Culture*. Bloomington: Indiana University Press.

Godshall, Jeffrey. 1983. "The traditional farmhouse of the Franconia Mennonite Community," *Pennsylvania Mennonite Heritage* 6:1:22–5.

Goertzen, Peter. n.d. *Mennonite Village Museum Booklet*. Steinbach, Manitoba: Mennonite Village Museum.

Goins, Charles R. and John W. Morris. 1980. *Oklahoma Homes: Past and Present*. Norman: University of Oklahoma Press.

Golany, Gideon S. 1988. *Earth-Sheltered Dwellings in Tunisia*. Newark, DL: University of Delaware Press.

Golany, Gideon S. 1989. *Urban Underground Space Design in China: Vernacular and Modern Practice*. Newark, DL: University of Delaware Press.

Golany, Gideon S. 1990. *Design and Thermal Performance: Below-Ground Dwellings in China*. Newark, DL: University of Delaware Press.

Golany, Gideon S. 1992. *Chinese Earth-Sheltered Dwellings*. Honolulu: University of Hawaii Press.

Gonzalez, Alberto Rex. 1943. "Arqeolologia del yacimiento indegena de Villa Rumipal (Provinciade Cordoba)," *Publicaciones del instituto de Arquelogia, Linquistica y Folklore de las Universidad de Cordoba. IV*.

Gonzalez, Alberto Rex. 1953. "Concerning the existence of the pit house in South America," *American Antiquity* 18:3:271–2.

Goodall, Harrison and Renée Friedman. 1980. *Log Structures: Preservation and Problem-Solving*. Nashville, TN: American Association for State and Local History.

Goss, Peter L. 1975. "The architectural history of Utah," *Utah Historical Quarterly* 43:3:208–39.

Gottmann, Jean. 1957. "Locale and architecture," *Landscape* 7:1:17–26.

Gowans, Alan. 1964. *Architecture in New Jersey*. Princeton: D. Van Nostrand.

Gowans, Alan. 1966. *Building Canada: An Architectural History of Canadian Life*. Toronto: Oxford University Press.

Greenlaw, Jean-Pierre. 1976. *The Coral Buildings of Suakin*. London: Oriel Press.

Gregor, Howard F. 1951. "A sample study of the California ranch," *Annals of the Association of American Geographers* 61:4:285–306.

Gresham, Colin A. 1963. "The interpretation of settlement patterns in north-west Wales," pp. 263–79 in Foster, I.L.L. and L. Alcock (eds.), *Culture and Environment: Essays in Honour of Sir Cyril Fox*. London: Routledge and Kegan Paul.

Grider, Sylvia Ann. 1975. "The shotgun house in oil boomtowns of the Texas panhandle," *Pioneer America* 7:2:47–55.

Grisebach, H. 1917. *Das Polnische Bauernhaus*. Berlin.

Gritzner, Charles F. 1971. "Log housing in New Mexico," *Pioneer America* 3:2:54–62.

Gritzner, Charles. 1974. "Construction materials in a folk housing tradition: Considerations governing their selection in New Mexico," *Pioneer America* 6:1:25–39

Groome, J.R. 1964. "Sedan-chair porches: A detail of Georgian architecture in St. George's," *Caribbean Quarterly* 10:3:31–3.

Guernsey Society. 1963. *The Guernsey Farmhouse*. London: De La Rue.

Haagensen, Hans. 1982. "A socio-architectural case study in north Thailand," pp. 103–14 in Izakowitz, K.G. and P. Sorenson (eds.), *The House in East and Southeast Asia*. London: Curzon Press.

Haase, Ronald W. 1992. *Classic Cracker: Florida's Wood-Frame Vernacular Architecture*. Sarasota: Pineapple Press.

Haile, Berard. 1942. "Why the Navaho hogan?" *Primitive Man: Quarterly Bulletin of the Catholic Anthropological Conference* 15:3–4:39–56.

Haile, Berard. 1954. *Property Concepts of the Navaho Indians*. Washington: Catholic University of America Press.

Hakansson, Tore. 1977. "House decoration among south Asian peoples," pp. 84–94 in Oliver, Paul (ed.), *Shelter, Sign and Symbol*. Woodstock, NY: Overlook Press.

Hall, Nick. 1981. "Has thatch a future?," *Appropriate Technology* 8:3:7–9.

Hammer, Kenneth. 1968. "The prairie sod shanty," *North Dakota History* 35:1:57–61.

Hance, William A. 1951. "Crofting settlements and housing in the outer Hebrides," *Annuals of the Association of American Geographers* 41:1:75–87.

Hannaford, Donald R. and Rivel Edwards. 1931. *Spanish Colonial or Adobe Architecture of California, 1800–1850*. New York: Architecture Book Publishing Company.

Hansen, Eric. 1995. "The water village in Brunei," *Aramco World* 46:3:32–9.

Hansen, Hans Jürgen. 1971. *Architecture in Wood: A History of Wood Building and its Techniques in Europe and North America*. New York: Viking Press.

Hanson, Shirley and Nancy Hubby. 1983. *Preserving and Maintaining the Older Home*. New York: McGraw Hill.

Harding, Joan. 1990. "Notes on the 16th century development of timber framed houses in Surrey," pp. 199–208 in Warren, John (ed.), *Wealden Buildings: Studies in the Timber-Framed Tradition of Building in Kent, Sussex and Surrey*. Horsham: Coach Publishing.

Harris, R. 1987. *Weald and Downland Open Air Museum Guidebook*. Singleton, Chichester: Weald and Downland Open Air Museum.

Harrison, Austen and S.R.P. Hubbard, 1949. "Maltese vernacular," *Architectural Review* 105:77–80.

Harrison, Henry S. 1973. *Houses: The Illustrated Guide to Construction, Design, and Systems*. Chicago: Realtors National Marketing Institute.

Harrison, Paul. 1976. "Troglodyte life in Goreme," *Geographical Magazine* 48:8:451.

Hartley, Marie and Joan Ingilby. 1971. *Vanishing Folkways: Life and Tradition in the Yorkshire Dales*. New York: A.S. Barnes.

Harvey, John. 1975. *Mediaeval Craftsmen*. New York: Drake Publishers.

Haslova, Vera and Jaroslav Vajdio. 1974. *Folk Art of Czechoslovakia*. New York: Arco Publishing.

Hay, Frances S. 1924. "The house and geography," *Journal of Geography* 23:6:225–33.

Heath, Kingston. 1988. "Defining the nature of vernacular," *Material Culture* 20:2:1–8.

Hegstad, Sveinulf. 1997. "Wooden houses," pp. 47–55 in Bratrein, Havared D. (ed.), *Northern-Norway: A Way of Life*. Tromso: University of Tromso and Tromso Museum.

Hekker, Robert C. 1975. "Farmstead villages in the Netherlands," *Vernacular Architecture* 4:7–12.

Hemp, F.N.U. 1939. "Dwelling-sites, Hautes Alpes," *Antiquity* 13:89–91.

Henderson, Arn, Frank Parman and Dortha Henderson. 1978. *Architecture in Oklahoma: Landmarks and Vernacular*. Norman, OK: Point Riders Press.

Henderson, Martha L. 1992. "Maintaining vernacular architecture on the Mescalero Apache reservation," *Journal of Cultural Geography* 13:1:15–28.

Henkes, Rollie. 1976. "Where the soddy survives," *The Furrow* 81:6:30–1.

Herman, Bernard L. 1987. *Architecture and Rural Life in Central Delaware*. Knoxville: University of Tennessee Press.

Herrmann, Maria. 1977. "The restoration of historic Fredericksburg," *Rice University Studies* 63:3:119–39.

Hicks, David T. 1966. "The architecture of the high Atlas Mountains," *Arena* 82:85–7.

Hill, Michael and Sally Birch. 1994. *Cotswold Stone Homes*. Phoenix Mill, Gloucestershire: Sutton Publishing.

Hilton, R.N. 1956. "The basic Malay house," *Journal of the Malayan Branch of the Royal Asiatic Society* 29:3:134–55.

Hinshalwood, Sophia Gruys. 1981. "The Dutch cultural area of the Mid-Hudson Valley," unpublished PhD dissertation, Rutgers University, New Brunswick, NJ.

Hiroa, Te Rangi. 1930. *Samoan Material Culture*. Honolulu: Bishop Museum.

Hirt, Howard F. 1982. "Caste and urban house type in south India: Brahmin houses in Tamilnadu and Karnataka," pp. 125–45 in Noble, Allen G. and Ashok K. Dutt (eds.), *India: Cultural Patterns and Processes*. Boulder, CO: Westview Press.

Hoagland, Alison K. 1993. *Buildings of Alaska*. New York: Oxford University Press.

Holan, Jerri. 1990. *Norwegian Wood: A Tradition of Building*. New York: Rizzoli.

Homes, Inett. 1978. "The agricultural use of the Herefordshire house and its outbuildings," *Vernacular Architecture* 9:12–16.

Hoover, J.W. 1931. "Navajo nomadism," *Geographical Review* 21:3:29–45.

Hoskins, W.G. 1960. "Farmhouses and history," *History Today* 10:5:333–41.

Howe, L.E.A. 1983. "An introduction to the cultural study of traditional Balinese architecture," *Archipel* 25:137–58.

Hubka, Thomas. 1985. "A good stand of buildings," *Maine History News* 21:4:8–9 & 11.

Hudson, John. 1975. Frontier housing in North Dakota," *North Dakota History* 42:4–16.

Hugh-Jones, Stephen. 1985. "The maloca: A world in a house," pp. 76–93 in Carmichael, Elizabeth, Stephen Hugh-Jones, B. Moser and D. Tayler (eds.), *The Hidden Peoples of the Amazon*. London: British Museum Publications.

Huguenot Historical Society. 1964. *Stone Houses of the Paltz Patentees*. New Paltz, NY: Huguenot Historical Society.

Humphrey, Caroline. 1974. "Inside a Mongolian tent," *New Society* 30:630:273–5.

Hulan, Richard H. 1975. "Middle Tennessee and the dogtrot house," *Pioneer America*. 7:2:37–46.

Hulan, Richard H. 1977. "The dogtrot house and its Pennsylvania associations," *Pennsylvania Folklife*. 27:1:25–32.

Hunter, John M. 1967. "The social roots of dispersed settlement in northern Ghana," *Annals of the Association of American Geographers* 57:2:338–49.

Hussey, E.C. 1876. *Victorian Home Building: A Trancontinental View*. Watkins Glen, NY: American Life Foundation (reprinted 1976).

Hutslar, Donald A. 1971. "The log architecture of Ohio," *Ohio History* 80:3–4:171–271.

Huyler, Stephen P. 1982. "Rural wall decorations: A comparison of four villages," pp. 80–90 in Pieper, Jan and George Michell (eds.), *The Impulse to Adorn*. Bombay: MARG Publications.

Innocent, C.F. 1916. *The Development of English Building*. Cambridge: Cambridge University Press.

Ionescu, Grigore. 1957. *Archtectura Populara Romineasca*. Bucharest(?): Editura Technica.

Irving, Robert (ed.). 1985. *The History and Design of the Australian House*. Melbourne: Oxford University Press.

Isham, Norman and Albert F. Brown. 1900. *Early Connecticut Houses*. Providence: Preston and Rounds (reprinted 1965).

Islam, Nazrul, Khadem Ali and Shahnaz Huq. 1981. *A Survey of Housing in a Bangladesh Village*. Dhaka: Centre for Urban Studies.

Jack, W. Murray. 1955. "Old houses of Lagos," *Nigeria Magazine* 46:96–117.

Jackson, J.B. 1953. "Pueblo architecture and our own," *Landscape* 3:20–5.

Jackson, J.B. 1984. *Discovering the Vernacular Landscape*. New Haven, CT: Yale University Press.

Jackson, Peter and Anne Coles. 1975. "Bastakia wind-tower houses," *Architectural Review* 158:51–3.

Jackson, Richard H. 1980. "The use of adobe in the Mormon cultural region," *Journal of Cultural Geography* 1:1:82–95.

Jacquet, Pierre. 1963. *The Swiss Chalet*. Zurich: Orell Fussli Verlag.

Jaderborg, Elizabeth. 1981. "Swedish architectural influence in the Kansas Smoky Valley community," *Swedish Pioneer Historical Quarterly* 32:1:65–79.

Jain, Kulbshan. 1980. "Form – a consequence of context," *Process Architecture* 15:17–34.

Jain, Kulbshan. 1983. "Havelli facades: concepts of embellishment," *MARG* 34:4:45–54.

Jain-Neubauer, Jutta and Jyotindra Jain. 1983. "Wall decorations of a mobile people," *MARG* 34:4:33–42.

Jans, Jan. 1969. *Landelijke bouwkunst in Oost-Nederland*. Enshede: Firma M.J. Van der Loeff.

Janse, H. 1970. *Houten Huizen, een unieke bouwwijze in Noord-Holland*. Zaltbommel: Europese Bibliotheek.

Jeancon, Jean Allard and F.H. Douglas. 1931. *The Plains Indian Tipi*. Denver: Denver Art Museum (Leaflet no. 19).

Jenkins, Paul B. 1923. "A 'stove-wood' house," *Wisconsin Magazine of History* 7:189–92.

Jett, Stephen C. 1978. "Navajo seasonal migration patterns," *The Kiva* 44:1:65–75.

Jett, Stephen C. 1980. "The Navajo homestead: situation and site," *Yearbook of the Association of Pacific Coast Geographers* 42:101–17.

Jett, Stephen C. 1987. "Cutural fusion in Native-American architecture: The Navajo Hogan," pp. 243–56 in Ross, Thomas E. and Tyrel G. Moore (eds.), *A Cultural Geography of North American Indians*. Boulder, CO: Westview Press.

Jett, Stephen C. and Virginia E. Spencer. 1981. *Navajo Architecture: Forms, History, Distributions*. Tucson: University of Arizona Press.

Jochelson, Waldemar. 1906. "Past and present subterranean dwellings of the tribes of northeastern Asia and northwestern America," *International Congress of Americanists* 15:115–28.

Johnson, Warren. 1995. "Keeping cool," *Aramco World* 46:3:10–17.

Jones, G.I. 1984. *The Art of Eastern Nigeria*. Cambridge: Cambridge University Press.

Jones, Larry. 1979. "Utah's vanishing log cabins," *Utah Preservation/Restoration* 1:1:48–50.

Jones, Steven L. 1985. "The African-American tradition in vernacular architecture," pp. 195–213 in Singleton, Theresea A. (ed.), *The Archaeology of Slavery and Plantation Life*. Washington, DC: Smithsonian Institute Press.

Jones, Sydney R. 1918. *Old Houses in Holland*. London: The Studio Ltd.

Jope, E.M. and G.C. Dunning. 1954. "The use of blue slate for roofing in medieval England," *Antiquaries Journal* 34:209–17.

Jopling, Carol F. 1988. *Puerto Rican Houses in Sociohistorical Perspective*. Knoxville: University of Tennessee Press.

Jordan, Terry. 1978. *Texas Log Buildings: A Folk Architecture*. Austin: University of Texas Press.

Jordan, Terry and Matti Kaups. 1989. *The American Backwoods Frontier: An Ethnic and Ecological Interpretation*. Baltimore: Johns Hopkins University Press.

Jordan, Terry, Matti Kaups and Richard M. Lieffort. 1986–87. "Diamond notching in America and Europe," *Pennsylvania Folklife* 36:2:70–8.

Jordan, Terry G. and Jon T. Kilpinen. 1990. "Square notching in the log carpentry tradition of Pennsylvania extended," *Pennsylvania Folklife* 40:1:2–18.

Jorre, Georges. 1967. *The Soviet Union: The Land and its People*. New York: John Wiley.

Just, Peter. 1984. "Houses and house-building in Donggo," *Expedition* 26:4:30–46.

Kana, N.L. 1980. "The order and significance of the Savunese House," pp. 221–30 & 346–7 in Fox, James J. (ed.), *The Flow of Life: Essays on Eastern Indonesia*. Cambridge, MA: Harvard University Press.

Kane, Harnett T. 1944. *The Bayous of Louisiana*. New York: William Morrow.

Kanvinde, Achyut. 1971. "Regional housing traditions," *Architectural Review* 150:372–3.

Karni, Michael and Robert Levin. 1972. "Northwoods vernacular architecture: Finnish log building in Minnesota," *Northwest Architect* (May/June) 92–9.

Kauffman, Henry J. 1954/55. "The riddle of two front doors," *The Dutchman* (later *Pennsylvania Folklife*) 1:27.

Kauffman, Henry J. 1972. *The American Fireplace*. Nashville: Thomas Nelson.

Kauffman, Henry J. 1975. *The American Farmhouse*. New York: Hawthorn Books.

Kaups, Matti. 1976. "A Finnish savusauna in Minnesota," *Minnesota History* 45:11–20.

Kawashima, Chuji. 2000. *Japan's Folk Architecture: Traditional Thatched Farmhouses*. Tokyo: Kodansha International.

Kear, V.A. 1971. *Sod Houses and Dugouts in North America*. Colby, KS: Prairie Printers.

Kelly, J. Frederick. 1924. *The Early Domestic Architecture of Connecticut*. New Haven, CT: Yale University Press.

Kempe, David. 1988. *Living Underground: A History of Cave and Cliff Dwelling*. London: Herbert Press.

Kevlin, Mary Joan. 1984. "Plank house construction in Ithaca, New York," *Newsletter of Historic Ithaca and Tompkins County, New York* 2:4:I–IV.

Kiefer, Wayne E. 1972. "An agricultural settlement complex in Indiana," *Annals of the Association of American Geographers* 62:487–506.

Kilpinen, Jon. T. 1995. "The front-gabled log cabin and the role of the Great Plains in the formation of the Mountain West's built landscape," *Great Plains Quarterly* 15:19–31.

King, Anthony D. 1977. "The Bengali peasant hut: Some nineteenth century accounts," *AARP, Art and Archeology Research Papers* (June) 70–8.

King, Anthony D. 1984. *The Bungalow: The Production of a Global Culture*. London: Routledge and Kegal Paul.

King, Geoffrey. 1976. "Some observations on the architecture of southwest Saudi Arabia," *Architectural Association Quarterly* 8:1:20–9.

Kipling, Lockwood. 1911. "The origin of the bungalow," *Country Life in America* 19:8:308–10.

Kirk-Greene, Anthony. 1963. *Decorated Houses in a Northern City*. Kaduna: Baraka Press.

Klammer, Paul W. 1960. "Collecting log cabins," *Minnesota History* 37:71–7.

Klammer, Paul W. 1963. "Building with logs," *Gopher Historian* (Fall) 13–17.

Kleinert, Christian. 1976. "House types and settlement pattern in the Nepal Himalayas," pp. 199–205 in Singh, R.L. et al. (eds.), *Geographic Dimensions of Rural Settlements*. Varanasi: National Geographic Society of India.

Kloberdanz, Timothy J. 1980. "Plainsmen of three continents: Volga German adaptation to steppe, prairie, and pampa," pp. 54–72 in Luebke, Frederick C. (ed.), *Ethnicity on the Great Plains*. Lincoln: University of Nebraska Press.

Kluckhohn, Clyde, W.W. Hill and Lucy W. Kluckhohn. 1971. *Navaho Material Culture*. Cambridge, MA: Harvard University Press.

Knapp, Ronald G. 1986. *China's Traditional Rural Architecture: A Cultural Geography of the Common House*. Honolulu: University of Hawaii Press.

Knapp, Ronald G. 1989. *China's Vernacular Architecture: House Form and Culture*. Honolulu: University of Hawaii Press.

Knapp, Ronald G. 1990. *The Chinese House*. Hong Kong: Oxford University Press.

Knapp, Ronald G. 2003. *Asia's Old Dwellings: Traditional, Resilience, and Change*. Hong Kong: Oxford University Press.

Kniffen, Fred. 1960. "To know the land and its people," *Landscape* 9:3:20–3.

Kniffen, Fred. 1968. *Louisiana: Its Land and People*. Baton Rouge: Louisiana State University Press.

Kniffen, Fred. 1969. "On corner-timbering," *Pioneer America* 1:1:1–8.

Kniffen, Fred and Henry Glassie. 1966. "Building in wood in the eastern United States," *Geographical Review* 56:1:40–66.

Knuffel, Werner E. 1973. *The Construction of the Bantu Grass Hut*. Graz: Akademische Druck und Verlags anstalt.

Koch, William E. 1982. "Log homes in Kansas," pp. 25–30 in Chinn, Jennie E. (ed.), *Folk Roots*. Manhattan, KS: University for Man.

Koenigsberger, Otto and Robert Lynn. 1965. *Roofs in the Warm Tropics*. London: Lund Humphries.

Koop, Michael and Stephen Ludwig. 1984. *German-Russian Folk Architecture in Southeastern South Dakota*. Vermillion, SD: State Historical Preservation Center.

Koos, Greg and William D. Walters, Jr. 1986. "The Eliel Barber house and American vertical plank wall construction," *PAST – Pioneer America Society Transactions* 9:71–7.

Kostof, Spiro. 1985. *A History of Architecture: Settings and Rituals*. New York: Oxford University Press.

Krause, Aurel. 1956. *The Tlingit Indians*. Seattle: University of Washington Press.

Kriesis, Anthony. 1948. "Tradition in evolution: the persistence of the classical Greek house," *Architectural Review* 103:267–8.

Krissdottir, Morine. 1982. "Ingolf's pillars: The changing Icelandic house," *Landscape* 26:2:7–14.

Kucukerman, Onder. 1988. *Turkish House: In Search of Spatial Indentity*. Istanbul: Turkiye Turing ve Otomobil Kurumu (Turkish Touring and Automobile Association).

Kuper, Hilda. 1946. "The architecture of Swaziland," *Architectural Review* 100:20–4.

Kuzela, Z. 1963. "Folk architecture," pp. 302–9, vol. 1, in Kubijovyc, Volodymir (ed.), *Ukraine: A Concise Encyclopedia*. Toronto: University of Toronto Press.

Laius, Otto. 1885. *Das Friesische Bauernhaus*. Strasburg: Karl J. Trübner.

Lange, Merike. 1995. "Estonian open air museum as a reflector of Estonian history and architecture," *Acta Scansenologica* 7: 60–4.

Langsam. Walter E. and William Gus Johnson. 1985. *Historic Architecture of Bourbon County, Kentucky*. Georgetown, KY: Historic Paris-Bourbon County, Inc. and Kentucky Heritage Council.

Lanier, Gabrielle M. and Bernard L. Herman. 1997. *Everyday Architecture of the Mid-Atlantic: Looking at Buildings and Landscapes*. Baltimore: Johns Hopkins University Press.

Laoust, E. 1935. "L'habitation chez les transhumants du Maroc Central," *Collection Hesperis* 6.

Lari, Yasmeen. 1989. *Traditional Architecture of Thatta*. Karachi: Heritage Foundation.

Larsson, Anita. 1989. "Traditional versus modern housing in Botswana – An analysis from the user's perspective," pp. 503–25 in Bourdier, Jean-Paul and Nezar Alsayyad (eds.), *Dwellings, Settlements and Tradition: Cross-Cultural Perspectives*. Lanham, MD: University Press of America.

Larsson, Anita and Viera Larsson. 1984. *Traditional Tswana Housing: A Study in Four Villages in Eastern Botswana*. Stockholm: Swedish Council for Building Research.

Lasius, Otto. 1885. *Das Friesische Bauernhaus*. Strasburg: Karl J. Trubner.

Latham III, James A. 1977. *Mississippi Folk Houses*. Washington, DC: National Endowment for the Humanties.

Laws, Bill. 1995. *Traditional Houses of Rural Spain*. New York: Abbeville Press.

Lay, K. Edward. 1982. "European antecedents of seventeenth and eighteenth century Germanic and Scots-Irish architecture in America," *Pennsylvania Folk Life* 32:1:2–43.

Lazistan, Eugen and Jan Michalov. 1971. *Drevene Stavby na Slovensku*. Bratislava(?):Osveta.

Lebreton, Clarence. 1982. "Material culture in Acadia," pp. 429–76 in Daigle, Jean (ed.), *The Acadians of the Maritimes*. Moncton, New Brunswick: Centre d'Estudes Acadiennes.

Ledohowski, Edward M. and David K. Butterfield. 1983. *Architectural Heritage: The Eastern Interlake Planning District*. Winnipeg: Manitoba Department of Cultural Affairs and Historical Resources.

Lee, David R. 1969a. "Factors influencing choice of house type: A geographic analysis from the Sudan," *Professional Geographer* 21:6:393–7.

Lee, David R. 1969b. "The Nubian house: Persistence of a cultural traditional," *Landscape* 18:1:36–9.

Lee, David R. 1974. "Mud mansions of northern Sudan," *Ekistics* 227:244–6.

Lee, David R. 1983. "Reconsidering traditional housing," *Landscape* 27:2:28–33.

Lee, Molly and Gregory A. Reinhardt. 2003. *Eskimo Architecture:Dwelling and Structure in the Early Historic Period*. Fairbanks: University of Alaska Press and University of Alaska Museum.

Lee, Sang-hae. 1991. "Continuity and consistency of the traditional courtyard house plan in modern Korean dwellings," *Traditional Dwellings and Settlements Review* 3:1:65–76.

Lehmer, Donald J. 1939. "Modern jacales of Presidio," *El Palacio* 46:183–6.

Lehr, John C. 1973. "Ukrainian houses in Alberta," *Alberta Historical Review* 21:4:9–15.

Lehr, John C. 1975. "Changing Ukrainian house styles," *Alberta History* 23:1:25–9.

Lehr, John C. 1976. "Ukrainian vernacular architecture," *Canadian Collector* 11:1:66–70.

Lehr, John C. 1980. "The log buildings of Ukrainian settlers in western Canada," *Prairie Forum* 5:2:183–96.

Lehr, John C. 1981. "Colour preferences and building decoration among Ukrainians in western Canada," *Prairie Forum* 6:2:203–6.

Leiby, Adrian C. 1964. *The Early Dutch and Swedish Settlers of New Jersey.* Princeton: D. Van Nostrand.

LeMoal, G. 1960. "Les habitations semi-souterraines en afrique de l'ouest," *Journal de le Societé des Africanistes* 30:193–203.

Lerche, Grith 1973. "Timber framed buildings in Denmark," *Vernacular Architecture* 4:12–17.

Lesley, Robert W. 1972. *History of the Portland Cement Industry in the United States.* New York: Arno Press (originally published in 1924).

Levin, Michael D. 1971. "House form and social structure in Bakosi," pp. 143–52 in Oliver, Paul (ed.), *Shelter in Africa.* London: Barre and Jenkins.

Lewandoski, Jan Leo. 1985. "The plank framed house in northeastern Vermont," *Vermont History* 53:2:104–21.

Lewcock, Ronald. 1976. "Towns and buildings in Arabia: North Yemen," *Architectural Association Quarterly* 9:1:3–19.

Lewcock, Ronald B. 1980. "The need for special studies of third world architecture," *Architectural Association Quarterly* 12:1:26–9.

Lewcock, Ronald and Gerard Brans. 1977. "The boat as an architectural symbol," pp. 107–16 in Oliver, Paul (ed.), *Shelter, Sign and Symbol.* Woodstock, NY: Overlook Press.

Lewis, Peirce. 1975. "Common houses, cultural spoor," *Landscape* 19:2:1–22.

Lewis, Thomas R. 1981. *Near the Long Tidal River: Readings in the Historical Geography of Central Connecticut.* Washington: University Press of America.

Lim, Jee Yuan. 1987. *The Malay House: Rediscovering Malaysia's Indigenous Shelter System.* Pulau Pinang: Institut Masyarakat.

Lin, Heng-tao. 1975. "Taiwan's traditional Chinese houses," *Echo Magazine* 5:11:23–7, 54 & 56.

Lindley, Kenneth. 1965. *Of Graves and Epitaphs.* London: Hutchinson.

Ling, Arthur George. 1936. "Peasant architecture in the northern provinces of Spain," *Journal of the Institute of British Architects* 27:845–63.

Liphschitz, Nili and Gideon Biger. 1994. "The wooden houses of the American colony in Jaffa, Eretz Israel," *Geography Research Forum* 14:97–108.

Littlejohn, James. 1960. "The Temne house," *Sierra Leone Studies* 14:63–79.

Lodge, Olive. 1936. "Villages and houses in Jugoslavia," *Geography* 94–106.

Lloyd, John. 1969. "The Norwegian laftehus," pp. 33–48 in Oliver, Paul (ed.), *Shelter and Society.* New York: Frederick A. Praeger.

Long, Amos, Jr. 1965. "Pennsylvania Summer-Houses and Summer-Kitchens," *Pennsylvania Folklife* 15:10–19.

Long, Barbara B. 1981. *Hometown Architecture.* Des Moines: Central Iowa Regional Association of Local Governments.

Lounsbury, Carl. 1977. "The development of domestic architecture in the Albemarle Region," *North Carolina Historical Review* 54:1:17–48.

Lounsbury, Carl. 1983. "Vernacular construction in the Survey," pp. 183–95 in Stamm, Alicia and C. Ford Peatross (eds.), *Historic America: Buildings, Structures, and Sites.* Washington, DC: Library of Congress.

Loveday, Amos J., Jr. 1983. *The Rise and Decline of the American Cut Nail Industry.* Westport, CN: Greenwood Press.

Lowenthal, David. 1975. "Past time, present place: Landscape and memory," *Geographical Review* 65:1:1–36.

Lowie, Robert H. 1922. "The material culture of the Crow Indians," *American Museum of Natural History, Anthropological Papers* 21:3.

Lucas, A.T. 1956. "Wattle and straw mat doors in Ireland," *Studia Ethnographica Upsaliensia* 11:16–35.

Lung, David. 1991. *Chinese Traditional Vernacular Architecture*. Hong Kong: Regional Council.

Lyford, Carrie A. 1945. *Iroquois Crafts*. Lawrence, KS: Bureau of Indian Affairs.

Maas, John. 1969. "Where architectural historians fear to tread," *Journal of the Society of Architectural Historians* 28:1:3–8.

MacCauley, Clay. 1884. *The Seminole Indians of Florida*. Washington, DC: Bureau of American Ethnology, Smithsonian Institute.

McClintock, Walter. n.d. *The Blackfoot Tipi*. Los Angeles: Southwest Museum (Leaflet #5).

McCourt, Desmond. 1960–62. "Cruck trusses in North-west Ireland," *Gwerin* 3:165–85.

McCourt, Desmond. 1964–65. "The cruck trusses in Ireland and its West-European connections," *Folkliv* 28–9:64–78.

McCourt, Desmond. 1970. "The house with bedroom over byre: A long-house derivative?," *Ulster Folklife* 15–16:3–19.

McDaniel, George W. 1982. *Hearth and Home: Preserving a People's Culture*. Philadelphia: Temple University Press.

McGhee, Robert. 1984. "In the land of the plank houses," *Canadian Heritage* (May/June) 13–17.

McIlwraith, Thomas F. 1983. "Altered buildings: Another way of looking at the Ontario landscape," *Ontario History* 75 (June) 110–34.

McIntosh, R.J. 1974. "Archeology and mud-wall decay in a west African village," *World Archaeology* 6:154–71.

McKim, Wayne. 1985. "House types in Tanzania: A century of change," *Journal of Cultural Geography* 6:1:51–77.

Macrae, Marion and Anthony Adamson. 1963. *The Ancestral Roof*. Toronto: Clarke, Irwin.

McRaven, Charles. 1980. *Building with Stone*. New York: Lippincott and Crowell.

McRaven, Charles. 1985. "Chinking log walls," *Fine Homebuilding* (April/May) 48–51.

Mahapatra, Sitakant and Nityananda Patnaik. 1986. *Patterns of Tribal Housing*. Bhubaneshwar: Academy of Tribal Dialects and Culture.

Mahr, August C. 1945. "Origin and significance of Pennsylvania Dutch barn symbols," *Ohio Archaeological and Historical Quarterly* 54:1–32.

Malcolm, L.W.G. 1923. "Huts and villages in the Cameroon, West Africa," *Scottish Geographical Magazine* 39:21–7.

Mann, Dale and Richard Skinulis. 1979. *The Complete Log House Book*. Toronto: McGraw Hill Ryaeson.

Manucy, Albert. 1962. *The Houses of St. Augustine*. St. Augustine, FL: St. Augustine Historical Society.

Marh, Bhupinder Singh. 2004. "Three rural house types of the Ravi river valley," pp. 60–74 in Grover, Neelam and Kashi Nath Singh (eds.), *Cultural Geography : Form and Process*. New Delhi: Concept.

Maringer J. 1980. "Dwellings in Ancient Japan: Shapes and cultural context," *Asian Folklore Studies* 39:1:115–23.

Marshall, Howard W. 1981. *Folk Architecture in Little Dixie: A Regional Culture of Missouri.* Columbia: University of Missouri Press.

Marshall, Howard W. 1986. "The Pelster housebarn: Endurance of Germanic architecture on the Midwestern frontier," *Material Culture* 18:2:65–104.

Martin, Charles E. 1984. *Hollybush: Folk Building and Social Change in an Appalachian Community.* Knoxville: University of Tennessee Press.

Mason, R.T. 1973. *Framed Buildings of England.* Horsham: Coach Publishing House.

Mathiassen, Therkel. 1928. *Material Culture of the Iglulik Eskimos.* Copenhagen: Gyldendalske Boghandel, Nordisk Forlag.

Megas, George A. 1951. *The Greek House: Its Evolution and its Relation to the Houses of the Other Balkan Peoples.* Athens: Ministry of Reconstruction.

Megaw, B.R.S. 1962. "The 'Moss houses' of Kincardine, Perthshire, 1792," *Scottish Studies* 6:87–93.

Meggitt, M.J. 1957. "House building among the Mae Enga, western highlands, Territory of New Guinea," *Oceania* 27:3:161–78.

Meirion-Jones, Gwyn I. 1981. "Cruck construction: The European evidence," pp. 39–55 in Alcock, N.W. (ed.), *Cruck Construction: An Introduction and Catalogue.* London: Council for British Archaeology.

Meirion-Jones, Gwyn I. 1982. *The Vernacular Architecture of Brittany.* Edinburgh: John Donald.

Melvin, Bruce L. 1932. *Farm and Village Housing.* Washington, DC: President's Conference on Home Building and Home Ownership.

Mendele, Ferenc. 1991. *Holloko: The Collection of Historic Buildings.* Budapest: Hungarian Tourism Service.

Metraux, Alfredo. 1929. "Contribution à l'ethnographie et à l'archeologie de la province de Mendoza, Argentine," *Revista del Instituto de Etnologia de la Universidad Nacional de Tucuman I.*

Metraux, Alfred. 1949–51. "L'Habitation paysanne en Hati," *Bulletin de la Societe Neuchateloise de Geographie* 55:3–14.

Metson, Norma. 1945. "Farming in New Zealand: The farm home," *New Zealand Journal of Agriculture* 71:4:357–70.

Mikesell, Marvin W. 1985. *Northern Morocco: A Cultural Geography.* Westport, CN: Greenwood Press.

Milbauer, John. 2004. "Common houses in eastern Oklahoma," *Material Culture* 36:1:1–17.

Miles, Douglas. 1964. "The Ngadju longhouse," *Oceania* 35:1:45–57.

Miller, T.A.H. 1949. *Adobe or Sun-Dried Brick for Farm Building.* Washington: US Department of Agriculture (Farmers' Bulletin #1720).

Milliet-Mondon, Camile. 1982. "Certain aspects of housing in Nepal," pp. 151–67 in Izikowitz, K.G. and Per Sorensen (eds.), *The House in East and Southeast Asia.* London: Curzon Press.

Mills, David B. 1982. *The Evolution of Folk House Forms in Trinity Bay, Newfoundland.* St. Johns: Department of Culture, Recreation and Youth.

Mills, G.E. and D.W. Holdsworth. 1975. "The B.C. Mills prefabricated system: The emergence of ready-made buildings in Western Canada," *Canadian Historic Sites* 14:127–69.

Mindeleff, Cosmos. 1898a. "Navaho houses," *Annual Report for 1895–96, Bureau of American Ethnology* 17:2:475–517.

Mindeleff, Cosmos. 1898b. *Origin of the Cliff Dwellings*. New York: American Geographical Society (Bulletin #30).

Mindeleff, Victor. 1891. *A Study of Pueblo Architecture*. Washington, DC: Smithsonian Institute (Eighth Annual Report of the Bureau of American Ethnology).

Mishra, Shiv Narain. 1969. "Human dwellings in Sonpar region (U.P.): A geographical analysis," *National Geographical Journal of India* (March) 8–23.

Moe, John F. 1978. "Concepts of shelter: The folk poetics of space, change and continuity," *Journal of Popular Culture* 11:1:221–53.

Mollison, Elizabeth. 1978. "Farmhouses and cottages in Quercy-2. Their plans and interiors," *Vernacular Architecture* 9:2:35–9.

Moogk, Peter N. 1977. *Building a House in New France*. Toronto: McClelland and Stewart.

Morgan, John T. 1986. "The decline of log house construction in Blount county, Tennessee," unpublished PhD dissertation, University of Tennessee, Knoxville.

Morgan, John T. 1990. *The Log House in East Tennessee*. Knoxville: University of Tennessee Press.

Morgan, Lewis H. 1965. *Houses and House-Life of the American Aborigines*. Chicago: University of Chicago Press (Originally published as vol. IV of *Contributions to North American Ethnology*. Washington: Government Printing Office, 1881).

Morisset, Gerard. 1958. "Quebec: The country house," *Canadian Geographical Journal* 57:6:178–95.

Morse, Edward S. 1886. *Japanese Homes and their Surroundings*. New York: Dover Publications (reprinted 1961).

Motto, Sytha. 1973. *Old Houses of New Mexico and the People Who Built Them*. Albuquerque: Calvin Horn.

Moughtin, J.C. 1964. "The traditional settlements of the Hausa people," *Town Planning Review* 35:31–4.

Moughtin, J.C. 1985. *Hausa Architecture*. London: Ethnographica.

Mturi, Amini. 1984. "The conservation of the African architectural heritage," *Monumentum* Part I 27:3:181–96, Part II 27:4:275–84.

Mueller, Esther L. 1972. "Log cabins to Sunday houses," pp. 51–9 in Hudson, Wilson M. (ed.), *Diamond Bessie and the Shepherds*. Austin, TX: Encino Press.

Mukerji, A.B. 1962. "Jat house types," *Geografia* (Winter) 27–37.

Munro, Neil. 1963. *Ainu Creed and Cult*. New York: Columbia University Press.

Murdock, George Peter. 1934. *Our Primitive Contemporaries*. New York: Macmillan.

Myrthe, A.T. 1967. *Ambrosio de Letinez or the First Texian Novel*. Austin: Steck Company (facsimile reproduction of 1842 edition).

Nabokov, Peter. 1978. "Kickapoo," pp. 50–3 in Kahn, Lloyd (ed.), *Shelter II*. Bolinas, CA: Shelter Publications.

Nabokov, Peter. 1981. *Adobe: Pueblo and Hispanic Folk Traditions of the Southwest*. Washington, DC: Smithsonian Institute.

Nabokov, Peter and Robert Easton. 1989. *Native American Architecture*. New York: Oxford University Press.

Naismith, Robert J. 1985. *Buildings of the Scottish Countryside*. London: Victor Gollancz

Nash, Judy. 1991. *Thatchers and Thatching*. London: B.T. Batsford.

Nash, Roy. 1923. "The houses of rural Brazil," *Geographical Review* 13:3:329–44.

National Slate Association. 1926. *Slate Roofs*. Fair Haven, VT: Vermont Structural Slate Company (reprinted 1977).

Negoita, Jana. 1986. *The Village Museum*. Bucharest: Meridiane Publishing House.

Nelson, Lee H. 1991. "How hand-wrought nails were made from bar iron in the 18th century," *Cultural Resource Management* 14:4:18–19.

Nelson, Walter R. 1969. "Some examples of plank house construction and their origin," *Pioneer America* 1:2:18–29.

Newman, Thomas M. 1974. "Native peoples and shelters," pp. 5–29 in Vaughan, Thomas (ed.), *Space, Style and Structure: Building in Northwest America*. Portland: Oregon Historical Society.

Newton, Ada J. 1964. "The history of architecture along the Rio Grande as reflected in the buildings around Rio Grande City, 1749–1920," unpublished MA thesis, Texas College of Arts and Industries.

Nguyen, Van Huyen. 1934. *Introduction a l'étude de l'habitation sur Pilotis dans l'Asie du Sud-est*. Paris: Librairie Orientaliste Paul Geuthner.

Nishi, Midori. 1967. "Regional variations in Japanese farmhouses," *Annals of the Association of American Geographers* 57:2:239–66.

Noble, Allen G. 1981. "Sod houses and similar structures: a brief evaluation of the literature," *Pioneer America* 13:2:61–6.

Noble, Allen G. 1984. *Wood, Brick and Stone: The North American Settlement Landscape Volume 1 Houses* and *Volume 2 Barns and Farm Structures*. Amherst: University of Massachusetts Press.

Noble, Allen G. 1991."House types in Blota, Poland and a source of North American I-houses," *PAST – Pioneer American Society Transactions* 14:1–9.

Noble, Allen G. 1992a. "Migration to North America: Before, during, and after the nineteenth century," pp. 3–25 in Noble, Allen G. (ed.), *To Build in a New Land: Ethnic Landscape in North America*. Baltimore: Johns Hopkins University Press.

Noble, Allen G. 1992b. "The German Russian Mennonites in Manitoba," pp. 268–84 in Noble, Allen G. (ed.), *To Build in a New Land*. Baltimore: Johns Hopkins University Press.

Noble, Allen G. 1996. "Introducing the Dutch landscape of southwestern Michigan," *PAST – Pioneer America Society Transactions* 19:11–18.

Noble, Allen G. 2003. "Patterns and relationships of Indian houses," pp. 39–69 in Knapp, Ronald (ed.), *Asia's Old Dwellings: Tradition, Residence, and Change*. Hong Kong: Oxford University Press.

Noble, Allen G. and Brian Coffey. 1986. "The use of cobblestones as a folk building material," *P.A.S.T – Pioneer American Society Transactions* 9:45–51.

Noble, Allen G. and Deborah Phillips King. 1989. "Here today, gone tomorrow: Determining the disappearance rate of agricultural structures in Pike county, Ohio", pp. 272–82 in Walls, Robert E. and George H. Schoemaker (eds.), *The Old Traditional Way of Life: Essays in Honor of Warren E. Roberts*. Bloomington, IN: Trickster Press.

Noble, Allen G. and Hubert G.H. Wilhelm (eds.). 1995. *Barns of the Midwest*. Athens, OH: Ohio University Press.

Norris, H.T. 1953. "Cave habitations and granaries in Tripolitania and Tunisia," *Man* 53:82–5.

Norsk Folkemuseum, Dept of Cultural History. 1996. *Norsk Folkemuseum, The Open Air Museum*. Oslo: Norsk Folkemuseum.

Norton, John. 1986. *Building with Earth*. London: Intermediate Technology Publications.

Nwafor, J.C. 1979. "Traditional rural houses of Nigeria," *Nigerian Field: The International Field Studies Journal of West Africa* 44:50–64.

Nwe, Than Than. 2003. "Dwellings of Myanmar: Ceremony, ritual, and life," pp. 221–33 in Knapp, Ronald D. (ed.), *Asia's Old Dwellings*. Hong Kong: Oxford University Press.

O'Danachair, Caoimhin. 1945. "The questionnaire system," *Bealoideas* 15:203–17.

O'Danachair, Caoimhin. 1956. "Three house types," *Ulster Folklife* 2:22–6.

O'Danachair, Caoimhin. 1957. "Materials and methods in Irish traditional building," *Journal of the Royal Society of Antiquaries of Ireland* 87:1:61–74.

O'Danachair, Caoimhin. 1964. "The combined byre-and-dwelling in Ireland," *Folklife* 2:58–75.

O'Dea, Shane. 1982. "Simplicity and survival: vernacular response in Newfoundland architecture," *Newfoundland Quarterly* 78:3:19–31.

Ojo, G.J. Afolabi. 1967. "Traditional Yoruba architecture," *African Arts* 1:3:14–17 & 70–2.

Oliver, Basil. 1929. *The Cottages of England*. London: B.T. Batsford.

Oliver, Paul. 1969. *Shelter and Society*. New York: Fredrick A. Praeger.

Oliver, Paul. 1977. *Shelter, Sign and Symbol*. Woodstock, NY: Overlook Press.

Oliver, Paul. 1987. *Dwellings: The House Around the World*. Austin: University of Texas Press.

Oliver, Paul. 1989. "Handed down architecture: tradition and transmission," pp. 53–75 in Bourdier, Jean-Paul and Nezar Alsayyad (eds.), *Dwellings, Settlements, and Tradition: cross-cultural perspectives*. Lanham, MD: University Press of America.

Oliver, William. 1843. *Eight Months in Illinois*. Newcastle upon Tyne: W.A. Mitchell (reprinted 1968 by University Microfilms, Ann Arbor, MI).

Olson, Ronald. 1927. *Adze, Canoe and House Types of the Northwest Coast*. Seattle: University of Washington Press.

O'Malley, James R. and John B. Rehder. 1978. "The two-story log house in the Upland South," *Journal of Popular Culture* 11:4:904–15.

Ondaatje, Kim and Lois Mackenzie. 1977. *Old Ontario Houses*. Toronto(?): Gage Publishing.

Opolovnikov, Alexander and Yelena Opolovnikov. 1989. *The Wooden Architecture of Russia*. New York: Harry N. Abrams.

Oringderff, Barbara. 1976. *True Sod*. North Newton, KS: Mennonite Press.

Otterbein, Keith. 1975. *Changing House Types in Long Bay Cays: The Evolution of Folk Housing in an Out Island Bahamian Community*. New Haven, CT: Human Relations Area Files.

Ozkan, Suha and Selahattin Onur. 1977. "Another thick wall pattern: Cappadocia," pp. 95–106 in Oliver, Paul (ed.), *Shelter, Sign and Symbol*. Woodstock, NY: Overlook Press.

Page, Gordon B. 1937. "Navajo house types," *Museum Notes* (Museum of Northern Arizona) 9:9:47–9 + 8 plates.

Parachek, Ralph E. 1967. *Desert Architecture*. Phoenix: Parr of Arizona.

Parsons, James J. 1991. "Giant American bamboo in the vernacular architecture of Colombia and Ecuador," *Geographical Review* 81:2:131–52.

Patel, Kalkans. 1987. "An enduring form of dwellings in Gujarat," *Man in India* 67:3:276–86.

Patterson, T.G.F. 1960. "Housing and house types in County Armagh," *Ulster Folklife* 6:8–17.

Patty, Ralph L. and L.W. Minium. 1933. *Rammed Earth Walls for Farm Buildings*. Brookings, SD: Agricultural Experiment Station, South Dakota State College (Bulletin #277).

Paul, Bimal Kanti. 2003. "Dwellings in Bangladesh," pp. 91–111 in Knapp, Ronald G. (ed.), *Asia's Old Dwellings*. Hong Kong: Oxford University Press.

Paulsson, Thomas. 1959. *Scandinavian Architecture*. Newton, MA: Charles T. Branford.

Pavlides, Eleftherios and Jana Hesser. 1989. "Sacred space, ritual and the traditional Greek house," pp. 275–93 in Bourdier, Jean-Paul and Nezar Alsayyad (eds.), *Dwellings, Settlements and Tradition: Cross-Cultural Perspectives*. Lanham, MD: University Press of America.

Pawar, R.S. 1984. "Cultural ecology of Marwari Gujar house types of the lower Chambal Basin," *Geographical Review of India* 46:2:42–8.

Payne, Geoffrey. 1980. "The Miri longhouse in Assam," *Process: Architecture* 15:67–70.

Peate, Iorwerth C. 1963. "The Welsh long-house: A brief re-appraisal," pp. 439–44 in Foster, I.L. and L. Alcock (eds.), *Culture and Environment*. London: Routledge and Kegan Paul.

Peate, Iorwerth C. 1964. "The long-house again," *Folk Life* 2:76–9.

Penoyre, John and Jane Penoyre. 1978. *Houses in the Landscape: A Regional Study of Vernacular Building Styles in England and Wales*. London: Faber and Faber.

Perrin, Richard W.E. 1961. "German timber farmhouses in Wisconsin: Terminal examples of a thousand-year building tradition," *Wisconsin Magazine of History* 44:199–202.

Perrin, Richard W.E. 1963. "Wisconsin 'stovewood' walls," *Wisconsin Magazine of History* 46:215–19.

Perrin, Richard W.E. 1963–64. "Boulders, cobblestones, and pebbles: Wisconsin's fieldstone architecture," *Wisconsin Magazine of History* 47:136–45.

Perrin, Richard W.E. 1967. *The Architecture of Wisconsin*. Madison: State Historical Society.

Petersen, Albert J. 1970. "German-Russian Catholic colonization in western Kansas: A settlement geography," unpublished PhD dissertation, Louisiana State University, Baton Rouge.

Petersen, Albert J. 1976. "The German-Russian house in Kansas: A study in persistence of form," *Pioneer America* 8:1:19–27.

Peterson, Charles. E. 1941. "Early Ste. Genevieve and its architecture," *Missouri Historical Review* 35:2:207–32.

Peterson, Charles E. 1948. "Early American prefabrication," *Gazette de Beaux-Arts* (6th series) 33:37–46.

Peterson, Charles. E. 1965. "Prefabs in the California gold rush, 1849," *Journal of the Society of Architectural Historians* 24:4: 313–24.

Petherbridge, Guy. 1978. "The house and society," pp. 193–208 in Michell, George (ed.), *Architecture of the Islamic World*. London: Thames and Hudson.

Philippides, Dimitri. 1983. *Greek Traditional Architecture*. Athens: Melissa Publishing House

Phillipps, William J. 1952. *Maori Houses and Food Stores*. Wellington: Dominion Museum (Monograph #8).

Phleps, Hermann. 1982. *The Craft of Log Building*. Ottawa: Lee Valley Tools Ltd.

Piggott, Stuart. 1945. "Farmsteads in central India," *Antiquity* 19:154–6.

Pillsbury, Richard. 1976. "The construction materials of the rural folk housing of the Pennsylvania culture region," *Pioneer America* 8:2:98–106.

Pillsbury, Richard. 1977. "Patterns in the folk and vernacular house forms of the Pennsylvania culture region," *Pioneer America* 9:1:12–31.

Pitman, Leon. S. 1973. *A Survey of Nineteenth Century Folk Housing in the Mormon Culture Region*. Ann Arbor, MI: University Microfilms.

Pocius, Gerald L. 1983. "Architecture on Newfoundland's southern shore: Diversity and the emergence of New World forms," *Society for the Study of Architecture in Canada, Bulletin* 8:12–19.

Porphyrios, Demetrius. 1971. "Traditional earthquake resistant construction on a Greek island," *Journal of the Society of Architectural Historians* 30:31–9.

Post, Lauren. C. 1962. *Cajun Sketches: From the Prairies of Southwest Louisiana*. Baton Rouge: Louisiana State University Press.

Pramar, V.S. 1983. "Traditional woodwork in secular architecture," *Marg* 34:4:21–32.

Pratt, Ned, Wendy Nichols and Don Weber. 1980. *The Shotgun House*. Louisville, KY: Preservation Alliance of Louisville and Jefferson County.

Price, Wayne. 1989. "The Schwarz-Krueger wine cellar-housebarn," *PAST – Pioneer America Society Transactions* 12:39–46.

Prussin, Labelle. 1970. "Sudanese architecture and the Manding," *African Arts* 3:4:12–19 & 64–7.

Prussin, Labelle. 1974. "An introduction to indigenous African architecture," *Journal of the Society of Architectural Historians* 33:3:182–205.

Prussin, Labelle. 1995. *African Nomadic Architecture: Space, Place and Gender*. Washington, DC: Smithsonian Institution Press and the Museum of African Art.

Quiney, Anthony. 1990. *The Traditional Buildings of England*. London: Thames and Hudson.

Radford, A. and G. Clark. 1974. "Cyclades: Studies of a building vernacular," pp. 64–82 in Doumanis, Orestis B. and Paul Oliver (eds.), *Shelter in Greece*. Athens: Architecture in Greece Press.

Radig, Werner. 1966. *Das Bauernhaus in Brandenburg und im Mittelelbegiet*. Berlin: Akademie-Verlag.

Ragette, Friedrich. 1974. *Architecture in Lebanon: The Lebanese House During the 18th and 19th Centuries*. Beirut: American University of Beirut.

Raglan, Lord. 1963. "The origin of vernacular architecture," pp. 373–87 in Foster, I.L. and L. Alcock (eds.), *Culture and Environment*. London: Routledge and Kegan Paul.

Raglan, Lord. 1964. *The Temple and the House*. New York: W.W. Norton.

Raine, David F. 1966. *Architecture – Bermuda Style: A Short Survey of Architecture in the Bermudas*. Bermuda: Longtail Publishing.

Ramm, H.G., R.W. McDowall and Eric Mercer. 1970. *Shielings and Bastles*. London: HMSO.

Rapoport, Amos. 1967. "Yagua, or the Amazon dwelling," *Landscape* 16:3:27–30.

Rapoport, Amos. 1969. "The pueblo and the hogan," pp. 66–79 in Oliver, Paul (ed.), *Shelter and Society*. New York: Praeger.

Rapoport, Amos. 1977. "Australian aborigines and the definition of place," pp. 38–51 in Oliver, Paul (ed.), *Shelter, Sign and Symbol*. Woodstock, NY: Overlook Press.

Rapoport, Amos. 1980. "Vernacular architecture and the cultural determinants of form," pp. 283–305 in King, Anthony (ed.), *Buildings and Society*. London: Routledge and Kegan Paul.

Rau, John E. 1992. "Czechs in South Dakota," pp. 285–306 in Noble, Allen G. (ed.), *To Build in a New Land*. Baltimore: Johns Hopkins University Press.

Ray, Dorothy Jean. 1960. "The Eskimo dwelling," *The Alaska Sportsman* 26:13–15 & 61–2.

Rees, Roland and Carl J. Tracie. 1978. "The prairie house," *Landscape* 22:3:3–8.

Rempel, John. I. 1967. *Building with Wood*. Toronto: University of Toronto Press.

Reuther, Oskar. 1910. *Das Wohnhaus in Bagdad und anderen Stadten des Irak*. Berlin: Ernest Wasmuth A.G.

Richardson, A.J.H. 1973. "A comparative historical study of timber building in Canada," *Bulletin of Association for Preservation Technology* 5:3:77–102.

Richmond, I.A. 1932. "The Irish analogies for the Romano-British barn dwelling," *Journal of Roman Studies* 22:96–106.

Ricketson, Oliver G., Jr. 1927. "American nail-less houses in the Maya bush," *Art and Architecture* 24:27–36.

Rider, Bertha C. 1965. *The Greek House*. Cambridge: Cambridge University Press.

Riley, Robert B. 1985a. "Square to the road, hogs to the east," *Places* 2:4:72–9.

Riley, Robert B. 1985b. "Square to the road, hogs to the east," *Illinois Issues* 11:7:22–6.

Ritchie, T. 1967. *Canada Builds: 1867–1967*. Toronto: University of Toronto Press.

Ritchie, T. 1971. "Plankwall framing: A modern wall construction with an ancient history," *Journal of the Society of Architectural Historians* 30:1:66–70.

Ritchie, T. 1974. "The use of planks in wall construction," *Bulletin of the Association for Preservation Technology* 6:3:26–34.

Ritchie, T. 1979. "Notes on dichromatic brickwork in Ontario," *APT Bulletin* 11:2:60–75.

Rivière, Georges H. 1954. "Folk architecture: Past, present and future," *Landscape* 4:1:5–12.

Roark, Michael. 1992. "Storm cellars: imprint of fear on the landscape," *Material Culture* 24:2:45–53.

Roark, Michael and Brian McCutchen. 1993. "Stack houses: A German tradition in eastern Missouri," *PAST – Pioneer America Society Transactions* 16:63–8.

Roberts, Warren. 1972. "Folk architecture," pp. 281–93 in Dorson, Richard M. (ed.), *Folklore and Folklife: An Introduction*. Chicago: University of Chicago Press.

Roberts, Warren. 1976. "Some comments on log construction in Scandinavia and the United States," pp. 437–50 in Degh, Linda, Henry Glassie and Felix J. Oinas (eds.), *Folk Lore Today: A Festschrift for Richard M. Dorson*. Bloomington: Indiana University.

Robinson, Philip. 1985. "From thatch to slate: Innovation in roof covering materials for traditional houses in Ulster," *Ulster Folklife* 31:21–35.

Robinson, Willard B. 1981. *Gone from Texas: Our Lost Architectural Heritage*. College Station: Texas A & M University Press.

Rodger, Allan. 1974. "The Sudanese heat trap," *The Ecologist* 4:3:102–6.

Roe, Frank G. 1958. "The old log house in western Canada," *Alberta Historical Review* 6:1–9.

Roe, Frank G. 1970. "The sod house," *Alberta Historical Review* 18:3:1–7.

Ron, Zvi. 1977. "Stone huts as an expression of terrace agriculture in the Judean and Samarian hills," unpublished PhD dissertation, Tel-Aviv University, Tel-Aviv.

Ron, Zvi D. 1982. "Climatological aspects of stone huts in traditional agriculture in a Mediterranean region," *Israel Journal of Earth Sciences* 31:111–21.

Rose, A.J. 1962. "Some boundaries and building materials in southeastern Australia," pp. 255–79 in McCaskill, Murray (ed.), *Land and Livelihood: Geographical Essays in Honour of George Jobberns*. Christchurch: New Zealand Geograpical Society.

Roth, Walter E. 1909. "Australian huts and shelters," *Man* 27–8:49 and plate D.

Roy, Robert. L. 1977. *How to Build Log-End Houses*. New York: Drake Publishers.

Ruede, Howard. 1966. *Sod House Days*. New York: Cooper Square Publishers.

Ruitenbeek, Klaas. 1986. "Craft and ritual in traditional Chinese carpentry," *Chinese Science* 7:1–23.

Rushton, William F. 1979. *The Cajuns*. New York: Farrar Straus Giroux.

Rutter, Andrew F. 1971. "Ashanti vernacular architecture," pp. 153–71 in Oliver, Paul (ed.), *Shelter in Africa*. London: Barre and Jenkins.

Salinas, Iris Milady. 1991. *Arquitectura de los Grupos Etnicos de Honduras*. Tegucigalpa: Editorial Guaymuras.

Salzman, L.F. 1952. *Building in England, Down to 1540*. London: Oxford University Press.

Samizay, Rafi. 1974. "Herati housing in Afghanistan," *Ekistics* 38:227:247–51.

Sandklef, Albert. 1949. *Singing Flails*. Helsinki: Suomalainen Tiedekaakatemia. (FF Communications #136).

Sandon, Eric. 1977. *Suffolk Houses: A Study of Domestic Architecture*. Woodbridge: Baron Publishing.

Sands, Carolyn. 1980. "Frontier architecture of the Big Sioux valley: 1865–1885," pp. 29–44 in Huseboe, Arthur R. (ed.), *Big Sioux Pioneers*. Sioux Falls, SD: Nordland Heritage Foundation, Augustana College.

Sanford, Dena Lynn. 1991. "Finnish homesteads in Montana's Little Belt Creek Valley: Korpivaara's vernacular building tradition," unpublished MSc thesis, University of Oregon, Eugene.

Sanford, Trent E. 1950. *The Architecture of the Southwest*. Westport, CN: Greenwood Press.

Scargill, Ian. 1974. *The Dordogne Region of France*. Newton Abbott: David and Charles.

Scherman, L. 1915. "Wohnhaustypen in Birma und Assam," *Archiv fur Anthropologie* 42:203–34 + 10 pp. of plates.

Scheuermeier, Paul. 1943. *Bauernwerk in Italien: Der Italienischen und Ratoromanischen Schweig* (2 vols.). Erlenbach-Zurich: Eugene Rentsch Verlag, 2 vols.

Schmertz, Mildred F. 1974. "Upgrading barns to be inhabited by people," *Agricultural Record* 115:117–22.

Schmidt, Carl. F. 1958. "The cobblestone houses of central New York state," *Journal of the American Institute of Architects* 29:229–35.

Schmidt, Carl F. 1966. *Cobblestone Masonry*. Scottsville, NY: privately printed.

Schoenauer, Norbert. 2000. *6,000 Years of Housing*. New York: W.W. Norton.

Schwatka, Frederick. 1883. "The igloo of the Inuit," *Science* 2:182–4, 216–18, 259–62, 304–6 & 347–9.

Schwerdtfeger, Friedrich W. 1972. "Urban settlement patterns in northern Nigeria (Hausaland)," pp. 547–56 in Ucko, Peter J., Ruth Trigham and G.W. Dimbleby (eds.), *Man, Settlement and Urbanism*. Cambridge, MA: Schenkman.

Scofield, Edna. 1936. "The evolution and development of Tennessee houses," *Journal of the Tennessee Academy of Science* 11:4:229–40.

Sculle, Keith A. 1989. "The Canadian connection to Illinois: The Joseph Steffens house in Carroll County," *Bulletin of the Illinois Geographical Society* 31:1:33–45.

Seaborne, H.V.M. 1963. "Small stone houses in Northamptonshire," *Northamptonshire Past and Present* 3:4:141–50.

Seaborne, H.V.M. 1964. "Cob cottages in Northamptonshire," *Northamptonshire Past and Present* 3:5:215–25.

Sen, Jyotirmoy and Sakti Prasad Dhar. 1997. "Bhotpotty: A study in settlement geography," *Geographical Review of India* 59:3:249–58.

Sewan, Olga G. 1995. "The methods of designing and arranging open-air museums in the Russian north," *Acta Scansenologica* 7:86–90.

Shah, Mayank. 1980. "Nomadic movements and settlements of the Rabaris," *Process: Architecture* 15:49–66.

Sharkey, Olive. 1985. *Old Days, Old Ways: An Illustrated Folk History of Ireland*. Dublin: O'Brien Press.

Sharp, Mildred J. 1921. "Early cabins in Iowa," *The Palimpsest* 2:16–29.

Shaw, Alison. 1988. *A Pakistani Community in Britain*. Oxford: Basil Blackwell.

Shedd, Nellita S. 1974. "Cobblestone buildings in southern Wisconsin," *Antiques Journal* (April) 19–22 & 48.

Shelgren, Olaf W., Jr., Cary Lattin and Robert W. Frasch. 1978. *Cobblestone Landmarks of New York State*. Syracuse, NY: Syracuse University Press.

Sheppard, June A. 1966. "Vernacular buildings in England and Wales: A survey of recent work by architects, archaeologists and social historians," *Institute of British Geographers Transactions* 40:21–37.

Sherman, William C. 1974. "Prairie architecture of the Russian-German settlers," pp. 185–95 in Sallet, Richard (ed.), *Russian-German Settlements in the United States*. Fargo: North Dakota Institute for Regional Studies.

Shetelig, Haakon and Hjalmar Falk. 1937. *Scandinavian Archaeology*. Oxford: Clarendon Press.

Shichor, Michael. 1987. *Michael's Guide: Argentina, Chile.* Tel Aviv: Inbal Travel Information Ltd.

Shortridge, James R. 1980. "Traditional rural houses along the Missouri-Kansas border," *Journal of Cultural Geography* 1:1:105–37.

Shotridge, Louis and Florence Shotridge. 1913. " Chilkat houses," *Museum Journal, University of Pennsylvania* 4:81–100

Shufeldt, R.W. 1892. "The evolution of house-building among the Navajo Indians," *Proceedings of the U.S. National Museum* 15:279–82 + 3 plates.

Shumway, E.W. 1954. "Winter quarters, 1846–1848," *Nebraska History.* 36:115–25.

Shurtleff, Harold R. 1939. *The Log Cabin Myth: A Study of the Early Dwellings of the English Colonists in North America.* Cambridge, MA: Harvard University Press.

Sickler, Joseph S. 1949. *The Old Houses of Salem County.* Salem, NJ: Sunbeam Publishing.

Sigurdsson, Gisli. 1971. "The turf farm: Now a relic of the past," *Atlantica and Iceland Review* 9:1:33–41.

Simons, Mary Joan. 1982. "Radiographic inspection of plank house construction," unpublished MA thesis, Cornell University, Ithaca, NY.

Simpson, Pamela H. 1990. "The architecture of Rockbridge County, chapter 1; Or, how does a house mean," *Proceedings of the Rockbridge Historical Society* 10:77–86.

Simpson, Pamela. 1992. "Windows, closets, taxes and Indians: Architectural legends and myths," *Arris* 3:23–34.

Sinclair, Colin. 1953. *The Thatched Houses of the Old Highlands.* Edinburgh: Oliver and Boyd.

Sinclair, Peter. 2004. "From the journal," *Hudson Valley Vernacular Architecture Newsletter* 6:8:1–6.

Sinclair, Peter. 2005. "From the editor," *Hudson Valley Vernacular Architecture Newsletter* 7:6:1–2.

Singh, Jai Pal and Mumtaz Khan. 2002. *Mythical Space, Cosmology and Landscape: Towards a Cultural Geography of India.* Delhi: Manak Publications.

Singh, Mehar. 2004. "The changing rural house type of Punjab," pp. 75–96 in Grover, Neelam and Kashi Nath Singh (eds.), *Cultural Geography: Form and Process.* New Delhi: Concept.

Singh, R.L. 1957. "Typical rural dwellings in the umland of Banaras (India)," *National Geographical Journal of India* 3:2:51–64.

Singh, Tebir. 1965. "A case study of house types in village Kurali," *Geographical Observer* (Meerut) 11–14.

Singleton, William A. 1952. "Traditional house-types in rural Lancashire and Cheshire," *Transactions of the Historic Society of Lancashire and Cheshire* 104:75–92.

Sinha, Amita. 1989. "Woman's local space: Home and neighborhood in northern India," *Women and Environments* 11:2:15–18.

Sizemore, Jean. 1994. *Ozark Vernacular Houses.* Fayetteville: University of Arkansas Press.

Skolle, John. 1962–63. "Adobe in Africa : Varieties of anonymous architecture," *Landscape* 12:15–17.

Sledge, John S. 1990. "Shoulder to shoulder ... Mobile's shotgun houses," *Gulf Coast Historical Review* 6:56–64.

Smaal, A.P. (ed.). 1979. *Looking at Historic Buildings in Holland.* Baarn: Bosch and Kenning.

Smith, Arnold. C. 1962. *The Architecture of Chios.* London: Alec Tiranti.

Smith, Fred T. 1980. "Architectural decoration of northeastern Ghana," *Ba shiru* (Dept. of African Languages and Literature, University of Wisconsin) 11:1:24–32.

Smith, J.T. 1963. "The long-house in Monmouthshire: A reappraisal," pp. 389–415 in Foster, I.L. and L. Alcock (eds.), *Culture and Environment.* London: Routledge and Kegan Paul.

Smith, Peter. 1963. "The long-house and the laithe-house: A study of the house-and-byre homestead in Wales and the West Riding," pp. 415–38 in Foster, I.L. and L. Alcock (eds.), *Culture and Environment.* London: Routledge and Kegan Paul.

Smith, Peter. 1967. "Rural housing in Wales," pp. 767–813 in Thirsk, Joan (ed.), *The Agrarian History of England and Wales, Volume IV.* Cambridge: Cambridge University Press.

Smith, Peter. 1979. "The architectural personality of the British Isles," *Archaeologia Cambrensis* 129:1–36.

Smith, Peter. 1989. "Houses and building styles," pp. 95–150 in Owen, D. Huw (ed.), *Settlement and Society in Wales.* Cardiff: University of Wales Press.

Smith, Terence P. 1979. "Refacing with brick tiles," *Vernacular Architecture* 10:33–6.

Smole, William J. 1976. *The Yanamamo Indians.* Austin: University of Texas Press.

Soebadio, Haryati. 1975. "The documentary study of traditional Balinese architecture: Some preliminary notes," *Indonesian Quarterly* 3:86–111.

Spence, R.J.S. and D.J. Cook. 1983. *Building Materials in Developing Countries.* Chichester: John Wiley.

Spencer, Joseph E. 1947. "The houses of the Chinese," *Geographical Review* 37:254–73.

Spencer, Virginia. E. and Stephen C. Jett. 1971. "Navajo dwellings of rural Black Creek valley, Arizona-New Mexico," *Plateau* 43:4:159–75.

Stacpoole, John. 1976. *Colonial Architecture in New Zealand.* Wellington: A.H and A.W. Reed.

Stahl, Paul-Henri. 1972. "L'habitation enterrée dans la région orientale du Danube," *L'Homme* 12:4:37–61.

Stalfelt-Szabo, Helene and Matyas Szabo. 1979. "The architecture of Bekevar," pp. 210–56 in Blumenstock, Robert (ed.), *Bekevar: Working Papers on a Canadian Prairie Community.* Ottawa: National Museums of Canada.

Stanford, Deirdre. 1975. *Restored America.* New York: Praeger.

Stayton, Kevin L. 1990. *Dutch by Design.* New York: Phaidon Universe.

Stell, Christopher. 1965. "Pennine houses: An introduction," *Folk Life* 3:5–24.

Sternberg, Frances R. 1984. "Housetypes in the landscape of the Brasilian Amazon," paper presented at the annual meeting of the Association of American Geographers (April).

Stevens, Bryan J. 1980/81. "The Swiss bank house revisited: The Messerschmidt-Dietz cabin," *Pennsylvania Folklife* 30:2:78–86.

Stevenson, J.J. 1880. *House Architecture.* London: Macmillan.

Steward, Norman R. 1965. "The mark of the pioneer," *Landscape* 15:1:26–8.

Stewart, Hilary. 1984. *Cedar: Tree of Life to the Northwest Coast Indians.* Seattle: University of Washington Press.

Stewart, Janice S. 1972. *The Folk Arts of Norway.* 2nd edition. New York: Dover.

Stokhuyzen, Frederick. 1963. *The Dutch Windmill.* New York: Universe Books.

Straight, Stephen and Myles Mustoe. 1996. "Temporary buildings: Where are they going, where have they been?," *Journal of Geography* 95:2:73–80.

Subhashini, A.V. 1987. "Tharavads: Kerala's Nair homes," *The India Magazine of her People and Culture* (July) 52–63.

Subramanyam, K.M. 1938. "Four main house types in South India: their geographical controls," *Journal of the Madras Geographical Association (India Geographical Journal)* 13:2:168–75.

Sullivan, Linda F. 1972. "Traditional Chinese regional architecture: Chinese houses," *Journal of the Hong Kong Branch of the Royal Asiatic Society* 12:131–49.

Swithenbank, Michael. 1969. *Ashanti Fetish Houses.* Accra: Ghana Universities Press.

Szabo, Albert and Thomas J. Barfield. 1991. *Afghanistan: An Atlas of Indigenous Domestic Architecture.* Austin: University of Texas Press.

Taggart, Kathleen M. 1958. "The first shelter of early pioneers," *Saskatchewan History* 11:3:81–93.

Talbot, P. Amaury. 1916. "Note on Ibo houses," *Man* 14:129.

Talib, Kaizer. 1984. *Shelter in Saudi Arabia.* New York: St. Martin's Press.

Tate, Bryan. 2002. "Sullivan county log homes," *Material Culture* 34:2:41–53.

Taut, Bruno. 1958. *Houses and People of Japan.* Tokyo: Sanseido.

Tebbetts, Diane. 1978. "Traditional houses of Independence County, Arkansas," *Pioneer America* 10:1:37–55.

Tewari, A.K. 1966. "A house type in Jaunsar-Himalaya," *Australian Geographer* 10:1:35–46.

Thomas, F.L.W. 1869. "On the primitive dwellings and hypogea of the Outer Hebrides," *Proceedings of the Society of Antiquaries of Scotland.*

Thompson, Robert F. 1983. *Flash of the Spirit: African and Afro-American Art and Philosophy.* New York: Random House.

Thomsen, Jorgen Rahbek. 1982. "Two houses in Thailand," pp. 81–102 in Izikowitz, K.G. and P. Sorensen (eds.), *The House in East and Southeast Asia.* London: Curzon Press.

Tisdale, E.S. and C.H. Atkins. 1943. "The sanitary privy and its relation to public health," *American Journal of Public Health* 33:1319–22.

Tishler, William. H. 1979. "Stovewood architecture," *Landscape* 23:3:28–31.

Tishler, William. H. 1982. "Stovewood construction in the upper Midwest and Canada: A regional vernacular architectural tradition," pp. 125–36 in Wells, Camille (ed.), *Perspectives in Vernacular Architecture.* Annapolis, MD: Vernacular Architecture Forum.

Tishler, William H. and Christopher S. Witmer. 1984. "The housebarns of east-central Wisconsin," pp. 102–10 in Wells, Camille (ed.), *Perspectives in Vernacular Architecture II.* Columbia: University of Missouri Press.

Tonna, Jo. 1989. "The interpenetration of high and folk traditions in Malta," pp. 161–81 in Bourdier, Jean-Paul and Nezar Alsayyad (eds.), *Dwellings, Settlements and Tradition: Cross-Cultural Perspectives.* Lanham, MD: University Press of America

Too, Lillian. 1996. *The Complete Illustrated Guide to Feng Shui.* New York: Barnes and Noble.

Trefois, C.V. 1937. "La technique de la construction rurale en bois," *Folk* 55–72.

Tremblay, Marc-Adelard, John Collier, Jr., and Tom T. Sasaki. 1954. "Navaho housing in transition," *America Indigena* 14:3:187–219.

Tremearne, A.J.N. 1910. "Hausa houses," *Man* 99:177–80.

Trewartha, Glenn T. 1945. *Japan: A Physical, Cultural and Regional Geography.* Madison: University of Wisconsin Press.

Trimble, Stanley W. 1988. "Ante-bellum domestic architecture in middle Tennessee," *Geoscience and Man* 25:97–117.

Trindell, Roger T. 1968. "Building in brick in early America," *Geographical Review* 58:484–7.

Trisch, F.J. 1943. "False doors on tombs," *Journal of Hellenic Studies* 63.

Tuan, Yi-Fu. 1989. "Traditional: What does it mean?" pp. 27–34 in Bourdier, Jean-Paul and Nezar Alsayyad (eds.), *Dwellings, Settlements and Tradition: Cross-Cultural Perspectives.* Lanham, MD: University Press of America.

Turnbull, Colin M. 1965. *Wayward Servants: The Two Worlds of the African Pygmie.* Garden City, NY: Natural History Press.

Ua Danachair, Caoimhghin. 1945. "Some primitive structures used as dwellings," *Journal of the Royal Society of Antiquaries of Ireland* 75:204–14.

ud-Din, Israr. 1984. "House types and structures in Chitral District," pp. 265–89, vol. 1, in Miller, K.J. (ed.), *International Karakoram Project.* Cambridge: Cambridge University Press.

Upton, Dell. 1979. "Toward a performance theory of vernacular architecture: Early tidewater Virginia as a case study," *Folklore Forum* 12:2–3:173–96.

Upton, Dell. 1983. "The power of things: Recent studies in American vernacular architecture," *American Quarterly* 35:3:262–70.

Upton, Dell. 1991. "Architectural history or landscape history?," *Journal of Architectural Education* 44:195–9.

van den Hurk. 2005. "Letter," *Hudson Valley Vernacular Architecture Newsletter* 7:6:2.

van Ravenswaay, Charles. 1977. *The Arts and Architecture of German Settlements in Missouri.* Columbia: University of Missouri Press.

Vastokas, Joan Marie. 1967. *Architecture of the Northwest Coast Indians of America.* Ann Arbor, MI: University Microfilms.

Verity, Paul. 1971. "Kababish nomads of northern Sudan," pp. 25–35 in Oliver, Paul (ed.), *Shelter in Africa.* London: Barrie and Jenkins.

Villeminot, Alain. 1958. "The Japanese house in its setting," *Landscape* 8:1:15–20.

Vlach, John Michael. 1975. "Sources of the shortgun house: African and Caribbean antecedents for Afro-American architecture", unpublished PhD thesis, Indiana University, Bloomington.

Vlach, John Michael. 1976a. "The shotgun house: An African architectural legacy, Part I," *Pioneer America* 8:1:47–56.

Vlach, John Michael. 1976b. "The shotgun house: An African architectural legacy, Part II," *Pioneer America* 8:2:57–70.

Vlach, John Michael. 1976c. "Affecting architecture of the Yoruba," *African Arts* 10:1:48–53 & 99.

Vlach, John Michael. 1977. "Shotgun houses," *Natural History* 86:51–7.

Volders, Jean Louis. 1966. *Bouwkunst in Suriname*. Hilversum: G. van Saane.

Vreim, Halver. 1937. "The ancient settlements in Finnmark, Norway," *Folkliv* 2–3:169–204.

Vryonis, Speros. 1975. "Local history and folklore from the village of Vasilikadhes in the district of Erissos, Cephalonia," pp. 397–424 in *Essays in Memory of Basil Laourdas*. Athens: Gregories.

Wace, A.J.B. and R.M. Dawkins. 1914–15. "The towns and houses of the archipelago," *Burlington Magazine for Connoisseurs* 26:99–107.

Wagstaff, J.M. 1965. "Traditional houses in modern Greece," *Geography* 50:58–64.

Waite, Diana. S. 1976. "Roofing for early America," pp. 135–49 in Peterson, Charles E. (ed.), *Building in Early America*. Radnor, PA: Chilton Book Co.

Walker, Bruce. 1977. *Clay buildings in North East Scotland*. Dundee: Scottish Vernacular Buildings Working Group.

Walker, Bruce. 1979. "The vernacular buildings of north east Scotland: An exploration," *Scottish Geographical Magazine* 95:45–60.

Walker, Bruce. 1989. "A Donegal building type: Farmhouse or farm building," *Ulster Folklife* 35:1–7.

Walker, Ralph. 1940. "The Japanese house," *Pencil Points* 1:332–42.

Walters, Derek. 1988. *Feng Shui: The Chinese Art of Designing a Harmonious Environment*. New York: Simon & Schuster.

Walton. James. 1948. "South African peasant architecture: Southern Sotho folk building," *African Studies* 7:4:139–45.

Walton, James. 1951. "Corbelled stone huts in southern Africa," *Man* 82:45–8.

Walton, James. 1952. "The oval house," *Antiquity* 26:135–40.

Walton, James. 1956. "Upland houses: The influence of mountain terrain on British folk building," *Antiquity* 30:142–8.

Walton, James. 1957. "The Skye house," *Antiquity* 31:155–62.

Walton, James. 1960–62. "Cruck trusses in the Dordogne," *Gwerin*. 3:3–6.

Walton, James. 1962. "The corbelled stone huts of southern Europe," *Man* 62:33–4 & plate D.

Wan Abidin, W.B.B. 1981. *The Malay House: Rationale and Change*. Cambridge, MA: MIT Press.

Warburton, Miranda. 1985. *Culture Change and the Navajo Hogan*. Ann Arbor, MI: University Microfilms.

Warren, John and Ihsan Fethi. 1982. *Traditional Houses in Baghdad*. Horsham: Coach Publishing House.

Waterman, Thomas T. 1950. *The Dwellings of Colonial America*. Chapel Hill: University of North Carolina Press.

Waterson, Roxana. 1989. "Migration, tradition and change in some vernacular architectures of Indonesia," pp. 477–501 in Bourdier, Jean-Paul and Nezar Alsayyad (eds.), *Dwellings, Settlements and Tradition: Cross-Cultural Perspectives*. Lanham, MD: University Press of America

Waterson, Roxana. 1990. *The Living House: An Anthropology of Architecture in South-East Asia*. Singapore: Oxford University Press.

Watson, Penelope S. 1984. "Eighteenth-century patterned brickwork in Connecticut," *Connecticut Antiquarian* 36:1:4–12.

Weaver, Williams Woys. 1986. "The Pennsylvania German house: European antecedents and New World forms," *Winterthur Portfolio* 21:4:243–65.

Webb, George. W. 1975. "A comparative study of traditional houses in the Caroline Islands," *Journal of Geography* 74:2:87–103.

Weeks, Christopher. 1996. *An Architectural History of Harford County, Maryland*. Baltimore: Johns Hopkins University Press.

Weiss, Richard. 1959. *Häuser und Landschaften der Schweiz*. Erlenbach-Zurich: Eugen Rentsch.

Weller, H.O. 1922. *Building in Cob and Pisé de Terre*. London: HMSO.

Wells, Malcolm B. 1968. "Down under down under . . . or how not to build underground," *Progressive Architecture* (March) 164–5.

Welsch, Roger L. 1967. "The Nebraska soddy," *Nebraska History* 48:335–42.

Welsch, Roger L. 1968. *Sod Walls: The Story of the Nebraska Sod House*. Broken Bow, NB: Purcells.

Welsch, Roger L. 1970. "Sandhill baled-hay construction," *Keystone Folklore Quarterly* 15 (Spring) 16–34.

Welsch, Roger L. 1980. "Nebraska log construction: Momentum in tradition," *Nebraska History* 61:3:310–35.

Wenzel, Marian. 1972. *House Decoration in Nubia*. London: Duckworth.

Weslager, C.A. 1969. *The Log Cabin in America*. Brunswick, NJ: Rutgers University Press.

West, H.G. 1951. "The house is a compass," *Landscape* 1:2:24–7.

West, Robert C. 1987. *Thatch*. Newton Abbot: David and Charles.

Westmaas, Rory. 1970. "Building under our sun," pp. 128–58 in Searwar, L. (ed.), *Co-op Republic: Guyana, 1970*. Georgetown: Government of Guyana.

Whyte, Ian D. 1975. "Rural housing in lowland Scotland in the seventeenth century: The evidence of estate papers," *Scottish Studies* 19:62–5.

Wilcoxen, Charlotte. 1984. *Seventeenth Century Albany: A Dutch Profile*. Albany, NY: Albany Institute of History and Art.

Wilhelm, Hubert G.H. 1971. "German settlement and folk building practices in the Hill Country of Texas," *Pioneer America* 3:2:15–24

Williams, Hattie Plum. 1916. "A social study of the Russian German," *University Studies of the University of Nebraska* 16:3:127–227.

Williams, Michael Ann. 1984. *Marble and Log: The History and Architecture of Cherokee County, North Carolina*. Murphy, NC: Cherokee County Historical Museum.

Williams, Michael Ann. 1990. "Pride and prejudice: The Appalachian boxed house in southwestern North Carolina," *Winterthur Portfolio* 25:217–30.

Williams, Michael Ann. 1991. *Homeplace: The Social Use and Meaning of the Folk Dwelling in Southwestern North Carolina*. Athens, GA: University of Georgia Press.

Williams, Michael Ann. 2001. "Vernacular architecture and the park removals: Traditionalization as justification and resistance," *Traditional Dwellings and Settlements Review* 13:33–42.

Wilmsen, Edwin N. 1960. "The house of the Navaho," *Landscape* 10:1:15–19.

Wilson, Eugene M. 1970. "The single pen log home in the South," *Pioneer America* 2:1:21–8.

Wilson, Chris. 1991. "Pitched roofs over flat: The emergence of a new building tradition in Hispanic New Mexico," pp. 87–97 in Carter, Thomas and Bernard L. Herman (eds.), *Perspectives in Vernacular Architecture IV*. Columbia: University of Missouri Press.

Wilson, Kenneth M. 1976. "Window glass in America," pp. 150–64 in Peterson, Charles E. (ed.), *Building Early America*. Radnor, PA: Chilton Book Co.

Wilson, Mary. 1984. *Log Cabin Studies: The Rocky Mountain Cabin*. Ogden, UT: Forest Service, US Department of Agriculture.

Winberry, John J. 1974. "The log house in Mexico," *Annals of the Association of American Geographers* 64:1:54–69.

Winberry, John J. 1975. "Tejamanil: The origin of the shake roof in Mexico," *Proceedings of the Association of American Geographers* 7:288–93.

Wonders, William C. and Mark A. Rasmussen. 1980. "Log building of West Central Alberta," *Prairie Forum* 5:2:197–217.

Wood, Margaret. 1965. *The English Mediaeval House*. London: Phoenix House.

Woodburn, James. 1972. "Ecology, nomadic movement and the composition of the local group among hunters and gatherers: An East African example and its implications," pp. 193–206 in Ucko, Peter J., Ruth Tringham and G.W. Dimbleby (eds.), *Man, Settlement and Urbanism*. Cambridge, MA: Schenkman.

Wooley, Carolyn Murray. 1974. "Kentucky's early stone houses," *Antiques* (March) 590–600.

Works, Martha Adrienne. 1985. "Development and change in the traditional landscape of the Mayo Aguaruna, eastern Peru," *Journal of Cultural Geography* 6:1:1–18.

Wright, Martin. 1958. "The antecedents of the double-pen house type," *Annals of the Association of American Geographers* 48:2:109–17.

Wulff, Inger. 1982. "Habitation among the Yakan, a Muslim people in the southern Philippines," pp. 137–50 in Izikowitz, K.G. and Per Sorensen (eds.), *The House in East and Southeast Asia*. London: Curzon Press.

Yang, Martin C. 1965. *A Chinese Village: Taitou, Shantung Province*. New York: Columbia University Press.

Yde, Jens. 1965. *Material Culture of the Waiwai*. Copenhagen: National Museum of Copenhagen.

Yuan, Lim Jee. 1981. *A Comparison of the Traditional Malay House and the Modern Housing-Estate House*. Tokyo: United Nations University.

Zelinsky, Wilbur. 1953. "The log house in Georgia," *Geographical Review* 43:2:173–93.

Zialcita, Fernando Nakpil. 1997. "Traditional houses," pp. 46–56 in *Filipino Style*. London: Thames and Hudson.

Zink, Clifford W. 1987. "Dutch framed houses in New York and New Jersey," *Winterthur Portfolio* 22:4:265–94.

Zurick, David and Nanda Shrestha. 2003. "Himalayan dwellings: A cultural-environmental perspective," pp. 15–38 in Knapp, Ronald G. (ed.), *Asia's Old Dwellings*. Hong Kong: Oxford University Press.

Index